William Connor Sydney

England and the English in the eighteenth century

Chapters in the social history of the times. Vol. 1

William Connor Sydney

England and the English in the eighteenth century
Chapters in the social history of the times. Vol. 1

ISBN/EAN: 9783337203603

Printed in Europe, USA, Canada, Australia, Japan

Cover: Foto ©ninafisch / pixelio.de

More available books at **www.hansebooks.com**

ENGLAND AND THE ENGLISH

IN THE EIGHTEENTH CENTURY

VOL. I.

PREFACE.

THE scope and intent of these volumes are sufficiently indicated upon their title-page. They consist of a series of short chapters embodying the results of a study of the manners, the customs, the daily life, the occupations, and the general social condition of the English people in the eighteenth century, an age which, in spite of its close proximity to that in which we live, and in spite of the many books which have been written to illustrate its history, is still, perhaps, more imperfectly known and understood than any of those to which it immediately succeeded.

That the specification of every source of information which has been consulted would hardly have been possible, will be obvious, nevertheless the work contains few, if indeed any, statements of importance which are unaccompanied by the means whereby their accuracy can be tested by such as may be desirous of so doing.

If such a pendant to historical literature shall be found instrumental in casting even a very slight semblance of the glow and colour of reality over a century which now exists only in print, and in conveying easily to the minds of its readers that knowledge of commonplace detail and everyday life which, however apt to be neglected by professed students of the past, is yet the very kind of knowledge that is calculated to invest history with reality and vividness, the object in presenting it as a candidate for the favour of the public will have been fully attained.

LONDON : *May* 1891.

CONTENTS

OF

THE FIRST VOLUME

——◦◦◦◦——

VOL. I.   a

CHAPTER IV.

DRESS AND COSTUME.

CHAPTER V.

AMUSEMENTS AND PASTIMES, PUBLIC AND PRIVATE.

CHAPTER VI.

LONDON COFFEE-HOUSES, TAVERNS, AND CLUBS.

CHAPTER X.

WARS AND RUMOURS OF WARS.

ENGLAND AND THE ENGLISH

IN THE

EIGHTEENTH CENTURY.

———◦◦◦———

CHAPTER I.

INTRODUCTORY.

THE England to which it is proposed to introduce the reader in the following pages is the England of the eighteenth century. He will be transported, in imagination at least, into that strange, quaint old world in which Pope, Addison, Gay, Goldsmith, Fielding, Lord Chesterfield, Dr. Johnson, Horace Walpole, Lady Mary Wortley Montagu, Mrs. Delany, and Mrs. Elizabeth Robinson, not to mention a host of other major and minor celebrities, lived, moved, and had their being. He will be carried back to the days when beaux strutted about Pall Mall and St. James's Street attired in richly-embroidered velvet coats, sporting cocked hats and lace cravats, and priding themselves on 'the nice conduct' of ten-guinea clouded canes ; to days when belles deemed it no disfigurement to stick patches on their faces, to wear pyramidical head-dresses, or to shop on Ludgate Hill and in St. Paul's Churchyard, or to take the air in St. James's Park, attired in hooped petticoats, carrying huge decorated fans, accompanied by black boys and curly lap-dogs ; to days when 'the quality,' as people of rank and position were ordinarily styled, repaired to the haunts of gaiety and pleasure in sedan chairs and gilded chariots ; when travellers possessed of the stoutest hearts quailed at the prospect of continuing their journey after the shades of night had fallen ; when every highway of importance was studded with gibbets and constituted a happy hunting-ground for armed and mounted desperadoes ; when stage coaches, pack-horses, and waggons afforded the only means of communication between places situated far apart ; when it would sometimes be found necessary to harness a team of strong oxen to the cumbersome family coach in order to drag it through the sloughs and narrow miry lanes ; when the rich veins of coal and iron had scarcely been opened ; when the great manufactures had barely emerged into existence ; and when as yet neither steam, electricity, gas, the post, the newspaper press, nor a hundred other kindred agencies favourable to the comfort and happiness of the people, had begun to make their enormous power known and felt throughout the length and breadth of the land.

The reader will be invited to undertake a short mental pilgrimage over the kingdom, pausing as he does so to make note of the condition of the roads along which he passes, to take cognisance of the homes and haunts of the peasantry, to mark the peculiarities of dialect, and to observe the various trades and handicrafts, the manners, customs, recreations, and tastes of the people.   He will be led to the court and the manor-house, and thence to the mansion and the cottage.   He will be conducted through the streets of the capital—to its theatres, its ridottos, its masquerades, its auctions, its toyshops, and its bear-gardens.   For his inspection, the churches, the gaols, the dens of the astrologers and fortune-tellers will all be unroofed, after the manner of Asmodeus in the ' Diable Boiteux ' of Le Sage.   He will be invited to walk over the houses, to examine the furniture, to rummage the wardrobes contained in them, and to summon into existence specimens of the different classes of English society from the king on his throne to the humblest subject in the realm.   And if this has the result of opening his eyes a little, well will it be.   We are so accustomed to the innumerable conveniences peculiar to a highly civilised state of society, of which the wealthy and the indigent participate in a greater or lesser degree, as of the air which they breathe, that we are apt not only to undervalue them but even to overlook them altogether. It is well, therefore, that the present generation should be occasionally made to realise the value of that which it thus thanklessly enjoys. Far below their true worth are good and safe roads, well lighted streets, cheap and speedy methods for the conveyance of life and property, great discoveries and striking improvements, estimated in this our day.

Few of those to whom it was permitted to cross the deep gulf which separates this century from the one which preceded it now linger among us. Fewer still are able to say anything from personal knowledge about the social life of England before the year 1800, in an age which is in character although not in time, so very far removed from our own. The extraordinary strides which scientific progress has made, and the revolutions which have been effected in the means of locomotion have not merely completely altered many customs, but have eradicated very much that was peculiar in our modes of living. It can hardly be expected that so complete a transition from the old order to the new will readily occur again. Men having ceased to wonder at their own experience will probably soon cease to believe that things in the world around them were not always what they seem to them at present.

There is a certain class of people, who were perhaps never more numerous than they are now, who delight to pose in the character of *laudatores temporis acti.* It is from such that society hears periodically the most pathetic lamentations over the degeneracy of these latter days, and sighs the most plaintive for the return of bygone ages. With something akin to regret they dwell on the 'Merrie England' of their forefathers ; their waking hours are haunted by beatific visions of those far away times when ' the extremes of exuberant wealth and luxury, of pale-faced poverty and squalid want,' to adopt their own language, were almost, if not entirely unknown. One of our greatest bards has told us that it is distance which lends enchantment to the view. And the remark is true, for, to minds at all capable of reflection lamentations and regrets alike of this kind appear to be founded upon conceptions altogether erroneous ; since the more closely the candle is held up to what by a strange figure of speech it is the fashion to call 'the good old times,' the less reason will be found for either envy or admiration of them—indeed the inevitable conviction that will force itself upon the inquirer will be this, that 'the good old times' were in point of actual fact very bad times, and that those in which our lot happens to be cast are not such evil ones as they are commonly represented. What one of the most illustrious of English historians observed nearly half a century ago remains true even to this day—namely, that 'the more carefully we examine the history of the past, the more reason shall we find to dissent from those who imagine that our age has been fruitful of new social evils. The truth is that the evils are, with scarcely an exception, old. That which is new is the intelligence which discerns and the humanity which remedies them.'

The pleasure derived from the present possession of advantages is considerably heightened when they are compared with the disadvantages which were endured in the last age. There is nothing which tends to dull delight and to obliterate gratitude so much as custom. As Sydney Smith once said, 'It is of some importance at what period a man is born.' People who live in these luxurious times are far too apt to undervalue many benefits which they possess, and are far too prone to ignore the startling contrast which exists between the light of the present age and the darkness of the past. Who that is now whirled in less than three hours from London to Bristol, or to Manchester in five, would care to entrust his limbs to a stage coach accomplishing the distance in as many days? Or who would care to consume seven hours out of the twenty-four in making a voyage in a packet from Dover to Calais, or from Brighton to Dieppe? Who that in the capital nowadays walks through streets lighted by gas and electricity would feel any intense desire to return to the miserably lamp-lighted streets of eighteenth-century London? The habit of walking on well-paved thoroughfares begets forgetfulness of the pebbly narrow streets of the age anterior to the present. So, too, the possession of an efficient police force renders men utterly insensible to the woes of foot passengers to whom no better protection—if such it deserves to be called—was vouchsafed than lazy beadles and tipsy watchmen. The working classes (albeit they perpetually grumble and strike) would be in a far more contented frame of mind than they are could they but realise one half of the discomforts and privations that their predecessors endured without repining, the poor fare on which they subsisted, the restrictions by which they were hampered, and the scanty wages that they earned. Let him turn in which direction he may, where will the mechanic to-day find things in anything like the same state in which they were in the last century? Can he lay his finger upon a commodity consumed by all classes of the people that is not either of better quality or of improved manufacture? Can he point to any article of male or female wearing apparel, worn even by the poorest of the population, that is not at the present day of a quality far superior to that which was then in general use among the wealthy? And may not the same be truly said with respect to food? Will it be denied that inferior substitutes for bread made of wheaten flour have long since passed out of use? Will it be denied that the masses live upon nothing, or at any rate expend their earnings upon nothing as the mainstay of their subsistence, except the best and the costliest of all the commonly cultivated productions of the soil? Will it be contended that the numerous other articles of daily consumption, such as tea, coffee, and sugar, for example, have not from being the luxuries of the few become the necessaries of the many; or that houses, cottages, and mansions, tenanted by people of all degrees, both externally and internally have been equally changed and improved; or that every article of furniture, every article intended either for use or for ornament, contained in them, has been changed, and that decidedly for the better; or that the intellectual needs of the masses have never been ministered to more assiduously by those agencies which civilise the conduct of men and prevent them from sinking to the level of the brute creation—the lecture halls, free public libraries, mechanics' institutes, and recreative evening classes? Surely not. It would be no easy task to enumerate the many things which in the last century were seldom seen, and are now possessed in greater or smaller measure by nearly everybody; the many things not then in vogue, but which have since passed into daily use, to our "exceeding refreshment," as Robinson Crusoe would say; the many more things which were not even in existence, and which, if not enjoyed by the entire community, are at all events enjoyed by no inconsiderable portion of it. Once more. If the visits of the heavenly bodies were like those of angels, few and far between, no small amount of wonder and interest would be excited in mortal minds in their exits and their entrances; but, because they set their watch in the sky on almost every clear night, few condescend to elevate their eyes in order to gaze at them. Much the same is the attitude which present-day folk adopt in regard to the past. If it be impossible to gauge all the benefits at present enjoyed, it is not impossible to recognise this, that times associated as they are with so many flagrant evils and so many discomforts have no claim whatever, in the name of common sense, to the title of 'the good old times.' To all the previous ages the present stands indebted for the advantages it now possesses, and failure to appreciate them can result only from despising the day of small things.

CHAPTER II.

THE LONDON OF OUR GREAT-GRANDFATHERS.

Changes in the aspect of the metropolis since the accession of George III.
—Condition of its thoroughfares in the last century—'The art of walking
the streets'—Taking the wall—Inconveniences endured by foot-passengers—Signboards—A city shower—Sedan chairmen—Pall Mall—Night-
side of Old London—Linkboys and watchmen—The state of Westminster—Of Fleet Ditch—Decayed houses—Condition of various localities
described—Bird's-eye view of the metropolis in the Georgian era.

IT is the special object of the present chapter to sketch in
brief outline as accurately and comprehensively, in so far as the
materials available for the purpose will permit, the condition
and topographical aspect which the vast and ever-increasing
capital of the British Empire presented about the time of the
accession of George III., the era from which the prosperity
of the kingdom began to increase in a marvellous ratio. The
changes which had taken place over the metropolis in the
sixty years before that date were neither very extensive nor
were they very important; but such was not the case in the
forty years that followed. Yet although an Act for the paving
of Westminster was passed in 1762, and another for the
improvement of the Strand and St. James's Street three years
later, fully half a century elapsed before anything approaching
a complete reformation made itself perceptible. A rough
sketch of London, therefore, at the epoch when the sceptre
passed from the hands of George II. into those of his successor, may serve a useful purpose in two ways—in the first place
as forming a fitting prelude to the subject by showing very
decidedly the vast strides which the metropolis has made on
the road of improvement, and, secondly, from the possibility
of its being the means of enabling the reader to understand

some facts contained in subsequent chapters, which would perhaps otherwise fail to lend themselves readily to his compre-
hension, or perhaps even to his belief.

It sounds like the reiteration of an already well-worn truism,
to say that there is probably no other city in Europe, certainly
none in the United Kingdom, which has undergone during the
last three-quarters of a century of its existence more extraordinary metamorphoses and improvements than London.   Yet so
it is.   The capital, undoubtedly, still stands where it did then ;
but in almost every other respect it is as much transformed as
an ancient residence that had been almost entirely reconstructed
from kitchen to garret.   The historian of the ' Decline and Fall
of the Roman Empire ' remarks that the description composed
in the Theodosian age of the many stately mansions in which
Rome abounded might almost excuse the exaggeration of the
poet that the Eternal City contained a multitude of palaces,
and that each palace was equal to a city.   Signs are not wanting
that some such destiny as this is reserved for the metropolis
of England in the immediate future.

In these days a new generation has arisen, the grandchildren
and great-grandchildren of those who were in the prime of life
when George III. ascended the throne.   They know and see
London as it now is ; but few people living have before their
mind's eye the appearance which it wore in the days of their
eighteenth-century ancestors.   What sweeping changes old Father
Time, that most irresistible of all reformers, has silently laboured
to accomplish in this particular direction will be readily apparent
to anyone who will take the trouble to collate with care the
contemporary maps and engravings purporting to represent the
London of the Georgian era with those which represent the
London of the present day.   By a series of gradual and successive revolutions, entire streets and immense blocks of dilapidated houses have been demolished, in order to make room for
the new spacious and imposing thoroughfares which have been
formed on their sites ; in addition to numerous railway-stations,
banks, offices, squares, crescents, and churches.   Before the
progress of alteration and amelioration, the labyrinthine mazes
of fœtid alleys, the dingy courts, the squalid dens of crime

and misery, and innumerable other abominations, reeking of
poverty, hunger, and destitution, which then flourished almost
beneath the very shadow of kingly palaces, have in great part
vanished, never, it is devoutly to be hoped, to reappear ; while
on the other hand desolate commons and fields which were then
appropriated to pasturage have been converted, as by the wand
of some Arabian magician, into long rows of lofty buildings,
magnificent in their outward aspect. William Maitland, were
he to renew once more life's fitful fever, would hardly recognise the city which he so diligently and carefully catalogued
some one hundred and fifty or more years ago ; and if he
would not, it is a moral certainty that his contemporaries,
among whom Dr. Johnson, Goldsmith, Boswell, and William
Hogarth may be specially mentioned, would experience the
same difficulty.

Looking backwards from the vantage-ground of time upon
the age which closed with the year 1799, it requires no small mental effort to realise that London, at the coronation of George III.,
was, and for many a year afterwards continued to be, marred by
numerous disfigurements which it had inherited from preceding
eras. By far the greater part of its streets and courts, to start with,
were built in a very irregular fashion; numbers of ancient gabled
houses which, by an accident of their position, had escaped
the great conflagration of 1666, were still standing in them ;
and tradespeople encroached to a most unwarrantable extent
upon the footway with their bulks, their bow windows, and
their great glass doors. Not a few of the principal thoroughfares still remained unpaved ; and, as a consequence of this,
every shopkeeper and householder paved the space in front of
his door entirely in accordance with his own peculiar ideas.
Such pavements as were in existence consisted of round stones
taken fresh from the quarry, and thrown down at random ; so
that it was almost next to impossible for wayfarers to find repose
for the soles of their feet.[1] Some of the streets of the capital,
it is true, were paved with freestone ; but to have done so on
any extended scale would have entailed considerable expense,
as the stone had to be brought from a very long distance, and

[1] J. P. Grosley, *Tour to London* (1765), i. 23-26.

that was not then deemed worthy of serious consideration.
The middle of a thoroughfare was either generally full of
cavities which harboured water and filth—removed only at
the convenience of the scavengers—or else was occupied by
a succession of dirty puddles, five or six inches deep, which,
when stirred up by the cart-wheels and horses' hoofs, smothered
the pedestrian from head to foot, filled the passing coaches
and carriages when their windows were not closed, and daubed
all the lower parts of shop and house-fronts. On either
side of every thoroughfare ran a miry ditch, in the truest
sense of the word, commonly called 'the kennel,' that, during
the prevalence of tempestuous weather, was often swollen
well-nigh to overflowing, and in hot weather positively pesti-
lential, by reason of the various fumes emitted by the heaps
of garbage and rubbish, 'of all hues and odours,' of which
it was made the receptacle. Through these veritable morasses,
when they had attained 'full tide,' it afforded infinite gratification to coachmen and carters to urge their horses, and to splash
purposely every decently-dressed person they met on the way..
Well might the poet Gay counsel the London pedestrians ever
to be watchful to maintain the wall—by which he meant that
they should keep as closely as they possibly could to the shop
and house-fronts.[1] This was one of the golden rules of 'the art
of walking the streets' which no person outside the precincts of
Bedlam at that time would so much as have dreamed of
despising. Dr. Johnson relates that, when his mother lived in
London, there were two sets of people, those who gave the
wall and those who took it—the peaceable and the quarrel-
some ; and that when he returned to Lichfield in 1737, after
sojourning in London, she asked him whether he was one of
those who gave the wall or of those who took it. ' Now,' said
he, ' it is fixed that every man keeps to the right ; or, if one is
taking the wall, another yields it, and it is never a dispute.'

[1] Gay, *Trivia*, ii. The poet also furnishes elaborate hints as to whom to
'give' and whom to 'refuse' the wall to (b. i.). Gay's curious little poem
was originally published in 1716, but much of what he says in it respecting
the state of the London streets and outdoor life in general was applicable
not only at the particular date of which this chapter treats, but also until
the commencement of the present century.

In order to render transit across the streets within the bounds of possibility, small causeways, raised a little above the level, and composed of large broad stones picked out for the purpose, were constructed.[1] Kerbstones were as yet unthought of, and rows of posts formed the only lines of demarcation between the foot and carriage ways.[2] Although these footpaths barely afforded space for more than one person to pass at a time, the passenger's only chance, or rather certainty of safety, lay in keeping steadily within them, notwithstanding the danger he momentarily ran of being sent floundering head first into 'the kennel,' or thrust heavily against 'the wall' by some ruffianly sedan chairman, thus proving the value of the caution which Gay administered to foot passengers :—

> Though expedition bids, yet never stray
> Where no ranged posts defend the rugged way ;
> Here laden carts with thundering waggons meet,
> Wheels clash with wheels and bar the narrow street.[3]

If it happened that a pedestrian, compelled by the urgency of his business to exchange the footpath for the carriage way, turned out into the latter from the space between two posts, ten chances to one if some advancing vehicles would not necessitate his speedy return to the place he came from ; and in that case he had no course open to him but to leap over or stoop beneath the chain or rail which was commonly continued from the top of one post to that of another. In accomplishing this feat he might congratulate himself if he escaped without a sprained arm or a dislocated ankle.[4]

The elaborately carved and coloured signboards, loaded with lead and iron, which cut such grotesque figures in the paintings of Hogarth, projected conspicuously, in the absence of numbers (a system not enforced until the succeeding century), at unequal distances across the streets, from the door lintel or window of every shop and house, on both sides of the way, from Whitechapel to the Haymarket, and from the Borough to Clerkenwell, betokening the name and profession of the owner,

---

[1] Boswell's *Life of Johnson,* ciii.   [2] Grosley, *Tour,* i. p. 33.
[3] *Trivia,* ii.   [4] J. Pugh, *Life of Jonas Hanway,* p. 127.

obstructing the view, and preventing the free circulation of the air.[1] When the wind blew high the luckless pedestrian, as he threaded the crowded streets and alleys of the city, heard with dismay the dissonant creaking of these signboards as they swung to and fro upon their rusty hinges above his head, and, if he were proficient in weather lore, regarded it as the certain herald of a shower.[2] No sooner was the welkin observed to be overcast than everybody prepared for the coming storm, and as, until quite the latter end of the eighteenth century, it was considered a sign of great effeminacy to be seen carrying that most indispensable guard from chilly showers to present-day folk—to wit, an umbrella—the gentlemen got into coaches and chairs, or sought the kindly shelter of the coffee-houses and taverns ; the ladies, under the pretence of buying and cheapening goods, crowded the shops of the linendrapers ; the booksellers, with prudent foresight, hastened to remove their stock from off their rails and shops ; the hosiers took down their poles hung with stockings ; and the Thames watermen clothed their tilt-boats with blue, in the hope of tempting a fare.[3] When the clouds began to drain their fleeces in right real earnest, the tiles rattled with the smoky shower, hundreds of dragon-mouthed water-spouts poured from on high, and these, added to the kennels hastening to disgorge their trophies into the Fleet Ditch, the bursting of water-pipes, and the dirty and unsavoury streams emptied by careless domestics out of garret windows, combined to pour merciless cascades upon the unfortunate heads of passers-by, as they endeavoured to steer their way past the hogsheads rolled down from drays by porters, the barrels lowered by the brewers into open cellars by means of ropes, past the combs and other articles strung on twines dangling in the air, or through a maze of carts, coaches, wheelbarrows, and their bawling owners. Nor did people find themselves a whit the better off by proceeding to their destinations in coaches or chairs. Every thoroughfare of any importance

[1] J. Pugh, *Life of Jonas Hanway*, pp. 129–140. John Spranger's *Proposal for Paving the Streets*, 1756.

[2] *Trivia*, b. i. p. 11 ; Swift's *Lines descriptive of a City Shower.*

[3] *Trivia*, i.

was so constantly impeded by an array of vehicles, all wedged
in one behind the other, that they found it ten times preferable
to get out and walk, leaving coachmen and chairmen to fight
and quarrel to their hearts' content.[1]   At the time Gay wrote,
and indeed long afterwards, the only street regulation that was
in force appears to have been one by which the sedan chairmen
were confined to the middle of the road ; for, says he :

> Let not the chairman with assuming stride
> Press near the wall and rudely thrust aside ;
> The laws have set him bounds, his servile feet
> Should ne'er encroach where posts defend the street.

Pall Mall, alone of all the localities in the metropolis at this
time, seems to have been comparatively secure, although even
there the pedestrian was not wholly free from the inconveniences occasioned by bad paving.   Gay, when apostrophising this
particular locality, exclaims :—

> O bear me to the paths of fair Pall Mall,
> Safe are thy pavements, grateful is thy smell !
> At distance rolls along the gilded coach,
> Nor sturdy carmen on thy walks encroach ;
> No lets would bar thy ways were chairs deny'd,
> The soft supports of laziness and pride ;
> Shops breathe perfumes, thro' sashes ribbons glow,
> The mutual arms of ladies and the beau.
> Yet still e'en here, when rains the passage hide,
> Oft the loose stone spirts up a muddy tide
> Beneath thy careless foot ; and from on high,
> Where masons mount the ladder, fragments fly ;
> Mortar and crumbled lime in showers descend ;
> And o'er thy head destructive tiles impend.[2]

When all the annoyances and inconveniences which have
been enumerated are taken into account it is hardly to be
wondered at that London citizens dreaded the bare thought of
taking their walks abroad even in clear daylight, more especially
when such mishaps as those which Gay has so graphically
portrayed in the second book of his ' Trivia ' are added to
the number :—

> I've seen a beau in some ill-fated hour,
> When o'er the stones choak'd kennels swell the show'r,

---

[1] Twiss's *Life of Lord Chancellor Eldon*, i. p. 49.   [2] *Trivia*, ii.

> In gilded chariot loll ; he with disdain
> Views spatter'd passengers all drench'd in rain,
> With mud fill'd high the rumbling cart draws near,
> Now rule thy prancing steeds, laced charioteer !
> The dustman lashes on with spiteful rage,
> His pond'rous spokes thy painted wheel engage,
> Crush'd is thy pride, down falls the shrieking beau
> The slabby pavement crystal fragments strow,
> Black floods of mire th' embroidered coat disgrace,
> And mud enwraps the honours of his face.

But the fury of the elements and an encounter with carts and chairmen were very far from being the worst evils which passengers were forced at that time to endure in the London streets. Disastrous accidents occurred at night from all kinds of obstacles carelessly or purposely placed in the road, such for instance as unprotected heaps of earth or stones, thrown up while repairs were being effected, to say nothing of cellars and common sewers which 'kept a lulling murmur.' Mark the testimony of Gay upon this head :—

> Where a dim gleam the paly lanthorn throws
> O'er the mid pavement, heapy rubbish grows,
> Or arched vaults their gaping jaws extend,
> Or the dark caves to common sewers descend,
> Oft by the winds extinct the signal lies,
> Or smother'd in the glimmering socket dies
> Ere night has half rolled round her ebon throne ;
> In the wide gulph the shatter'd coach o'erthrown
> Sinks with the snorting steeds, the reins are broke,
> And from the crackling axle flies the spoke.[1]

Far too many of these accidents were the result of the arrangements for lighting the London streets during the eighteenth century, which were, as may be imagined, miserably insufficient, and so tardy was the legislature in making more effectual provision, that no systematic lighting of them can be said to have really taken place until George III. had been seated on the throne nearly a decade. Maitland said justly that the lighting of London was worse than that of any other great city. The light, such as it was, was derived mainly from several thousands of small tin vessels, which were half filled

---

[1] *Trivia*, ii.

with whale oil of the worst quality that could possibly be procured, supplied with bits of cotton twist for wick and enclosed in globes of semi-opaque glass. Such lamps were either stuck upon posts placed at long intervals in the Strand, Cheapside, Pall Mall, and other important thoroughfares, or were suspended from iron rods which jutted out horizontally from the sides of shops and private dwellings, and served to shed a faint glimmer of light, or rather to make the darkness visible at street corners and crossings from sundown to midnight, when they were religiously extinguished, if they had not in the meantime rendered this duty unnecessary by extinguishing themselves. For the purpose of trimming, snuffing, cleansing, and lighting the 'lamps' each wardmote enlisted the services of a contingent of greasy clodhopping fellows. of whom typical specimens may be seen in Hogarth's series of paintings depicting the Rake's Progress, and in Pyne's 'Book of Costume.' A distinguishing characteristic of these lamplighters was that of invariably spilling the oil upon the heads of those who passed them while they stood upon their ladders, and occasionally breaking a head by dropping a globe. Though the lamps were usually lighted soon after dark, they were, owing to their being unprovided with reflectors, totally inadequate to dispel the Cimmerian gloom in which London was shrouded in the winter months. The consequence was that during the greater part of the twenty-four hours life and property were left to the uncontrolled dominion of robbers and murderers. The inhabitants of the outlying districts of the metropolis sat in the shadow of darkness from Lady Day to Michaelmas when the pale moon declined to shed her silvery light ; consequently those who either from choice or necessity stirred out after dark, generally engaged torch-bearers, linkmen or linkboys to light them on their way going or returning. This, however, was an undertaking attended with considerable risk : far more often than not these 'servants of the public' were hand and glove with footpads and highwaymen, and would rarely think twice on receiving a signal from such accomplices of extinguishing the link and slipping away, leaving the terrified fare or fares, as the case might be, to their tender mercies—a little

delinquency which did not succeed in escaping the notice of
that lynx-eyed professor of ambulation who has been frequently
quoted in this chapter, and moved him to utter his voice of
warning against employing them.

> Though thou art tempted by the linkman's call
> Yet trust him not along the lonely wall,
> In the midway he'll quench the flaming brand,
> And share the booty with the pilf'ring band.[1]

That the foregoing assertions owe nothing to the exaggeration of the poet is confirmed by the testimony of the following paragraph extracted from the Historical Chronicle of the
'Gentleman's Magazine' for 1760, under date of Tuesday,
December 23 :—

> A remarkable robbery was committed near Moorfields by a
> linkman, who having offered his service to a country gentleman to
> light him through the fog, decoyed him into a bye-place, and with
> an accomplice, after thrusting the link in his face, took from him
> great-coat, watch, and money.

The ironwork over the front entrances of the houses in all
the fashionable quarters of the capital was furnished with huge
extinguishers up into which the linkbearers thrust their smoking
flambeaux, and until within a comparatively recent period
several specimens of these extinguishers might have been seen
in a few of the older London squares.

From its western extremity at Hyde Park Corner to its
eastern extremity at Whitechapel, London was guarded by
neither police, patrol, nor regular troops. The sole guardians
or rather non-guardians of life and property during the
night season were divers sleepy-headed old watchmen (an
infinitely greater nuisance than they were a protection),
who were despatched on their 'beats' at intervals from the
watch-houses or temporary gaols built in cylindrical form
like ·a modern Martello tower.[2] These officials were selected
from the dregs of the people, and their primary qualifications

[1] *Trivia*, ii.
[2] So late as 1797 the number of London watchmen, according to a
German traveller named D'Archenholz, did not exceed 2,000.

for so responsible a post would appear to have been those of advanced age and sheer incapacity. Apparelled in thick heavy great-coats, and armed with poles, rattles, and lanterns, the watchmen perambulated the streets crying the hour after the chimes, taking precautions for the prevention of fire, proclaiming (in tones the reverse of melodious) tidings of foul or fair weather, and awakening at daybreak all those who intended to set out on a journey.[1] At intervals the drowsy citizen would be snatched from the tender embrace of 'tired Nature's sweet restorer' by some such cry as 'Pa-a-st eleven o'clock, and a ra-a-iny night,' or 'Pa-a-st one o'clock, and a sho-o-wery mo-o-orning.' Then a lull, broken presently by loud cries for 'help' and 'mercy,' followed by the springing of rattles, telling the affrighted listener that 'all the savage soul of fight was up,' and that not many yards from his house door a fierce hand-to-hand conflict was being waged between the aged guardians of the night and some desperate gang of street thieves or mischief-loving 'bricks' or 'bloods.'

Occasionally it would happen that one of these poor old men would be caught napping in his box at early dawn by a company of fine gentlemen 'flown with insolence and wine,' returning home after a protracted celebration of bacchanalian orgies. One of the number would instantly suggest the over-turning of the box, and this resolution being passed unani-mously, some choice spirit would push heavily against the shelter and turn it topsy-turvy. Having accomplished this praiseworthy exploit, the gang would take to their heels, leaving the unfortunate tenant of the box to scramble out of it in the best way he could. At other times a watchman would be sent on a wild goose chase by the oft-reiterated cry of 'Watch ! W-a-a-tch !' and wander up hill and down dale only to discover at the end of his perambulation that he was the victim of a hoax. Small indeed was the protection afforded by the watchmen at the best of times, but much less so in the long dark nights of winter. Then, either one of two things happened : they became the butts of the fine gentlemen who were never so

---

[1] Grosley, *Observations on England*, i. p. 49 ; Saunders Welch, *Obser-vations on the Office of Constable*, pp. 12 15.

completely in their element as when teasing, insulting, and beating them, or else in three cases out of four they became the pliant instruments of the light-fingered fraternity, permitting them to commit robberies before their very eyes with perfect impunity. What was said of the London watchmen in the first quarter of the present century, before Sir Robert Peel had laid before the public his scheme for the formation of an efficient metropolitan police force, would have been equally applicable at any time during the eighteenth century—namely, that no human being had the smallest confidence in them ; that scenes of collusion, tricks, compromises, knaveries of all kinds in which they had borne lot and parcel were brought to light daily ; that none of the magistrates reposed the least faith on their statements, unless they were supported by the evidence of other people ; that the feeling against them was strong exactly in proportion as opportunities of learning their real habits had been abundant ; and finally, that their existence was a nuisance and a curse.[1] Watchmen never quitted their respective ' beats.' A person might be robbed, nay, might be murdered, by footpads within a dozen yards of the boundaries of one parish, yet the watchmen would never trouble themselves to run to his rescue. And why? Simply because he was being robbed or murdered beyond their jurisdiction. With this, all or nearly all London citizens were fully satisfied—the old ways, the old habits, the old customs sufficed for them. Of innovation they had a perfect dread, and rather than fly to ills they knew not of they preferred to bear those they had. Thus for many years after they were first penned (1738) the following lines in Dr. Johnson's poem of ' London ' continued to be daily exemplified :—

> Prepare for death if ere at night you roam,
> And sign your will before you pass from home ;
> Some fiery fop with new commission vain,
> Who sleeps on brambles till he kills his man,
> Some foolish drunkard, reeling from a feast,
> Provokes a broil, and stabs you for a jest !

The services of shoeblacks, or ' gentlemen trading in blackball,' as the Earl of Chesterfield once described them,

[1] *Quart. Rev.* vol. xxxvii.

were greatly in request during the last century. They usually took up their quarters at the street corners, provided with a ball of blacking, of which the chief ingredients were oil and soot contained in a pipkin, a three-legged stool, a pair of hard brushes, and a cast-off periwig, wherewith they removed the covering of mud with which the shoes of pedestrians were only too thickly coated. The poet Gay in addressing a member of the shoeblacking fraternity in his poem of 'Trivia : or the Art of Walking the Streets,' says :—

> Go thrive ; at some frequented corner stand,
> This brush I give thee, grasp it in thy hand ;
> Temper the soot within this vase of oil,
> And let the little tripod aid thy toil.
> On this methinks I see the walking crew
> At thy request support the miry shoe :
> The foot grows black that was with dirt embrown'd,
> And in thy pocket jingling halfpence sound.[1]

The only public vehicles in use in the public streets were sedan chairs and hackney coaches. The former, which derived their name from the little town of that name in the Ardennes, were extensively patronised by the metropolitan *habitués*, beaux and belles alike, when proceeding to the innumerable Court drawing-rooms, royal levees, theatres, balls, and assemblies. Sedan chairs were so constructed as to admit of the roof being pushed up in order to allow of their occupants standing upright in them, and closed tightly down when they had taken their seats. People of quality usually kept their own chairs, which were fitted up and decked out in the most lavish and extravagant manner, emblazoned with their coat-of-arms, lined with silk or satin, and placed regularly in the hall ready for use. This sometimes caused them to become the prey of street thieves. One of these courtly vehicles is introduced into Hogarth's series, 'A Modern Rake's Progress,' wherein the man of fashion may be seen proceeding to the levee at St. James's Palace. The anonymous writer of a life of Jonathan Wild, which purported to be an authentic biography, relates that a couple of thieves, meeting together, stole the young Duchess of Marlborough's chair as she was visiting in Piccadilly, while her chairmen and

---

[1] *Trivia*, iii.

footmen had gone to a neighbouring alehouse. One of her servants immediately applied to Wild, who told him that if he would leave ten guineas he might have the chair next day. The servant made some difficulty of leaving the money beforehand, but Wild told him he was a man of honour, and scorned to wrong him ; and, indeed, his character was by this time established as a man that dealt honourably in his way, so the man ventured at last to leave the money ; whereupon Mr. Wild bade him direct the Duchess's chairmen to attend the morning prayers at Lincoln's Inn Chapel, and there they should find the chair, which the fellows did accordingly ; and they found the chair with the crimson velvet cushion and damask curtains all safe and unhurt. The sedan chairmen were for the most part of Irish nationality, and are described as a thick-set, thick-legged race of men, who when engaged in the exercise of their calling contrived to render themselves in every way as obnoxious as possible, digging their chair-poles into the ribs of the passers-by, or squeezing them against the wall. Dean Swift alludes to these ' playful' habits on their part in his ' Journal to Stella,' under date of February 10, 1710, wherein he says that 'the chairmen that carried me squeezed a great fellow against the wall, who wisely turned his back and broke one of the side glasses into a thousand pieces. The hackney coaches, which stood in stands and places where people knew to send for them, seem to have been not only very numerous but very cheap, and moreover ready at a moment's notice. These slow, dirty, rickety vehicles were constructed to hold four people, and were drawn by two horses. The fare was one shilling per mile. So capacious were the coaches that six people could easily be accommodated within them, and when they contained that number the driver received an extra fee. A Swiss traveller, B. L. de Muralt, who visited London early in the reign of George II., was inclined to believe that this was one of the advantages which it enjoyed over the French capital. The slow pace at which the hackney coaches rumbled along proved of inestimable assistance to footpads and highwaymen, who frequently waylaid them, and robbed their occupants.

Yesterday morning, about four o'clock, a gentleman and lady going home from Carlisle House in a hackney coach were stopped near the great house lately belonging to the D. of Newcastle, the corner of Great Queen Street, by three footpads, who robbed the gentleman of his watch and seven guineas. They made the lady pull off her gloves, and finding she had no rings of value, told her they would give her no further trouble and made off.[1]

Daniel Defoe, in the record of his 'Tour through England,' in his notice of the capital, when speaking of the coffee-houses in which the localities of Pall Mall and St. James's abounded in the first half of the eighteenth century, observes :—'We are carried to these places in chairs, which are here very cheap—a guinea per week, or a shilling per hour—and your chairmen serve you for porters, to run one's errands as your gondoliers do at Venice ;' and Dean Swift, in his lines descriptive of a city shower, shows that the pleasure of traversing the streets in a chair was not unalloyed :—

> Boxed in a chair the beau impatient sits,
> While spouts run clattering o'er the roof by fits,
> And ever and anon, with frightful din,
> The leather sounds, he trembles from within.

Largely as sedan chairs were utilised by the nobility and gentry, they do not seem to have been exempt from the depredations of town thieves, since it is recorded that in 1726 the Earl of Harborough's chair was waylaid in Piccadilly in the forenoon, and that one of the chairmen pulled a pole out of the chair and knocked down one of the villains, while the Earl, stepping out, drew his sword, and put the others to flight, but not before they had raised their wounded companion, whom they took off with them.

The state of Westminster, which in the eighteenth century had not been altogether swallowed up in the general vortex of London, was equally bad. Its streets were narrow, dirty, ill-paved, often loathsome, and we are assured on the authority of Goldsmith that often in the midst of the footway a great puddle might have been seen moving lazily along. Almost within the precincts of Westminster Abbey there still existed a remnant of Elizabethan London, a network of alleys called the 'Bermudas.' Close by stood Porridge

[1] *Public Advertiser*, Jan. 31, 1778.

Island, famous for its cookshops, where the fine gentlemen who went in a chair every evening to the rout, dined off pewter plates.[1]   Down to 1750 the Houses of Parliament could be approached only by way of King Street and Union Street, both of which were in such a miserable state that it was found absolutely necessary to cast faggots into the ruts on the days on which the King proceeded to the House of Lords, in order that the progress of the lumbering, unwieldy state coach, which required no fewer than eight horses to drag it along, might be facilitated.   St. Margaret's Street, which had been formed out of a thoroughfare known as St. Margaret's Lane, was so narrow that the inhabitants were forced to place poles four feet high between the footpath and the carriage-way, 'to preserve passengers from injury and from being covered with the mud which was splashed on all sides in abundance.'[2] No wonder that on January 27, 1741, during the progress of a debate in the Commons on the Bill for paving and cleansing the streets of Westminster, Lord Tyrconnel rose and gave it as his opinion that 'the filth of some parts of the town and the inequality and ruggedness of others, could not but in the eyes of foreigners disgrace our nation and incline them to imagine us a people not only without delicacy, but without government, a herd of barbarians or a colony of Hottentots.'   'The passenger,' he continued, 'is everywhere surprised or endangered by unexpected chasms, or offended or obstructed by mountains of filth . . . . such as a savage would look on with amazement, and that the grievance was without remedy, was to him a sufficient proof that no magistrate had the power to remove it.'[3]   So decayed and tottering were many of the houses in the city proper, that it was far from uncommon for a short paragraph such as the two here following to make its appearance in the daily papers of the time :—'A house in Queen Street, Lincoln's Inn Fields, which had been lately repaired, and two in Gracechurch Street, which showed no signs of craziness, suddenly tumbled down to the ground.'   Or as this :—'An old lodging-house in Plumtree Court, Broad Street, St. Giles's, fell down, by which accident seven poor wretches were crushed to death, and many were desperately maimed. There being other houses in the court in like tottering condition, the mob assembled in a few days afterwards and pulled them down.' Stonecutter Street and Shoe Lane were full of such empty and dilapidated houses, and within their walls crept poor and destitute creatures to find shelter and to die oftentimes of starvation. The reader will scarcely be surprised after reading this to learn that swine fed in the streets and lanes of the city. In a paragraph of that valuable compilation the 'Annual Register,' under date of December 31, 1760, it is stated that a 'great many hogs were lately seized by the churchwardens, overseers, and constables of the parish of St. George's, Hanover Square, and sold for the benefit of the poor, agreeable to the 8th and 9th of William III., which makes all hogs forfeited that are bred, fed, or kept in houses or the paved streets.'

Let us suppose a pedestrian who wished to perambulate the metropolis started from Tyburn turnpike, which stood on the high road to Oxford (the present Oxford Street), at the entrance of Hyde Park, where now the Marble Arch stands, hard by a commodious inn known as the 'Pillars of Hercules.' The sites of the palatial residences which thence fringe the Uxbridge Road on the right-hand side, and which occupy an angle between it and the Edgware Road, would then have presented to his gaze an extensive waste, dotted with squatters' huts. The entire locality was one that was loathed and detested by all respectable people until 1783, and indeed long afterwards, by reason of the ominous name of Tyburn gallows, where deserters were commonly shot, and where on Monday mornings men, women, and even children were executed by the dozen for petty larceny, and in vindication of other offended laws. Within sight was the burying-ground of St. George's, Hanover Square, now eclipsed by Stanhope Street and Albion Street, and a few old houses on each side of the Edgware Road, in addition to some ale-houses of very picturesque appearance, screened by high elms, with long troughs for watering the teams of the hay-waggons on their way to and from market.[1]

[1] Henry Angelo's *Reminiscences*, i. p. 230.

It was at one of these houses that the sheriffs and other officials used to dine after attending the executions. Within a mile from Tyburn turnpike the pedestrian would then have found himself literally among green fields, farmhouses, and babbling brooks.[1] Bayswater was a tiny hamlet surrounded by fields and tea-gardens, and thence on towards Acton and Brentford there stretched a tract of ' delicate pleasant country.'[2] Paddington was as remote and rustic a village as any in the English shires, being ' from the amenity of its scenery much resorted to by the lovers of the picturesque.' Acres of it were covered by fields which afforded pasture for droves of cattle, and among them it was possible to forget any proximity to the busy haunts of men. Marylebone in 1760 was a small village distant from the city about a mile. Sir Samuel Romilly mentions in his ' Memoirs ' that he removed his family thither on one occasion during the summer, in order that they might breathe a purer air than that of London. What is now known as High Street, Marylebone, was covered with houses, semi-detached, chiefly tenanted by 'families who kept their coaches.'[3] Leaving Kilburn on the right, and crossing the fields to the left, the pedestrian would have reached (after a pleasant stroll along a road such as it now would be only possible to see fifteen or twenty miles from town) a beautiful suburban village lying a little to the west of Hampstead. This was Frognal. Around Hampstead itself, then verily ' a place of groves,' and Highgate, to which the same description would have applied, stretched enclosed cornfields, green pastures, verdant meadows, and thickly-planted hedgerows. A proof of the healthy repute of the first of these two localities is afforded by the fact that in 1748 Mrs. Samuel Johnson engaged lodgings there, whither her husband also occasionally resorted for the benefit of the country air.[4]

But we have wandered too far afield. Let us return. Presuming the visitor to London taking his way down the Oxford Road from Tyburn turnpike in the direction of St. Giles's Pound, he would have noticed the houses fairly numerous on

[1] James Boaden, *Memoirs of Mrs. Inchbald*, ii. p. 99.
[2] Ralph Thoresby's *Diary*, ii. p. 132.
[3] Henry Angelo's *Reminiscences*, i. p. 231 ; Romilly, *Memoirs*, i. p. 9.
[4] Boswell's *Life*, ed. 1793, i. p. 210.

the right-hand side, but not so numerous on his left. Streets
in which to-day it would be impossible to find breathing room
for one or two sickly plants or shrubs, were then resplendent
with flowers and trees. Hanover and Portman Squares had
been built about twenty years. Portman Place was in process
of erection. Baker Street was not yet in existence, and consequently fields stretched between it and the New Road.
Cavendish Square, built about 1720, was enclosed by a dwarf
brick wall surmounted by a heavy wooden railing, and the site
of Harley Street was Harley Fields, memorable as being one of
the numerous scenes of George Whitefield's evangelistic labours.[1]
In the rear of Rathbone Place was a large pond (designed to
resemble the reservoir in the Green Park) surrounded with
walks. At the upper end of this was a sluice, and fronting it a
house much celebrated for the manufacture of Bath buns and
Tunbridge-water cakes. Thence a row of huge venerable elms
led to a famous house of public entertainment called the 'Cock
and Pye,' surrounded by extensive grounds and an ingenious
maze, one path of which led into Tottenham Court Road.[2]
Tottenham Court Road itself, beyond Whitefield's Tabernacle
(which was built in 1754 upon the site of a deep pond, called
the 'Little Sea'), had hedges which in summer were redolent of
hawthorn. A turnstile opened into the Crab Tree Fields which
extended almost uninterruptedly to the 'Adam and Eve Tavern'
(the then aspect of which may be seen in Hogarth's 'March to
Finchley') and thence onwards to the 'Mother Red Cap.'
Near Union Street stood a cottage with a garden before it, immediately behind which extended a walk lined on either side by
elm trees, commanding views of the distant hills of Harrow,
Highgate, and Hampstead. Crossing the New Road by a
turnstile at the entrance of a meadow, a footpath led to a tavern
long since consigned to the custody of oblivion, known as 'The
Queen's Head and Artichoke,' a little beyond which was another
turnstile that led to the 'Jew's Harp' House, Tavern, and Tea
Gardens. Along by-paths over extensive fields where snipe were
occasionally shot, the pedestrian reached Kentish Town, then

[1] J. T. Smith, *Life and Times of Nollekens*, i. p. 131.
[2] Moser's 'Vestiges,' *Europ. Mag.* vol. iv. pp. 170-171.

literally a secluded village, containing 'about one hundred houses,' chiefly detached from each other, scattered promiscuously by the roadside, and inhabited by people 'who kept their coaches.'

Behind the grounds of Montagu House, the site of which is now occupied by the British Museum, lay Lamb's Conduit Fields (in summer time the resort of base-ball players [1]), extending westwards to Lisson Grove and Paddington, northwards to Primrose Hill, Chalk Farm, Hampstead, and Highgate,[2] eastwards to Battle Bridge, Islington, and St. Pancras ; and in order that this prospect might not be destroyed, the north side of Queen Square, the building of which had been begun in the reign of Anne, was allowed to remain open. The Foundling Hospital stood quite by itself, with the isolated burying grounds for the parishes of St. George the Martyr and St. George's, Bloomsbury, in its rear. The spacious gardens attached to Bedford House (which then occupied the north side of Bloomsbury Square) reached those of Montagu House. The ground immediately behind the north-west end of this building was occupied by a farm, while that lying further away was covered by fields (the occasional resort of duellists) between which and the distant hills was uninterrupted freedom of air.[3] It is probable that streets and roads to the extent of something like three miles lie between these two localities at the present time.

Still pursuing his course towards Holborn, the visitor reached the termination of Oxford Road at Tottenham Court Road, and plunged into the ancient limits of St. Giles's, noting as he did so, 'an inrailed column upon which seven dials counted the day' for the benefit of the inhabitants of a group of seven streets adjoining this abominable district which then constituted part and parcel of the parish of St. George's, Bloomsbury, and of which New Oxford Street now occupies the site. St. Giles's at that era was the licensed Alsatia of beggary and wretchedness, and its poverty-stricken and disreputable condition caused

[1] J. Strutt, *Sports and Pastimes* ; J. T. Smith, *Life and Times of Nollekens*, i. pp. 32-33, 37, 41.

[2] Dodsley's *Environs*, 1761, v. p. 240. Hatton, *New View*, p. 67.

[3] Miss Hawkins's *Memoirs*, i p. 52; Smith's *Book for a Rainy Day* ; Twiss's *Life of Lord Chancellor Eldon*, p. 354.

it to become a synonym for everything in the shape of coarseness, brutality, and ugliness. The entire district was a perfect labyrinth of courts and alleys, tenanted by beggars, thieves, and tramps, who crowded together in one hideous chaos of filth, disease, and gin. The rookeries and mouldy and dilapidated houses in Seven Dials, which were the resorts of French refugees and the outcasts of society, chiefly Irish, were chockfull of the vilest social horrors. One of Smollett's heroes, it may be remembered, was rescued from the hands of the soldiers by 'two Tatterdemalions from the purlieus of St. Giles's, and between them both there was but one shirt and a pair of breeches.' The scenes, too, of some of Hogarth's most celebrated pictures are laid in St. Giles's—particularly that of Gin Lane, which has for its background the church of St. George, Bloomsbury, built in 1731. The whole extent of this horrible district abounded in dens and kitchens where swarms of footpads and highwaymen congregated, and enjoyed complete immunity from the approach even of the Bow Street runners, the only police force then in existence, migrating to similar colonies in other parts of the town as their ranks swelled. It was in these kitchens that robberies were daily planned, where all ill-gotten gains were divided or gambled for, and where if deemed expedient the victims of foul play might be safely stowed away beneath false floors or double ceilings. The locality between the south side of High Holborn and Lincoln's Inn Fields was known as Whetstone Park, a formidable criminal colony, the rendezvous of the most desperate and abandoned characters whom the law either would or could not dare to touch.[1] From the back of Field Lane onwards as far as Saffron Hill, a ruinous district of dilapidated houses and rats' castles cumbered the ground, which among the many sinks of iniquity and vice abounding in London at this period maintained its supremacy ; where from generation to generation scores of young boys and girls were bred, nursed, and educated in crime, even to the pitch of moral lycanthropy ; where from the days of Elizabeth the tribe of canters, chaffers, and slop-mongers had led the dodge and

---

[1] Parton's *History of St. Giles in the Fields*, passim ; Archer's *Vestiges* ; Blizard's *Reflections on Police*, pp. 30–32.

had handed down in an academy of thieves, the science, the mystic symbolism, and occult nomenclature of their craft. One of the scenes in Hogarth's series of 'Industry and Idleness' is significantly distinguished as the Blood Bowl House, Chick Lane, which was an important part of this hateful locality. One wonders when pondering these facts what could have possessed the poet Gay to apostrophise London in the pages of his 'Trivia' as

> Happy Augusta! law-defended town!
> Where tyranny ne'er lifts her purple hand,
> But liberty and justice guard the land!

Between Bridewell Dock and Holborn and what is now called Farringdon Street, lay a canal called Fleet Ditch, the long gloomy Fleet Prison, and the Fleet Market. The Ditch at this time extended no higher than Fleet Bridge, all above being arched, covered over and converted into Fleet Market. The prison (razed to the ground by the 'No Popery' rioters of twenty years later) lay on the east side of the market (the east side of the present Farringdon Street), and took its name from the river which had once flowed by it. The rules or liberties of its inmates were the north side of Ludgate Hill, and the Old Bailey up to Fleet Lane, thence to the market and all the east side along by the prison itself to the bottom of Ludgate Hill.[1]

The Fleet Ditch in 1760 was navigable for barges by the assistance of the tide from the Thames as far as Fleet Street. Despite the vast sums of money expended upon it, Fleet Ditch continued until long after this date, as it had done in the past, to be a perfect disgrace to the city and a byword among men for filth and uncleanliness. Readers of the 'Dunciad' will remember that it was—

> To where Fleet Ditch with disemboguing streams
> Rolls the large tribute of dead dogs to Thames,
> The king of dykes, than whom no sluice of mud
> With deeper sable blots the silver flood,

that the votaries of Dulness were driven to their sports. Swift's details, penned some years earlier, in his lines descriptive of a city shower, are a trifle too realistic for quotation, but the

---

[1] Dodsley's *London*, ii. pp. 305-309.

nourishing effect of this muddy and genuine ditch may be gathered from the following paragraph which appeared in the Historical Chronicle of the 'Gentleman's Magazine,' under date of Tuesday, August 14, 1736 :—

A fatter Boar was hardly ever seen than one taken up this day coming out of Fleet Ditch into Thames. It proved to be a Butcher's near Smithfield Bars, who had mist [*sic*] him 5 months, all which Time it seems he had been in the common Sewer, and was improv'd in Price from 10*s*. to 2 guineas.

The unprotected state of the Ditch is evidenced in the subjoined paragraph extracted from the same source :—

On the 11th of January, 1763, a man was found in Fleet Ditch, standing upright and frozen to death. He appeared to have been a barber at Bromley in Kent. He had come to town to see his children, and had mistaken his way in the night and slipped into the ditch, and being in liquor he could not disentangle himself.

The fields which in the days of James I. stretched away from the rear of Gray's Inn to the northern heights remained as they had been in times past. Twenty years after the date to which this chapter has especial reference, Sir Samuel Romilly could say in writing to his sister from the chambers he was then occupying in No. 7 Gray's Inn Square, that, even in the depth of winter, the moment the sun peeped out he was in the country.[1] If it were possible for him to behold it now he would feel tempted to exclaim with Horace, *Tempora mutantur !* It was by the Gray's Inn Lane that the coach bearing 'Tom Jones' entered London to put up at the 'Bull and Gate' in Holborn. Something of the semi-rural character of the surrounding neighbourhood in the reign of George III. is indicated in the following paragraph, which appeared in the issue of the *Daily Courant* for November 12, 1765 :—

Friday afternoon, about two o'clock, a hare crossed the New Road near Dobney's bowling-green, ran to the New River Head, and from thence to Coldbath Fields, where in some turning among the different avenues she was lost. She appeared to have been hard run, by her dirty and shabby coat.

St. Pancras, where nearly half a century previously Swift had laid the scene of his 'Tale of a Tub,' still preserved a

---

[1] *Memoirs*, i. p. 139.

rural air—the graveyard surrounding the old church (in some parts entirely overgrown with docks and nettles) enclosed only by a low hand-rail and commanding extensive views of the surrounding country, besides an uninterrupted prospect of Whitefield's Tabernacle, Montagu House, Bedford House, and · Baltimore House.[1] Islington was a charming suburb, an isolated village, surrounded by open fields, and renowned for its dairies and purity of air, which induced many wealthy people to make it their abode. Such paragraphs as those subjoined are far from uncommon in newspapers of the period :—

Yesterday the corpse of Esq. Jervis, a stock-broker at the Exchange, who died worth 50,000*l.*, lay in state at his house at Islington, and this morning was carried thence to be interred at North Mimms in Hertfordshire.

Yesterday, died at the Shepherd and Shepherdess, near St. Luke's', Old Street, *where he went for the recovery of his health,* Mr. George West, surgeon, in Bow Churchyard, Cheapside.

Within easy reach of ' The Angel,' in the midst of solitary fields, wherein cows might be seen feeding in hundreds,[2] stood five spas, or fashionable lounges, all within walking distance of each other. These Spas, which were much frequented not only by the London citizens and their families, but also by many of the nobility, were Merlin's Cave, the New Tunbridge Wells, Islington Spa, Bagnigge Wells, and Sadler's Wells, the waters yielded being mostly chalybeate. The site of Coldbath Square was then Coldbath Fields ; Exmouth Street stands upon what were the notorious Spa Fields, which from the south end of Rosoman Street to Pentonville and from St. John Street Road to the Bagnigge Wells Road, were devoted to the pasturage of cows.[3] Canonbury was a hamlet of Islington, and the number of ' transitory visitants ' who selected it as their abode ' for fresh air or to pursue their literary labours in retirement,' was not represented by unity. It is long since the eyes of newspaper readers were greeted by such an advertisement as this :—

April 11, 1780. At Canonbury Mansion House, near Islington. Elegant Apartments to Let, genteelly furnished by G. Delfosse.

[1] J. T. Smith's *Book for a Rainy Day*, pp. 64, 65, *seq.*
[2] Baird, *Ag. Middx.* p. 12.
[3] J. Britton's *Autob.* i. p. 62 ; S. Lewis's *Hist. Islington*, pp. 31–37.

·This situation is so well known to the Faculty that they have constantly with great success recommended it, where a pure fine air
necessary for recovery and establishment of health. Its contiguity
to the principal parts of the metropolis, and the conveniency of a
sixpenny stage every hour to the City, Holborn, Temple Bar, and
parts adjacent, render it exceedingly convenient.

The now densely-populated district of Clerkenwell was then
thinly inhabited, and abounded in tea gardens, mulberry gardens,
and mineral spas. In the vicinity stood a court of several narrow
alleys, filled with small huttish kind of houses, chiefly inhabited
by thieves and vagabonds, named Blueberry Alley, notorious
for its constant supply to Tyburn.[1] Mount Pleasant was not
then the forbidding region that it now is. Near at hand was a
place of public resort called Hockley-in-the-Hole, which possessed an evil reputation, chiefly by reason of its bear garden,
besides being full of ruinous old houses, some of which tumbled
down daily. The City Road was completed and opened for traffic
in 1761, and was a fine level thoroughfare, railed in on both sides,
and commanding on the right-hand side a fine prospect of Finsbury Fields, which then constituted a kind of vast metropolitan
gymnasium—the resort of archers, wrestlers, runners, boxers,
jugglers, and merry-andrews, and of mountebanks and charlatans
who there erected their booths and dispensed their never-failing
remedies. In Cripplegate was the notorious Grub Street, 'much
inhabited by writers of small histories, dictionaries, and temporary poems.' The site of what is now known as Finsbury Square
was then known as the Upper Moorfields. Separated at first by
a palisade, but afterwards by a low wall, was another space extending from the south side of the present Finsbury Square to
South Place and Eldon Street, and called the Middle Moorfields. The ground extending from South Place to the City
Wall, and from about Broad Street to Finsbury Pavement, was
known by the name of Lower Moorfields.[2] That the state of
the surrounding neighbourhood was anything but satisfactory is
evident from a newspaper correspondent so late as 1774, who in
drawing the attention of the city commissioners for the lighting
and paving to the lower part of Philip Lane, London Wall,

---

[1] S. Curwen's *Journal and Letters.*
[2] Dodsley's *London*, v. x.

stated that it 'had sunk down, and lay in a very bad condition, as most of the dirt from the upper part of the lane settled there, and was a great nuisance, being taken away but once a week.' The Upper and Middle Moorfields were encircled by trees. The Lower Moorfields were divided by very strong but clumsy wooden rails into four different squares, each containing a large grass-plot, surrounded on either side by a row of trees. Between these squares (which were called 'the quarters') were gravel walks ; and one extending from east to west, with a row of trees on each side, was denominated the City Mall, wherein a great concourse of well-dressed citizens of both sexes customarily took the air every Sunday noon in fine weather and on evenings ;[1] the fashionable beaux who frequented the Mall at such times never failing to give their gold-laced, three-cornered hats what was known as 'the Moorfields cock.'[2] Situated in the parish of St. Mary, Whitechapel, near the Tower of London, was the district called 'Rag Fair,' where old clothes and frippery were sold. Thomas Pennant, the antiquary, who well knew this locality, said of it that 'the articles of its commerce by no means belied the name, and that there was no expressing the poverty of the goods, nor yet their cheapness.'[3]

Fully three-fourths of the space now covered by houses in Hoxton, De Beauvoir Town, Kingsland, Clapton, Homerton, and Hackney was occupied by fields owned by market-gardeners and dairymen. So favoured was the latter suburb by wealthy citizens in the early part of the century, that Defoe, when writing his 'Tour,' thought it sufficiently worth while to place on record that there were then nearly a hundred coaches kept in it. The surrounding neighbourhood was hedged with desperate characters, whose operations sometimes assumed the form indicated in the subjoined paragraph :—

Sunday, October 4, 1789.—About seven o'clock in the morning the nephew of John Lomax, Esq., of Homerton, was attacked on his way to Hackney by two villains, who knocked him down, robbed him of his watch and money, and attempted to murder

---

[1] *London and its Environs*, vol. v. p. 10.
[2] Pink's *Hist. Clerkenwell*, ed. Wood.   [3] *Lond.* p. 433.

him. While he lay on the ground, one of the villains cried out,
'Kill him! kill him!' At which instant a stroke was aimed at his
throat with a knife, which cut through several folds of a silk
handkerchief which he fortunately had about his neck. In endeavouring to defend his throat, the ends of two of his fingers were
almost severed. On a gentleman's servant opening the back door
of a garden, the villains made off.[1]

At that epoch East London generally was widely different from
what it is now. Stepney, which has long been incorporated with
the metropolis itself, was then simply a rural hamlet surrounded
by fields, stretching away in the direction of Ilford, while Mile
End and Bethnal Green partook largely of the same character.

The space lying between Westminster and Millbank—at
this day densely covered with houses—was, in the days of
George III., a desolate tract known as the 'Downs,' or Tothill
Fields; or 'Tuttle Fields,' as they were called in the language
of the riff-raff who mostly frequented them, to hunt ducks in
the summer and to skate in the winter months. It was the
Campus Martius of metropolitan blackguardism; the haunt
of bull-baiters, badger-drawers, prize-fighters, and the like.
Beyond Tothill Fields stretched, almost as far as Chelsea,
another desolate region, covered with market-gardens, cabbage-
grounds, stagnant ditches, and patches of stunted grass.

Vauxhall Bridge did not exist. Its construction was not
even contemplated. Millbank Penitentiary Prison as yet was
slumbering in the deep of Time. The district now designated
Belgravia was as yet very little better than a swamp. The sites
of Eaton Square and the streets adjoining were then occupied,
partly by the lands of Ebury Farm, and partly by market-gardens
bounded by mud-banks, and a wide open space called the
'Five Fields;' where rank grass and weeds grew luxuriantly,
and where at night lay in wait footpads and other questionable
characters, as they had done in the days when the talk of the
town ran on the 'Tatler' and the 'Spectator.' The district round
Pimlico (then noted for its ale) was principally covered with
osier-beds, tea-gardens, and waste bog. Close by was situated
Stratton's Ground, a playing-field for the boys of Westminster
School. Drinking tea at Pimlico was quite an institution; and

[1] *Gent. Mag.* 1789.

hundreds of the working-classes patronised the neighbourhood for the sake of inhaling the pure air of its fields.

Through pleasant green fields and nurseries the pedestrian might have walked to Chelsea, where there was not only a flourishing physic garden belonging to the Society of Apothecaries, but a famous coffee-house kept by one Don Saltero, and an establishment at the bottom of Jews' Row, renowned for the excellent quality of its buns and custards.[1] Near, too, stood an old ale-house, known as 'Jenny's Whim,' surrounded by a garden and bowling-green, whither parties constantly resorted to enjoy a day's amusement in eating strawberries, cream, cake and syllabub;[2] a circumstance which provoked Gay to say—

> Then Chelsea meads o'erhear perfidious vows,
> And the press'd grass defrauds the grazing cows.

No bridge spanned the Thames between Fulham and Putney. Along the riverside dwelt numbers of boat-builders, watermen, and alehouse keepers. Here and there, on the road to Fulham and Parson's Green, a gentleman's house might be seen. Within a short space of time the pedestrian arrived at Kensington, with its gravel-pits, then some considerable distance from the metropolis, whither the consumptive were often sent for recovery by their physicians. Still pursuing his way along the road shaded by trees he would have reached Knightsbridge, where several farmhouses and a maypole would have saluted his gaze. From Knightsbridge a brisk walk brought him to Hyde Park Corner, close by which stood a commodious inn known as the 'Pillars of Hercules;' at which, it may be remembered, Fielding makes Squire Western take up his quarters on his visit to the capital in quest of Sophia.[3] The present Park Lane was then known as Tyburn Lane, and Mayfair, destined in later days to be 'a seat of the most elegant population,' was a district called Shepherd's Market, which was annually the scene of a low metropolitan carnival, frequented by the tag-rag and bobtail of the town. Piccadilly extended on the south side of Hyde Park as far as it does at present; a turnpike stood facing St.

[1] Gay's *Trivia*; Swift's *Journal to Stella.*
[2] *Maids of Honour.* A tale, *temp.* George I.
[3] *Tom Jones*, p. 16, c. 2.

George's Hospital, and at the termination of Constitution Hill
stood a fine old brick building called Buckingham House.
There were no houses in existence at this time on the west
of St. George's Hospital, and the ground was occupied by the
warehouses of stonemasons in much the same manner as the
Euston Road is now. 'Sorry I am;' remarks Ralph, in his
'Critical Review of Public Buildings,' 'that the shops and
yards of the statuaries in Piccadilly afford a judicious foreigner
such flagrant opportunities to arraign and condemn our taste.'[1]
Entering St. James's Park, the pedestrian would have beheld
innumerable bagwigs, ruffles, and hoop petticoats on the Mall,
which lay on the north side, and in the Birdcage Walk, which
lay on the south side. The next important point would have
been Leicester Fields, which, until long after the accession of
George III., was one among the rendezvous of the chuck-
farthing players. Near at hand, on the north of a neglected
open space, stood the King's Mews, behind which was a horse-
pond, where all pickpockets captured in the neighbourhood
were customarily ducked.[2] So greatly did this locality abound
with indigent French refugees, harried out of their own land
by persecution, 'that it was an easy matter for a stranger to
imagine himself in France.'[3] The pedestrian now turned into
St. Martin's Lane, the lower part of which then extended as
far as the Strand, and came to a termination nearly opposite
Northumberland House, a pile which has since disappeared.
Around St. Martin's Church was a rookery, the local habitation
of all the thieves and low characters within five miles. Thence
emerged the desperadoes by whom highway robberies were
perpetrated to such an extent. Trafalgar Square and the
National Gallery were among the improvements that were to
be. In the Strand, there still stood the last remaining land-
mark of the peculiar jurisdiction of the City (which now exists
only in the memory), Temple Bar; the outlet from which,
narrow and inconvenient to the last degree, was known by the
name of the 'Pass,' under which it is frequently mentioned
in the 'Spectator.' Upon the top of the 'City Golgotha,' as

[1] Ed. 1783, p. 185
[2] J. T. Smith, *Antiq. R.*   [3] Maitland, *Hist. Lond.*

D 2

the Bar was sometimes called, bleached a row of grinning skulls of the chief actors in the Jacobite insurrections of 1715 and 1745 ; people curious in such matters being enabled to enjoy a peep at them, as Horace Walpole mentions, by the aid of spy-glasses, at the small charge of one halfpenny. Where Burleigh Street now stands, a block of buildings known as Exeter 'Change stood, containing two walks below stairs and as many above, with shops fitted with casement windows on each side for sempsters, milliners, hosiers, &c. Wild beasts were exhibited in rooms upstairs.

On the north side of the Strand stood a narrow passage called 'Butcher Row' (originally a meat market), a filthy slum, which consisted of a stack of wretched old wooden houses, with one story overhanging the other.[1] The row was a place of considerable traffic, containing numerous shops and taverns, all kept in what in earlier days had been the abodes of princes and ambassadors, and long constituted a great nuisance and impediment. White Friars teemed with hovels and lay-stalls, and a large tract lying between Fleet Street and the Thames, 'heaped with filth and ruins,' afforded hiding-places to a numerous swarm of the most degraded poor.

The Thames was a great silent highway between London and Westminster. Hundreds of red-stockinged watermen, who literally possessed charters for barbarity and extortion, plied their wherries up and down its stream, saluting passengers of all grades with volleys of scurrilous raillery and abuse.[2] Steam-boats there were none, but the river was much used by plea-sure-parties bound for Ranelagh, Vauxhall, Cuper's Gardens, Folly House, an establishment at Blackwall, and the Folly, a sort of floating coffee-house and tavern on a very large vessel (said to have been the hulk of a ship of war or frigate), which was moored on the water nearly opposite Hungerford Stairs, abreast of Cuper's Gardens.

Save by ferry, the only way through which access could be gained to the Surrey side of the river was by the London and Westminster Bridges. The former, as late as the accession of

[1] Mozer's 'Vestiges,' *Europ. Mag.*, vol. xlii. pp. 9-11.
[2] Grosley, *Tour to London.*

George III., was still lined at frequent intervals on both sides by lofty houses of many stories (chiefly tenanted by pin and needle makers), with ponderous arches overhead to save them from falling in. It was beneath one of these arches that there turned a water-wheel, which supplied the metropolis in great part with water. The way available for foot and vehicular traffic was practically a series of short low tunnels, which were simply perilous to foot-passengers, who could proceed in safety only by following in the muddy wake of the carts and carriages as they crawled along. Pennant, who well remembered the street on London Bridge, describes it as 'narrow, irksome, and dangerous to passengers from the multitude of carriages.' There were no posts to preserve the pathway as in other streets ; consequently, whenever the bridge was much thronged (which was not unfrequently the case in the middle of the day, owing to the perpetual passage of coaches and carriages), pedestrians were often an hour before they finally succeeded in making their way across, and but for several open spaces guarded by iron palisades, there was absolutely nothing to indicate to them that, instead of walking through an unusually crowded thorough-fare, they were actually crossing the river Thames.[1] The strength of current at this point may be inferred from Thomas Pennant, who, writing in his well-known ' History of London,' published in 1787, states that, having occasion to proceed by boat from Westminster along the river, he alighted at the Old Swan Stairs, through fear of adding to the many thousands who had lost their lives in dashing down the rapids at London Bridge, and walked to Billingsgate, where he re-embarked.[2] The commerce of the Thames was chiefly conducted by means of the London Dock and the East India Docks.

By whatever way the traveller made his way across the river, he would not have failed to notice how thickly enveloped the city was in heavy smoke. This sable curtain was occasioned partly by the prodigious quantities of matter uncon-

[1] Gonzales' *Voyage to England*, 1731, p. 47 ; *Narrative of a Journey through England*, 1752 ; Brayley's *Londiniana*, ii. 256.
[2] Pennant, *London*, p. 340; J. T. Smith's *Antiq. R.* ; R. Thomson, *Chronicles of London Bridge*.

sumed in the process of combustion, in the centres of manufactures situated along the banks of the Thames;[1] and partly
by the coal burnt in glass-houses, in earthenware manufactories,
and in the gunsmiths' shops and dyers' yards.   M. Grosley,
who visited England in 1765, bears testimony to the ill-effects
produced by the smoke upon both the exteriors and interiors
of private houses and public buildings.

Crossing Westminster Bridge into Surrey, the visitor might
have proceeded to Wandsworth, annually the scene of the mock
election of the sham 'knight' or 'mayor' of Garratt Lane, a
small village situated on the road to Tooting, a ceremony which
half the population of the metropolis turned out to see, to the no
small emolument not only of the local idlers and tavern-keepers,
but of all the thieves and vagabonds for seven miles round.   The
road to Greenwich exhibited for several miles houses and fields.
The ancient archiepiscopal palace of Lambeth was at this date
surrounded by an Augean stable of filth and vice, a labyrinth
of courts and alleys, as bad as could be, some of them afford-
ing the privileges of sanctuary to insolvent debtors, who
emerged from their retreat only on Sunday, when they could
plead and claim immunity from arrest.   The spot destined
in later days to be occupied by the Nine Elms railway station
was then a space of fields, between which and Southwark,
or the Borough, as it is generally termed—then, as now,
densely inhabited by the scum of the population—stretched
St. George's Fields, an open space of very considerable extent;
which during the summer was infested by footpads, and during
the winter inundated for several consecutive months.   It was
in these very fields that, in 1780, the fanatical Lord George
Gordon harangued the mob of some 20,000 strong, who afterwards created those fearful disturbances which are known to all
students of our annals as the 'No Popery' riots.   Situated in
the midst of St. George's Fields, about a mile from the Southwark end of Westminster Bridge, there might have been seen 'a
neat little regular town, consisting of one street, surrounded by
a very high wall and including an open piece of ground.'   This

---

[1] Grosley, *Tour to London*, i. p. 44.

was the King's Bench Prison, which was attached to the Court of the same name, and wherein were confined all such as had been charged with contempt of the Courts of King's Bench, Chancery, Common Pleas, and the High Court of Admiralty. On St. Margaret's Hill, Southwark, stood another well-known prison, the Marshalsea; where pirates were confined along with such debtors for whom no accommodation could be provided within the precincts of the Fleet. A fourth prison, which was known as the Compter, or prison of the city's Court of Record, stood in Mill Lane, Tooley Street.

From Blackfriars Bridge to the Elephant and Castle at Newington there were not, including both sides of the road, fifty habitations. The Magdalen Hospital was an isolated building in the midst of fields. The bun-houses were known to every child in the metropolis, and a *lactarium*, or movable milk booth, much resorted to by people of delicate health, was usually stationed in a field a few yards to the right of the turnpike near the Obelisk. Towards the close of the American War, many speculative builders in the metropolis were practically ruined, and the road from Blackfriars Bridge to the Obelisk presented for years a melancholy scene of half-finished shells of houses, technically termed carcases, all crumbling to ruin, and long rows of arches designed for the cellars of houses, the foundation of which constituted the limits of the ruined builder's pecuniary liability.[1]

To the east of Newington turnpike a marsh was plainly visible. Newington Causeway was then what its name implied, a paved thoroughfare across a tract of marshy land. Newington Butts was simply an archery ground. Rotherhithe was a mere village known as Redriff, and Bermondsey, which was noted for a mineral spa that had been discovered in its vicinity, answered to the same description. Both Camberwell and Clapham were mere villages, surrounded by fields of which the hedges were 'perfumed by sweet-smelling blossoms'[2] and in which such events as the following not unfrequently took place :—

[1] Place MSS. Add. MSS. Brit. Mus. **27,826.**
[2] S. Curwen's *Journal and Letters*, p. **349.**

Wednesday night last, Captain Lambert was stopped by three footpads between Clapham and Peckham and robbed of a um of money and his gold watch.[1]

The present Old Kent Road was known as Kent Street Road. It was a continuation of the long narrow Kent Street in the Borough, and constituted the great highway between the south-eastern portion of England and the capital. Rocques's map of London, published in 1750, exhibits it lined with hedgerows, but Smollett, writing sixteen years later, describes 'the avenue to London by way of Kent Street' as 'a most disgraceful entrance to such an opulent city;' and was of opinion that 'a foreigner, in passing through this beggarly and ruinous suburb, conceived such an idea of misery and meanness as all the wealth and magnificence of London and Westminster were afterwards unable to destroy.'

At this period certain districts of London were the seats of peculiar crafts or professions. In Fleet Street and Ludgate Hill, for example, were to be found the shops of the most eminent linen drapers; St. Paul's Churchyard, Paternoster Row, Temple Bar, and Piccadilly swarmed with the shops of the booksellers; milliners established themselves in Change Alley and in the immediate vicinity of the Exchange; Westminster Hall was full of hucksters' booths; Leadenhall was the great market for the sale of beef; Newgate Market was resorted to on account of its mutton; St. James's for veal; Clare Market was much resorted to by country butchers and higglers on the market days, which were Wednesdays and Saturdays; Pall Mall and Shire Lane were the grand marts for perfumery; Cranbourne Street and Leicester Alley for coachbuilders and goldsmiths; Thames Street for cheese; Covent Garden, as now, for fruit and vegetables; Little Britain and Moorfields were the earthly paradises of bibliophiles and zealous antiquaries, who there rummaged among the booksellers' stalls for rare tomes, and very frequently, like Ralph Thoresby, succeeded in finding them; Seven Dials was the classic home of ballad-mongers; Monmouth Street, ostensibly a depôt for cast-off wearing apparel, afforded great facilities for the disposal of stolen and ill-gotten goods ; while Change Alley, Cornhill, sounded and resounded for hours together with quotations of prices and advertisements, and with a ceaseless hubbub caused by the crowds of stockbrokers and sharejobbers by which it was frequented.[1]   Leadenhall Market was accounted the finest shambles in Europe, and contained at the period of Gonzales' visit one hundred standing stalls for the sale of beef alone. The court or yard was on Tuesdays a market for leather, to which the tanners resorted ; on Thursdays the waggons from Colchester and other parts rolled in, bearing baize, and the fellmongers with their wool ; on Fridays a market was opened for the sale of raw hides, and on Saturdays for beef and other provisions.   There was a third market at Leadenhall for the sale of herbs, roots, and fruit.   The chief markets in Smithfield were those for live cattle, nor, as the author of the work usually attributed to Gonzales observes, were there anywhere better riding horses to be purchased if the buyer had skill, despite a great deal of jockeying and sharping used by the dealers in horse-flesh.[2]   In the neighbourhood of Smithfield was Cloth Fair, full of decayed and rotten houses, the sudden fall of which frequently occasioned such a disaster as that indicated in the newspaper paragraph subjoined :—

Yesterday morning the body of an elderly gentlewoman, who was advertised in the paper, was taken out of the ruins in Middle Street, Cloth Fair, mangled in a shocking manner. We understand she was going in Long Lane towards Smithfield, when an over-driven ox affrighted her back into Cloth Fair, where she unfortunately retired for safety ; but, at the very instant, two houses gave way, and buried her in the ruins.

The capital at the accession of Queen Anne, including the city, Westminster, and Southwark, was almost confined to the lower part of the valley of the Thames.   From east to west it extended five miles, and from north to south its greatest breadth was under two miles.   At the close of the eighteenth century, calculating one continued junction of buildings, London could

---

[1] Gay, *Trivia*, b. ii. ; Macky, *Journey* ; Ralph Thoresby's *Diary*, ii. pp. 33, 121, 126.
[2] *Public Advertiser*, April 21, 1790.

not have been less than eight miles in length and three miles at its extreme breadth.

Many years ago, the great Dr. Arnold of Rugby, in writing to a pupil who had gone to reside in Tasmania, said that he could always better fancy the actors in distant lands when he had a distinct idea of the scenes amid which they were acting. Should the reader entertain the same opinion with respect to distant times, the foregoing sketch of the London of his great-grandfathers, rough and imperfect as it is, will not have been drawn in vain.

CHAPTER III.

SOME PHASES OF TOWN LIFE.

The population of London during the eighteenth century—Isolation of the various districts—Its causes and effects—The daily life of a Beau—'Bloods,' 'Frolics,' and 'Macaronies'—Eighteenth-century hours—The belle of fashion and her mode of life—Conversation—Swearing—Excessive drinking—Eminent hard drinkers—The classes and the masses—Life of the commonalty—Places of amusement and entertainment—Fashionable residential localities—The Mall in St. James's Park—'Shoemaker's holiday'—Wedding and funeral customs—Marrowbones and cleavers—Lying in state—Insecurity of life and property—The life of the streets—Thieves and their practices—Vails-giving—Footmen.

THE mode of living both among the upper and lower grades of society in London during the last century closely resembled in some respects that of the present day. In other respects, however, there is a marked difference. The nobility in general were much the same as they are now, and were distinguished from others by their palatial dwelling-places, lavishly furnished, by the magnificence of their equipages, and by the sumptuousness of their tables. The gentry were generally remarkable for their wealth and refinement, but pressed very closely upon the heels of the nobility as regarded their extravagant manner of living. The same may be said of the mercantile classes. Coarseness and brutality, as might be expected, distinguished the lower classes in a pre-eminent degree. In 1700 the metropolis, which now contains upwards of four millions of people, contained only five hundred and fifty thousand and odd souls. By 1750 the population had increased by not more than fifty thousand. Half a century later the capital did not contain one million of inhabitants. Though the extent of the city was commensurately limited, the inhabitants of the various

districts which it comprised were not only almost totally un-
acquainted with each other but were quite distinct in their
habits, manners, and characteristics. Obviously this common
ignorance originated in the complete lack of communication
which then existed, and which precluded one section of the
community from paying frequent visits to the other section.
It must be clearly borne in mind that a walk from Tyburn
Turnpike to Mile End Green, or from Mile End Green to
Tyburn Turnpike, was not then an easy accomplishment. To
be conveyed thither in a hackney-coach or a sedan-chair, then
the sole means of conveyance, was not only very tedious but
very expensive. Thus each district of London was comparatively isolated. Such a state of isolation tended to produce
peculiarities. These peculiarities were never corrected, and
the consequence was that those resident in the districts situated
to the west of Temple Bar differed as much from the house-
holders and shopkeepers of Bishopsgate Without, Whitechapel,
Stepney, and the other localities which lay on the Essex side
of the city as they now do from the peasantry of Brittany or
the Western Pyrenees.

Judging from those curious memoranda of the passing hour,
the budgets of family correspondence and the diaries kept by
the careless, light-hearted, and too often light-headed idlers of
the day, who spent the best part of their lives in the capital, it
would seem as if they seldom or never imposed any very great
restraints upon themselves as to the time of rising. Roughly
speaking, a fine gentleman of the Georgian era ordinarily began
the day about ten o'clock in the forenoon by a general reception of visitors in his dressing chamber, having first fortified
himself for that arduous task by swallowing a cogue of Nantsey.
When the last batch of callers had taken their departure he
rose and placed himself under the superintendence of his
valet for about two hours. Now was brought into requisition
his extensive assortment of perfumery—oil of Venus, spirit of
lavender, atar of roses, spirit of cinnamon or eau-de-luce—
among others—with which the various articles of attire were
severally and carefully sprinkled. Then, as now, there were
in vogue certain sweetly-scented soaps which were largely

patronised by fashionable beaux, and with a cake of one of these he freely lathered his hands and face. He next dabbed his face with scented powder till it was as white as that of a miller, and plastered his hair with scented pomatum, and having perfumed his pocket-handkerchief with rose or jessamine water, tied his cravat and adjusted his periwig, he finally sat down to dine about three, either alone or in company with his friends. The repast concluded, he buckled on his sword, brushed his hat with great care, gave it the 'cock,' placed it with much ceremony on his head, and for a brief space surveyed himself in the mirror. When quite satisfied with his appearance the beau took up his cane, ordered a sedan-chair, and proceeded in state to some coffee-house in the neighbourhood of St. James's (generally White's), where for about an hour he aired his political views, or tickled the ears of the company with choice samples of his wit and pleasantry, intermingled with jests from the newest play or the gist of the latest scandalous story that had been circulated. Then this 'killing creature,' having first smeared his upper lip with snuff, hailed a chair and was borne along to the door of the playhouse, where, instead of attending to the performance (his mind would have recoiled with horror at the thought !), he wandered from pillar to post, now laughing and chatting with his friends, and then pulling out by turns his watch and pocket-handkerchief. When the play concluded the beau usually repaired either to the coffee-house or to the residence of some boon companions, with whom he spent the remainder of the night, lending a hand at crimp, ombre, loo, or whist, over bowls of punch and bottles of claret, until the small hours of the following morning—not unfrequently being conducted reeling home by a friendly watchman, bribed with sixpence for the purpose. The sketch here presented is of course open to slight modification, for absolute likeness in individuals it is impossible to find anywhere, but that this was the mode of the age in its main outlines is incontestable.

Every age of a nation's history is characterised by what in the German language is called the 'Zeitgeist,' a term corresponding to the 'spirit of the age,' in our own tongue, a mould or form into which all the ordinary mortals of the period fall, and which is relieved only by strong individual character. A Chesterfield or a Horace Walpole, for example, though falling generally into the habits of the time, would have presented a somewhat different aspect from this of the stereotyped beau of the early Georgian era.

There is introduced into the third chapter of the third book of Fielding's novel of 'Joseph Andrews,' a character named Wilson, who entertains the company assembled at a rural alehouse with an extract from the journal of one day of his life as a man of fashion in the capital, and which is worth reproducing here, because, although fictitious, it may be taken as a fair sample of the way in which a certain class of beaux apportioned the hours of their day in the first half of the eighteenth century :—

In the morning [he writes], I arose, took my great stick, and walked out in my green frock, with my hair in paper, and sauntered about till ten. Went to the auction ; told Lady B. she had a dirty face, laughed heartily at something Captain G. said (I can't remember what, as I did not very well hear it), whispered to Lord ——, bowed to the Duke of ——, and was going to bid for a snuffbox, but did not for fear I should have it ; 2 to 4 dressed myself ; 4 to 6 dined ; 6 to 8 coffee-house ; 8 to 9 Drury Lane playhouse ; 10 to 12 drawing-room.

To this short excerpt may be appended another illustrative of the same point. It occurs in John Macky's 'Journey through England,' written in 1714, and published in 1722 :—

We rise by nine, and those that frequent great men's levées find entertainment at them till eleven. About twelve the *beau monde* assembles in several coffee or chocolate houses. We are carry'd to these places in chairs or sedans. If it is fine weather we take a turn in the Park till two, when we go to dinner. The general way is to make a party at the coffee-house to go dine at the tavern, where we sit till six, when we go to the play, except you are invited to the table of some great man. After the play the best company generally go to Tom's and Will's coffee-houses, near adjoining, where there is playing picket, and the best of conversation till midnight.

Besides the clubs and the coffee-houses there were in London at this period several fashionable lounges, the chief of which was 'Betty's,' a celebrated fruit shop in St. James's, where men of rank met for the purpose of eating strawberries and discussing the news of the day.[1]

The beaux of the period were roughly divisible into three classes or groups. There was one class familiarly known as 'bloods,' apt with the gloves, and mighty in the use of the broadsword, who acted the parts severally of fine gentlemen at balls and assemblies, sharpers in the gambling-hells, and bullies at places of public resort. A second class of beaux passed under the name of 'frolics,' gentlemen who displayed their powers to great advantage in crippling or maiming the watchmen, in running tavern drawers through the body, and making bonfires of their cloaks. A not uncommon antic (strange and unaccountable as it seems) in which the 'frolics' would manifest their regard for the fair sex sometimes, is alluded to by the Earl of Cork in a paper which he contributed to the 'Connoisseur' in 1754. In the course of his remarks he states that upon one occasion he was present

at an entertainment where a celebrated lady of pleasure was one of the party ; her shoe was pulled off by a young man, who filled it with champagne and drank it off to her health. To this delicious draught he was immediately pledged by the rest, and then to carry the compliment still farther, he ordered the shoe itself to be dressed and served up for supper. The cook set himself seriously to work upon it ; he pulled the upper part of it (which was of damask) into fine shreds and tossed it up in ragout ; minced the sole, cut the wooden heel into very thin slices, fried them in butter, and placed them round the dish for garnish. The company testified their affection for the lady by eating very heartily of this exquisite impromptu.

The 'macaronies' constituted a third class of beaux which made its appearance in the capital towards the close of the American War. These extraordinary creatures rendered themselves conspicuous by wearing their hair in long curls, eye-glasses, red-heeled shoes, and by an extreme fondness for importing wholesale the tastes and fashions prevalent in continental society, in which for a time they had usually moved during the course of 'the grand tour.' Walpole mentions in one of his letters that the 'Macaronies' of his acquaintance were in the habit of carrying two watches—one to indicate

[1] Jesse's *Selwyn*, i. 230.

what the time *was*, and the other to indicate what it was *not* ; while General Burgoyne in his comedy of 'The Maid of the Oaks,' produced in 1774, causes a character, Lady Bab Barbloon, to say that the 'Macaronies' of her acquaintance added to other accomplishments that of being able to whistle songs through their toothpicks. To sketch by means of words the entire character of these autocrats of fashion would far transcend the powers of the pen, and consequently, in order to gain anything like an adequate idea of them, those sepulchres of departed fashion, the productions of the contemporary caricaturists, must be consulted.

Walpole in a letter to a friend thus describes a day of his life in the reign of George III. : 'I had been at the Duke of Cumberland's levée, then at the Princess Amelia's drawing-room ; from thence to a crowded House of Commons ; to dinner at your brother's ; to the opera ; to Madame Seilern's ; to Arthur's ; and to supper at Mrs. George Pitt's.' A 'mincing air' was one of the very marked characteristics of fashionable gentlemen of the last century. Miss Hawkins, when describing the personal appearance of Horace Walpole, takes occasion to observe : 'He always entered a room in that style of affected delicacy which fashion had made almost natural, viz. *chapeau bas* between his hands as if he wished to compress it, or under his arm, knees bent, and feet on tip-toe, as if afraid of a wet floor.'[1]   Here is the record of three days in the life of the Rt. Hon. W. Windham, M.P. for Norwich, 1784 :—

Jan. 22, 1784.—Did not rise till an hour after I ought. Got to the ice between one and two ; pleasant skating. Called on my way home on Lady Cornewall. Dined at Coleman's—company Mr. Elliot, Dr. Wharton, and Thom, Dr. King, Sir Joshua. Went afterwards to the Club—Dr. Brocklesby, Mr. Cook, Mr. Allen, Daines Barrington. Went to Brookes's and supped—Fox, Fitzpatrick, Hare, Sheridan, and late in the evening G. Selwyn.

23rd.—Skated in the morning. Went afterwards to Legge's, and went afterwards to Brookes's, where I stayed till the House of Commons broke up between two and three in the morning.

Feb. 4th.—Steevens called just after breakfast ; went with him to Sir Joshua and Burke's to settle engagement. Went with D. Burke to Kensington Gardens to skate, and stayed there with unusual satisfaction till near three, when I was obliged to come

---

[1] *Memoirs*, i. 106.

away, having engaged to dine with Steevens at Wood's, to go
afterwards to the pit, ' Measure for Measure.' After the play went
with Miss Kemble to Mrs. Siddons's dressing-room ; met Sheridan
there, with whom I sat in the waiting-room, and who pressed me
to sup at her house with Fox and G. North.' [1]

It is not easy to fix the precise hours at which fashionable
as well as other folk resident in London during the last century were in the habit of taking their meals. The usual
breakfast-hour seems to have been between eight and eleven.
The dinner-hour varied greatly. Swift, who frequently recorded
for the information of Stella particulars of the dinners he enjoyed at the houses of the nobility, speaks of dining in 1710
with Secretary St. John at three o'clock in the afternoon, and
with Lord Treasurer Harley an hour later. Macky, as the
reader will have noticed in the extract from his tour printed on
page 46, fixed the dinner-hour in Queen Anne's reign at two
o'clock. When Fielding began to write his novels (early in
the reign of George II.) dinner was served at four. From
Horace Walpole's correspondence it would appear that about
1765 people of rank customarily sat down to dine between
three and five. Mrs. Papendiek, writing in the latter quarter of
the eighteenth century, mentions that the dinner-hour for private families at that time was two, for company three o'clock.
Moritz, a Lutheran pastor sojourning in England in 1782,
mentions that in Westminster breakfasts were not taken earlier
than ten o'clock in the morning, and that dinners were usually
eaten between four and five. ' The farther you go from the
court,' wrote Moritz, ' into the city, the more regular and
domestic the people become ; and there they generally dine
about three o'clock, or as soon as the business of Change is
over.' Wilhelm von Archenholz, a Prussian captain, who
visited England two years later, says that in London tradesmen
dined at one o'clock, merchants and people of middling rank
at three, and the nobility at four or five.[2] Gouverneur Morris
speaks of dining with the Marquis of Lansdowne in May,
1790, after six.[3] Sir John Hawkins, commenting, in a book

---

[1] Windham's *Diary*, ed. by Hon. Mrs. Baring, pp. 203, 204.
[2] *Picture of England*, p. 315.   [3] *Diary*, i. p. 333.

which was published in 1787, on the hours then kept by London society, said that from the play the company were 'generally able to get away by eleven, the hour of assembling at other places of amusement, that from these the hour of retirement was three, which gave till noon the next day, nine hours, for rest, and after that sufficient time for a ride, auctions, or shopping, before five or six, the dinner hour.'[1] Professor Pryme of Cambridge, who was born in 1781, has recorded in his autobiographic memoranda that the customary dinner-hour for good families in 1794 was two o'clock ; for dinner-parties between three and four.[2] In the last few years of the century the dinner-hour for fashionable society got later than ever. Lord Eldon mentions that in 1789 lawyers dined in time to begin their evening labours between six and seven.[3] His lordship also says that he remembered the Duchess of Gordon asking Mr. Pitt to dine with her at eight o'clock in the evening, and his begging to be excused on the ground that he had arranged to sup with the Bishop of Lincoln.

This digression has almost caused the omission of all notice of the belle of fashion, who has a claim on the attention for a brief space. A fashionable lady in the last century seldom awoke until nearly noon, and, when she did, signalised the fact by three violent tugs at the bell and as many raps with the slipper on the floor, for her black servant to place at her bedside chocolate and cream, of which she would drink two, perhaps three, ' dishes.' Before the cups and saucers had been cleared away, the belle's intimate friends and acquaintances (male as well as female) would begin to arrive, and would be ushered into her chamber, where she would exchange salutations with them, devise plans for the day's arrangements, and participate in all the trifling matters which go to make up a meeting of the kind. The fourth of Hogarth's series of pictures depicting Marriage à-la-Mode represents the dressing-room levée of a fashionable couple in the first half of the eighteenth century. To the left the bridegroom sits sipping

---

[1] *Life of Johnson*, p. 262.   [2] *Autobiographic Recollections*, p. 21.
[3] Twiss's *Life of Lord Eldon*, i. p. 199.

his chocolate, surrounded by his friends and admirers, while the *friseur* is engaged in the task of curling the locks of his spouse, who is listening with rapt attention to the utterances of the councillor who lounges on a sofa by the side of her dressing-table. Within a short time the Sir Fopling Flutters, 'the Dapperwits, and Themises would make way for mercers, mantua makers, lacemen, milliners, haberdashers, and other ministers to female *parure*, who in their turn had to give place to quite a small army of duns and creditors presenting their bills. As soon as the belle had succeeded in getting rid of these 'nuisances'—a very difficult task sometimes—she arose and proceeded to put on all her charms, and, with the assistance of her maid, perhaps managed by dint of great exertion to complete her toilette by about three o'clock. While Betty was engaged dressing her hair 'my lady' fondled her lapdog or prattled to her parrot, her monkey, or squirrel. She then went down to dinner and wearied her guests, if any happened to be present, with worn-out jokes and 'phrases battered, stale, and trite.'[1] The second important point in the belle's programme was that of paying a visit, in company with her lapdog and monkey, either to some of the many toy shops, or the auction-rooms where articles of vertu, cockle shells, looking-glasses, dogs, snuffboxes, rings, masks, spectacles, and fancy china, for which beaux and belles had a perfect mania, and Oriental knick-knacks of all descriptions, were bought and sold. A poet of the time speaks of fashionable dames as taking

> their wonted range
> Through India shops to Motteux's or the Change,
> Where the tall jar erects its stately pride
> With antic shapes in China's azure dy'd ;
> There careless lies a rich brocade unroll'd,
> Here shines a cabinet with burnish'd gold.[2]

The India shops, which corresponded to the bazaars of modern days, were the principal repositories in the capital of curiosities of furniture and costly wearing apparel, and were so named by reason of the predominance of articles of exclusively Indian manufacture. The next step was to hail a chair

Swift, *Fashionable Ladies' Life.* [2] Dodsley, *The Toy Shop,* 1735.

E 2

and frequent the playhouse or the opera ; and, when tired of this, to return home to tea at six.   It was fashionable for ladies to take tea with one another by turns in the evening, and it was tacitly understood that tea would be followed by games at cards.   One after another the ladies would make their appearance, and over 'the cups that cheer but not inebriate,' discussed every conceivable subject, from religion to coquetry. Tea over, card-playing began, and continued with the exception of a short interval for supper till the voice of the drowsy watchman, bawling the morning hours, roused them to don their hoods and cloaks, and to wend their steps in the direction of their respective abodes.   If the weather proved so unfavourable that a belle was compelled to stop at home, she racked her brains to kill the time, and if she failed in this, had recourse to the bottle.   'Palestris in her drawing-room is supported by spirits to keep off the return of spleen and melancholy, before she can get over half of the day, for the want of something to do, while the wench in the kitchen sings and scours from morning to night.'[1]   The same remark which applied to the sketch which has been drawn of the beau applies also to this of the belle.   There were many women who passed the days of their lives far differently.   Among the fair correspondents of Samuel Richardson, the author of 'Clarissa Harlowe,' was Lady Bradshaigh.   This estimable woman, who resided with her husband, Sir Roger Bradshaigh, at Hague, near Wigan, in Lancashire, rendered the novelist upon one occasion the following account of the manner in which her days were usually spent :—'I rise about seven, sometimes sooner ; after my private duties, I read or write till nine ; then breakfast ; work and converse with my company till about twelve ; then if the weather permit, walk a mile in the garden, dress and read till dinner ; after which sit and chat till 4 ; from that till the hour of tea-drinking, each day variety of employments.'[2]   It may well be believed that there were many like-minded, but for every one there were ten whose mode of living differed little, if at all, from that which has just been indicated.   Between husbands

[1] *Tatler*, No. 248.
[2] Richardson's *Correspondence*, ed. Mrs. Barbauld, vol. vi. pp. 54-55.

and wives in general at this time hardly any unanimity as regards tastes and recreations can be said to have existed.

The conversation of people who moved in the polite circles of eighteenth-century London seldom extended to such topics as Shakespeare, taste, and the musical glasses. Cowper, when a law student in the Temple, contributed to the pages of the 'Connoisseur' an excellent essay on the subject which he afterwards expanded into his delightful poem entitled 'Conversation.' In that essay he expressed his conviction that it was vain to look for conversation where it might be expected in the greatest perfection—among people of fashion. 'There,' he wrote, 'it is almost annihilated by universal card-playing, insomuch that I have heard it given as a reason why it is impossible for our present writers to succeed in the dialogue of genteel comedy, that our people of quality scarce ever meet but to game.'[1] Dr. Priestley endorsed what Cowper said when he declared that the majority of men of quality in his time had no other resource but that of gaming. Swearing was of the essence of conversation in fashionable society, and was quite as common as it was fashionable. To curse and swear habitually would seem to have been considered as indispensable an accomplishment as the minuet. It is scarcely possible to point to any voluminous novel written during this period, having for its professed object the delineation of fashionable manners with exactitude and fidelity, that will not be found full of strange oaths, exhibiting all the various grammatical degrees, 'indifferent,' 'bad,' 'worse,' 'vile,' from the first chapter to the last. Addison found the practice in vogue among the fashionable society of Queen Anne's time, and censured it severely in the 'Spectator' as a reproach to the British nation. His censures, however, produced no effect, seeing that for more than half a century after he had ceased to write, some of the oaths with which fashionable dames were in the habit of emphasising their utterances would have almost thrown into the shade those which proceeded out of the mouth of Hotspur's wife. Indeed, Dr. Young went so far as to say that the accents of the average 'lady of quality' in his time were invariably graced by an oath

[1] *Conn.* Sept. 6, 1756; Archenholz, *Picture of England*, p. 262.

in order to supply 'the vacancies of sense,' and, considering
how very deficient many women of the period were in that respect, there was doubtless much truth in the remark. By an
Act passed in June 1746, a person convicted of cursing or
swearing, if a day labourer, common sailor, soldier, or seaman,
was to pay one shilling ; every person under the degree of
gentleman two shillings ; and every other person of or above
the degree of gentleman, five shillings ; for the second offence
to pay double ; and for every subsequent offence treble the
sum first inflicted. Offenders who refused to pay the penalty
could be committed to the House of Correction and be kept
to hard labour for 10 days. What effect this measure had
produced upon society by the time of George III. may be
inferred from the fact that a precocious Etonian (George
Canning) writing in an amateur periodical entitled 'The
Microcosm,' started in 1786, asserted that the practice of swearing pervaded all stations and degrees of men, from the peer to
the porter, and from the minister to the mechanic.

Nay [he says] even the female sex have to their no
small credit caught the happy contagion ; and there is scarce
a mercer's wife in the kingdom but has her innocent unmeaning
imprecations, her little oaths 'softened into nonsense,' and with
squeaking treble, mincing blasphemy into odsbodikins, slitter-
kins, and such like, will swear you like a sucking dove, ay, an
it were any nightingale.

Drunkenness characterised the upper classes of society
during the last century to a much greater extent than might be
supposed.[1] Addison, Steele, and Pulteney were all notoriously
addicted to the bottle. Goldsmith, Parnell, Churchill, Henry
Fox, and Lord Holland were never better pleased than when
they were engaged in driving round the cheerful bowl. And not
less so was the Earl of March, and Lord Carteret and the set in
which he moved. Even Sir Philip Francis, the reputed author
of the 'Letters of Junius,' is not above suspicion in this respect.
In all times of their tribulation fashionable gentlemen sought
comfort in liquor. 'I dined at Holland House,' wrote the
Right Hon. Richard Rigby, the Paymaster of the Forces, upon

---

[1] A man who drew the line at the third bottle was deemed little better
than a milksop.—*Life and Times of Frederick Reynolds*, i. p. 88.

one occasion to Selwyn, ' where, though I drank claret with the master of it from dinner till two o'clock in the morning, I could not wash away the sorrow he is in at the shocking condition his eldest boy is in.' It is stated by Mrs. Delany in her auto-biography, that Lord Bolingbroke, when in office, sat up whole nights drinking, and that in the morning, having bound a wet napkin round his forehead and eyes, to drive away the effects of intemperance, he hastened without sleep to his official busi-ness. This would scarcely be credited were it not for the fact that Mrs. Delany had access to the best sources of informa-tion, and doubtless derived her knowledge at first hand.

About the time that the American War drew to a termi-nation drunkenness increased among members of English Society in a marked degree. This was doubtless traceable to the very bad example which they found in the heir-appa-rent. Brinsley Sheridan, William Pitt, Lord Chancellor Eldon, Lord Stowell, and Professor Porson could each empty the con-tents of six bottles at a sitting, and did so repeatedly. Nor was society then at all scandalised at this. ' At the rehearsal on Wednesday night,' wrote Gilly Williams to George Selwyn from White's Coffee House, on Friday, January 11, 1765, ' of the speech at Lord Halifax's, Lord Lichfield came extremely drunk, and proposed amendments and alterations to the no small amusement of the company.'[1] The Earl of Carlisle, writing to George Selwyn in November 1771, accounts for a headache which he suffered at Lord Clermont's dinner on the ground that he drank all the red wine within his reach. Sir Gilbert Elliot, first Earl of Minto, in writing to his wife on March 8, 1787, tells her that from the opera he went to Mrs. Crewe's, ' where there was a large party, and pleasant people, among them, for example, Tom Pelham, Mundy, Mrs. Sheridan, Lady Palmerston, &c., besides all which were three young men so drunk as to puzzle the whole assembly.'[2] The names of these three indecorous youths, it may be added, were Orlando Bridgman, Charles Greville, and Charles Gifford. The last of the trio, unfortunately for himself, had then recently entered

[1] *Selwyn Corresp.* i. 352.
[2] *Life and Letters of Sir Gilbert Elliot*, ed. Countess of Minto, i. p. 135.

into possession of an estate worth about five thousand pounds per annum, and was engaged in endeavouring to squander it within one or two years at most.[1] In a letter dated Monday, April 2, 1787, Sir Gilbert Elliot discloses to his spouse the fact that the London belles of fashion were in the habit of imbibing something stronger than water. 'On Saturday,' says he, 'I dined at Lady Palmerston's. . . . Mrs. Cholmondeley came in just after dinner and called for a bottle of champagne, and was in one of her high-spirited humours.' It was not so very long before this that the same writer had expressed his inability to conceive how the men of business and the great orators of the House of Commons contrived to reconcile their inordinate consumption of liquor with their Parliamentary duties.

Men of all ages [he wrote] drink abominably. Fox drinks what I should call a great deal, though he is not reckoned to do so by his superiors, Sheridan excessively, and Grey more than any of them, but it is in a much more gentlemanly way than our Scotch drunkards, and is always accompanied with lively clever conversation on subjects of importance. Pitt, I'm told, drinks as much as anybody.

Most people have either heard or read something concerning the excesses of George IV. when Prince of Wales, but not all are aware that at the bacchanalian revels over which he presided at Carlton House he frequently drank wine to an excess that can only be termed bestial, excusing himself for so doing on the pretext that he was subject to nervous debility. It is asserted by Sir Nathaniel Wraxall that the heir-apparent's drinking excesses at the banquets held at his residence in Pall Mall more than once nearly proved fatal to him.

His Royal Highness has been [says he], as I know, critically rescued from suffocation, when the delay of half an hour or even a shorter time would have rendered unavailing all assistance. . . . As his father at an early part of his reign had been caricatured under the figure of 'Farmer George' . . . so the prince was portrayed in the shops of Bond Street as a 'Voluptuary in the Agonies of Indigestion,' his waistcoat unbuttoned, his respiration impeded by repletion, and the board before him covered with bottles of maraschino or cedrate.[2]

---

[1] Frederick Reynolds, in his amusing autobiography, bears testimony to the liquor ordinarily consumed at the Horse Guards about the same period (ii. pp. 87-89).   [2] Wraxall's *Memoirs*, ed. Wheatley, v. p. 364.

Where did the fashionable folk of London fix their residence in the last century? Principally in the west-central district of the capital, or, to speak more definitely, in a somewhat circumscribed extent of space between Piccadilly and the Oxford Road. Peter's Court, St. Martin's Lane, was 'a very handsome and genteel place, with good houses, well contrived, with little gardens to them.' Strype, speaking of Great Russell Street in 1720, calls it 'a very spacious and handsome street, inhabited by the nobility and gentry, especially on the north side. In its passage it saluteth Southampton House, Montagu House, and Thanet House, all these the seats of noblemen.' As late as the reign of George II., Covent Garden was a place where numbers of the nobility possessed town houses. 'The Lady Wortley Montagu,' so runs a paragraph in the issue of the 'Morning Advertiser' for March 6, 1730, 'who has been greatly indisposed at her house in Covent Garden for some time, is now greatly recovered, and takes the benefit of the air in Hyde Park every morning by advice of her physicians.' Rathbone Place, Great Titchfield Street, Foley Place, Great Portland Street, and Charlotte Street were all accounted fashionable. In connection with the last-named locality, it is worth mentioning that Richard Wilson, the celebrated Welsh landscape-painter, who died at the age of sixty-nine in May 1782, told one of his friends when taking the lease of a house in Charlotte Street, Fitzroy Square, that he liked the place, 'because no building interposed between it and the open country.'[1] Long since has the 'open country' which his eyes beheld disappeared beneath acres of bricks and mortar.

Among other haunts of fashion in the last century ranked Soho Square, where, it may be remembered, the worthy Worcestershire knight Sir Roger de Coverley customarily resided when in town; Cavendish Square, which was laid out in 1717; Hanover Square, which was built in 1731, and the numerous streets situated in the adjoining neighbourhood; Grosvenor Square, Grosvenor Place, built in 1767; St. James's Square, Hatton Garden, Bedford Row, Bedford Square, Russell Square, Bloomsbury Square, Golden Square, Red Lion Square, round

[1] T. Wright, *Life of R. Wilson*, p. 5.

about Lincoln's Inn Fields, Bow Street, Bury Street, and Berners Street. The newspaper obituary paragraphs of the time often afford a clue to the localities in which fashionable people fixed their abodes. Thus, in 1773 : 'Suddenly, at her house in Lisle Street, Leicester Fields, Lady Sophia Thomas, sister of the late Earl of Albemarle.'

All through the century the Mall in Hyde Park continued to be a favourite daily promenade for people of quality, who went thither in their lumbering coaches or on foot. 'No frost, snow, nor east wind,' observed the 'Tatler' in 1711, 'can hinder a large set of people from going to the Park in February, nor dust and heat in June'; and in 1776 the stranger to the metropolis was informed by Sir John Fielding, in his 'Guide to London,' that the park was 'the usual place of exercise in a morning for fine gentlemen and ladies, who resort thither to see and be seen,' during the season, which extended from the beginning of December till the end of May.

For those who believed in the advantages of physical exercise there were numerous promenades 'where they might walk abroad and recreate themselves,' such for example as St. James's Park, where, as Goldsmith said, 'if a man were splenetic, he might every day meet companions with whose groans he might mix his own, and pathetically talk of the weather'; the noble gardens of the Inns of Court, some of the companies' halls, and the Charterhouse Garden—the only qualification requisite for admission being that of 'a genteel appearance,'[1] to say nothing of the multifarious medicinal spas and other places of resort of which more will be said in subsequent chapters. Ten was the usual hour in London for retiring to rest. Winter and summer it seems to have been customary for many London merchants to leave town on the Saturday for their country houses a few miles out, to return the following Monday at Change time.

Of those who occupied the stately mansions situated in the west end of the town, they who dwelt in the east end at this time knew nothing or next to nothing, save by report. As to the existence of any bond of sympathy between these two poles

---

[1] *Present State of Great Britain,* 1738.

of London life there was little or none, and consequently when chance threw the denizens of them in each other's way they regarded each other with a curiosity akin to that which would be excited at this day by the presence of a Hottentot stalking in Rotten Row or Grosvenor Square. The inhabitants even of the city proper and the west end of the town kept at a respectful distance from one another. Very few merchants lived out of the city; their residences were mostly attached to their counting-houses, and their credit depended in no small degree upon their observance of these limits.[1] Charles Macklin, the veteran actor, who died in 1797, remembered well the first migration of merchants from the city. This could not have been earlier than the reign of George I. or thereabouts, and extended then only as far as Hatton Garden. 'None,' wrote he, 'but men who had secured a large fortune, and whose credits were beyond the smallest censure, durst take this flight.' Members of the legal profession lived mostly in the Inns of Court, or about Westminster Hall. Most actors of any eminence resided in the immediate vicinity of the two theatres; in such localities as Great and Little Russell Streets, King Street, Bow Street, Vinegar Yard, and in numerous little courts which then existed in the neighbourhood of Covent Garden.[2]

The commonalty of London in their daily life followed that of their superiors to a greater or lesser degree. Most citizens rose much earlier than they do now. As no part of London was then situated more than a quarter of an hour's walk from fields and hedgerows, invalids made a point of getting up and drinking milk at the cow-houses, or asses' milk, which was sold in large quantities in St. James's Park, at Knightsbridge, and in other spots, or of breakfasting at the numerous huts erected for the accommodation of early risers. Some London citizens would even attend morning prayers in such churches where the practice had not fallen into disuse, and after breakfasting with their families, repaired about ten to their own particular coffee-houses, where they spent on an average about an hour over their coffee and tobacco, perusing 'The Daily,' 'The Public,' 'The Ledger,'

---

[1] *Memoirs of C. Macklin*, p. 72.
[2] Boaden's *Memoirs of Mrs. Inchbald*, i. p. 230.

'The Chronicle,' 'The London Evening,' 'The Whitehall Evening,' the seventeen magazines, and the two reviews. Then they either returned home or transacted business. At two o'clock they went on Change, where they remained about two hours ; lounged awhile on their return home in the coffee-house, and dined about four. Down to the latter end of the reign of George II. dinner concluded the day, the remaining hours being given over to the society of friends at home, to walks, or to places of amusement.

This was the same nearly all the year round, varied on Sundays perhaps by a visit to church or chapel in the morning, the usual hour for which was ten o'clock, and by amusing themselves in the afternoon in a variety of ways. They formed water parties to Greenwich, to Dagenham Beach, Hampton Court, or Richmond. They visited Highgate Hill, where with a jocularity not very refined the burlesque oaths were administered to them over the horns at the Gate House Inn. They swallowed new buns, custards, and coffee at Don Saltero's Coffee House in Chelsea, or at the numerous resorts in and around ' the pleasant village of Islington,' where near the turnpike stood the 'Three Hats,' renowned for the feats of horsemanship which were on week-days exhibited in its proximity ; the White Conduit House and tea gardens, which then stood on what is now the east side of Penton Street, Clerkenwell [1] ; Sadler's Wells tea and bun house (limned in Hogarth's 'Evening') ; Prospect House, Phillips' New Wells ; the New Red Lion Cockpit, the Mulberry Gardens, the Shakespeare's Head Tavern, the Jubilee Gardens, or the New Tunbridge Wells. The houses of entertainment multiplied to meet the demand as the population increased. There were the Apollo, Fuch's Grotto Garden, the Dog and Duck Gardens, St. George's Fields ; the Queen of Bohemia's Head, Turnham Green ; China Hall, Rotherhithe ; Cumberland Gardens, Vauxhall ; Spa Tea Gardens, in Grange Road, near Southwark ; Smith's Tea Gardens, Vauxhall ; Kendal House, Isleworth ; New Wells, Goodman's Fields ; Marble Hall, Vauxhall ; Staton's Tea Gardens, Marylebone ; the 'Queen's Head and Artichoke,' Marylebone Fields ; Ruckholt House, near Wan-

[1] Bentham's *Works*, ed. Bowring, x. p. 34.

stead ; the Castle, at Kentish Town ; the Grotto Garden, Rosamond Row; the St. Helena Tea Gardens, Bermondsey; the Angel, at Upper Holloway ; and Spring Gardens, at Newington and Stepney. The tea gardens which were to be found on the outskirts of London, especially the northern outskirts, in the last century, were as the sands of the sea-shore for multitude ; and a writer in one of the leading periodicals soon after the accession of George III., computed the number of people who visited them each Sunday alone at two hundred thousand, and as none of them would depart without having disbursed at least half-a-crown, twenty thousand pounds might fairly be taken to represent the sum total of what would sometimes be expended by this number of people.[1] These resorts were only nominally tea gardens, as it is very evident malt liquors were largely supplied by those who kept them, and doubtless any other beverage for which customers chose to ask.[2]

Failing the tea-gardens, how did people amuse themselves? By visiting the regalia and the lions in the Tower of London, which were restrained with iron bars and a cage 'under a postern on the south side' ; the British Museum ; the Museum of the Royal Society in Gresham Street ; Cox's Museum in Lincoln's Inn Fields ; Humphrey's Grand Museum of Natural History, No. 71 St. Martin's Lane ; the waxen effigies in Westminster Abbey ; with the great variety of pleasing entertainments at Astley's Riding School, near Westminster Bridge ; Mrs. Salmon's Waxwork Show, a sort of permanent exhibition (like that of Madame Tussaud's in later days), held at the sign of the 'Salmon,' near the Horn Tavern in Fleet Street ; Mr. Lever's Museum, Leicester House ; and until 1770, strange as it may seem, by watching the antics of the ill-fated inmates of the Bethlehem Hospital in Moorfields, near Bishopsgate. Plaster models and exhibitions of pictures never failed to draw crowds of spectators. Horace Walpole, mentioning three exhibitions of this kind in 1770, says that the rage to see them was so great that it was impossible sometimes for anybody to pass through the streets where they

[1] Quoted by Sala, *Life of Hogarth*, p. 257.
[2] *Place MSS. Add. MSS. Brit. Mus.* 27, 829.

chanced to be.[1] To all these must be added the attractions of
several annual fairs, notably Tottenham and Mayfair, and Horn
Fair, held on the outskirts of a valley near Charlton in Kent.

The drunkenness which we have had occasion to notice in
the upper classes spread to the lower classes. The number of
distilleries, beginning with Anne, steadily increased under the
Hanoverian monarchs. It was at an early stage of the reign of
George I. that the pernicious habit of gin-drinking struck root .
in the English taste, and 'small as is the place which the fact
occupies in English history, it was probably, if we consider all
the consequences that have flowed from it, the most momentous
event in that of the eighteenth century—incomparably more so
than any event in the purely political or military annals of the
country.'[2] The medical faculty were not slow in perceiving
that with the increased taste for gin poverty and disease would
increase in a proportionate rate among the poor of the capital.
The justices of the peace for the county of Middlesex in 1736
presented a petition to Parliament setting forth

that the drinking of Geneva had for some years past greatly increased, especially among the people of inferior rank, and that the
constant and excessive use thereof had destroyed thousands of
people, that it had contributed to the spread of thieving and other
enormities, and that it had resulted in the halter gracing the necks
of many.[3]

Dr. Martin Benson, Bishop of Gloucester, was of the same
opinion. Writing from Westminster to his right reverend
brother Berkeley of Cloyne, on February 18, 1752, he said :—

Your lordship calls this the freest country in Europe. There
is indeed freedom of one kind in it, more, it is to be hoped, than
in any other—a most unbounded licentiousness of all sorts ; a dis-
regard to all authority, sacred and civil ; a regard to nothing but
diversion and vicious pleasures. There is not only no safety of
living in this town, but scarcely in the country now, robbery and
murder are grown so frequent. Our people are now become, what
they never before were, cruel and inhuman. Those accursed
spirituous liquors which, to the shame of our Government, are so
easily to be had, and in such quantities drunk, have changed the

---

[1] Walpole's *Letters to Sir H. Mann*, ii. 97.
[2] Lecky, *Hist. of England in Eighteenth Century*, i. 479.
[3] *Parl. Hist.* vol. ix.

very nature of our people. And they will, if continued to be drunk, destroy the very race of the people themselves.[1]

Chief among other beverages popular during the century were porter, salep, rum, brandy, Hollands (smuggled into the country), Dorset beer and Oxford ale. The increase in the number of distilleries led to a corresponding increase in the number of inns and taverns, nowhere so rapidly as in London, where the drunkenness of the lower classes was already frightful to contemplate. It was stated in the House of Commons in 1736, during the debate on the Spirituous Liquors Bill, that in the report of the king's justices of the peace, at Hick's Hall, there were then within Westminster, Holborn, the Tower, and Finsbury division (exclusive of London and Southwark), 7,044 houses and shops wherein Geneva and other spirituous liquors were publicly sold by retail, of which they possessed an account, and that they believed it was very far short of the true number.[2] Painted boards were suspended from the door of almost every seventh house inviting the poor to get intoxicated for a penny, and dead drunk for twopence, straw whereon to lie until they had slept off the effects of the first bout and were ready to start afresh being given them for nothing. It was the horrible effects of gin which he beheld on all sides around him that furnished Hogarth with the idea that he worked out in his picture of 'Gin Lane.' The drunkenness of England grew worse and worse till it culminated in the passing of a Gin Act in 1736, which produced no effect. Thirteen years later it was computed that there were within the bills of mortality more than 17,000 gin-shops. Fielding, the novelist, in a pamphlet discussing the increase of crime, published when the century had just completed half its course, declared that gin constituted the chief sustenance of more than 100,000 people in the capital alone, and said that if it continued for twenty years longer at the same rate there would be few left among the lower classes to drink gin at all.

Roderick Random was told on his first visit to the metro-

---

[1] *Life and Letters of Bishop Berkeley*, ed. Prof. Fraser, iv. pp. 332–333.
[2] *Parl. Hist.* ix. p. 1094. See also the grim array of facts contained in the *Place MSS. Add. MSS. Brit. Mus.*, 27, 829.

polis by the good-natured Scotch chandler who let him an
apartment over his shop, that there were two ways of eating
and drinking for men of his condition—'the one more credit-
able and expensive than the other : the first is to dine at an
eating-house frequented by well-dressed people only ; and the
other is called diving, practised by those who are either obliged
or inclined to live frugally.' The young inexperienced surgeon
expressed his willingness to dive, if it were not infamous.
Whereupon his landlord told him that he had seen 'many a
pretty gentleman with a laced waistcoat dine in that manner
very comfortably for threepence-halfpenny, and go afterwards
to the coffee-house, where he made a figure with the best lord in
the land.' This settled the point, and Roderick Random found
himself dining off shin of beef 'surrounded by a company
of hackney coachmen, chairmen, draymen, and a few footmen
out of place or on board wages.' In after days, Smollett makes
his hero dine at an ordinary. Ordinaries, although they do
not seem to have been popular, were numerous, and abounded
not only in the city but in the environs. 'There was a very
good ordinary of two dishes and pastry kept at about this time
(five-and-twenty years ago) at Highbury Barn, at 10*d*. per head,
including a penny to the waiter ; and the company generally
consisted of literary characters, a few Templars, and some
citizens who had left off trade.'[1] Charles Macklin, the celebrated actor, relates in his 'Memoirs' that the ordinaries of the
day between 1730–35 were 'from 6*d*. to 1*s*. per head ; at the
latter there were two courses, and a great deal of what the
world calls mixed company in the mixed way. There were
private rooms for the higher order of wits and noblemen where
much drinking was occasionally used.'[2] Ordinaries did not
enjoy half so much public patronage as the chop-houses. 'In
these common refectories,' says a writer in the issue of the
'Connoisseur' for June 6, 1750, 'you may always find the
jemmy attorney's clerk, the prim curate, the walking physician,
the captain upon half-pay.' It was considered part of the
fashionable education of a young gallant for him to eat his way

---

[1] *Europ. Mag.* vol. xxiv. 172.   [2] *Ibid.* p. 70.

at an ordinary, and to continue to attend it if he desired to avoid the cost of housekeeping. Calipash and calipee, it may be noted, were very toothsome at the 'Crown' and the 'King's Arms,' beefsteaks and gills of ale were to be had at Dolly's, Betty's, and Horseman's in Ivy Lane, while a writer in the 'Connoisseur,' 1755, advises 'a mutton-chop behind St. Clement's, or, if preferred, an extempory sausage or black pudding over the farthing fries at Moorfields or the Horse Guards.'

There was still a great consumption of tobacco in London at this period, though not nearly so much as there had been in the preceding century. It is related of Dr. Johnson that though he never smoked he had a high opinion of its sedative influence, and during his tour in Scotland he emphatically declared to Boswell that smoking had gone out of fashion, and that he was unable to account for a habit which, in his opinion, 'required so little exertion, and yet preserved the mind from total vacuity,' having fallen into comparative desuetude.[1] Croker, in his edition of 'Boswell's Life of Dr. Johnson,' published the year after the accession of William IV., appends to this assertion a note in which he states that while the habit of drinking to excess had greatly diminished within living memory, there had been a revival of the habit of smoking, which he considered had in all probability originated in the military habits of Europeans while the French wars were in progress.

It was only with difficulty that Horace Walpole in his declining years could bring himself into conformity with the late hours of London society. Writing from Arlington Street to his friend Sir Horace Mann on February 6, 1777, he said :—

Everything is changed, as always must happen when one grows old and is prejudiced to one's old ways. I do not like dining at nearly six, nor beginning the evening at ten at night. If one does not conform one must live alone, and that is more disagreeable and more difficult in town than in the country, where old useless people ought to live.[2]

Servants, domestic and public.—Of the chairmen and watchmen mention has already been made. Domestic servants

[1] Croker's *Boswell*, pp. 106–282.
[2] *Letters*, ed. Cunningham, vi. 410.

attached to the households of the upper classes were distinguished primarily for aping the manners of their masters and mistresses, and, so far as the first half of the eighteenth century is concerned, the Rev. James Townley's famous farce 'High Life Below Stairs,' in which their extravagance and affectation were most cleverly ridiculed, is far removed from a caricature. The dress of domestic servants attached to the households of the middle classes seems to have been plain and good, and insolence was not a characteristic of them. Coachmen wore, as a mark of distinction, an upper coat adorned with a long cape of two or three rows fringed, and in point of outward appearance there was no perceptible difference between the coachman of a merchant and that of a nobleman. Nor could even waiting-maids and ladies'-maids, when attending their masters and mistresses in places of amusement, be easily distinguished from them. In 1765 the average wage of a servant maid was six guineas, besides one guinea for tea, while a good plain cook could at this time command twenty guineas a year. The wages of all servants were considerably augmented by the 'vails,' a species of 'blackmail,' which they received, or rather exacted, from the friends and relatives of the families in which they lived.

House-rents were high, and houses themselves internally much less comfortable than they are now. The wines that were mostly drunk were port, Bordeaux, and Burgundy; also a white wine composed of sloes and blackberries gathered in the hedges round the metropolis.

Poverty, though not on the increase, continued to exist to a sad extent throughout the metropolis. Much of it might have easily been prevented, and was due to early and improvident marriages, to unthrifty habits, and to drunkenness. On the other hand a vast amount of poverty was due to the lack of employment. Hundreds who were able and willing to work could not find in London any means of subsistence. In these circumstances crime increased to an appalling extent; for the ranks of the regular London thieves were always being reinforced by the dangerous and desperate from all parts of the Empire.

The middle-class habitants of London dressed well and lived well ; yet everything was excessively dear, if the testimony of foreign visitors, who are generally very observant, may be accepted. Small tradesmen in particular, though their earnings might be considerable, could live only from hand to mouth. M. Grosley mentions that, during his sojourn in London in 1765, he was charged twopence-halfpenny or threepence per pound for bread, fourpence-halfpenny a pound for coarse meat, from eightpence to ninepence a pound for roasting-beef, tenpence per pound for bacon, elevenpence per pound for butter, and sevenpence-halfpenny per pound for candles.[1] Grosley speaks in high terms of the English bread, the consumption of which, he noticed, was chiefly occasioned at breakfast and tea, and was cut in slices so thin, that it did as much honour to the address of the person who cut it as to the sharpness of the knife. With the roast and boiled meat that was served up on the tables in English households M. Grosley was much disappointed, having been prepared for something much better than he found. The game was remarkable for softness and flabbiness, the veal exhibited all the imperfection of flesh not quite formed, the mutton had nothing to recommend it save its fat, and even the beef was exceedingly fat. To soups he found the English utter strangers, and to what passed in his own country under the name of *bouillé.* Broth was occasionally made for sick people. The various sorts of garden-stuff were proportionately dear with other articles of food. Such vegetables as were grown about London—the cabbages, the radishes, the leeks, and the spinach—he mentions were all more or less impregnated with the sea-coal smoke, and that this gave them a most disagreeable taste, that was invariably communicated to the meat with which they were boiled. The cleanly habits of the London denizens were to be not unfavourably compared with those of the Hollanders. The plate, the hearthstones, the doors, the staircases, the street-doors, the locks, and the huge brass knockers, were duly scoured till they shone. The houses internally were mostly wainscoted with deal, a material of which the stairs and floors were chiefly

[1] *Observations on England,* i. p. 67.

composed, and which was also washed and scrubbed daily with scrupulous care.

The writer of some very interesting 'Table Talk' concerning celebrated and illustrious British characters, printed in the September number of the 'European Magazine,' 1793, says, in speaking of Oliver Goldsmith and his sayings and doings, that there was nothing which he enjoyed better than what he used facetiously to term a 'shoemaker's holiday' :—

> Three or four of his intimate friends [says the writer] rendezvoused at his chambers to breakfast about ten o'clock in the morning ; at eleven they proceeded, by the City Road and through the fields, to Highbury Barn to dinner ; about six o'clock in the evening they adjourned to White Conduit House to drink tea ; and concluded the evening by supping at the Grecian or Temple Exchange coffee-houses, or at the Globe in Fleet Street. . . . The whole expenses of this day's fête never exceeded a crown, and oftener from three-and-sixpence to four shillings, for which the party obtained good air and exercise, good living, the example of simple manners, and good conversation.[1]

There was scarcely a day but at least one marriage or funeral took place in the capital, and these ceremonies were then invariably accompanied by certain customs which happily accompany them no longer. Thus the stranger in London, who happened to be passing through Cheapside or Ludgate Hill, would behold a row of drummers standing in martial file, and dinning the ears with their 'vellum thunder,' and another row of butchers, making before the houses of the newly married, on the morning after the wedding, if they thought they would be remunerated for their pains, a kind of wild Janissary music. The marrow-bone and cleaver players are introduced into Hogarth's picture representing the festivities attendant on the marriage of the industrious apprentice with his master's daughter, at the parental residence on Fish-street Hill. Professor Lichtenberg in alluding to this custom in his curious and exhaustive 'Commentary on the Works of Hogarth,' published at Göttingen between 1794 and 1799, says :—

> They perform it by striking their cleavers with the marrowbones of the animals they have slain. To comprehend that this

music is—we shall not say supportable, for that is not here the question—but that it is not entirely objectionable, we shall observe that the breadth of the English cleaver is to that of the German in nearly the same proportion as the diameter of the English ox is to that of Germany.[1]

The books of the Marrow-Bones-and-Cleavers Society for the parish of St. George, Hanover Square (the famous temple in the Georgian era for fashionable marriages) are yet in existence, and for the year 1745 alone it appears that their receipts amounted in all to three hundred and eighty pounds, disbursed in guineas by the couples who had been married within the walls of St. George's church. That which was at first regarded as a gratuity, came, in process of time, to be recognised as a right, and such proportions did the burden assume, that the aid of Parliament was at last invoked for its removal.

London funerals in the last century were accompanied by many external indications of bereavement now happily obsolete. First, the brass street-door knocker was carefully encased in flannel, and a mute took up his stand at the door. The friends and relatives of the deceased were bidden by deep black-edged cards, decorated with death's heads and cross-bones, and hour-glasses, and other ghastly insignia of mortality. The hearse, emblazoned with emblems and crowned with nodding plumes of ostrich-feathers, was followed by unwieldy black coaches drawn by horses of the same sombre colour. The corpse was religiously laid out, and no pains were spared to make it appear to all who had known it in life as charming as possible. Large numbers of yellow wax tapers were placed in sconces around the room in which the coffin lay; the walls were hung with sable cloth; and the mourners were presented with wine-glasses of claret, bread, cake, or biscuits, and quarts of ale. Gloves were also distributed, and sometimes even whole suits of mourning and rings were bestowed upon them. If the funeral took place at night, there was of course another outlay for numerous flambeaux-men to hold lighted torches in branches of four. All ranks and conditions of London society at that time observed the absurd custom in London of lying-in-state.

[1] *Ausführliche Erklärung der Hogarthischen,* &c.

The body of the poet Gay was, on his death, exposed to the vulgar gaze in Exeter Change, in the Strand, and that of the dramatist Congreve in Westminster Abbey. Walpole, writing to Sir Horace Mann, under date Nov. 1, 1760, tells him that the mob, who never gulled curiosity about Lady Coventry, 'went to the number of ten thousand only to see her coffin.'[1] Writing to the Earl of Hertford under date of March 27, 1764, he says:—

I had sent to know how Lady Macclesfield did. Louis (his valet) brought me word that he could hardly get into St. James's Square, there was so great a crowd to see my lord lie in state. At night I met my Lady Milton at the Duchess of Argyll's, and said in joke, 'Soh, to be sure, you have been to see my Lord Macclesfield lie in state'—thinking it impossible. She burst out into a fit of laughter, and owned she had. She and my Lady Temple had dined at Lady Betty's, put on hats and cloaks, and literally waited on the steps of the house in the thick of the mob, while one person was admitted and let out again for a second to enter, before they got in.'[2]

Goldsmith satirised this silly fashion in one of his best essays in the 'Citizen of the World,' also in the first act of his comedy of 'The Good-natured Man,' wherein he causes Croaker to observe :—' Well, well, be a good child and say no more ; but come with me, and we shall see something that will give us a great deal of pleasure, I promise you—old Huggins, the curry-comb maker, lying in state. I am told he makes a very handsome corpse and becomes his coffin pro-digiously.' Pope had ridiculed the candle-burning practice in the third epistle of his ' Moral Essays,' by saying of a notorious miser, who in life begrudged the expense of a farthing rush-light—

When Hopkins dies a thousand lights attend
The wretch who, living, saved a candle's end.

A London funeral procession in 1784 is thus described in the journal of an American refugee who was residing in the capital at the time :—

June 19.—At one o'clock the funeral procession of Sir Bernard Turner, sheriff, passed through Bishopsgate Street amidst great

---

[1] Walpole's *Letters*, ed. Cunningham, iii. 358.   [2] *Ibid.* iv. 212.

crowds, though much lessened by the delay, which the populace mistook for its being laid aside. The body had been arrested after it was put into the hearse, in the street, for a considerable debt, which was afterwards compromised ; on whose or what account is variously stated. The hearse was preceded by two lines of the Artillery Association, headed by an officer and five privates abreast, their firelocks reversed, marching in slow pace ; muffled drums beating, trumpets sounding, and other instruments playing the 104th Psalm tune. The hearse was adorned with large flowing plumes of ostrich-feathers, just before which was led the horse of the deceased, dressed in black ; on the saddle were laid the hat, sword, and boots crossed. A small detachment of the Artillery Company followed the carriage of the deceased and those of his brother sheriffs ; after which the whole closed in by fourteen carriages, each drawn by two pair of horses. The whole was to proceed some miles, to Tottenham, solemn and pompous in the extreme.[1]

One very great drawback to the comfort of town life in the last century was the perpetual danger in which people ran of being robbed, and even murdered, in the public streets. Modern townsfolk can hardly realise that such was the case ; but the fact remains that it was so. As soon as the evening shades prevailed in London, both in winter and summer, the highway-men and footpads emerged from their retreats in the capital like so many bats, in order to begin without delay their work of depredation and plunder, for which unlimited facilities ex-isted, in consequence of an inefficient staff of watchmen, and by reason of the inadequate lighting of the streets. Some evidence of the manner in which these desperadoes exercised their calling is subjoined, and the list might easily be extended to almost any length. The insecurity of life and property in the reign of George II. may be gathered from the address upon the subject which, in 1744, the then lord mayor presented to that sovereign. In this document it was set forth that ' divers confederacies of evil-disposed persons, armed with bludgeons, pistols, cutlasses, and other dangerous weapons, infested not only the private lanes and passages, but likewise the public streets and places of usual concourse, committing most daring outrages upon his Majesty's subjects.' So great was the con-tempt in which highwaymen held the city constables and other

[1] *Journal of S. Curwen*, p. 407.

guardians of the public peace, that they would ride into Hyde Park in the dusk of the evening, fasten their horses to its railings, and sally forth in the direction of the town, for the purpose of waylaying chairs, carriages, and pedestrians. William Shenstone, 'the poet of the Leasowes,' being on a visit to the metropolis in 1744, wrote thus in March of that year to his friend the Rev. William Jago :—

· London is really dangerous at this time : the pickpockets, formerly content with mere filching, make no scruple to knock people down with bludgeons in Fleet Street and the Strand, and that at no later hour than eight o'clock at night. But in the Piazzas, Covent Garden, they come in large bodies armed with *couteaus*, and attack whole parties, so that the danger of coming out of the play-houses is of some weight in the opposite scale, when I am tempted to go to them oftener than I ought.'

In the nineteen years which followed, highwaymen increased in number, so that the 'Annual Register' for 1763 records, under the month of October, that 'a horse patrol, under the direction of Sir John Fielding, is fixed upon the several roads near the metropolis, for the protection of his Majesty's subjects. The patrol consists of eight persons well mounted and armed.'

One night in the beginning of November, 1749 [says Horace Walpole, in the 'Short Notes' of his own life], as I was returning from Holland House by moonlight, about ten at night, I was attacked by two highwaymen in Hyde Park, and the pistol of one of them going off accidentally razed the skin under my eye, left some marks of shot on my face, and stunned me. The ball went through the top of the chariot, and if I had sat an inch nearer to the left side must have gone through my head.[1]

One of the ruffians to whom Walpole alludes was the notorious James Maclean, called 'the gentleman highwayman,' who was executed at Tyburn on the 3rd of October in the following year. Writing from his residence in Arlington Street on September 20, 1750, to Sir Horace Mann, Walpole says :—

I was sitting in my own dining-room on Sunday night—the clock had not struck eleven—when I heard a loud cry of 'Stop thief!' A highwayman had attacked a post-chaise in Piccadilly, within fifty yards of this house : the fellow was pursued, rode over

---

[1] Walpole's *Letters*, ed. Cunningham, i. 67

the watchman, almost killed him, and escaped. I expect to be robbed one night in my own garden at Strawberry.[1]

The same writer complains (in 1752) that in London 'one is forced to travel, even at noon, as if one was going to battle'; [2] and thirty years later (August 20, 1782), in a letter addressed to the Hon. W. S. Conway, declares that nobody in the neighbourhood of Strawberry Hill, where he was then residing, 'dare stir after dusk, nor be secure at home'; and that people were robbed and murdered if they did 'but step over the threshold to the chandler's shop for a pennyworth of plums.'[3] The community at large became heartily sick of being thus exposed to the thieving and murdering fraternities. As yet nothing had been done to check them. Towards the latter end of the year 1753, a gang of street robbers to the number of about fourteen, who divided themselves into parties, committed a series of audacious robberies, and perpetrated such barbarities, that they occasioned general alarm throughout the town, insomuch that citizens were unable to move out of doors after nightfall. The king issued a proclamation offering a hundred pounds reward for each of these violaters of the public peace, but without effect. At length, when public indignation had been roused to the highest pitch, a zealous and active police magistrate who presided at Bow Street, and who in the midst of his official drudgery found time for the writing of novels which still keep his memory green, received a message from the then Duke of Newcastle, through the king's messenger, desiring him to attend upon his Grace at his mansion in Lincoln's Inn Fields, with a view of devising some plan in order to bring these desperadoes to justice. In the introduction to the very last work he wrote, which was entitled 'The Journal of a Voyage to Lisbon,' Henry Fielding has supplied full particulars of the scheme. He there states that, although on the eve of setting out for Bath, whither he had been recommended by the king's surgeon to proceed in consequence of the bad state of his health, he complied with the duke's

---

[1] Walpole's *Letters*, ed. Cunningham, ii. p. 228.   [2] *Ibid.* p. 280.
[3] *Ibid.* viii. pp. 268, 276.

request. When Fielding called, the duke was unable to see him, but

His Grace [says the novelist] sent a gentleman to discourse with me on the best plan which could be invented for putting an immediate end to those murders and robberies which were every day committed in the streets : upon which I promised to transmit my opinion, in writing, to his Grace, who, as the gentleman informed me, intended to lay it before the Privy Council. Though this visit cost me a severe cold, I notwithstanding set myself down to work, and in about four days sent the duke as regular a plan as I could form, with all the reasons and arguments I could bring to support it, drawn out in several sheets of paper ; and soon received a message from the duke, by Mr. Carrington, acquainting me that my plan was highly approved of, and that all the terms of it would be complied with. The principal and most material of those terms was the immediately depositing 600*l.* in my hands ; at which small charge I undertook to demolish the then reigning gangs, and to put the civil policy into such order that no such gangs should ever be able, for the future, to form themselves into bodies, or at least to remain any time formidable to the public. I had delayed my Bath journey for some time, contrary to the repeated advice of my physical acquaintance and the ardent desire of my warmest friends, though my distemper was now turned to a deep jaundice ; in which case the Bath waters are generally reputed to be almost infallible. But I had the most eager desire of demolishing this gang of villains and cut-throats, which I was sure of accomplishing the moment I was enabled to pay a fellow who had undertaken for a small sum to betray them into the hands of a set of thief-takers, whom I had enlisted into the service, all men of known and approved fidelity and intrepidity. After some weeks the money was paid at the Treasury, and within a few days after 200*l.* of it had come to my hands, the whole gang of cut-throats was entirely dispersed, seven of them were in actual custody, and the rest driven, some out of town and others out of the kingdom.[1]

It is necessary to remark that this dispersion was purely local as well as temporary. Such members of the gang as were able to effect their escape merely shifted for a little while the scene of their nefarious operations. About the time of the accession of George III., in 1760, the state of affairs was as bad as it had been before, and so it continued until long after the termination of the American War ; nothing whatever being done in the meantime to provide for the public security by those from whom such measures might reasonably be supposed to have emanated.

[1] Introd. pp. 19 22. Ed. 1755.

, And here slight reference to the causes of these highway robberies may not be out of place. Fielding, who, it should be borne in mind, was fully a hundred years in advance of his time on many points, and on none more so than on the subject of legal reform, devotes a section in that brochure from which citations have previously been made in this chapter—namely, 'An Inquiry into the Causes of the late Increase of Robbers, &c.'—to a very thoughtful consideration of the subject. Foremost in the list of them he placed what he called 'the great torrent of luxury which of late years hath poured itself into the nation';[1] and the too frequent and expensive diversions among the lower kinds of people '—masquerades in particular—which he stigmatised as being ' no other than the temples of lewdness and all kinds of debauchery.' He also complained loudly of the drunkenness occasioned by the inordinate consumption among the lower orders of society of 'the strongest intoxicating liquors, and particularly by that poison called gin,' which he had strong reasons for believing was, at the time he wrote, the principal sustenance of upwards of a hundred thousand people in the capital alone. The gaming, which he declared was 'a school in which most highwaymen of great eminence had been bred;' the improper regulation of what were called the poor in the kingdom, arising partly from the abuse of some laws, and partly from the total neglect of others; the ease and safety with which stolen goods could be disposed of; the probability of escaping from punishment; the difficulties which attended prosecutions; and the encouragement given to robbers by the frequency of pardon, were among other of the reasons that Fielding assigned for the increase of robbers.

Have not some of these committed robberies in broad daylight [he exclaims] in the sight of many people, and have afterwards rode solemnly and triumphantly through the neighbouring towns without any danger or molestation? This happens to every rogue who has become eminent for his audaciousness, and is thought to be desperate, and is in a more particular manner the case of great and numerous gangs, many of which have for a long time committed the most open outrages in defiance of the law. Officers of justice have owned to me that they have passed by such with warrants in their

---

[1] *Inquiry*, p. 18.

pockets against them without daring to apprehend them ; and indeed they could not be blamed for not exposing themselves to sure destruction : for it is a melancholy truth that at this very day a rogue no sooner gives the alarm within certain purlieus than twenty or thirty well-armed villains are found ready to come to his assistance.[1]

Was any effectual remedy ever applied ? None whatever. And within less than fifty years after the grave had closed over Fielding, Dr. Patrick Colquhoun, an acting magistrate for Westminster and the Home Counties, published his famous ' Treatise on the Police of the Metropolis,' a work containing appalling details of the various crimes and misdemeanours by which both private and public property, as well as the security of London, were not only injured but endangered, and in which remedies were suggested for their prevention.   The picture Dr. Colquhoun drew was a most extraordinary and startling one, and evoked no inconsiderable amount of comment in many quarters.   Of course it was but natural that the critics when they came to examine Dr. Colquhoun's treatise should have imputed to him a host of mis-statements and exaggerations, more especially when they found him estimating the loss arising from the burglaries, highway robberies, and small thefts in the capital alone at nine hundred and ninety-nine thousand pounds, and that in the year of grace 1796.   But wisdom is justified of her children.   Colquhoun's statements were very soon proved to be in strict accordance with the facts, and some idea of the very great impression that his volumes produced upon the mind of the public is evidenced by the fact that during the four years which followed their publication they ran through five editions.   In the case of such a book popularity is surely a high criterion of merit.

Now let the reader peruse the three following paragraphs, all transcribed from *one* issue of the ' Public Advertiser' (Thursday, February 12, 1761), and having done so, let him reflect upon the absurdity of those well-intentioned people whom nothing pleases better than to extol ' the good old times.'

One evening last week the Hamstead [*sic*] caravan was robbed the other side of Kentish Town, near the ' Half-Way House,' by a

---

[1] *Inquiry*, p. 94.

single highwayman. There were ten gentlemen in the caravan. At going up he seemed intimidated, and presenting his pistol, desired one of them to take off his hat and collect round the company, who were so obliging as to collect twenty guineas. For two Sunday nights past some housebreakers have attempted to break into houses at North End, Hampstead, but the inhabitants fired at them, and made them desist.

On Friday last, Mr. Adams, of Ham, near Richmond, was stopped by two footpads on East Sheen Common, and robbed of five guineas. There are so many thieves infest the road in that neighbourhood that people are afraid of stirring out after dark.

On Wednesday night, about nine, Mr. Stanton and Mr. Lovell were robbed going to Deptford in a chariot, of twenty guineas and their watches, by six footpads, armed with horse pistols.

Mrs. Harris, writing to her son, the first Earl of Malmesbury, under date of February 6, 1773, tells him that

a most audacious fellow robbed Sir Francis Holburne and his sister in their coach, in St. James's Square, coming from the opera. He was on horseback, and held a pistol close to the breast of one of the Miss Holburnes for a considerable time. She had left her purse at home, which he would not believe. He has since robbed a coach in Park Lane.[1]

It was not so very long before this occurrence that Lady Grey and Lady Scott, while returning in a chariot from Lady Holderness's rout, were stopped between Green Street and New Norfolk Street by a highwayman, who robbed each of them of her purse. So near town as Kensington, it was customary at this time on Sunday evenings for a bell to be tolled at intervals, in order that the visitors to the Gardens, and other people in the neighbourhood who might be returning to the city, could assemble in a band sufficiently numerous for common protection. The 'Public Advertiser' for April 27, 1774, contains the following record :

Sunday, one of the Richmond stages was stopped at Kew Green by four footpads, who robbed the passengers of their watches and money.

Monday evening, as Mr. Beaumont, of Red Lion Street, Holborn, was returning from Uxbridge in a post-chaise, he was stopped near Acton turnpike by a highwayman, who robbed him of about six pounds.

Monday night, at half-past eight, two gentlemen on their way to

---

[1] *Letters of the First Earl of Malmesbury*, i. p. 258.

town in a post-chaise, were robbed near the four-mile stone at Hammersmith, by two highwaymen, who took from them a watch, and what little money they had about them. The road from Turnham Green to Hammersmith has lately been much infested by a set of gentlemen who support themselves in extravagance by making depredations on the traveller ; for though much frequented, the great number of avenues to it are found very favourable to their escape.

Sunday night, a gentleman and lady were stopped in their carriage on Blackheath by two highwaymen, who took from the gentleman six guineas and a watch; the lady being much frightened, they politely took their leave without robbing her.[1]

Early in September 1776, Alderman Sawbridge, the then lord mayor of London, while travelling with his suite in a carriage and four from Kew, was stopped near Turnham Green, a mile east of Brentford, and relieved of his possessions in the sight of all his retinue by a single highwayman, who vowed that he would shoot the first person that dared to offer any resistance.[2]

The 'Morning Post' of Thursday, May 14, 1778, states that :—

Yesterday; Price a Custom House officer and Andrews master of a public house in Marybone Street, were charged with a highway robbery at the public office in Bow Street by Mr. Selby and Mr. Eccles. Mr. Selby deposed that on Sunday evening he was stopped near Acton, about ten o'clock, by two men well mounted ; one held a pistol to his throat, whilst the other thrust his pistol to his ear and demanded his money ; after some little altercation he gave them a watch and five guineas and they made off.

Horace Walpole, writing to Sir Horace Mann in 1781, tells him that Lady Browne and himself were both robbed by a single highwayman while proceeding to a *soirée* at the house of the Duchess of Montrose, near Twickenham Park, her ladyship exclaiming after the knight of the road had taken his departure :—'I am in terror lest he should return, for I have given him a purse with only bad money that I carry on purpose.'

The 'Morning Chronicle' for January 2, 1782, states that—

The inhabitants of Hoxton near the Ivy House have entered into a military association for the protection of their persons and

---

[1] *Public Advertiser,* July 27, 1774.   [2] *Gent. Mag.* vol. xlvi. p. 433.

properties against the attacks of a desperate set ·of fellows, who have struck a terror in those parts.

Visitors to the 'pleasant village of Islington' were seldom allowed to proceed home without molestation, as the newspapers of the age conclusively prove.

The 'London Chronicle' for March 9, 1782, records that—

Last Saturday night, about eight o'clock, as Mr. Grindall, watchmaker, in Holborn, was going up to his lodgings at Islington, he was stopped in the Spa Fields near Merlin's Cave by three footpads who robbed him of a guinea, some silver, and his watch. They also robbed him of his handkerchief, in which were two fowls and a piece of bacon, which he intended for his next day's dinner. They told him if he offered to give information of them or make the least noise they would rip him up ; they ran off towards Coldbath Fields.——Monday night, as a young man was returning from Newington Green, he was attacked on the footway leading to Islington by four footpads who robbed him of his watch, eight guineas, and some silver.——Saturday night, five footpads stopped a gentleman near Taylor's Buildings, Islington, and robbed him of 4*l.*

The 'Morning Chronicle' of March 25, 1782, states that—

On Thursday evening last, as Mr. Heath, of Milk Street, with two ladies, were coming to town from Islington in a coach, they were attacked by five footpads armed with bludgeons, cutlasses, &c., who robbed them to the amount of three or four guineas, and made off.

The 'London Chronicle' for March 16 of the same year records that—

On Saturday Mr. Rogers and his brother, brewers at South End, were stopped in their carriage near Lewisham, in Kent, by two highwaymen who robbed them of their watches and money. One of the gentlemen fired a pistol, and killed one of the highwaymen on the spot, and the other had his horse stabbed by a soldier in making his escape.

Walpole, writing to Sir Horace, November 26, 1782, says :—

Your sister-in-law, Mrs. Mann, was robbed about ten days ago in New Park, between three and four in the afternoon; the prudent matron gave the highwayman a purse with very little money, but slipped her watch into the bag of the coach. The cavalier, not being content, insisted on more. The poor girl, terrified, gave him not only her own pinchbeck watch, but her grandmother's concealed gold one.[1]

A paragraph in the 'Times' for September 15, 1790 states that—

> So daring are the street robbers become that on Monday evening, a few minutes after five o'clock, two ladies were knocked down within a few seconds of each other, and robbed by four men in Coventry Street (one of the most public in London). The method these ruffians took was to strike the ladies violently on the legs, and when they fell, one of them secured their arms while the other rifled their pockets.
>
> *The Monster!*—On Monday last many ladies who had been assaulted and brutally wounded in the streets, appeared at the public office in Bow Street, in consequence of notice that a person was in custody suspected to be the wanton assassin.[2]

The paragraph immediately foregoing is a transcript from a morning journal for April 1790, and the truth of what it says is confirmed by Sir Gilbert Elliot, first Earl of Minto, who in writing to his wife in the same month of that year tells her that fashionable society was greatly concerned at the Monster's evil doings. That these outrages were of common occurrence is proved by the fact that when chronicled in the newspapers of the day they are described in ordinary language. One outrage succeeded another with such rapidity that the public became perfectly callous.

Five years before the eighteenth century draws to its close, the danger to which the public safety in and out of London was exposed, appears to have been as great as it was fifty years earlier. Here is a list of highway robberies extracted from a newspaper bearing date of February 28, 1795 :—

> Last Sunday night, as Mr. Lukin, of Long Acre, was returning to town over Wandsworth Common, he was stopped by two highwaymen, and on refusing to deliver his money, one of the highwaymen discharged a pistol at him, but it missed. Mr. L. then discharged a pistol at the robbers, on which they rode off. On Monday, as Mr. Sutton, of Salisbury, in company with his brother, was travelling to London on horseback, they were stopped by two highwaymen near Virginia Waters, and robbed of their cash and their watches.——Monday evening, as Mr. Cross, of Twickenham,

---

[1] Walpole's *Letters*, viii. 310 ; *Miss Berry's Journal*, ii. p. 434.
[2] *Public Advertiser*, April 21, 1790 ; Von Archenholz, *Picture of England*, pp. 297-298.

was travelling between Sunbury and Hampton, he was stopped by two highwaymen, who robbed him of his cash and watch, with which they got clear off.

A paragraph in the 'Times' for January 6, 1797, records that :

On Monday evening last Mr. Adamson, of Clapham, was stopped near Matrimony Hill by two footpads, who after treating him with a great deal of cruelty, robbed him of his money and a quantity of cloth.

In the year 1785 a pamphlet was published by Dilly, an eminent bookseller in the Poultry, under the following title :. 'Desultory Reflections on Police, &c. by William Blizard, F.S.A., Surgeon to the Honourable Artillery Company.' Blizard, who was afterwards knighted, was a skilful surgeon, a man well known in his day, and greatly respected. He states that during the American war, when the enemies of this country avowed their intention of invasion, many gentlemen of character and property in the city of London formed themselves into a company under the title of the London Military Foot Association. In the year 1781 most of the members incorporated themselves with the Honourable Artillery Company, and the Association ceased. Blizard's statements exhibit a very lax state of society, the absence of everything like a regular police, the monstrous venality even at this time of justices of the peace and their officers, and the impunity with which they as well as the thieves committed their depredations. The number of crimes then committed must have been enormous. The difficulty, too, of apprehending criminals, the uncertainty of bringing them to justice, and the protection which was afforded to them by the thief-takers, are all set forth in their naked reality. The description of the drunkenness, riots, assaults, vagabondage, and blackguardism about the streets and the environs of the metropolis, in public-houses and tea gardens, would now scarcely receive credit were it not indisputably substantiated by contemporary literature. Such things as these were not recorded at the time ; they were of so common occurrence as frequently to pass unnoticed in print. Sir William Blizard's pamphlet, though brief, incomplete, and relating to but a very limited period, is yet of considerable value to the student of the age. It was the production of a good, a kind, and an honest man, whose tastes, moral perceptions, and regard for truth had not been vitiated by birth and breeding among such scenes as those which he describes. Nor can one rise from its perusal without the conviction that its historical record may justly claim a very extended margin of inference which the moderation of the writer wisely left to the imagination of his readers.

Much of the life of the London streets in the eighteenth century has been stereotyped for posterity by Gay in the pages of his 'Trivia,' and by William Hogarth in his series of pictures depicting the four parts of the day. They, for all time, have made posterity familiar with the Billingsgate damsels carrying their fishy wares on their heads through the streets, with the milk-maids chalking their gains upon the street doors, the barbers in their aprons, the perfumers, the bakers, the chimney-sweepers skulking along, the drawl of the small-coal man, with the clang of the dustman's bell, the chandlers bearing baskets brimfull of tallow, the cross-grained butchers with their greasy trays and their hands dyed with blood. It is long since it was possible to see a wretch undergoing the stern discipline of the pillory. Brokers have ceased the wearing of 'spacious beaver hats,' and gentlemen of quality no longer seek to avoid the dun of 'the Fleet Street draper.' The last of the ancient race of chairmen, who might then have been seen in any numbers standing outside White's, as also the giants who performed the astonishing feat of striking the hours on the old clock of St. Dunstan's in Fleet Street, have passed away. The 'crowds of apprentices' are seen no longer. The ranks of the flower and herb sellers are rapidly diminishing, the mackerel criers are in process of extinction, while the rosemary sellers, and the oyster tubs ranged in rows beside the posts 'where Fleet Ditch with muddy current flows,' are equally things of the past. The pedestrian nowadays may walk for twenty years from Hyde Park Corner to Mile End at midnight, without the least fear of being insulted by street robbers, knocked down and plundered, or of being exposed to the insolence of abusive rascals who after provoking his resentment by opprobrious language, would afterwards haul him before a magistrate, not hesitating even at wilful perjury to make a prey of him, which was then an incident of common occurrence. No traveller now need fear passing through 'the roads of Drury's mazy courts and dark abodes,' nor need hesitate at taking his way 'where Catherine Street descends into the Strand.' The ballad-singers have ceased to bawl their ditties and to dive their hands into the pockets of those who stayed to listen. The rakes, 'kindlers of riot and enemies of sleep,' have vanished, and mischief-loving gentlemen, familiarly known as 'Nickers,' who delighted to break the windows of their auditors with showers of halfpence, the Scourers, the Mohocks, and their legitimate descendants, from whose blows neither watchman nor female was safe, are no more.

A chapter devoted to the manners of the town may not inaptly contain some notice of its various frauds and tricks of thieves, if it should serve only to show that they are much the same in all ages. One class of gamblers cheated passers-by with their eyes open by inviting them to 'prick in the belt' or the 'garter' for a wager. Another class of men, generally poorly clad, pretended to find papers full of gold rings, which they took care to pick up in the sight of a passenger, whose opinion they asked. This being given, they at once poured out a pitiful tale about not having broken their fast for a whole day, regretted that they had not picked up a piece of bread and cheese, and ended with a request that the bystander or bystanders would become purchasers. The usual result was that some silly bird would swallow the bait, and pay the rascal a guinea for half a dozen brass rings which had been carefully washed over for the purpose.[1] Another dodge, which often proved successful, was that called 'guinea dropping.' The plan was to pick up a bright yellow coin, or a half-crown or shilling, before the gaze of some gaping country clown, and immediately to ask his opinion as to whether it were silver or not. Replying in the affirmative, the clown would be invited to share the good fortune

[1] Sir John Fielding's *Observations on Extracts from the Penal Laws* 1762.

of the finder in a neighbouring alehouse, where he would be introduced to the friends and acquaintances of the sharper, who on the first opportunity would suggest card-playing and fleece the unwary countryman of every penny he had about his person and every article of value.[1]   Sometimes the sharpers would vary their operations in the manner indicated in the following paragraph :—

On Monday afternoon a country-looking man was inveigled by a sharper into a public-house in Ludgate Street, who, calling for a shillingsworth of punch, asked him to drink, pretending he knew him and some of his relations in Lancashire ; but while they were in discourse, two other sharpers entered the room and joined company, one of whom pulled out of his pocket a large purse full of counters, as is supposed, which he said were guineas, and proposed the old stale trick of hushing in the hat, which the countryman not being aware of, they not only took him in for 19s. 6d., but left him to pay the reckoning, which was all he had except a single farthing.[2]

Another set of sharpers took up their quarters outside the doors of inns.   As soon as a porter received instructions to deliver a box or parcel which had arrived from the country, the sharper mentally noted the direction, and sent his companion immediately to the house, there to await its arrival.   Meeting the porter within a few yards of the house, the confederate would abuse him for his tardiness, tell him that he was just coming to fetch it, and that he had a very great mind to send him empty away.   Hereupon the porter would humbly beg pardon, and the sharper, inwardly exulting at his success, would give him a trifle, take possession of the parcel, and decamp with it the moment the porter had gone his way.   Sir John Fielding, a zealous Bow Street magistrate in the reign of George III., in a small work upon the state of the metropolis, enumerates numbers of the tricks practised by London thieves in his time. Servants who had been in the employ of tailors, mantua-makers, milliners, &c. would think nothing of obtaining goods in the name of their late masters and mistresses, long after they had quitted their service.   In the neighbourhood of Charing Cross, St. Clement's Church, and Ludgate Hill, passengers would be decoyed by ' duffers ' to wend their way down obscure alleys

[1] Sir John Fielding's *Observations*, &c.
[2] *British Chronicle*, 3-8 June, 1778.

to buy cheap handkerchiefs and waistcoats. Another set of cheats commonly frequented the yards into which coaches and waggons deposited their passengers, for the purpose of following baskets, bundles, or portmanteaus put into hackney coaches, and frequently succeeded in getting possession of them by sending the porter to deliver some message or to procure a bottle of wine, promising to take care of their goods during their absence, or otherwise by tracking them to the door of the house, and personating the servant. Others gained a livelihood by walking into alehouses and desiring the landlord to send a gallon of ale to some neighbour whose name they had learned, and to bring change for a counterfeit guinea, which was usually sent by the hands of a little boy. The sharper's plan was to waylay the boy, receive from him the change and the liquor, then to send him back to fetch a pipe, and in the meanwhile to walk off. It was a common practice, according to Sir John Fielding, for thieves to carry a parcel of old books to the town residence of some family known to be away, and to represent to the servant who opened the door that they had called from the bookseller for the second subscription, which if not paid, their master or mistress's order would be cancelled. This ruse often ended in the unwary servant parting with a guinea. Another dodge consisted in discovering the name of some gentleman's servant, as well as the place of his or her nativity, and then calling to inform him or her that a parcel directed to one of that name lay at a certain inn till called for. A demand would then be made for the money for carriage, and for this, if the servant was foolish enough to pay it, a note for the removal of the goods would be given. To watch servants' masters out, and then to call in the guise of a coffee-house waiter for their master's great-coat or in that of a tailor's apprentice or journeyman for a suit of clothes to alter, was another dodge to which London thieves often successfully resorted at that time.

Not the least among the numerous evils which disgraced society during the greater part of the eighteenth century was the custom, already mentioned, of giving vails to servants. Dr. William King, principal of St. Mary Hall, Oxford, in writing a series of autobiographical memoranda, about 1760, makes some interesting observations concerning vails-giving. 'How much,' wrote he,

> are foreigners astonished, when they observe that a man cannot dine at any house in England, not even with his father or his brother, or with any other of his nearest relations, or most intimate friends and companions, unless he pay for his dinner! But how can they behold without indignation or contempt a man of quality standing by the guests, while they are distributing money to a double row of his servants! . . . I remember a Lord Poor, a Roman Catholic peer of Ireland, who lived upon a small pension which Queen Anne had granted him : he was a man of honour and well esteemed, and had formerly been an officer of some distinction in the service of France. The Duke of Ormonde had often invited him to dinner, and he as often excused himself. At last the duke kindly expostulated with him, and would know the reason. My lord Poor then honestly confessed he could not afford it ; 'but,' says he, 'if your Grace will put a guinea into my hands as often as you are pleased to invite me, I will not decline the honour of waiting upon you.' This was done and my lord was afterwards a frequent guest in St. James's Square.[1]

The absurdities, inconveniences, national disputes, and many other pernicious consequences to all ranks of the English people, to which this detestable custom gave rise, form the subject of no fewer than eight discourses by the eminent philanthropist Jonas Hanway. In these discourses, which were published in 1760, Hanway proved that no person of distinction could then accept an invitation to dinner without carrying a number of shillings, half-crowns, and sometimes even guineas and half-guineas, with which to fee the servants of his host, from the butler downwards, at parting—a custom which bore terribly hard upon people possessed of small incomes. The result was that servants became proverbial for their rapacity, standing in rows when distinguished visitors took their departure to demand their vails, which ranged from a guinea downwards. 'I have known a captain of a man-of-war,' wrote Hanway, 'who has not been possessed of 10*l.* a year independent of his pay, give five guineas for sleeping two nights at a nobleman's seat.'[2] By this means a man who depended upon his wits, was com-

---

[1] *Anecdotes of His Own Times*, ed. 1819, pp. 50, 54.
[2] Hanway's *Eight Letters to the Duke of Devonshire on Vails Giving*, p. 21.

pelled to act upon a level with a man of fortune, or to be excluded from a house where his company was really desired.
That which had originally been conceded as a voluntary gift,
became eventually an appendage to servants' wages, many of
them indeed regarding the former as of far greater importance
than the latter.   Vails-giving became at last a grievance which
required the interposition of the Legislature for its abolition,
and it is worthy of mention that Hanway's pamphlet contributed largely to the removal of so obnoxious an impost.

Some information respecting the manners of town society
in the closing years of the eighteenth century may be gained
from a perusal of Hannah More's 'Thoughts on the Manners
of the Great,' which was published anonymously in 1787.
From this little work it appears that the conventional falsehood
styled the lie of 'Not at home,' was then not unknown.   Sunday
concerts had crept into vogue, as well as Sunday gaming.
There was also a perceptible increase of work for the hairdressers on the same day.   The authoress deals severely with
the petty mischief of card-money, in other words the payment
of servants' wages by their furnishing the means of diversion for
the guests of their masters, of the lowering of the standard of
right, of the cool indifference displayed towards the gravest
offences, of the affected tenderness and indulgent toleration
manifested towards the most shameful profligacy, and of much
more besides, all tending to show that London society in the
latter quarter of the eighteenth century was little better, if at all,
than it was under William III. and Anne.   The duties of footmen
and servants are admirably summed up by Robert Dodsley in
his poem entitled 'The Footman,' which is printed among others
in his 'Muse in Livery.'   This poem, which is cast in the form
of an epistle to his friend Wright, indicates that a footman was
required to rise early, and to set himself to the task of cleaning
glasses, knives, and plate.   This done he brightened his own
buckles, blacked his shoes, powdered his wig, brushed his
clothes, and then attended his lady's maid, and after complying
with her orders, flying here, there, and everywhere, 'with services and how-d'ye does,' returned home, when it was his next
duty, as soon as the scent from spits and kettles saluted his

nostrils, to lay the cloth, to place the plate, glass, and china ware on the sideboards, to decant the ale, beer, and wine, and to wait at the table after the dishes had been placed upon it and the guests had taken their places. When the afternoon had sped by, the hour for tea-drinking had arrived, whereupon the kettle having been filled, the water boiled, the cream provided, and the biscuits piled, the duty devolved upon the footman of ranging in order and with decorum—

> The Lilliputian equipage
> Of dishes, saucers, spoons, and tongs
> And all th' et cetera which thereto belongs.

By the time tea was over, the hour for visiting had drawn nigh, and while the chairmen prepared the chair, the footman provided himself with a lighted flambeau, with which he strutted along through the streets, crying with a steady voice, 'By your leave, sir! Have a care!' proceeding from place to place, rapping loudly at each door at which he was bidden to rap, and inquiring whether the master or mistress was within. If at home, he halted, and while his lady ascended to the drawing-room, the footman directed his steps to the hall, where in company with his brethren, he drank small beer, and amid oaths and peals of laughter, joined in the coarse raillery directed against his lords and ladies, exposed their faults, and tattled scandal, until his services were again required to wend his steps in some other direction, the play, assembly, or opera. The footman's working day ended after he had conducted his master or mistress home to supper. Sir John Fielding, one of the king's justices of the peace for the counties of Middlesex, Essex, and Surrey, and for the city and liberty of Westminster, writing of London in 1776, used words with which this chapter may fittingly conclude :—

So numerous are the inconveniences of residing in town, so many the temptations to evil, so shameful the venality and luxury there in fashion, and consequently so exorbitant the expenses of it, that we must heartily recommend it to every gentleman of moderate fortune to reflect seriously with how much more grace and dignity he may support himself and family in the country at a far less charge, reviving the old British hospitality, enjoying salutary air and exercise, and bidding fair to be a long time a blessing to his neighbours himself and his posterity.

CHAPTER IV.

DRESS AND COSTUME.

NOTWITHSTANDING the ban under which philosophy has always placed the vanity of dress, it has never failed to engross the constant attention of civilised humanity. It does so now, it did so in the last century, and from the closing years of the reign of William III. down to 1799, the dress and costume worn by men and women in England passed through transitions so numerous and so frequent, that neither the historian, the essayist, nor the painter has been successful in preserving all of them. Like the fabled sea-god Proteus struggling in the arms of Telemachus on the Pharic coasts, it passed from shape to shape with the velocity of thought. In the face of this, it will be manifest that any attempt to detail the multifarious fantastic alterations which the eighteenth century wrought in the costume of English society with anything approaching completeness would require researches far too extensive for the limits of a single chapter. All that it is possible to do here, therefore, will be to pass in brief review the styles which male and female attire most commonly assumed during the four reigns which the century comprises, freely according *place aux dames*.

For the first few years during which Queen Anne wielded the sceptre, the ladies of this land dressed very much in the

same way as in the reign of her predecessor, 'adding or sub-
tracting minor decorations which did not materially affect their
tout ensemble.' About the year 1711, however, the good taste
of the Queen induced her to discontinue the wearing of those
monstrous fashionable head-dresses, sadly misnomered *commodes,* which were (as may be learnt from a reference to the
' Lady's Dictionary') frames of wire, two or three storeys high,
fitted to the head, and covered with tiffany or some other thin
silk. Why the appellation of commodes should have ever
been applied to obvious inconveniences passes the understanding, for no name could possibly have been more appropriate to the style of coiffure which they represented than that
of 'tower,' or ' Bow steeple,' names which the wits bestowed
upon them in derision. Addison, who with Steele endeavoured,
through the medium of the 'Spectator,' to correct what was
amiss in the fashions of his day, thus alluded to the change :—

There is not so variable a thing in nature as a lady's head-
dress. Within my own memory I have known it rise and fall
within thirty degrees. About ten years ago it shot up to a very
great height, insomuch that the female part of our species were
much taller than the men. The women were of such enormous
stature that we appeared as grasshoppers before them. At present
the whole sex is in a manner dwarfed and shrunk into a race of
beauties that seem almost another species. I remember several
ladies who were once very near seven feet high, that at present
want some inches of five. How they came to be thus curtailed I
cannot learn. Whether the whole sex be at present under any
penance which we know nothing of, or whether they have cast
their head-dresses in order to surprise us with something of that
kind which shall be entirely new, or whether some of the tallest of
the sex, being too cunning for the rest, have contrived this method
to make themselves appear sizeable, is still a secret, though I find
most are of opinion they are at present like trees new lopped and
pruned, that will certainly sprout up and flourish with greater heads
than before.

Nor was Mr. Spectator very far out in the conjecture he thus
hazarded, seeing that shortly after the accession of George III.
female head-gear rose to more exaggerated and ridiculous
heights than ever, reaching the climax of absurdity between
the years 1763 and 1780, when the head was usually surmounted with a high cushion, over which the front hair—

reduced to a cloudy hue by a mixture of powder and grease—
was combed to meet that behind, and when strained tight
was surrounded by ribbons and jewels or artificial flowers, or
adorned with a plume of feathers standing frequently half a yard
in height. It was about this time that the celebrated Duchess
of Devonshire supported in her hair two ostrich-feathers (each
more than an ell in length) which had been presented to her
by Lord Stormont, and as her Grace wielded absolute sway
over the then existing fashions, the craze for towering feathers
became well-nigh universal.[1] The poet Rogers, in speaking of
the preposterous size of the female head-dresses prevalent in his
youth, once told the company at a dinner-table that he well
recollected, on one occasion, going to Ranelagh in a coach,
accompanied by a lady who was obliged to sit upon a stool
placed in the bottom of it, on account of the height of her
head-dress precluding her from occupying the regular seat.[2]
George Colman the younger, describing the head-gear of the
spouse of his tutor, a parson named Fountayne, who kept
a famous boarding establishment at Marylebone in the last
quarter of the eighteenth century, says that—

Although she rejected powder and pomatum (which were universally worn), she nevertheless so far conformed with the prevalent
female fashion as to erect a formidable messuage or tenement of
hair upon the ground-plot of her pericranium. A twopenny toupee,
pulled up all but the roots, and strained over a cushion on the top
of her head, formed the centre of the building; tiers of curls served
for the wings, a banging *chignon* behind defended the occiput like
a buttress, and the whole fabric was kept tight and waterproof,
as with nails and iron cramps, by a quantity of long single and
double black pins.[3]

According to some accounts, this hideous fashion was first
introduced by the unfortunate Marie Antoinette, and entailed
hours of suffering under the *friseur,* who not unfrequently
failed entirely to give satisfaction. From a letter written by
Hannah More to one of her sisters from London in 1776, it

[1] Stone, *Chronicles of Fashion,* ii. 436 ; *Life of Nollekens,* i. 61 ; J. T.
Smith, *Book for a Rainy Day,* pp. 35–36 ; *Life and Times of Nollekens,*
i. 18 ; *Correspondence of the First Earl of Malmesbury,* i. 296 ; Miss
Burney's *Evelina,* c. xix.
[2] *Recollections of the Table Talk of Samuel Rogers,* p. 24.
[3] *Random Records,* p. 35.

appears that some ladies went to the length of wearing a large quantity of fruit in their head-dresses, others four or five ostrich feathers of different colours at the back of their perpendicular caps.[1] Visiting some relations at Bungay, in Suffolk, in April 1777, Hannah met a number of damsels who, she declared, had amongst them on their heads, 'an acre and a half of shrubbery, besides slopes, grass-plats, tulip-beds, clumps of peonies, kitchen-gardens, and greenhouses.'[2] It is stated that this now scarcely credible but fashionable folly was abolished through the instrumentality of Garrick, who appeared in the character of Sir John Brute, dressed in female attire, with his cap decorated with a profusion of every kind of vegetable, a huge carrot being dependent from each side. The picture-galleries in many of our historic mansions bear testimony to the truly frightful phantasy of head-gear to which the despotic and exacting canons of fashion required fashionable belles to conform. It is perpetuated, for example, in some of the finest handiwork of Thomas Gainsborough ; and it may be mentioned that, while this master of English portraiture was slowly fighting his way to fame and competence at Bath, there resided in the same city a *friseur* who was far more honoured and far better paid than the painter. So high was the esteem in which this *friseur* was held by the leaders of *bon ton*, that they would employ no one else ; with the result that they were often compelled to submit to his operations whole days before they were to appear at some grand ball or brilliant fête, and to rest at night in an upright position, lest they should damage or destroy his work by lying down. Under date of November 1, 1779, the 'Gazetteer and New Daily Advertiser' records that a young lady of Grantham, in looking over some papers with a lighted candle in her hand, set fire to her head-dress. Her cries alarmed some of the neighbours, who 'hastened to her relief ; and happily put an end to the dreadful conflagration without any other material injury than the loss of a large *mountain* of hair, wool, powder, pomatum, &c.' By way of variety, fashionable belles not unfrequently bound up kitchen-

---

[1] Roberts's *Memoirs of H. More*, i p. 65.   [2] *Ibid.* p. 100.

garden stuff into their hair, the flower of the scarlet-runner being considered particularly suitable for the adornment of their locks.

The second abomination in point of female costume of which the eighteenth century witnessed the birth was that 'sevenfold fence,' the hoop, which for so many years afforded such a rich theme for the lively pens of wags and satirists. The manufacture of this famous article, which was the precursor of the crinoline, has been generally ascribed to the inventive genius of a certain Mrs. Selby, concerning whom nothing definite appears to be known beyond the fact that she was a noted London mantua-maker, who died in January 1717. Wearers of the hoop pleaded in excuse of its absurdity that it rendered them cool in summer by admitting a free circulation of the air.[1] In the reign of Anne, the hooped petticoat— which was no more a petticoat than Diogenes' tub was his breeches [2]—attained such enormous proportions that the editor of the 'Tatler' felt in duty bound to ridicule the innovation. Forthwith Mr. Bickerstaff (*i.e.* Sir Richard Steele) inserted in the pages of that journal the bogus 'humble petition of William Jingle, coachmaker and chairmaker, of the city of West-minster,'

which showeth, that upon the late invention of Mrs. Catherine Crossditch, mantua-maker, the petticoats of ladies were too wide for entering into any coach or chair which was in use before the said invention.   That for the service of the said ladies, your petitioner has built a round chair in the form of a lantern, six yards and a half in circumference, with a stool in the centre of it, the said vehicle being so contrived as to receive the passenger by opening in two in the middle, and closing mathematically when she is seated.   That your petitioner has also invented a coach for the reception of one lady only, who is to be let in at the top.   That the said coach has been tried by a lady's woman in one of these full petticoats, who was let down from a balcony, and drawn up again by pulleys, to the great satisfaction of her lady and all who beheld her.[3]

On another occasion Mr. Bickerstaff enlivened his readers by reporting the imaginary proceedings of a court established

[1] Noble's *Continuation of Granger.*   [2] *Ibid.*
[3] Malcolm, *Anecdotes of London in Eighteenth Century,* ii. 321.

for the special consideration of the hooped petticoat by a jury of matrons :—

> The court [he wrote] being prepared for proceeding on the cause of the petticoat, I gave orders to bring in a criminal who was taken up as she went out of the puppet-show about three nights ago, and was now standing in the street with a great concourse of people about her. Word was brought me that she had endeavoured twice or thrice to come in, but could not do it by reason of her petticoat which was too large for the entrance of my house, though I had ordered both the folding doors to be thrown open for its reception.

Eventually the wearer, 'a young damsel,' contrives to get into the court, and at the close of a humorous mock trial, Mr. Bickerstaff pronounces the petticoat 'a forfeiture,' though in order to show that he does not pass sentence from interested motives, he sends it as a present to a widow lady of his acquaintance blessed with five daughters, desiring she would make *each* a petticoat of it. The good-tempered 'Spectator,' like his merry contemporary the 'Tatler,' was never tired of inveighing against hoop petticoats or remonstrating with their wearers, and so when furnishing his readers with an account of the way in which he passed the Sabbath at the country seat of Sir Roger de Coverley, he causes the good old knight to observe when conducting him round the picture gallery : 'You see, sir, my great-grandmother has on the new-fashioned petticoat, except that the modern is gathered at the waist. My grandmother appears as if she stood in a large drum, whereas the ladies now walk as if they were in a go-cart.' The march of time did not at all affect the hoop petticoat, since so late as 1745 the writer of a pamphlet entitled 'The Enormous Abomination of the Hoop Petticoat' expressed his conviction that the fair sex by reason of their partiality for these articles had become an intolerable nuisance. The pamphleteer's wrath appears to have been particularly excited at beholding a young girl of seventeen taking up the whole side of a street with her hollow standing petticoat, and another damsel walking down 'the middle aisle' of a church after receiving the sacrament with one corner of her petticoat touching the pews on the right hand, and the other those on the left. The difficulty which a belle when propped

up on high-heeled shoes and attired in 'this requisite and inde-
scribable mode of dress,' as Tate Wilkinson called it, customarily
experienced in getting into a sedan-chair is cleverly illustrated
by Hogarth in his picture representing 'Taste à-la-mode.'[1]
Mrs. Pendarves writing to Mrs. Anne Granville in January
1738-9 tells her that the hoops then fashionable were made
of the richest damask with gold and silver, fourteen guineas a
hoop.[2] The same lady writing from Pall Mall to Mrs. Dewes on
January 21, 1746-7, says 'the only thing that seems general
are hoops of an enormous size, and most people wear vast
winkers to their heads. They are now come to such an extravagance in those two particulars, that I expect soon to see
the other extreme of thread paper heads and no hoops.'[3]

The ladies' trains, although by no means so cumbersome
and objectionable as their hooped petticoats, nevertheless came
in for a fair share of abuse at the hands of the censors of
fashion. Goldsmith, under the *nom-de-guerre* of a 'Citizen of
the World,' administered a sharp castigation to them when he
told his imaginary correspondent in the Celestial Empire that

what chiefly distinguishes the sex at present is the train. As
a lady's quality or fashion was once determined here by the circumference of her hoop, both are now measured by the length of
her tail. Women of moderate fortunes are contented with tails
moderately long, but ladies of true taste and distinction set no
bounds to their ambition in this particular. I am told the lady
mayoress on days of ceremony carries one longer than a bell-
wether of Bantam, whose tail, you know, is trundled along in a
wheelbarrow.

Referring to its extravagance, the same writer observes :—'A
lady's train is not bought but at some expense, and after it has
swept the public walks for a few evenings is fit to be worn no
longer.'

I have seen [says another writer of the times] young ladies
spirited enough to let their trains trail along the flagstones of
Bishopsgate Street and Whitechapel. It is true they have a
little damaged the edges of their dignity by it ; but what signifies
a fine woman putting on fine clothes, if she don't wear them as she

---

[1] *Mirror*, p. 90.
[2] *Autobiog. and Corr. of Mrs. Delany*, 1st series, vol. ii. 25.
[3] *Ibid.* ii. 451.

should do? Besides, how can we, as aptly as Simonides did, compare a woman to a peacock, unless she bears herself in consequence at every step by the sweep of her tail. This sweep at the bottom is grown too common ; for it was but last night, that my next door neighbour, who takes in stays to repair, hired a parish girl for her servant, and I heard her this morning tell the wench where I live that she had sent an Irish poplin to the scourers, and it was to be made up with ruffle cuffs ; but yet for all that she would not appear in it at church if it had not *the true quality sweep* at the bottom.

In imitation of the male sex the belles of the eighteenth century wore wigs, to which they gave the fanciful name of *têtes* or heads. These were huge concoctions of horse-hair stiffened with pomatum and sprinkled with powder, and, as Miss Fanny, a character in the 'Old Maid,' observes, would, ' when properly made up with pins and paste, *keep* a month very well.'

The fashionable ladies exhibited all the colours of the rainbow. The varieties of cloth being then exceedingly scanty, the upper ranks could distinguish themselves from the lower only by the adoption of French finery. This they learned from dolls dressed in the height of the prevalent fashion by Parisian *modistes*, and sent over to English milliners.[1] During the reign of Queen Anne scarlet cloaks with coloured hoods were largely worn by ladies when out walking. In George I.'s time, black and white beaver hats were widely worn. About 1731 high-crowned hats became the politest distinction of fashionable undress.[2] Between 1745 and 1746 gipsy hats crept into vogue, and shortly afterwards small bonnets tied beneath the chin became the rage. The large necklace remained in use, though not constantly worn, but the wearing of earrings was discontinued. The bodice was worn open in front, and fastened with gold or silver clasps ; the sleeves full. Spanish broadcloth trimmed with gold lace was still used by the fair sex. So also were furbelowed scarves. Riding habits were extensively patronised. The 'Whitehall Evening Post' for August 17, 1720, informed its readers that the princesses rode to Richmond in riding-habits, &c. Judging from an advertisement of one stolen in 1751—'white fustian turned up with blue and laced with

---

[1] *Corr. of Countess of Suffolk*, ed. Croker.
[2] Malcolm's *Aspects of London in the Eighteenth Century*, ii. 331.

silver'—the ladies' riding-habits must have occasionally presented a very attractive appearance. Horace Walpole in his
'Anecdotes of Painting' says that in the reign of George I.
the habits of the times were shrunk into awkward coats and
waistcoats for the men, and for the women two tight-laced
round hoops and half-a-dozen squeezed plaits of linen to which
dangled behind two unmeaning pendants, called lappets, not
half covering their straight-drawn hair.[1]

The dress usually worn by ladies in the reign of George II.
seems to have been a gown heavily brocaded, the waist reduced
to a point, a huge hoop, embroidered shoes with high heels,
pointed at the toes. The sleeves of the gown were wide, and
ruffled cuffs hung from the elbows. Hanging sleeves depended
from the backs of the gowns worn by young ladies. The neck
and shoulders were usually covered with fine handkerchiefs,
woven either of French lawn or cambric, which was most extravagantly worn until 1747, when Parliament stepped in and
enacted that 'all persons who wore cambric or lawn on any
garment or apparel after the 24th day of June, 1748, should
forfeit to the informer the sum of five pounds.' Mrs. Pendarves
writing from Brook Street to Mrs. Anne Granville under date
of January 23, 1738-9, with reference to the finery worn on the
Prince of Wales's birthday, says :—

I never saw so much finery without any mixture of trumpery in
my life. Lady Huntingdon's, as the most extraordinary, I must
describe first :—her petticoat was black velvet embroidered with
chenille, the pattern a large stone vase filled with ramping flowers
that spread almost over a breadth of the petticoat from the bottom
to the top ; between each vase of flowers was a pattern of gold
shells and foliage embossed and most heavily rich ; the gown was
white satin, embroidered also with chenille mixed with gold ornaments ; no vases on the sleeve, but two or three on the tail . . . .
The next fine lady was Mrs. Spencer ; her clothes green paduasoy
covered all over the gown as well as the petticoat with a very fine
and very pretty trimming . . . . Lady Dysart was white gold
. . . . Mrs. Carteret in an uncut blue velvet, and all my Lady
Carteret's jewels ; Lady Carteret, white and gold, and colours ;
the Princess was in white satin, her head and stomacher a rock of
diamonds and pearls.[2]

---

[1] *Anecdotes of Painting*, ed. Wornum, ii. 644.
[2] *Autob. and Corr. of Mrs. Delany*, 1st series, ii. pp. 28-29.

I go to-morrow in my Irish-green damask and my worked head [says Mrs. Delany, writing from Pall Mall to her friend Mrs. Dewes, on January 15, 1746-7] on the Birthday, which is on Tuesday next, in a flowered silk I have bought since I came to town, on a pale-coloured figured ground ; the flowers, mostly purple, are mixed with white feathers. I think it extremely pretty and very modest.[1]

Writing to Mrs. Dewes of the birthday of the Princess of Wales, in November 1742, Mrs. Pendarves says :—

My lady [Granville] was in dark green velvet trimmed with ermine, and an ermine petticoat. Her daughter Fanny had a scarlet damask. Mrs. Spencer was in blue and silver. But our fair maid of honour [Hon. Elizabeth Granville, daughter of George, Lord Lansdowne] outshone them all, clad in rich pink satin, trimmed with silver. . . . In the evening I went to Lady North's, where I saw but few people. The Duchess of Montrose was in silver tissue ; Lady Scarborough in blue damask with a gold trimming. There were several very handsome flowered silks shaded like embroidery ; but the finest clothes were Lady Caroline Lennox's gold and colours on white.[2]

In 1762 French night-caps were worn, besides Ranelagh mob-caps (pieces of gauze or Leicester web, clouted to the head, crossed under the chin, and brought back to fasten behind, the two ends hanging like a pair of pigeon's tails). Another cap was the Mary Queen of Scots cap, which was edged down the face with French beads. Fly caps, too, fixed upon the forehead, forming the figure of an overgrown butterfly, resting upon its head with outstretched wings, and edged with jewels and precious stones.[3] High-heeled shoes were worn and embroidered stockings of divers hues. The height of the former fifty years previously had caused Steele to wax satirical, when he humorously advertised in the 'Tatler' a stage coach as departing from Nando's Coffee House every evening, when 'dancing-shoes not exceeding four inches high in the heel would be carried in the coach-box gratis.'

The magazine pages devoted to fashionable attire of 1774 speak of stomachers crossed with silver or gold cord ; fine laced ruffles ; shoes embroidered with satin, and ornamented with diamond roses ; small drop earrings and Turkey handker-

---

[1] *Autob. and Corr.*, 1st series, ii. c. viii.
[2] *Ibid.* p. 201.   [3] *London Chronicle*, 1-62, xi. 167.

chiefs.[1] The following year ladies wore their hair in small curls, with pearl pins, starred leaves, and large white or coloured feathers, and two drop curls at the ears. Round the neck, small pearls or collars ; Ranelagh tippets, or rattlesnake tippets, of fine blond stuck with flowers, and rows of beads hanging over the shoulders, satin slippers, worked gowns of all sorts worn over small hoops ; long cloaks, short aprons, and shoes with buckles. A lady's riding-habit is described as being made with blue buttons and frogs lined with silk; colours, the light mahogany, pearl greens, cinnamon and dark brown, light blue, lilacs, and white silks ; fantail hats with ribbons and feathers.

Women's costume became so grotesque in 1776 that a wag felt constrained to sing :—

> Give Chloe a bushel of horse-hair and wool,
>   Of paste and pomatum a pound,
> Ten yards of gay ribbon to deck her sweet poll,
>   And gauze to encompass it round.
>
> Of all the gay colours the rainbow displays,
>   Be those ribbons which hang on her head ;
> Be her flowers adapted to make the folks gaze,
>   And about the whole work be they spread.
>
> Let her flaps fly behind for a yard at the least,
>   Let her curls meet just under her chin ;
> Let these curls be supported to keep up the jest,
>   With an hundred instead of one pin.
>
> Let her gown be tucked up to the hip on each side,
>   Shoes too high for to walk or to jump.
> And to deck the sweet creature complete for a bride
>   Let the cork-cutter make her a rump.
>
> Thus finished in taste while on Chloe you gaze
>   You may take the dear charmer for life :
> But never undress her—for, out of her stays,
>   You'll find you have lost half your wife.[2]

Some slight effect was produced upon female attire by the great French Revolution of 1789, since before the close of that memorable year a high bonnet shaped like a sugarloaf, very much worn by the French peasantry, found its way into

[1] *Lady's Magazine*, March 1774.
[2] *Univers. Mag.* vol. l. p. 268.

England. Tight sleeves began to be worn, besides low bodices, and exceedingly high waists. The corsets were about six inches long and a slight buffon tucker of two inches high was the only defensive paraphernalia of fashionable belles between the necklace and the apron strings.[1]

Tight lacing was attended with very uncomfortable results. Lady Crewe once told Samuel Rogers that on returning home from Ranelagh she had rushed up to her bedroom, and desired her maid to cut her laces without delay for fear she should faint.[2]

The habit of snuff-taking was not by any means confined to the male sex, and it was the fashion for ladies of quality to carry jewelled snuffboxes about their persons. When time began to deal severely with the blushes upon their cheeks, and the lustre in their eyes, the frail beauties of the age strenuously endeavoured to restore them with the assistance of size and oil. It is said that the Countess of Coventry—*née* Maria Gunning— died prematurely from the effects of an over-application of cosmetics.[3] Some ladies, in order to enhance their attractions, even laid on superfine stucco, or better still, plaster of Paris, which had the reputation of lasting four weeks. Considering that paint concealed time's ravage, it is not surprising that it should have been so universally adopted. Far on into the reign of George III., ladies adhered to the practice of sticking several circular pieces of black silk or velvet on various parts of their faces. It had formerly denoted the politics of the wearer, but it had long lost its political significance. Goldsmith, alluding to this odd custom in the 'Citizen of the World,' observes :—

They like to have the face of various colours, as among the Tartars of Coreki, frequently sticking on little patches on every part of it, except on the top of the nose, which I have never seen with a patch. You'll have a better idea of their manner of placing these spots when I have furnished a map of an English face patched up to the fashion, which shall shortly be sent to increase your curious collection of paintings, medals, and monsters.

---

[1] *Times,* June 24, 1795.
[2] *Recollections of Table Talk of Rogers,* p. 24,
[3] Hor. Walpole, *Journ.* June 11, 1757.

No lady went equipped without a gold *étui* case, richly chased, provided with a thimble, a pair of scissors, and small bottles of scent and aromatic vinegar. No lady, moreover, went equipped without a fan, generally mounted with diamonds and inlaid with jewels.[1] During the reign of Queen Anne the ladies' fans, which had previously been mere fashionable accompaniments, became instruments of great power. So large were their dimensions that Sir Roger de Coverley was made to declare that he would have allowed the widowed lady to whom he paid his addresses the profits of a windmill for her fans Addison, who preached a long homily in the 'Spectator,' on this 'insignificant toy' went so far as to say that it required three months' assiduous practice to acquire proficiency in the art of 'fluttering the fan.' Thorough mastery of the art, however, was supposed to bring its own reward, since the fair mistress of it was enabled to express by its means any emotion which her breast experienced—anger, modesty, temerity, confusion, mirth, or love. All sorts of political emblems were painted on fans, and thus a glance would often suffice to ascertain the politics of the wearer. In 1710, while the trial of Dr. Henry Sacheverell was occupying public attention, the ladies who entertained high Anglican views caused the doctor's trial scene to be painted on their fans. No sooner did the narrative of the extraordinary adventures of Captain Lemuel Gulliver make its appearance than it took the whole reading world by storm, and the consequence was that every other fan bore a representation of some scene contained in it. When the 'Beggar's Opera' was put upon the stage public fancy was caught by it, and as a matter of course the fair sex felt constrained to have the words of their favourite songs from it inscribed on their fans. In the month of May 1753, Sylvanus Urban, gent., of the 'Gentleman's Magazine,' was favoured with a communication on the subject of fans which is worth transcribing. It ran to the following effect :—

Mr. Urban,—I shall here subjoin a list of a dozen designs, elegantly executed, which at a late celebration of the communion in a

---

[1] J. T. Smith, *Book for a Rainy Day*, pp. 12, 69 ; Smith, *Life and Times of Nollekens*, i. 17.

certain church of this metropolis were actually displayed by way of screens to so many pretty faces, disposed in a semi-circular arrangement about the Holy Table : 1, Darby and Joan with their attributes ; 2, Harlequin Pierrot and Columbine ; 3, the Prodigal Son, copied from the Rake's Progress ; 4, a rural dance, with a band of music consisting of a fiddle, a bagpipe, and a Welsh harp ; 5, the taking of Porto Bello ; the solemnities of a filiation ; 7, Joseph and his mistress ; 8, the humours of Change Alley ; 9, Silenus with his proper symbols and supporters ; 10, the first interview of Isaac and Rebecca ; 11, the Judgment of Paris ; 12, Vauxhall Gardens with the decorations and company.

Until that sumptuous despot Beau Nash prohibited the wearing of them in the evening rooms at Bath, most ladies of fashion when full dressed wore long or short aprons richly embroidered with Macklin (or Mechlin) or Brussels lace. For lace of this description the fair sex in general seems to have had a perpetual mania, and, as Swift observes, they 'knew to a groat the lowest price' when selecting it in the linen-drapers' shops on Ludgate Hill. Indeed the passion which English dames evinced for such finery so alarmed the fierce honest Protestantism of Malachy Postlethwayt, that he took occasion in a 'Dictionary of Commerce' which he published in 1751 to draw their attention to the significant fact that foreign lace was chiefly manufactured by nuns in Catholic countries, and that they might just as well endow convents as wear it. Contemporary plays and satires abound in allusions to the mania for lace. Ladies'-maids were even bribed with pieces of Flanders lace by their mistress' lovers, as Lucy, the maid, in Farquhar's 'Recruiting Officer,' when assuring her mistress, observes : 'Indeed, madam, the best bribe I had from the captain was a small piece of Flanders lace.' Swift, in his advice to a young lady, exclaims, 'When you are among yourselves how naturally after the first compliments do you entertain yourselves with the price and choice of lace !' The Countess of Hertford, writing to the Duchess of Pomfret in 1740, informs her that when Princess Mary, daughter of George II., was married she possessed 'only four fine laced Brussels heads, two loopt, and two grounded ; two extremely fine point ones, with ruffles and lappets, six French caps and ruffles.'[1] ·

---

[1] *Correspondence.*

The Rev. William Harris, writing from Grosvenor Square to Mrs. Harris, mother of the first Earl of Malmesbury, under date of October 31, 1745, entertains her with a brief account of the finery which he saw in the drawing-room at St. James's on the occasion of the birthday of the king, George II. :—

The Princess Amelia [he says] had on a white silk flowered with all sorts of colours, very gay, but not fine nor elegant. Princess Caroline's was a pink, with flowers of green, yellow, and silver, which looked extremely beautiful, and was in my own poor judgment by far the handsomest suit of any I saw. Lady Gower was the richest in her dress, white, with a vast deal of gold and silver brocade upon it. Lady Cardigan had white and scarlet striped damask, not very admirable, but she excelled as to jewels, having on a magnificent solitaire, and her stomacher all over diamonds.[1]

In reference to the marriage of Lady Ranelagh in 1749 the Countess of Shaftesbury, writing to James Harris, M.P., under date of February 11, says :—

Lady Ranelagh's clothes were extremely fine and pretty : they were a white and gold and colours, and looked very much like an embroidery. I think she said it cost 3*l.* 18*s.* a yard ; she went through all the presentment in the same. She had a straw-coloured nightgown, with silver and colours, that is extremely pretty, which cost 30*s.* a yard ; and at Lady Romney's rout, last Monday, she had on a white and gold.[2]

I cannot well describe all our dresses [wrote Mrs. Harris to her son at Berlin under date of January 18, 1774, with reference to a recent visit of the family to Court] ; mine is a decent, quiet, plain silk, no colour ; Gertrude's a pretty uncommon colour, plain, but whether blue or green is hard to say ; it is trimmed a great deal with gauze and shades of orange chenille ; Louisa has the same sort of silk : her colour is named *Dartois*, something like a salmon not in season, trimmed with gauze and Denmark green chenille.[3]

In November 1754 Mrs. Delany wrote to Mrs. Dewes :—

We have been very full of business in settling the jewels and clothes for the Birthday. The Duchess of Portland's is white and silver ground flowered with gold and silver, and a stomacher of white satin covered with her fine coloured jewels and all her diamonds. Lady Betty is to have a very fine spray of pearls, diamonds and turquoises for her hair, by way of pompon ; loops and stars of diamonds between for her stomacher ; her clothes white and silver mosaic ground flowered with silver, intermixed with a little blue.[4]

---

[1] *First Earl of Malmesbury*, vol. i. p. 13.   [2] *Ibid.* p. 74.
[3] *Ibid.* p. 280.   [4] *Autob. and Corr.*, 1st series, iii. p. 301.

On the same page this observant lady favours her correspondent with the attire of Lady Coventry dressed for chapel :—

A black silk made for a large hoop, a cobweb laced handkerchief, a pink satin long cloak lined with ermine, mixed with squirrel skins; on her head a French cap that just covered the top of her head, of blond, and stood in the form of a butterfly with its wings not quite extended, frilled sort of lappets crossed under her chin, and tied with pink and green ribbon.[1]

Mrs. Delany, writing to her friend Mrs. Dewes, on January 14, 1756, says, speaking of a 'new cousin,' Mrs. Spencer :—

She was married in a white and silver trimmed—I cannot remember the rest—only a pink satin with embroidered facings, and robings in silver done by Mrs. Glegg. Her first suit she went to court in was white and silver, as fine as brocade and trimming could make it; the second blue and silver, the third white and gold and colours, six pounds a yard; the fourth plain pink-coloured satin. The diamonds worth twelve thousand pounds; her earrings three drops, all diamonds, no paltry scrolls of silver. Her necklace most perfect brilliants, the middle stone worth a thousand pounds, set at the edge with small brilliants. Her cap all brilliants (made in the fashion of a small butterfly skeleton). Her watch and *étui* suited to the rest, and a seal of a Mercury cut in a very fine turquoise stone, set as a standing for a spaniel dog.[2]

Ladies in 1756 pinned their gowns rather closer than before. Hoops were as flat as if made of pasteboard, and as stiff ; and the shape sloped from the hip and spread out at the bottom. Heads were variously adorned, pompons with a few feathers, ribbons, or flowers ; lappets 'in all sorts of *curliwurlis*.' Long hoods were worn close under the chin, tied behind the earrings, went round the neck and tied with bows and ends behind.[3] Two years later plain bombazines were worn for mourning, broad-hemmed muslin, or white crape and Turkey gauze.[4] Readers of Smollett's novel ' Sir Launcelot Greaves ' will remember that the bride of the estimable baronet was attired 'according to the elegant taste of the times,' in a négligée of plain blue satin, the only ornament in her hair being a small sprig of artificial roses ;[5] and many who have perused ' Roderick

---

[1] *Autob. and Corr. of Mrs. Delany*, 1st series, iii. p. 301.
[2] *Ibid.* pp. 399, 401.   [3] *Ibid.* p. 403.   [4] *Ibid.*
[5] *Sir Launcelot Greaves,* c. xxv. p. 268.

Random' will not forget that Narcissa wore on her wedding-day 'a sack of white satin, embroidered on the breast with gold ; the crown of her head covered with a small French cap, from whence descended her beautiful hair in ringlets.'[1] Young girls of this period were usually clad in white, and wore 'a pink sash and red morocco shoes.'[2] Enough having now been said to show how multitudinous and changeable were ladies' costumes, and to prove the truth of the remark attributed to one of the wits of the time, that 'a large ship is sooner rigged by far than a gentlewoman made ready,' let us direct our attention to the dress worn by Englishmen during the eighteenth century.

The consideration of the *tout ensemble* of male costume may be deferred, while a glance is bestowed upon some of the numerous items of which it was composed. And first, with respect to wigs. These cumbrous and superfluous articles of attire were not donned, as might be supposed, to conceal the decay of the natural hair. Men who possessed excellent heads of hair invariably caused it to be clipped off, and a wig to be substituted, merely because it was the fashion to do so. The fashion was certainly not without one advantage, seeing that a man of business might easily despatch his wig to be dressed by a *friseur* in the next street, while he attended to the transaction of affairs in his own counting-house. Wigs assumed all shapes and sizes. To one made very full, and curled eighteen inches to the front, which was imported from France in 1702, the name of 'campaign' was applied. Marlborough's victory at Ramilies, in 1706, gave the name to 'a long, gradually-diminishing plaited tail,' to wigs with a huge bow at the top and a small one at the bottom, which instantly became fashionable. Noble, in his 'Continuation of Granger's History,' states

[1] *Roderick Random*, c. lxviii. p. 191.
[2] Gardiner, *Music and Friends*, iii. p. 4. To finery of these kinds the French Revolution effectually put an end. English society after that date began to adopt revolutionary attire. The ladies lowered their heads. Horsehair was discarded, and large curls spread over the face and ears. Caps were enlarged to an enormous size. Bonnets swelled in proportion. The wearing of the hoop was entirely discontinued except at Court. Silks were unanimously voted unfashionable, and printed calicoes and the finest white muslins sprang at once into favour.

that Lord Bolingbroke gave great offence to Queen Anne upon one occasion by appearing before her, in obedience to a hasty summons, wearing one of these ' Ramilies ties,' as they were called.   ' I suppose,' her Majesty is reported to have exclaimed, 'that his lordship will come to court the next time in his nightcap !'   The queen herself patronised full-bottomed wigs, 'charged with powder like a miller's,' which were most expensive, costing not unfrequently as much as forty guineas each.   How many varieties of wigs made their appearance at one time or another during the last century, may be left to the reader to ascertain from the following list :—Story wigs, bob wigs, busby wigs, scratch wigs, bag wigs, brown George wigs, riding wigs, nightcap wigs, periwigs, tie wigs, queue wigs, brown bob wigs, grizzle bag wigs, grizzle bobs, dark majors, brown bag wigs, grizzle majors, and grizzle ties. Fashionable beaux who were particular as to the appearance of their wigs always took care to carry in a side-pocket of their coats a tortoiseshell wig-comb, often inlaid with mother-of-pearl, for constant use.   It was hardly to be expected that these 'curled bushes of frizzled heare' would escape becoming the laughing-stock of the wits of the time and the editors of the satirical journals.   In No. 54 of the ' Tatler ' Isaac Bickerstaff, Esq. is found humorously advertising ' A stage-coach ' as departing 'from Nando's Coffee House for Mr. Tiptoe's Dancing School every evening,' in which, among other articles carried in the coach-box gratis, were ' periwigs not exceeding three feet in length.'   Tom Brown, a coarse but lively satirist, describes an eighteenth-century beau as possessing a periwig large enough to have loaded a camel, with a bushel of powder at least bestowed upon it ; while Goldsmith informed his imaginary Chinese correspondent that, to appear wise in England (about 1760), 'nothing was more requisite than for a man to borrow hair from the heads of all his neighbours and clap it like a bush on his own.'   ' The distributors of law and physic,' he adds, ' stick on such quantities that it is almost impossible, even in idea, to distinguish between the head and the hair.'   And here it may be remarked that wigs, by reason of their value and the expenditure involved in their manufacture, became as much in request among the light-fingered fraternity of the Georgian era as jewels, watches, or any other species of valuables. 'The thieves,' runs a paragraph in the issue of the 'London Weekly Journal' for March 30, 1717,

have got such villanous ways now of robbing gentlemen that they cut holes through the backs of hackney coaches, and take away their wigs, or the fine head-dresses of gentlewomen. So a gentleman was served last Sunday in Tooley Street. Wherefore this may serve as a caution to gentlemen or gentlewomen that ride single in the night time to sit on the fore-seat, which will prevent that way of robbing.

Another very common dodge to which professional thieves had recourse in relieving folk of their wigs was that of disguising themselves as bakers, and hoisting on their shoulders, through the busy quarters and crowded thoroughfares of the city, 'a sharp boy' concealed in a covered huge laden bread-basket. As soon as an attractive-looking periwig appeared in sight, an accomplice would run against the wearer while the boy, knocking off his hat, dexterously seized the wig and stowed it away within the basket,[1] with which the baker would move quickly away. The veracious historian Malcolm is careful to mention that when human hair was scarce 'a little *horse* hair supplied the parts least in sight,' and he adds that the demand among people 'of quality' for 'delicate and beautiful wigs' was so great that hair commonly sold at 3*l.* the ounce.[2] The fashion of wearing wigs among the male sex extended, ridiculous as it may seem, to young boys, especially the sons of gentlemen, attending the public schools.[3] In the year 1765, owing to a temporary freak on the part of some of the leaders of fashion, wigs suddenly began to vanish off the heads of both young and old. The consequence was that the large body of the London wig-makers, seeing nothing but beggary looming before them, resolved upon presenting a petition to the king (George III.) praying him to maintain their usage. Such a document was actually drawn up, and having been duly signed by

[1] J. T. Smith, *Life and Times of Nollekens*, ii. p. 58, 59.
[2] *Anecdotes of London in 18th Cent.* ii. p. 314.
[3] Malcolm's *Life of Clive*, ii. p. 183.

the wig-making fraternity, was carried on February 9, 1765, to St. James's Palace for presentation to the king, who received it graciously, and promised to do what he could to redress their grievances. Not a few of the petitioners, however, who attended on this occasion, so offended the mob who had assembled, by their inconsistency in wearing their own hair, that they were hauled out and shorn of their locks on the spot.[1] Wigs had grown to such a variety of shapes by Hogarth's time, that he humorously reduced them to five orders—the episcopal, aldermanic, &c. Speaking of the second of these orders he says :—

The first aldermanic wig has two ends, exactly like the dropsical legs of some overgorged glutton ; and the three-quarter face indicates Plenty, Porter, and Politics. On the brow domestical significancy is seated, a look necessary to each master who dozes in his arm-chair on the Sunday evening while his lady reads prayers to the rest of the family.

Full-bottomed wigs were first disused as a magisterial appendage by Alderman Harley, who filled the office of lord mayor in 1768; but they were not generally forsworn until the principles of the first French Revolution struck root in our soil. Then it was that English partisans began to manifest their approval of those principles by appearing in public without their wigs and in 'the fierce republican head of Brutus.' Thenceforward the use of wigs was mainly confined to Anglican Church dignitaries, to members of the legal profession, and to a few of those who strenuously opposed the advocates of change. By a strange perversity of fate they were doomed to gasp out their latest breath under the slings and arrows of the satirist. *Hæc data pœna diu viventibus.*

Ascending now from the wig to the hat, it may be observed that the crown was surrounded by the cocks which represented the brim. The cocked hat was a mark of gentility among the male sex in the eighteenth century, which was universally worn both by boys and men, being trimmed with gold or silver lace to match that with which their clothes were trimmed. 'My

[1] *Ann. Reg.* Feb. 1765, p. 64; Malcolm's *Anecdotes,* ii. pp. 349, 353.

mother,' wrote a correspondent to Johnson's 'Rambler,'[1] 'would rather follow me to the grave than see me tear my clothes and hang down my head, and sneak about with dirty shoes and blotted fingers, hair unpowdered and a hat uncocked.' The teachers of deportment in those days always bestowed particular care upon the ceremony of hat-cocking, and in number 194 of the periodical just mentioned, mention is made of a young gentleman who in a few days became such a perfect master of his hat that, with a careless nicety, 'he could put it on and off' without adjusting it by a second motion. A writer in the 'London Chronicle' for May 1762 observes :—

> Hats are now worn upon an average six inches and three-fifths broad in the brim, and cocked between Quaker and Kevenhuller. Some of their hats open before, like a church spout and the tin scales they weigh flower [*sic*] in ; some wear them rather sharper, like the nose of a greyhound ; and we can distinguish by the taste of the hat the mode of the wearer's mind. There is a military cock, and the mercantile cock ; and while the beaux of St. James's wear theirs diagonally over their left or right eye, sailors wear the sides of their hats uniformly tucked down to the crown, and look as if they carried a triangular apple pasty upon their heads.

In the year 1768 the King of Denmark visited these shores ; and in honour of the event, fashionable gentlemen reduced the hat to a diminutive form, and cocked it up very high behind, giving it the name of the 'Denmark cock.' Pigtails were worn till a later period. One appears at the back of one of the heads in Hogarth's picture depicting 'Taste in High Life.' The clerical hat was composed of felt, with a plain broad brim, surrounded by a cord. Towards the middle of the century, the hat assumed a broad projection over the forehead like a spout, edged with gold or silver lace. About the same time, too, 'the Cumberland cock' came into vogue, in honour of William, Duke of Cumberland, the form of which may be seen on his statue in Cavendish Square. By the year 1770 round hats had become fashionable, but it was long before they supplanted the cocked hats. Cocked hats were always worn by boys. Rogers remembered running about the field

---

[1] No. 109, 1751.

chasing butterflies in one.[1] In many remote country churches
there remain to this day the huge racks and pegs whereon
the heavy hats of our great-great-grandfathers were suspended
during the time of divine service. Hats in the eighteenth
century were by no means cheap, and when this fact is borne
in mind, the circumstance of Dean Swift bequeathing by last
will and testament his best beaver hat to his friend the Rev.
John Worrall, and his second best beaver hat to the Rev.
John Jackson, Vicar of Santry, loses much of its whimsicality.

Until 1795 every fashionable gentleman continued to wear
powder in his hair. In that year William Pitt, who had long
conceived that the revenue would be materially augmented if
some impost were to be laid upon an article which was so
largely consumed by fashionable folk of both sexes, succeeded,
despite some opposition, in levying a tax upon it. Instead,
however, of gaining his own ends thereby, he contributed to its
disuse in English society. The fashionable world could not give
up immediately what was so dear to it without a struggle, and
to evade the impost more than one speculator endeavoured to
manufacture powder out of other materials, in particular, Lord
William Murray, one of the Duke of Athol's sons, who in
1796 took out a patent for the extraction of starch from horse-
chestnuts. It was reserved, however, for Francis, Duke of
Bedford, and his friends to deal the fatal blow at the fashion
which had so long been prevalent, by undertaking to forfeit a
certain sum of money if any of them wore their hair either
tied or powdered within a certain period.[2] Walter Savage
Landor was probably the first undergraduate who departed
from the practice at Oxford. The poet, whose youthful en-
thusiasm had been fired by Jacobinism, entered Trinity College
in the memorable year 1793, when he was eighteen years of
age, wearing his hair without powder. 'Take care,' said his
tutor to him ; 'they will stone you for a republican.' 'The
Whigs were then unpopular,' said Landor in after life when
recounting this circumstance, 'but I stuck to my plain hair

[1] *Recollections of Table Talk of S. Rogers*, p. 7 ; Smith, *Life and Times
of Nollekens*, i. p. 40 ; Smith, *Book for a Rainy Day*, p. 12.
[2] Captain Jesse's *Life of Beau Brummel*, i. 47-50.

and queue tied with black ribbon.'[1] The disuse of powder of course pressed heavily upon the large number of hairdressers throughout the country, and their profits began to diminish in no slight degree. Numbers also of those individuals who only wore powder occasionally complained that they would be as highly rated as those who were in the constant practice of powdering. The exemptions were by many not deemed sufficient. Clergymen not possessing 100*l.* a year, subalterns in the army, and officers in the navy under the rank of masters and commanders, were the only persons in public characters exempted from it ; and in private families all the daughters except the two eldest.[2] One guinea per annum was the duty levied upon every person who wore hair-powder, an impost which—in the first year that it was levied, 1795—was estimated as at 200,000*l.*

The gentlemen, like the ladies, were exceedingly fond of lace. Lace ruffles were commonly worn by gentlemen as ornaments for the neck. In the reign of Anne two point lace cravats were considered enough for any young gentleman of quality. In 1751 the Earl of Chesterfield in writing to his son, bade him bring with him only two or three of his laced shirts. Point ruffles graced the hands of beaux till the close of the century. Twice the newspapers of 1780 recorded that during the Gordon riots a report was circulated through the metropolis that the Earl of Effingham, who had joined the rioters, had been mortally wounded, and that his body, which had been thrown into the Thames, had been recognised by the point lace ruffles he wore. William Varey, Esq., writing to George Selwyn from Ixworth Abbey on February 10, 1764, says :—

My absence from London prevented my seeing the ruffles. I daresay I shall like them, but the price is so trifling that it is of no consequence. I shall be obliged to you for four pair of Valenciennes, as good as people wear when they dress, but not too deep. The price I shall not regard, as they are always handsome and in fashion.[3]

---

[1] Forster's *Life of Landor* : *Works*, vol. i. p. 29.

[2] *Annual Register*, 1795 ; *Hist. of Europe*, p. 179; Malcolm's *Anecdotes*, ii. p. 356.

[3] Jesse's *Selwyn*, i. 270 ; *Life and Times of Nollekens*, p. 16. See also Malcolm's *Life of Lord Clive*, ii. p. 182.

Gold and silver watches of all whimsical shapes and forms, studded with jewels and precious stones, were very much worn by beaux. Graham, a noted London watchmaker who flourished during the early part of the eighteenth century, made many improvements in the watches of the time, and as they were very fashionable, a writer in the 'London Magazine' for 1753, when enumerating the make-up of a *Monsieur à la mode* does not forget to specify, among others,

> A repeater by Graham which the hours reveals,
> Almost overbalanc'd with knickknacks and seals.

The size of watches in the first half of the eighteenth century may be readily inferred from an entry in Lady Cowper's Diary under date of 1716, to the effect that Lord Winton, while a prisoner in the Tower, endeavoured to effect his escape by sawing an iron bar nearly in half by means of the spring of his watch.

To fashionable beaux diamond-hilted swords, and clouded canes with amber heads looped with silk tassels, were necessary appendages. The latter were usually suspended by a silken loop on a button of the coat, and dangled and bobbed in a very awkward manner against the knees of their wearers as they walked. Muffs too, odd as it may seem, were largely patronised by gentlemen at this time. The political upholsterer, as all readers of the 'Tatler' will remember, carried one.[1] Those who have attentively studied Hogarth's series representing 'The Rake's Progress' will recollect that the artist, ever true in the delineation of men and manners around him, has introduced muffs into the picture of the 'Woman Swearing at the Child,' where the husband wears one, which appears to be fastened by a hook to his girdle. Upon the person of the beau (said to have been intended for Lord Portmore) in the scene depicting 'Taste in High Life,' a muff may be seen, and likewise also in the scene entitled 'The Arrest of the Rake for Debt' while he is proceeding to court on a drawing-room day. Soon after the accession of George III. small muffs became the rage among gentlemen of quality, for

---

[1] *Tatler*, No. 155.

Horace Walpole, writing to George Montagu in December
1765, says, 'I send you a decent smallish muff that you may
put in your pocket, and it costs but fourteen shillings.' Silver-
fringed gloves were largely worn by fashionable beaux. It was
the invariable custom of Francis, the second Earl of Guildford,
who died at an advanced age in 1790, to wear a muff.[1] Both
Charles James Fox and Dr. Samuel Parr not unfrequently
appeared in one.[2] So late as 1794 the aged Dr. Josiah
Tucker, the then dean of Gloucester, would walk up the nave
of the cathedral to attend service with his hands in a small
muff in cold weather. That the muff was commonly used
is apparent from the following circumstance related of the
performance of the 'Devil upon Two Sticks,' at the Haymarket
in 1768 :—

The active part taken by Sir William Browne, President of the
College of Physicians, in the contest with the licentiates, occasioned
his being introduced by Foote into this comedy. Upon Foote's
exact representation of him with his identical wig and coat, tall
figure and glass stiffly applied to his eye, Sir William sent him a
card, complimenting the actor on having so happily represented
him, but as he had forgotten his muff he sent him his own.[3]

It might have been a fastidious lady of quality, instead of
the Earl of March, a famous sporting character, who, under
date of November 17, 1766, writing to George Selwyn (then
sojourning at Paris) said, 'The muff you sent me by the Duke
of Richmond I like prodigiously, vastly better than if it had been
tigré, or of any glaring colour—several are now making after
it ;'[4] or who, ten years later, entreats the same to bring him
'two or three bottles of perfume to put amongst powder, and
some patterns for velvets that are new and pretty.'

Walpole, writing to George Montagu under date of April
16, 1761, said :—

I have chosen you a coat of a claret colour, but I have fixed
nothing about the lace. Barrett had none of gauze but what were

[1] *Notes and Queries*, vol. vi. p. 282; Murphy's *Upholsterer.*
[2] *Notes and Queries*, vi. 517, vii. 392; Boaden's *Memoirs of Mrs. Siddons*, i. 152.
[3] *Biograph. Dramatica*, ii. p. 161, ed. 1812.
[4] *Selwyn's Correspondence*, vol. ii. p. 71.

as broad as the Irish Channel. Your tailor found a very reputable one at another place, but I would not determine rashly ; it will be two or three and twenty shillings the yard ; you might have a very substantial real lace which would wear like your buffet for twenty.[1]

It is quite clear that until about 1756, when Jonas Hanway, the eminent philanthropist, set the fashion of carrying an umbrella when walking in the streets,[2] its use among English people was confined exclusively to the female sex.   The only precaution which Gay, in his ' Trivia,' bids the pedestrian take 'when the bursting clouds in deluge pour,' is ' a surtout of kersey fine,' while to good housewives he commends 'the oily shed of the umbrella,' wherewith they will be enabled to walk 'safe through the wet on clinking pattens.'   That the use of umbrellas was far from general for fully fifty years after the publication of ' Trivia ' is proved first from the remark of a French traveller, named Grosley, in the published narrative of his travels in this country in 1765 : ' It is a rule with the people of London not to use, or suffer foreigners to use, our umbrellas of taffeta or waxed silk ;'[3] and secondly, from a letter written between 1775 and 1776 to one of his friends by Mr. Warry (who for many years filled the office of British consul at Smyrna in Asia Minor), in which he alludes to the envy and astonishment evinced by the villagers of Sawbridgeworth (a small parish in Hertfordshire, about four miles from Bishop's Stortford, where his father had a country seat), on beholding him hastening along the road with an umbrella which he had recently brought with him from Leghorn, to shelter his mother from a heavy summer shower that had detained her one Sunday in the church porch after service.[4]   Rogers recollected that in his youth, 1763-1773, most gentlemen's families in London possessed one umbrella—a huge thing, made of coarse cotton, which used to be taken out with the carriage, and which if a shower fell was held by the footmen over the heads of the ladies as they stepped into their carriages or alighted.   Another curious proof of the scarcity of umbrellas in eighteenth-century

[1] *Letters*, ed. Cunningham.
[2] Pugh's *Life of Hanway*, p. 221 ; Bailey's *English Dict.* 1736.
[3] *Tour to London*, i. p. 45.
[4] *Notes and Queries* ; Southey's *Commonplace Book*, i. p. 574.

London is afforded in the curious autobiography (published in
1790) of John Macdonald, a cadet of the family of Keppoch,
in Inverness-shire, who served in various capacities, chiefly as
footman or valet, several of the nobility. Speaking of his
return to London from Boulogne in the month of January,
1778, he says :—

> If it rained, I wore my fine silk umbrella ; then the people would
> call after me, 'What, Frenchman, why do not you get a coach?'
> In particular the hackney coachmen and hackney chairmen would
> call after me ; but I, knowing the men well, went straight on, and
> took no notice. At this time there were no umbrellas worn in
> London, except in noblemen and gentlemen's houses, where there
> was a large one hung in the hall, to hold over a lady or gentleman
> if it rained, between the door and the carriage. I was going to
> dine in Norfolk Street on Sunday. It rained, my sister had hold
> of my arm, and I had the umbrella over our heads. In Tavistock
> Street we met so many young men, calling after us, 'Frenchman,
> take care of your umbrella.' 'Frenchman, why do not you get a
> coach, monsieur ?' [1]

But long after this time umbrellas continued to be most
clumsy in shape, made of oiled cloth, and very flat, and were
carried by a ring fastened to the top, so that the handle often
got dirty. George Pryme, Professor of Political Economy at
Cambridge from 1828 to 1861, recollected that so late as 1797
there was but one umbrella in that town, this solitary one
being kept at a shop in Benet Street, where it was let out by
the hour.[2] The intense hatred with which British subjects at
that epoch regarded everything of Gallican manufacture doubtless accounts for the long disuse of the umbrella. Even pattens
were worn by the male sex, for we read that John Newton, the
friend of Cowper, was accustomed to trudge through the mud
in the rainy season from the parsonage to the parish church at
Olney, in Buckinghamshire, in a pair. Clogs were often worn
by ladies in the public streets.[3]

The physicians of the time were usually attired in a tie
wig, a scarlet cloak, black velvet coat, a gold-headed cane
shaped like a parish beadle's staff, deep ruffles, a sword, a

---

[1] *Life and Travels*, pp. 382–383.
[2] Prof. Pryme's *Autobiographic Recollections*, p. 46.
[3] Boaden's *Memoirs of Mrs. Inchbald*, i. 230.

snuffbox, and carried their cocked hats under the arm to denote their profession.[1] The Anglican clergy were ordinarily attired in accordance with the seventy-fourth canon—that is to say, in cassocks, black stockings, knee breeches, gown and bands— ordinarily, for the 'gentlemen of the gown' in the eighteenth century must have occasionally exercised some considerable latitude in their canonicals, since we find Dean Swift describing his dress in the 'Journal to Stella,' as 'light camlet faced with red velvet, and silver buckles,' and if we may credit the 'Flying Post' for June 14, 1722, Dr. William Talbot, the then Bishop of Durham, appeared on horseback 'at a review in the king's train in a lay-habit of purple with jack-boots, and his hat cocked, and a black wig tied behind him like a militant officer.'[2] John Horne Tooke, we are assured by his biographer, was never proud of a clergyman's garb, and had always an ambition to be a fine gentleman ; consequently it is not surprising to find that on one occasion he left with his friend Wilkes, the member for Middlesex, '1 suit of scarlet and gold, 1 suit of white and silver cloth, 1 suit of blue and silver camlet, 1 suit of flowered silk, 1 suit of black silk, and 1 black velvet surtout.'[3] In some autobiographic memoranda relating to the year 1765, Jeremy Bentham states that in that year his father received a visit from a clerical friend named John Lind, a writer of some eminence in his day. 'He came,' says Bentham, 'in his flowered dress with purple and gold and I know not what ; for he had a prodigious quantity of fine clothes, cut velvet embroidery, silver, gold, and all sorts of trappings.'[4] The rector of Aston in Derbyshire, in 1789, wore a suit made entirely of a cloth of light colour, edged with silver or gold lace, and his hair in a bag.[5] Charles Churchill, the poet, drew down upon himself the wrath of the Dean of Westminster for his breach of clerical propriety in laying aside the sober canonical habit and appearing in the extreme of fashion, attired in leather breeches, silk stockings, a blue coat, gold-laced hat and ruffles.

[1] Sir John Hawkins's *Life of Dr. Johnson*, p. 212.
[2] At this period the Bishops of Durham enjoyed within their own diocese many of the privileges of lords temporal.
[3] Reid's *Memoirs of Tooke*, p. 19.   [4] *Works*, ed. Bowring, x. p. 48.
[5] Gardiner's *Music and Friends*, iii. p. 167.

One of the most regular and voluminous correspondents of the sixth Viscount Strangford, who died in 1855, was Ernest, Duke of Cumberland, uncle of Queen Victoria. After his accession to the throne of Hanover in the year 1837 his Majesty always evinced the greatest interest in the fortunes of England, and being Conservative to the backbone, he naturally beheld with dismay the progress of dissent and radicalism ; nor is it surprising that he should have dwelt with regret upon the decay of old institutions, old customs, and old manners. Among his letters to Viscount Strangford is one dated January 1850, which is interesting, from the light it sheds upon certain proprieties of costume of the higher dignitaries of the Anglican Church towards the close of the eighteenth century :—

I maintain [he wrote], that the first change and shock in the ecclesiastical habits was the bishops being allowed to lay aside their wigs, their purple coats, short cassocks and stockings, and cocked hats when appearing in public ; for I can remember when Bishop Heard [*i.e.* Hurd] of Worcester, Courtenay of Exeter, and Markham, Archbishop of York, resided in Kew and its vicinity, that as a boy, I met them frequently walking about, dressed as I now tell you, in the fields and walks in the neighbourhood, and their male servants appeared equally all dressed in purple, which was the custom. The present Bishop of Oxford was the first who persuaded George IV. to be allowed to lay aside his wig, because his wife found him better looking without it. I recollect full well that the Bishop of London who succeeded Bishop Porteus (whose name I forget at this moment),[1] coming to St. James's to do homage to my father, which is the custom in the closet prior to the levée, when Lord Sidmouth was Secretary of State, and he came into the closet, where I was at the time, and informed his Majesty that the bishop was there, but that he had refused to introduce him, as he had not a wig. Upon which I remember full well, as if it were to-day, that the king replied, ' You were perfectly right, my lord, and tell the bishop from me that until he has shaven his head, and has provided himself with a wig suitable to his garb, I shall not admit him into my presence,' and he was forced to go home, and could not be admitted until the week following, when he appeared *en costume.*[2]

The military costume continued throughout the eighteenth century to be of a most absurd character. In the reign of Queen

[1] Dr. John Randolph, who occupied the see only four years, 1809–1813.
[2] Fonblanque's *Lives of the Lords Strangford through Ten Generations,* p. 183.

Anne, scarlet with blue facings was the regimental colour, and remained so until the reign of George II. All the English officers wore point or Mechlin lace cravats, a strange fashion, which provoked a satirical poet of the time to say :—

> To war the troops advance,
> Adorned and trim like females for the dance.
> Down sinks Lothario, sent, by one dire blow,
> A well dress'd hero to the shades below.

Richard Brinsley Sheridan also gave the fashion a sly hit in his amusing comedy of 'St. Patrick's Day,' produced in 1776, in the scene where the daughter of the Justice exclaims :— 'Dear ! to think how the sweet fellows sleep on the ground, and fight in silk stockings and lace ruffles ! '

The sugarloaf cap which was worn by the Grenadiers appears in Hogarth's print, 'The March to Finchley.' In the time of George II. black cockades were worn by the regiments. Soldiers also wore large quantities of powder, so much so, indeed, that a writer in the 'World' declared in 1755 that the consumption of powder by the British army would have sufficed to feed 600,000 persons per annum. As late as 1778 the flaps of the soldiers' coats extended almost as low as their ankles, and the waistcoat flaps came to the middle of the thigh ; and this, with white woollen breeches, stockings, shoes and buckles, completed their lower attire. Their hair, smothered in flour and pomatum, came to a termination in a long pigtail, which rolled upon their shoulders ; their heads were surmounted with a huge cocked hat, and their chins were propped up by rigid leather collars which almost prevented them from catching a glimpse of the ground on which they walked.[1]

The naval costume—colours white and blue—arose in the reign of George II., owing, it is said, to that monarch meeting the Duchess of Bedford one day attired in a riding habit of blue faced with white. The habit so greatly took his fancy that, having under consideration a uniform for the navy, he adopted white and blue as the colours.

The pages of ' Roderick Random ' contain an excellent

---

[1] Gardiner's *Music and Friends,* iii. p. 9.

word-portrait of a naval captain, in which several items of dress
are supplied.

Captain Whiffle was a tall, thin young man, dressed in this
manner: a white hat garnished with a red feather adorned his
head, from whence his hair flowed upon his shoulders in ringlets
tied behind with a ribbon. His coat, consisting of pink coloured
silk lined with white, by the elegance of the cut, retired backward
as it were, to discover a white satin waistcoat embroidered with gold,
unbuttoned at the upper part to display a brooch set with garnets,
that glittered in the breast of his shirt, which was of the finest
cambric, edged with right Mechlin. The knees of his crimson velvet
breeches scarcely descended so low as to meet his silk stockings,
which rose without spot or wrinkle on his meagre legs from shoes of
blue Meroquin, studded with diamond buckles, that flamed forth,
rivals to the sun! A steel-hilted sword, inlaid with gold, and decked
with a knot of ribbon which fell down in a rich tassel, equipped his
side; and an amber-headed cane hung dangling from his wrist. But
the most remarkable parts of his furniture were a mask on his face
and white gloves on his hands, which did not seem to be put on
with an intention to be put off occasionally, but were fixed with a
curious ring on the little finger of each hand.[1]

George II., at the marriage of Frederick Prince of Wales to
the Princess of Saxe Gotha, on April 27, 1736, was dressed in
a gold brocade turned up with silk, embroidered with large
flowers in silver and colours, as was the waistcoat; the buttons
and star were diamonds. On this occasion the Dukes of
Grafton, St. Alban's, Newcastle, and other noblemen were in
dresses of gold brocade, to the value of 500*l.* each; the Duke
of Marlborough was in a white velvet and gold brocade, upon
which was an exceedingly rich *point d Espagne;* other noblemen were in clothes flowered or sprigged with gold, and the
Duke of Montagu in a gold brocaded tissue.

The ordinary garb of middle-class men consisted of a large
bushy wig, tied at the ends; of a coat broad laced, with quarters
below the knees, the sleeves large and the cuffs half at the
elbows; of a waistcoat nearly as long as the coat, finely embroidered and fringed; of breeches buckled close upon the
knees; and of long stockings unhandsomely terminated by
large insteps to the shoes, which were decorated with small
buckles. The cravat was worn long, and was drawn through

[1] Chap. xxxiv.

the waistcoat buttonhole, and the wig was covered with a three-cocked hat laced. The costume worn by the working classes in London and the provinces consisted among men of a plain coat buttoned up the front, having huge pockets and short wide sleeves, with cuffs so capacious that a gallon of wheat might easily have been poured into them ; of a long waistcoat that reached nearly as low as the knees ; of a cocked hat, bob-wig, stockings made long enough to reach the top of the thigh, garters and high quartered shoes. Those who have seen Hogarth's 'Politician' will have a good idea of the dress worn by an ordinary well-to-do London tradesman of the eighteenth century, and those who have seen 'The Country Inn Yard' scene by the hand of the same master, will have looked upon what was the ordinary dress of a country girl at the same period.

The costume of boys, so late as 1794, was curious. The sons of gentlemen wore pea-green, sky-blue, or scarlet coats, richly embroidered, occasionally laced cravats, shirts, and ruffles, knee breeches, silk stockings, and silver buckles on their shoes.[1]

The shoebuckle of this period deserves a word of comment, seeing that it underwent every figure, size, and shape of geometrical invention, and passed through every form in the whole Euclidean zodiac. The manufacture of buckles contributed largely to the employment of Warwickshire and Staffordshire ingenuity during the last century. In 1781, all gentlemen ot *ton* sported on their shoes a large square buckle plated with silver, and as the ladies soon adopted the reigning taste 'it was difficult,' as Hutton, the historian of Birmingham, remarks, 'to discover their beautiful little feet, covered with an enormous shield of buckle, and men wondered to see the active motion under the massive load.' The massive load soon after this became unsupportable to both sexes. Strings came into fashion, and consequently a large class of ingenious artisans were compelled to suffer the loss of their usual employ-

---

[1] Prof. Pryme's *Autobiog. Recoll.* p. 21 ; J. T. Smith's *Book for a Rainy Day*, p. 32 ; J. Grimaldi's *Memoirs*, ed. Whitehead, p. 23 ; see also Reynolds's *Life and Times,* i. 57.

ment. In 1791 a deputation of master buckle-makers from the towns of Birmingham, Walsall, and Wolverhampton, obtained an audience of the Prince of Wales (afterwards George IV.) at Carlton House, where they presented a petition setting forth the distressed situation of thousands who had been engaged in the different departments of the buckle manufacture consequent upon the fashion which was then so prevalent of wearing strings. The Prince received his petitioners very graciously, and to mark his sympathy with their condition, promised not only to wear buckles on his own shoes, but to order the members of his household to do the same. The example of royalty, however, and the commands of royalty were alike nugatory when they were opposed to the dominion of fashion. The use of strings became more and more general, insomuch that by the close of the century the whole generation of fashions in the buckle line was extinct ; a buckle was not to be found on a woman's foot, nor upon the foot of any man except that of an aged one.

A writer, describing in a periodical of the time the process which transformed him from the character of a 'greenhorn' into that of a 'blood,' makes the following allusion to his attire :—

I cut off my hair and procured a brown bob periwig of Wilding, of the same colour, with a single row of curls put round the bottom, which I wore very nicely combed and without powder. My hat which had been cocked with great exactness in an equilateral triangle, I discarded, and purchased one of a more fashionable size, the fore corner of which projected near two inches further than those on each side, and was moulded into the shape of a spout.'[1]

'The London Evening Post,' for December 1738, contains a letter from a certain lady of fashion, who writes as follows with reference to the dress of certain gentlemen she observed at one of the theatres she visited :—

'Some of them had those loose kinds of great-coats on, which I have heard called "wraprascals," with gold-laced hats slouched in humble imitation of stage coachmen ; others aspired at being grooms, and had dirty boots and spurs, with black caps on and long whips in their hands ; a third wore

[1] *Adventurer*, No. 101, 1753.

scanty frocks, little shabby hats put on one side, and clubs in their hands.' The attire of a gentleman who had arrived in England from the French capital is thus described by the author of 'Joseph Andrews' :—' He had on a cut-velvet coat of a cinnamon colour, lined with a pink satin, embroidered all over with gold ; his waistcoat, which was cloth of silver, was embroidered with gold likewise.' The Countess of Shaftesbury, writing to James Harris, M.P. for Christchurch, Hants, under date of December 3, 1754, gives the following description of the 'birthday finery' of George II. worn by the gentlemen :—

And first for the Prince of Wales, who looked as blooming as his clothes—they were a blossom-coloured velvet with gold, and gold lace down before ; the waistcoat and cuffs a rich white and gold stuff. Prince Edward's was a yellow and silver velvet, with a silver lace before, turned up with white and silver cuffs, and the waistcoat the same. His Majesty (who, I hear, had told Mr. Shutz, [a fashionable German tailor of the day], he would have him bespeak him a very handsome suit, but not to make a boy or a fop of him) was in brown, very richly laced with silver, and turned up with a blue cuff laced, and a blue and silver waistcoat. The duke was in a lead-colour cloth, richly laced with silver.[1]

Referring in the course of the same letter to her nephew's clothes, the countess says that they were 'a white and silver velvet coat, and the waistcoat and cuffs a silver stuff with purple, a blossom and centre flowers, which looked soft and elegant.' From the same letter we learn that her lord's clothes were 'a very rich scarlet and gold velvet coat, waistcoat and breeches the same ; and mine, a gold stuff with purple spots on the ground, and coloured sprigs of flowers that looked like embroidery.'[2] Miss Hawkins, describing the personal appearance of Sir Samuel Prime, a resident of Twickenham, about 1760, says :—

His suit, including stockings, I recollect to have been all of one hue in summer, and that the lightest that could be called colour. In winter we saw him less frequently, but he was then clad in a brown that might be called snuff-colour. . . . The nicety of the disposition, of his cravat and ruffles, the exactitude with which his

---

[1] *Correspondence of the First Earl of Malmesbury*, i. p. 80.
[2] *Ibid.* i. p. 81.

stockings preserved their place in the obsolete form of roll-ups, and the *tout ensemble* seemed rather the labour of a sculptor than the adroitness of a valet.   Everything he wore or used—his stiff tipped gloves of the gauntlet form, his carpets, nay even his lady's lapdogs, were all performed to a degree that would be inappropriate to the better taste of the present age.[1]

The same authority supplies some particulars respecting another neighbour of hers, the young Marquis of Tweeddale.

His throat [she wrote] was dressed open, as was the fashion ; and very fine lace decorated his linen, which in his warm patriotism he would not wear without being first assured that it was of Scotch manufacture.   His dress was most commonly nankeen with a scarlet coat, his stockings white silk ; his buckles gold.[2]

I beg you will give my best compliments to Lord March [says the Hon. Henry St. John to George Selwyn, writing from Paris on December 22, 1770], and tell him I have obeyed his orders in regard to his coat.   I have chosen a pretty silk, and I think it and a chenille embroidery analogue to the *fourrure*, with olives, &c.[3]

It is but reasonable to suppose that the novels of the age reflect its manners and morals about as truly as those of our own day, and that they contain many traits of both manner and dress upon which reliance can be placed.   If this be granted, there can surely be no difficulty in accepting the subjoined enumeration in its main outlines as the contents of the wardrobe of a 'pretty fellow,' extracted from Smollett's 'Roderick Random' :—

My wardrobe [he says] consisted of five fashionable coats full mounted, two of which were plain, one of cut velvet, one trimmed with gold and another with silver lace ; two frocks, one of white drab with large plate buttons, the other of blue with gold binding ; one waistcoat of gold brocade, one of blue satin embroidered with silver, one of green silk trimmed with broad figured gold lace, one of black silk with fringes, one of white satin, one of black cloth, and one of scarlet ; six pair of cloth breeches, one pair of crimson, and another of black velvet ; twelve pair of white silk stockings, as many of black silk, and the same number of fine cotton ; one hat laced with gold *point d'Espagne*, another with silver lace scolloped, a third with gold binding, and a fourth plain ; three dozen of fine ruffled shirts, as many neckcloths ; one dozen of cambric handkerchiefs, and the like number of silk. . . . A gold watch with a

[1] *Memoirs*, i. 50–1.   [2] *Ibid.* i. p. 60.
[3] Jesse's *Selwyn*, iii. p. 4 ; Reynolds's *Life and Times*, ii. 39.

chased case, two valuable diamond rings, two mourning swords, one with a silver handle, and a fourth cut steel inlaid with gold, a diamond stock buckle, and a set of stone buckles for the knees and shoes ; a pair of silver-mounted pistols with rich housings, a gold-headed cane, and a snuffbox of tortoise-shell mounted with gold having a picture of a lady on the top.

Smollett in chapter viii. of 'Peregrine Pickle' describes the dress which was worn by Commodore Trunnion on the memorable morning when he accompanied Mrs. Grizzle to the altar :—

Best coat of blue broadcloth [we read], cut by a tailor of Ramsgate, and trimmed with five dozen of brass buttons large and small. His breeches were of the same piece, fastened at the knees with large bunches of tape ; his waistcoat was of red plush lapelled with green velvet and garnished with vellum holes ; his boots bore an infinite resemblance, both in colour and shape, to a pair of leather buckets; his shoulder was graced with a broad buff belt, from whence depended a huge hanger with a hilt like that of a back sword ; and on each side of his pommel appeared a rusty pistol rammed in a case covered with a bearskin.

The Laird of Auchinleck, in chapter viii. of his 'Life of Johnson,' mentions that in 1749, on the occasion of the production of his play of 'Irene,' the Sage of Fleet Street 'had a fancy that as a dramatic author his dress should be more gay than what he ordinarily wore ; he therefore appeared behind the scenes, and even in one of the side boxes, in a scarlet waistcoat with rich gold lace, and a gold-laced hat.' Black was never considered as full dress, and was worn only for mourning. Boys ordinarily wore their heads curled and powdered. Black solitaires were worn in place of the scarf. When Dr. Carlyle first saw William Shenstone, the poet of the Leasowes, in 1758, his appearance surprised him. And why ? 'For he was a large, heavy, fat man, dressed in white clothes and silver lace, with his grey hair tied behind and much powdered.'[1] Much money was often lavished by the fine gentlemen of the Georgian era upon the buckles of their shoes. John Thomas Smith, who for many years held the appointment of Keeper of the Prints in the British Museum, was told in 1825 by a gentleman named Packer, then in the eighty-seventh year of his age,

[1] *Autob. of Dr. Carlyle,* p. 570.

that the shoebuckles worn by the Hon. John Spencer, on the occasion of his marriage to a lady of the name of Poyntz in 1756, were alone worth 30,000*l.*[1]   In 1759 the suit which Horace Walpole wore on the occasion of the marriage of one of his relatives was of 'a white ground, with purple and green flowers,' one that had been purposely selected for him by Lady Townshend.

His dress in visiting is described by Miss Hawkins as being in summer, the season when she mostly saw him,

a lavender suit, the waistcoat embroidered with a little silver ; or of white silk worked on the tambour, partridge silk stockings and gold buckles, ruffles and frill, generally lace. . . . In summer no powder, but his wig combed straight, and showing his very pale forehead, and queued behind ; in winter, powder.[2]

Oliver Goldsmith, who was far from economical in the matter of dress, possessed in 1768, according to the books of Mr. William Filby, a tailor who dwelt 'at the sign of the Harrow,' in Water Lane, London, among other articles of apparel the following :—'Tyrian bloom satin grain and garter blue silk breeches,' *price*, as the wary Filby takes good care to note, 8*l.* 2*s.* 7*d.*   Also in 1769, 'a blue velvet suit, 21*l.* 10*s.* 9*d.*' Again, in 1773, 'a green half-trimmed frock and breeches, lined with silk ; in 1771 a queen's blue dress suit ; in 1769 a half-dress suit of rateen lined with satin ; a pair of silk stocking breeches,' and another pair of a bloom colour ; in 1771 'a frock suit lined half trimmed with gold sprig buttons ;' in 1772 'Princess stuff breeches, 1*l.* 7*s.*, blue velvet suit 21*l.* 10*s.* 9*d.*'[3]

Jeremy Bentham says that in the year 1765 fine colours were the order of the day, and that as an Oxford undergraduate he possessed, in that year, a pea-green coat, and green silk breeches 'bitterly tight,' which he first exhibited in a walk from the university city to Farringdon.   When Lord Villiers appeared at the Court of St. James's on a gala day in 1773, he was attired, according to Mrs. Delany, in a coat of pale

[1] Lady Llanover's *Autob. and Corr. of Mrs. Delany*, 3rd series, ii. p. 402.   See also Smith's *Life of Nollekens.*
[2] *Memoirs*, i. p. 106.
[3] Prior, *Life of Goldsmith*, p. 192 ; Forster, *Life of Goldsmith*, ii. 172-73.

purple velvet turned up with lemon colour, and 'embroidered all over with SS's of pearls as big as peas, and in all the spaces little medallions in beaten gold—real gold !—in various figures of cupids and the like.' On April 21 of the following year, Gibbon, the Roman historian, in writing to his friend Colonel Holroyd, mentioned that he was sitting at Boodle's attired in a 'fine velvet coat, with ruffles of his lady's choosing.' Boswell dining with the Thrales at Streatham on the first day of April 1781, met Sir Philip Jennys Clerk, who appeared to him to have 'the appearance of a gentleman of ancient family well advanced in life. He wore his own hair in a bag of goodly size, a black velvet coat, with an embroidered waistcoat and very rich lace ruffles.' Foreigners contrived to spend as much as they could upon dress during this period.

Foreigners of every learned or scientific profession practising here [says Angelo], were remarkable for their rich display of costume. Many of my father's friends and acquaintances whose finances made it expedient for two or three to club expenses for a furnished second floor in the back streets of Soho, yet contrived to pay thirty or forty pounds for a dress suit, laced ruffles, a bag and sword. Monsieur Petro (designated *le grand Petro*), an old friend of my father, whom I remember well whilst *maître de ballet* at the Italian Opera House, danced a minuet in a black velvet suit, with diamond-hilted sword and buckles and buttons of brilliants, before the Empress Catherine, at Petersburg.[1]

At the opening of the session of Parliament on November 11, 1783, the Prince of Wales wore 'a black velvet, most richly embroidered with gold, and pink spangles, and lined with pink satin. His shoes had pink heels ; his hair was pressed much at the sides, and very full frizzed, with two very small curls at the bottom.' Ernest, King of Hanover, writing to the sixth Viscount Strangford shortly before the Exhibition of 1851, told him that he 'well remembered the time when all peers never attended the House but dressed like gentlemen and peers,' and 'when no minister came down to the House, having announced a motion, without being full dressed, with his sword by his side.' [2]

[1] Angelo's *Reminiscences*, i. pp. 133-134.
[2] Fonblanque's *Lives of the Lords Strangford*, p. 185.

Sir Nathaniel Wraxall, describing the costume worn in the House of Commons by Charles James Fox, says : ' In 1781 he constantly, or at least usually, wore in that assembly a blue frock coat and a buff waistcoat, neither of which seemed in general new, and sometimes appeared to be threadbare.'[1] Of the Right Hon. Richard Rigby, Paymaster of the Forces, in 1781 he says, ' When in his place he was also invariably habited in a full dress suit of clothes, commonly of a purple or dark colour, without lace or embroidery, close buttoned, with his sword thrust through the pocket.'[2] Angelo, describing the attire of Wilkes, the famous patriot, says, ' his dress—for he was a celebrated beau—was usually either a scarlet or a green suit edged with gold.'[3] George Colman, the younger, describes his attire in 1781, which was in accordance with the fashions, as being ' a frock coat with gilt buttons, and large flapping lapelles, a cocked hat, powdered hair tied behind in a queue with curls in rollers ; a frilled and ruffled shirt, very light leather breeches, and boots.' His father's financier sported ' thin nankeen breeches and light-blue silk stockings.'[4] Colman also states that he had been presented to the vice-chancellor of the University of Oxford two years previously, for matriculation, wearing 'a grass green coat with the furiously bepowdered pate of an ultra-coxcomb.' When the Rev. C. P. Moritz, a Lutheran pastor of Berlin, stayed for about seven weeks in this country, in 1782, he noticed how much the English people ' Frenchified ' themselves.

The most usual dress (he says), is, in summer, a short white waistcoat, black breeches, white silk stockings, and a frock, generally of very dark blue cloth, which looks like black. Officers rarely wear their uniforms, but dress like other people, and are to be known to be officers only by a cockade in their hats.

Rogers recollected that down to 1786 it was the fashion to wear swords, and remembered seeing Haydn play at a concert in a tie wig with a sword buckled at his side. When Warren

---

[1] *Memoirs*, ed. Wheatley, ii. 2.
[2] *Ibid.* i. p. 421.   [3] *Reminiscences*, i. 55.
[4] *Random Records*, i. ; quoted by Peake, *Memoirs of Colman Family*, vol. ii.

Hastings entered Westminster Hall to begin his defence in May 1791, he wore 'a puce silk coat, a bag wig, and a diamond-hilted sword.'[1]   Samuel Curwen, an American refugee in England, being near Hyde Park Gate on August 3, 1775, saw their Majesties returning from the drawingroom ; the king 'in a sedan chair surmounted by a crown, dressed in very light cloth, with silver buttons ; the queen carried by two porters in a chair, dressed in lemon-coloured flowered silk on a light cream-coloured ground.'[2]   From about 1780 onwards, large curls were added to the head dress, and collars high and stiff to the gentlemen's coats, both continuing to increase until they became almost unbearable.   General Burgoyne ridiculed this fashion with peculiar effect in his comedy of the ' Heiress ' (1786), wherein Alscript being attired in the style then prevalent, to gratify the wish of his daughter, testily exclaims, ' My daughter maintains that all fashions are founded in sense : but, egad, the tightness of my wig and the stiffness of my cape, give me a sense of the pillory.'   The following is a description of 'a gay Lionel' as he appeared in 1789 :—

His coat was a bright grey mixture, approaching to white, with a black silk collar and silver cord buttons, black satin small-clothes, with sky-blue ribbed silk stockings.   At the knee-band was a small diamond buckle, and a larger and costly one ornamented the toe of the shoe.   Rich lace ruffles set off the hand, and a cocked hat surmounted a head of hair dressed in the height of French fashion.[3]

' My coat,' wrote Sir Gilbert Elliot, in February 1786, 'is drab and *vig-o-gne* [?] with steel buttons ; waistcoat of the same.'[4]   Dr. Johnson, accepting an invitation from his friend Thrale to visit Paris in company with him and his wife, in the summer of 1775, dressed 'in a suit of black and a bourgeois wig, but resisted their importunity to wear ruffles.'[5]   Johnson's attire in those years, and later when he was sitting for his bust to Nollekens, the eminent sculptor, consisted of the following items :—

[1] Gardiner's *Music and Friends*, i. 521.
[2] *Journal and Letters*, p. 34.
[3] Gardiner's *Music and Friends*, iii. p. 129.
[4] *Life and Letters*, i. p. 193.
[5] Hawkins's *Life of Johnson*, p. 517.

A stock and wristbands; his wig was what is called a ' Busby,' but often wanted powder. His hat a three-cornered one ; coats, one a dark mulberry the other brown, inclining to the colour of Scotch snuff ; large brass or gilt buttons, black waistcoat and small-clothes —sometimes the latter were corduroy ; black stockings, large easy shoes with buckles.[2]

In 1791 male attire changed almost insensibly from formality to ease. Sir Nathaniel Wraxall, writing of the dress worn in London about what he calls 'the era of Jacobinism and of equality in 1793 and 1794,' says :—

It was then that pantaloons, cropped hair, and shoestrings, as well as the total abolition of buckles and ruffles, together with the disuse of hair powder, characterised the men ; while the ladies having cut off those tresses which had done so much execution, exhibited heads rounded *à la victime et à la guillotine,* as if ready for the stroke of the axe.[3]

Sheridan corroborates this when he mentions that each fop appeared cropped and trimmed up, exposing head and ears. But it was long before the new costume succeeded in displacing the old.

Speaking of the morning dress of Beau Brummel, which was similar (in 1795) to that of every other gentleman, Captain Jesse observes :—

Hessians and pantaloons, or top-boots and buckskins, with a blue coat, and a light or buff-coloured waistcoat. His dress of an evening was a blue coat and white waistcoat, black pantaloons, which buttoned tight to the ankle, striped silk stockings, and opera hat.[4]

To be adorned, is a natural instinct. The bright colours with which flowers are adorned are their attraction to insects. Uncivilized races prefer that which is bright and glaring to that which is quiet in dress. Could the eighteenth century more than any other century have existed without the study of orna-ment ? Is it not the same in our own time ? Men and women, more especially the latter, are fond to excess of bright colours ; and if any improvement has been effected, it is, perhaps, in the

---

[1] Smith's *Book for a Rainy Day*, ed. 1861, pp. 67–68.
[2] *Memoirs,* i. 99 ; Trotter's *Memoirs of C. J. Fox,* i. 374
[3] *Life,* i. p. 62 ; Malcolm's *Anecdotes,* ii. pp. 355–56.

choice of more elegant forms.   While the human race exists, the time will perhaps never come when adornment will be despised.   The τὸ πρέπον, the *quod decet*, the *simplex munditiis*, was the admiration of classical antiquity, and deserves equally the attention both of this and of succeeding ages.

CHAPTER V.

Vauxhall and Ranelagh—Marylebone and Cuper's Gardens—Drums, Festinos, and Ridottos—Masquerades—Mrs. Cornelys's Entertainments in Soho Square—The Pantheon—The Opera—The Stage—Its glaring anachronisms—The London fairs: Bartholomew, Southwark, and Mayfairs—Giants and dwarfs—Miscellaneous exhibitions—Cock-fighting—Prize-fighting—Bear-baiting—Cricket and football—Bowls—Boxing—Archery, rowing, and ballooning.

IN a previous chapter it was incidentally mentioned that among the many centres of pleasure and amusement in the capital frequented by the aristocracy and better class citizens during the last century, Vauxhall and Ranelagh Gardens took the highest rank. Both, from the time they rose, were marked by fashion for her own. Both were the butterflies of the hour at the caprice of the world of gaiety. Both were sufficiently in the outskirts for the enjoyment of pure air. Both could be easily reached by land or water; and although, as Fielding observes, by reason of their price they were not entirely appropriated to the people of fashion, they yet were seldom frequented by any below the middle rank. Even royalty condescended to smile on both, and no wonder, seeing that their meetings often outshone the royal levées in point of magnificence and splendour. How people comported themselves in these halls of pleasure, and what they did, many paragraphs in the newspapers, many passages in the writings of the essayists and novelists enable us to form tolerably correct ideas.

Vauxhall Gardens, being the elder of the two, will be noticed first. Begotten of the fierce outbreak of debauchery consequent upon the reign of the martial saints in the latter part of the preceding age, Vauxhall continued throughout the eighteenth century to be one of the chief haunts of the metropolitan pleasure-seeker. There it was that Joseph Addison went, accompanied by the worthy old Worcestershire knight Sir Roger de Coverley, as related in number three hundred and eighty-three of the 'Spectator.' There it was that Goldsmith's 'Citizen of the World' exclaimed, 'Head of Confucius ! this is fine, this unites rural beauty with courtly magnificence.' There it was that Hogarth for suggesting paintings (some of which are still in existence) was presented with a perpetual ticket of admission, which was last used the year before the Queen's accession. There it was that Fielding's 'Amelia' was sent into ecstasies of pleasure with the beauty and elegance of the surroundings ; and there it was that Frances Burney was enabled to gather incidents which she afterwards enshrined in her once popular, but now forgotten, novels of fashionable life. The favourite mode of proceeding to the gardens was by water, and the scenes which old Father Thames must have witnessed on the occasion of high days and holidays were doubtless ones of great animation. How sneeringly does Matthew Bramble wax over Vauxhall ! In his opinion it was

an unnatural assemblage of objects fantastically illuminated in broken masses, seemingly contrived to dazzle the eyes and divert the imagination of the vulgar. Here a wooden lion, there a stone statue ; in one place a range of things like coffee-house boxes covered a-top, in another a parcel of alehouse benches ; in a third a puppet-show representation of a tin cascade ; in a fourth a gloomy cave of a circular form like a sepulchral vault half-lighted ; in a fifth a scanty slip of grassplot that would not afford pasture for an ass's colt. The walks which nature seems to have intended for solitude, shade, and silence, are filled with crowds of noisy people, sucking up the nocturnal rheums of an aguish climate, and through these gay scenes a few lamps glimmer like so many farthing candles.

Horace Walpole, writing to George Montagu under date of June 23, 1750, favours him with the following account of one of his visits to Vauxhall Gardens :—

We got into the best order we could, and marched to our barge, with a boat of French horns attending, and little Ashe singing. We paraded some time up the river, and at last debarked at Vauxhall ; there, if we had so pleased, we might have had the vivacity of our party increased by a quarrel. . . . Miss Spurre, who desired nothing so much as the fun of seeing a duel—a thing which, though she is fifteen, she has never been so lucky to see—took due pains to make Lord March resent this, but he, who is very lively and agreeable, laughed her out of this charming frolic with a great deal of humour. Here we picked up Lord Granby, arrived very drunk from Jenny's (a well-known tavern at Chelsea), where, instead of going to old Strafford's catacombs to make honourable love, he had dined with Lady Fanny, and left her and eight women and four other men playing at brag [1]

The hour at which fashionable people generally made their appearance was between nine and ten o'clock in the evening.

There is a very curious account of a visit to Vauxhall contained in a narrative of a journey through England in the year 1752, by an Irish gentleman whose name is not recorded. He says that in company with others he went to Queenhithe stairs, and found a number of boatmen. He got into one of their boats and arrived at Vauxhall at seven o'clock.

The garden [he wrote] strikes the eye prodigiously ; it is set with many rows of tall trees, kept in excellent order, among which are placed an incredible number of globe lamps, by which it is illuminated, and when they are lighted the sound of the music ravishing the ear, added to the great resort of company so well dressed and walking all about, would almost make one believe he was in the Elysian fields. . . . In the middle of the garden are two semicircles which appear like an amphitheatre, in which are placed a great number of small booths which may contain about six or eight people apiece, where they commonly refresh themselves with sweetmeats, wine, tea, coffee, or suchlike. The backs of these boxes or booths are adorned with curious paintings, all which are enlightened to the front with globes. They are all numbered, and very just attendance is given by a vast number of warders kept for that purpose. Near to this a grand orchestra, where the music plays in fine weather ; but this night the concert was held in a magnificent hall neatly furnished. At one side of the orchestra is a noble statue of Handel. The music no sooner began than we entered the hall, where fifty-four musicians performed. Mr. Lowe soon sang, whose character I need not here mention, and after him the inimitable Miss Burchell. . . . Whilst we were entertaining ourselves, we were informed of the new cascade being lighted. . . . A fine grotto saluted our eyes, surrounded by the statues of Neptune, a mermaid, and other sea pieces, a dolphin, &c., placed in very agreeable attitudes, behind

---

[1] Walpole's *Letters*, ed. Cunningham, vol. ii. p. 211.

which fell in cascades crystal water which was received by a spacious basin or reservoir, wherein were placed small fishes, &c., which spouted up the water.[1]

Oliver Goldsmith, writing in the 'Public Ledger' under the signature of a 'Citizen of the World,' describes his visit to Vauxhall in company with Beau Tibbs, Mrs. Tibbs, the man in black, and the pawnbroker's widow, and he treats us to an account of the little dispute which arose between the two ladies —how Mrs. Tibbs was for keeping the genteel walk of the garden, where she observed there was always the very best company ; the widow, on the contrary, who came but once a season, was for securing a good standing place to see the water-works, which she assured us would begin in less than an hour at the furthest. The water-works are described in the excerpt from the narrative of the Irish traveller cited in a foregoing paragraph.

The proprietor of Vauxhall in the early part of the reign of King George III. took little care for the public safety, and whenever the young exquisites of the day took it into their heads to be merry, under the exhilarating influence of the celebrated Vauxhall punch, they never failed to highly distinguish themselves by mad freaks. 'About one o'clock on Friday morning,' says a newspaper of May 1764, 'about fifty young bloods &c. tore up the railing, and did other damage at Vauxhall, occasioned by Mr. Tyers having railed in the dark walks.' The road home to the city was fraught with no end of danger to belated frequenters of the gardens. So late as 1777, the issue of the 'Daily News' for June 27, states that—

On Thursday night, as Captain Sainthill, with two gentlemen and three ladies were returning home from Vauxhall in a coach, they were attacked by five armed ruffians, between the grounds and the turnpike, who with horrid imprecations demanded their money and watches. One of the villains put his pistol to the breast of a lady, while another struck at a gentleman with his cutlass. The captain is much wounded on the hand. Another coach coming up the thieves ran off, after robbing only two of the company.

Vauxhall Gardens was a favourite resort of George IV. when Prince of Wales, and the subjoined advertisement which

---

[1] *Narrative*, ed. by H. Huth and W. C. Hazlitt, pp. 94-98.

appeared in the morning papers of June 1781, has reference to one of his numerous visits.

> By authority we inform the public that their Royal Highnesses, the Duke and Duchess of Northumberland, attended by their own band of music, intend honouring Vauxhall Gardens with their company this evening, and their Royal Highnesses have commanded the grand pavilion and the adjoining room to be kept entirely for themselves and their suite.

And in a newspaper of August 1, 1782, it is stated that—

> The Prince of Wales was at Vauxhall, and spent a considerable part of the evening in company with a set of gay friends ; but when the music was over, being discovered by the company, he was so surrounded, crushed, pursued, and overcome that he was under the necessity of making a hasty retreat. The sound of the bell for the opening of the cascade never raised such a commotion on a Saturday night as did his appearance. The ladies followed the prince— the gentlemen pursued the ladies ; the curious ran to see what was the matter ; the mischievous ran to increase the tumult, and in two minutes the boxes were deserted, the lame were overthrown, the well-dressed were demolished, and for half an hour the whole company were contracted into one narrow channel, and borne along with the rapidity of a torrent, to the infinite danger of powdered locks, painted cheeks, and crazy constitutions.

Henry Angelo, in his amusing 'Reminiscences' of the last century, describes Vauxhall Gardens about 1776, when the price of admission was a shilling—as 'more like a bear garden than a rational place of resort, and most particularly on Sunday evenings,' at which times it was crowded from four to six with gentry, girls of the town, apprentices, shopboys, and crowds of citizens with their lawless children. Mrs. Calderwood, in the journal of her excursion from Caledonia into England, says that she could not but think the entertainment provided at Vauxhall a vulgar one, and also that she could not fancy herself in genteel company while she heard a man calling 'Take care of your watches and pockets !' When a falling-off in the attendance of visitors became apparent to the proprietors of both Ranelagh and Vauxhall, they employed persons fashionably dressed to mingle with the throngs of people walking in the Mall in St. James's Park. It was the business of these 'decoy ducks,' as they were called, occasionally to give vent to a very audible 'What charming weather for Ranelagh!' (or Vauxhall) as the case might be.[1]

> I was last night at the masquerade at Vauxhall [wrote Sir Gilbert Elliot to his wife from, Bury Street, under date of Thursday, May 17, 1787], with the Palmerstons, the Culverdens, Miss Burney, Wardham, Pelham, &c. I went in despair, as I always do on such services, but it answered vastly well, and I was more amused than usual at such places. The buildings and decorations were really fine and well-designed. No heat, nor much cold ; a great many people but no crowd, on account of the extent of the ground. A good supper, and a blackguardish company with a dash of good company, and no riot while we stayed, which was past three o'clock ; but the Vauxhall *squeak* was just beginning, and people were becoming very tender and very quarrelsome.[2]

Three years later the price of admission to Vauxhall was raised from one shilling, and for several years afterwards fluctuated between two and three shillings. At last, in 1804, after a connection with the fast life of London, nearly a century and a half's duration, Vauxhall was demolished, and a portion of the grounds converted into the Old Men's Garden attached to Chelsea Hospital.

The great contemporary and formidable rival of Vauxhall was Ranelagh, which stood on the south side of Hans Place, Chelsea. Towards the latter end of the reign of William III. Viscount Ranelagh had a villa built at Chelsea, and gardens laid out on a tract of land lying to the east of the Royal Chelsea Hospital, which then lay within a pleasant drive from the city. He died in 1712, and his domain passed into the possession of his daughter, who twenty-one years later disposed of it to an eminent builder of the day, by whom it was again sold in lots. Soon after this, Lacy, the patentee of Drury Lane Theatre, and a foreigner named Rietti took a lease of the premises with the object of converting it into a place of amusement for the gay world which should be unequalled in its magnificence. The consequence was that the estate was vested in shareholders to the number of thirty-six, the extensive gardens and grounds by which it was surrounded were laid out to the very best advantage, and a Rotunda was erected on a similar

[1] *Recollections of Table Talk of S. Rogers*, p. 23.
[2] *Life and Letters*, i. pp. 166-7.

plan to that of the Pantheon at Rome. In May 1742 Ranelagh was opened with great *éclat*—a public breakfast forming the novelty—and from that time onwards it continued to be much frequented by those languid dandies the 'macaronies,' the 'jolly young bucks,' the 'rattles,' and other extraordinary specimens of humanity, who now live only in the pages of Miss Burney's fictions ; so much so, that in two years it had 'totally beat Vauxhall.' 'Yesterday,' says Mrs. Delany in a letter to Mrs. Dewes dated April 26, 1744, 'my brother gallantly attended Mr. Donnellan, Miss Dashwood, and myself, to breakfast at Ranelagh ; the day was clear but cold ; there was a great deal of company.'[1] The magistrates of London and Westminster suppressed the public breakfasts on the ground that they were detrimental to society. Then the fashionable world insisted on morning concerts, consisting chiefly of selections from oratorios. The introduction of ballets, masquerades, and other amusements of a questionable character was but a short step, and it was quickly made. This contributed in no small measure to its ultimate downfall. Dr. Johnson declared on his first visit to Ranelagh that its *coup d'œil* was the finest thing he had ever seen.[2] About the time that Smollett wrote his novel of 'Humphrey Clinker,' Ranelagh was in the zenith of its popularity, consequently it is not surprising to find a description of it incorporated into that amusing work :—

Ranelagh [Miss Lydia Melford tells her friend Miss Lætitia Wills, of Gloucester] looks like the enchanted palace of a genie, adorned with the exquisite performances of painting, carving, and gilding ; enlightened with a thousand golden lamps that emulate the noonday sun ; crowded with the gay, the rich, the happy, and the fair ; glittering with cloth of gold and silver lace, embroidery and precious stones. While these exulting sons and daughters of felicity tread this round of pleasure, or regale in different parties and separate lodges with fine imperial tea and other delicious refreshments, their ears are entertained with the most ravishing delights of music, both instrumental and vocal.

The price of admission was half-a-crown, and on entering the gentlemen customarily bought flowers for their own button-

---

[1] *Autobiog. and Corresp. of Mrs. Delany,* 1st series, ii. p. 199.
[2] Boswell's *Johnson,* ed. Croker.

holes and flowers to present to their lady friends and admirers.
Among the spectacles, as recorded by Angelo, was a number of
boats on a large sheet of water filled with men gaudily dressed
and armed with long poles, who endeavoured to push one
another into the water, victory being won by those who succeeded in ducking the greatest number of their opponents.[1]
The staple amusement, however, was a promenade concert, and
the chief attraction seems to have been the 'promenading' of
the 'genteel' walks, on account of the facility it afforded for
seeing 'the first persons of the kingdom,' who were accustomed
to make their appearance there in the cool of the evening,
dressed in the height of fashion. The performances of vocal
and instrumental music seem to have wasted their sweetness
on the desert air, for as Robert Bloomfield, the author of the
'Farmer's Boy,' says in a humorous description of the place
which he wrote towards the close of the century :—

> The music was truly enchanting,
>   Right glad was I when I came near it ;
> But in fashion I found I was wanting :
>   'Twas the fashion to walk and not hear it.

Notwithstanding this, the high price of admission (half-a-
crown : which included tea, coffee, punch, and other beverages),
the costliness of the refreshments, and the privilege of gazing
upon lords and ladies, counts and countesses, attracted the
genteel, or those who wished to be considered so, in great
numbers. These mortals never begrudged the money expended
in coach hire, and always took good care, like Mr. and Mrs.
Tibbs, 'to sit in none but a genteel box ; a box where they
might see and be seen.'[2] 'My landlady (a tailor's widow)
assured me,' says the Rev. C. P. Moritz, writing in 1782, 'that
she always fixed on some one day in the year, on which without
fail she drove to Ranelagh.'

The Irish traveller whose tour has been quoted in illustration
of Vauxhall did not omit to pay a visit to Ranelagh during his
stay in London in 1752. He states that at that time he found

[1] *Reminiscences*, ii.
[2] *Citizen of the World*, No. 71 ; *Reise eines Deutschen in England im
Jahre* 1782 ; Miss Burney's *Evelina*, xlvi.

the gardens, though small, yet laid out in a very judicious manner.
. . . The amphitheatre, which is very large, is built of timber ; all
around are booths, such as before mentioned at Vauxhall, though
a greater quantity of them, and [you] descend by one step into the
area, where several tea-tables are laid out ; over the booths rise
very stately windows, outside of which is a gallery encompassing
the whole. From the crown of the arches of the windows a cap or
cupola decreases gradually, till it terminates in a point above, out
of which the chimney of the great fire place below is conveyed.
The fire-place stands in the middle, from whence all the tea-tables
are supplied with water and coffee. The room is illuminated with
thirty-six branches of globe lamps, besides many others which are
put near the booths. The orchestra fronts the door, wherein was
an excellent band of music and a good organ.

The following is a copy of an advertisement relative to
Ranelagh, extracted from the ' Public Advertiser' of June 1,
1774 :—

This day, the 1st of June, will be performed a Concert of Vocal
and Instrumental Music, Admittance 2s. 6d. each person, Coffee
and Tea included. To be continued on Mondays, Wednesdays,
and Fridays. The doors to be opened at half past six. The Music
to begin at seven. A Horse Patrol to guard the Roads. Ladies
and Gentlemen may walk in the Rotunda, Gardens, &c. every Day
(Sundays excepted) at 1s. each.

'What are the amusements at Ranelagh?' inquires that
irritable old gentleman Matthew Bramble in a letter to
Dr. Lewis.

One half of the company are following one another's tails, in an
eternal circle, like so many blind asses in an olive mill, where they
can neither discourse, distinguish, nor be distinguished ; while the
other half are drinking hot water, under the denomination of tea,
till 9 or 10 o'clock at night, to keep them awake for the rest of the
evening. As for the orchestra, the vocal music especially, it is
well for the performers that they cannot be heard distinctly.

Captain Mirvan, in Miss Burney's novel of ' Evelina,' complains that Ranelagh is dull ; whereupon the fashionable Mr.
Lovel observes that it needs 'a certain acquaintance with high
life and something *d'un vrai goût* to be really sensible of its
merit. Those whose connections and so forth are not among
les gens comme il faut, can feel nothing but *ennui* at such a
place as Ranelagh.'[1] In spite of its many attractions, in spite

[1] Miss Burney's *Evelina*, ed. Ellis, c. xxiii.

too of its crowded fashionable assemblies, 'the magic Ranelagh,' as it was called by the Earl of Chatham, rapidly declined and fell about the era of the French Revolution, and from being one of the gayest of fashionable resorts became a shadow of its former glory.

Ranelagh and Vauxhall were not the only places of amusement of their kind. How many of the thousands who now daily traverse the grimy Waterloo Bridge Road are aware that they are treading the site of Cuper's Garden or Gardens (a sort of eighteenth-century Cremorne Gardens), where their great-grandfathers frequented an entertainment consisting of fireworks, illuminations, and music, 'particularly with the music of a Mr. Jones, a celebrated musician on the harp'? Not one in fifty. Yet so it was. Boydell Cuper was the proprietor, and his garden, which was often styled 'Cupid's Garden,' became notorious for the profligacy of the company by whom it was frequented, until 1753, when it was suppressed, the house continuing open as a tavern. The ownership of the ground belonged to the family of the Duke of Norfolk, and by one of this family it was granted to the principal and fellows of Jesus College, Oxford, and from them it was long rented by the Messrs. Beaufoy, the celebrated vintners, part of whose establishment was built upon it.[1]

How many of those too, it may be asked, who daily frequent the Marylebone Road know that on the space now occupied by Beaumont Street, Devonshire Street, and part of Devonshire Place, there existed from 1737 until about 1778 an extensive tract of ground which went by the name of Marylebone Gardens, where on payment of one shilling the genteel company (the Cecilias, Evelinas, and Captain Macheaths of the day) could walk, and feast themselves and their friends with tea, coffee, fruit tarts, almond cheesecakes, and fine Epping butter? Peradventure, very few. How many are aware that there then stood 'regular rows of young trees, the stems of which received the irons for the lamps at about seven feet from the ground '—that on either side of the walks

[1] Tanswell's *Lambeth*, p. 180; Brayley and Britton's *Hist. Surrey*, ii. 334-335.

were 'latticed alcoves'—that there stood a 'bow-fronted
orchestra with balustrades supported by columns '—that lights
were 'erected in the coachway from Oxford Road, and also on
the footpath from Cavendish Square to the entrance to the
gardens '—that the fireworks were 'splendid beyond conception '—that 'cascades, showers of fire, and air balloons were
most magnificently displayed ' ; and likewise that 'red fire was
introduced'? It might now be hardly credited, but the fact
remains that it was so.[1] One or two of the advertisements
relating to this once famous place of amusement are subjoined.

Marybone Gardens.—This day, June 2, will be performed a
Concert of Vocal and Instrumental Music. In the course of which
will be sung for the first time this season an Entertainment of Music
called 'The MAGNET.' The Vocal Parts by Mr. Reinhold, Miss
Wilde, and Miss Wewitzer. The celebrated Mons. Ladell, Musician
to the King of Portugal, will perform a Concert on the German
Flute. Admittance Two Shillings and Sixpence. The Doors will
be opened at Five o'clock. The Concert will begin at Half Past
Six o'clock. Subscription Tickets are ready for delivery at Mr. Pigue-
nits's Bookseller, Berkeley Square, and at the Bar of the Gardens,
at Two Guineas each. To-morrow Sig. Torre's Second Exhibition ;
when he will repeat the Forge of Vulcan, as it was performed at
the Marriage of his Royal Highness the Count d'Artois.[2] This Day
Signior Torre will exhibit the Forge of Vulcan under Mount Etna,
the Cavern of the Cyclops, and Flowing of the Lava.
Marybone Gardens will be open To-morrow Evening immediately after Five o'clock for Company to walk in. Tea, Coffee, and
other Refreshments may be had at the Bar. To prevent Improper
company each Person to pay sixpence at the Door.[3]

Marylebone Gardens, or 'Marybone' as the name was pronounced, stood at what is now the bottom of Harley Street.
Henry Angelo, who frequented them, says that in his day the
exhibition of fireworks under the direction of Signor Torre was
the great inducement for people to frequent them, and that,
though far inferior to Vauxhall, they had attractions adapted
more to the taste of the gentry than to that of the *haut ton.*
It was in these gardens that Mrs. Fountain, a celebrated beauty

[1] Smith's *Book for a Rainy Day,* pp. 32–57 ; Miss Burney's *Evelina,*
c. lii. ed. Ellis ; Malcolm's *Anecdotes,* ii. 289–92.
[2] *Public Advertiser,* June 2, 1774.   [3] *Ibid.*

in the early part of the eighteenth century, was saluted by the notorious highwayman Richard Turpin, who left her, saying— 'Don't be alarmed ; you may now boast that you have been kissed by Turpin.' Living as moderns do in comparatively calm and peaceful days, little do they think of the terrors which filled the breasts of respectable people when preparing to take their way home after an evening passed at one of these resorts. Vauxhall, Ranelagh, Marylebone, Cuper's Gardens, and every other place of amusement were the rendezvous of footpads and highwaymen, who as soon as the crowds began to direct their steps homewards, took up their stand in dark and lonely spots where visitors might be expected to pass, for the purpose of robbing and maltreating them. Hardly an evening passed without some persons returning home from these places in the gloom being waylaid and relieved of whatever valuables they carried on their persons. Page after page might be filled with the newspaper records of these assaults. So late as 1790 the programme of entertainment at Sadler's Wells never failed to conclude with some such announcement as this :—

Patrols of horse and foot are stationed from Sadler's Wells Gate along the New Road to Tottenham Court Road turnpike ; likewise from the City Road to Moorfields. Also to St. John's Street, and across the Spa Fields to Rosaman Row, from the hours of eight to eleven.

Similar announcements were appended to the advertisements of Vauxhall and Ranelagh, and the other resorts. Macklin, the veteran player, was of opinion that all the tea and pleasure gardens round London were the baiting places of footpads and highwaymen, and certainly the newspapers and other contemporaneous sources of information lend much countenance to his opinion.[1] One of the most notorious Ranelagh pickpockets in the closing decade of the century was George Barrington, who in dress and address was inferior to none and was equalled

---

[1] This is sufficiently authenticated by other evidence, as, for instance, by that of Francis Place, who says that so openly was thieving carried on in these gardens, that he had known the landlords of some of them actually produce for the inspection of the company, lumps of silver melted from valuables stolen by persons who were present.—*Add. MSS. Brit. Mus.* 27, 829.

by few. The mode of dressing the hair prevalent at this period, which has been already adverted to, greatly facilitated his disguises, which were sometimes clerical, sometimes military, or otherwise, just as the fancy happened to strike him. A contemporary asserts that Barrington always contrived to introduce himself to the best society, and to converse upon equal terms with men far superior to him in social position. Any lady who went to Ranelagh wearing ornaments of value was pretty certain to return home without them. Such losses were usually recorded in the newspapers on the following day, and were almost invariably accompanied by an observation to the effect that they were attributable to Barrington, who was known to have been present. London at last became too hot to hold him, and he transferred the scene of his operations.[1] At length, being convicted, he was transported to Botany Bay, as the penal settlement in New South Wales was then called, and died at a very old age at Paramatta.

We cannot, however, linger any longer among the gay and festive throngs which sweep through the long lustrous arcades of the old London pleasure gardens, since drums, festinos, hurricanes, and masquerades must now occupy our attention. The first three of these assemblies, which were really no more than overcrowded parties, continued in great favour throughout the eighteenth century, and at the time when Francis Coventry, the satirical author of 'The History of Pompey the Little,' flourished, they were, as he says, ' the highest object of female vainglory.'

The end thereof [wrote Coventry] is to assemble as large a mob of quality as can possibly be contained in one house, and great are the honours paid to that lady who can boast of the largest crowd. For this purpose a woman of superior rank calculates how many people all the rooms in her house laid open can possibly hold, and then sends about two months beforehand among the people one knows to bespeak such a number as she thinks will fill them.[2]

What was a ridotto? The following extract from a letter of Mrs. Pendarves to her friend Mrs. Anne Granville, dated Pall Mall, April 4, 1730, will supply the answer :—

[1] Gunning's *Reminiscences*, i. pp. 207-208 ; Barrington's *Memoirs*.
[2] *Hist. of Pompey the Little*, p. 214.

Last Thursday I went to the ridotto. I was engaged to go with my cousins Graham and Granville, and my Lady Lansdowne being of the party, I shuffled me off, and was resolved to go, though it was with some difficulty ; and that she might not think me destitute of company, I got one of the Bramstons. The hour it begins is nine, polite company does not come till eleven ; I was between both and went at ten. The room is set out in the same manner as for the masquerade ; it is the most entertaining sort of assembly, because you are at liberty to wander about as much as you please, and there is dancing, tea, coffee, chocolate, and all sorts of sweet-meats. Most of the ladies were in great distress for partners, for the greatest part of the clever men are gone to Newmarket. . . . There was a prodigious crowd ; they danced till half an hour after one.[1]

Festinos were much more attractive scenes. The following description of one held at Northumberland House in 1762 by the Duchess of Northumberland, in honour of the queen's brother, who was then on a visit to England, is extracted from a letter of Horace Walpole to G. Montagu, dated June 8, 1762 :—

Not only the whole house but the garden was illuminated, and was quite a fairy scene. Arches and pyramids of lights alternately surrounded the enclosure ; a diamond necklace of lamps edged the rails and descent, with a spiral obelisk of candles on each hand ; and dispersed over the lawn were little bands of kettledrums, clarionets, fifes, &c., and the lovely moon, who came without a card.[2]

But all these forms of amusement paled their ineffectual fires before the prevailing mania for masquerades, which first became fashionable under the famous Heydegger (who is mentioned by Pope in the ' Dunciad ') in the early part of the eighteenth century, when they were usually held during the season at ' the King's Theatre in the Haymarket.' Tickets were issued to those only who subscribed to them, at White's Chocolate House in St. James's Street, and no effort was spared to exclude the common herd. ' People of quality ' were re-quested through the newspapers to refrain from lending their names in order to obtain tickets for others ; or, if they had more than they required, to lose no time in sending them back

[1] *Autobiog. and Corresp. of Mrs. Delany,* 1st series, i. p. 253.
[2] Walpole's *Letters,* ed. Cunningham, iii. p. 512.

to the office in the Haymarket, where the money they had cost would be returned, so as 'to prevent their falling into bad hands.' It was Heydegger's invariable rule to advertise that for the prevention of all disorders and indecencies, 'a sufficient guard' would be 'appointed within and without the house,' and that 'strict orders' would be issued 'not to deliver any bottles and glasses from the sideboards, and to shut them up early.' But in spite of these precautions masquerades were productive of an infinitely greater amount of evil than good.

> The midnight orgy and the mazy dance,
> The smile of beauty and the flush of wine,
> For fops, fools, gamesters, knaves, and lords combine;
> Each to his humour—Comus all allows:
> Champagne, dice, music, or your neighbour's spouse.

The episcopal bench inveighed against their vices and follies. The poets and essayists lashed them. The grand jury of Middlesex at last presented those that were held at the King's Theatre, 'conceiving the same to be a wicked and unlawful design to carry on gaming, chances by way of lottery, and other impious and illegal practices.' Notwithstanding all this, masquerades appear from the newspapers and published correspondence of this period to have held their ground, and the nobility continued to patronise Heydegger in the first and Mrs. Cornelys in the second half of the century. Lord Chesterfield, writing to his friend Mrs. Howard under date of May 28, N.S., 1728, says: 'I considered you particularly last Tuesday, suffering the heat and disorders of the masquerade, supported by the Duchess of Richmond of one side, and Miss Fitzwilliam of the other.'[1] The issue of the 'Edinburgh Evening Courant' for February 20, 1727, contains a paragraph extracted from a London newspaper setting forth that 'the King and the Prince were last night at the masquerade.'[2] At a masquerade held in 1749, at which one of the maids of honour, Miss Chudleigh, subsequently the notorious Duchess of Kingston, attended in the guise of Andromeda, there were

---

[1] *Suffolk Correspondence*, ed. Croker, i. 290; Walpole's *Letters*, iv. 87.
[2] *Correspondence of Lady M. W. Montagu*, ed. Thomas, i. 496.

present the Princess of Wales, besides other members of the royal family.[1] Tradition asserts that it was the fascinations of masquerades that alone induced George I. to emerge from his habitual shyness and reserve. The story goes that at the first masquerade given in honour of him after his arrival in England, a masked lady invited the monarch to accompany her to one of the buffets for the purpose of drinking a glass of wine. The damsel, in blissful ignorance as to the identity of her partner, filled her bumper exclaiming, 'Here, Mask, the health of the Pretender;' and filling another glass handed it to his Majesty, who graciously accepting it observed, 'Madam, I drink with all my heart to the health of all unfortunate princes!'[2] Not all the political riots and squabbles of the times could check the progress of the masquerades and masqueraders. Walpole records that, in February 1770, when Wilkes, the member for Middlesex, had attained the acme of his popularity, the House of Commons adjourned to attend a subscription masquerade held at Soho. 'The mob was beyond all belief, and they held lighted torches to the windows of every coach, and demanded to have the masks pulled off and put on at their pleasure.' Fortunately the mob was civil and good humoured, and the carriages and their occupants were permitted to pursue their way without further molestation. The reader may be interested to know that it was Carlisle House in Soho (the town house of the Earl of Carlisle) that the legislators of England visited—a very famous temple of fashion, established by Mrs. Cornelys, whose history is not without interest. Mrs. Teresa Cornelys was a native of Germany, and for some years followed the profession of a singer in different towns on the Continent. Between 1756 and 1757, it is supposed, she came to England, and in 1762 she selected a large mansion known as Carlisle House, situated at the corner of Sutton Street on the east side of Soho Square, where she succeeded in catering for the pleasure-loving metropolis in

[1] At private masquerades the guests were obliged to exhibit their cards of invitation at the door in order that people who had invited themselves might be excluded from admission under the disguise of masks.
[2] Lloyd's *Memoirs of George IV.*, p. 43 ; Walpole's *Letters*, v. 228.

such a manner 'that no other public entertainments could pretend to rival its attractions.' Mrs. Cornelys began with subscription balls and grand concerts of vocal and instrumental music, and her success in the management of them raised her many enemies, who at one time threatened to put the Alien Act into force against her. In 1764 she caused her assembly rooms to be altered and re-ornamented at an outlay of 2,000*l.*, and in the following year instituted society nights and concerts, which were so numerously patronised that another door had to be erected in Soho Square. On Monday night, February 27, 1770, she ventured on a masquerade, at which the principal nobility and gentry of the kingdom, to the number of near 800, were present. On February 7, 1771, Mrs. Cornelys held another masquerade which was attended by the whole of the fashionable world of both sexes. The house was illuminated (according to the 'London Chronicle') in the most splendid and picturesque manner with nearly 4,000 wax lights, and 100 musicians were dispersed throughout the rooms. Meanwhile the informer had marked the high priestess of fashion for his prey. For ever on the watch for novelty, Mrs. Cornelys instituted during the course of the same year Harmonic Meetings, thereby placing herself in direct rivalry with the Italian Opera House. The proprietors were so annoyed that they instantaneously called upon Sir John Fielding, the presiding magistrate at Bow Street, to interfere. He did so, pronounced her 'guilty of the facts laid to her charge,' and fined her 50*l.* For the first time poor Mrs. Cornelys's speculations had resulted in a failure, and from that hour her influence over the fashionable world began to decline. To make matters worse a splendid building called the Pantheon was opened in May 1772, and fashionable folk, ever in quest of something new, withdrew in great numbers from the gatherings over which she presided. Not to be outdone Mrs. Cornelys started a masquerade in opposition. For a time she struggled with commendable heroism for the supremacy, and might have prevailed had not she and her temple of festivity been 'seized upon by the cold hand of merciless creditors,' to use the elegant language of the newspapers of the time. Not until 1774 did she come again before the fashion-

L 2

able world to woo its patronage. In the 'Public Advertiser' for Friday, April 22, of that year, she

respectfully acquaints the Nobility and Gentry that Tuesday next is fixed for her Annual Night, when she trusts that she shall be honoured with their Presence and Interest, promises on her part to pay such attention to Elegance and Novelty on the Occasion as may, in some Degree, entitle her to that Honour which she thus publicly presumes to ask and hope for. The tickets are now delivering out at the Office in Soho Square.

Mrs. Cornelys (says a paragraph in another column of the same journal) is making very great preparations for her Annual Night, which is to be on Tuesday next ; and no little Preparations, we are told, are making on the side of the Parties that are forming to attend it. In a word, it is thought that this will be the most splendid night that has been at Soho for some years, whether considered as to the brilliancy and number of the company present, or as to the entertainment itself.

The vigilance of her creditors soon compelled Mrs. Cornelys to retire again into private life. Withdrawing to rural Knightsbridge, she installed herself as 'vendor of asses' milk,' and fitted up a suite of rooms for public breakfasts. But even this scheme did not prosper. Mrs. Cornelys's creditors again rose up against her, and from them she sought the shelter of the Fleet Prison. In that haven of refuge, 'the world forgetting, by the world forgot,' she passed away on August 19, 1797, at a very advanced age.[1] Sir John Hawkins. when writing his 'Life of Dr. Johnson,' about ten years before she died, paid the following tribute to her memory, evidently in ignorance of the fact that she was then alive :—

For most of the refinements in our public diversions we are indebted to the late Mrs. Cornelys, to whose elegant taste for pleasure the magistrates of Turin and Brussels were so blind, and of her worth so insensible, that . . . they severally drove her out of both those cities. This hospitable country, however, afforded her an asylum, and in Westminster she was permitted to improve our manners.[2]

'Old Soho,' as Mrs. Cornelys's establishment was familiarly called, soon felt from its high estate, and the 'European Magazine' for the month of July 1789 prints a mournful 'Elegy

---

[1] Mackinlay's *Mrs. Cornelys's Entertainments.*
[2] *Life of Johnson,* p. 263.

on seeing Mrs. Cornelys's House in Ruins,' from the pen of Anthony Pasquin, otherwise John Williams, one of the Della Cruscan school.

In February 1765, a Scotchman whose real name was Macall, but who called himself Almack, opened an assembly room in King Street, St. James's, as a rival of Mrs. Cornelys's establishment. The opening night, February 12, is thus described by Horace Walpole :—

> The new assembly room at Almack's was opened the night before last, and they say is very magnificent, but it was empty ; half the town is ill with colds, and many were afraid to go, as the house is scarcely built yet. Almack advertised that it was built with hot bricks and boiling water ; think what a rage there must be for public places if this notice instead of terrifying could draw anybody thither. They tell me the ceilings were dropping with wet ; but can you believe me when I assure you the Duke of Cumberland was there—nay, had a levée in the morning, and went to the opera before the assembly !

After the collapse of Mrs. Cornelys, the Pantheon, 'a new winter Ranelagh on the Oxford Road,' a little to the front of Great Marlborough Street, which had been finished in January 1772 at a cost of 60,000*l.* by James Wyatt, became the *locus classicus* for masquerades, and continued so to be until 1792, when it was unfortunately burnt down in the early hours of a morning on which one of the severest frosts was experienced. The Pantheon, which Horace Walpole compared to Baalbec in all its glory, sprang into existence like the creation of the magician's lamp in the Arabian legend, and not with greater assiduity did the obedient genii apply themselves to its internal adornment than the builder and his colleagues. Henry Angelo considered it the most elegant and beautiful structure that had been erected in the British metropolis. George III. and the first nobility and ladies of fashion—the Duchess of Devonshire—were to be seen in character at the Pantheon masquerades, which it would seem were not always very edifying spectacles, since a writer in the 'Westminster Magazine' for May 1774, when giving a description of one he had witnessed within its walls, concludes by saying :—'In short, I am so thoroughly sick of masquerading from what I beheld there, that I do seriously decry them as subversive of virtue and every noble and domestic point of honour.' It is probable that the writer was alluding to the masquerade which, according to the 'Public Advertiser' of May 2, 1774, was given at the Pantheon by the club at Boodle's on May 3. The doors were to be opened at ten o'clock, and the supper rooms at one. The tickets of admission were to be obtained at Boodle's in Pall Mall on the delivery of the checks. The Rev. Dr. Campbell (an Irish beneficed clergyman, who wrote a 'Diary of a Visit to England in 1775'), while praising the dimensions and appearance of the Pantheon, specifies among the company 'the Prussian ambassador, Lord Stormont, the Duke of Cumberland, and Lady Grosvenor, a fine woman lost to all sense of modesty, Lord Lyttelton, and Lady Archer, painted like a doll, but handsome with her feathers nodding like the plumes of Mambrino's helmet.'[1]

The dances most in vogue during the last century were the country dance and the minuet. Just before dancing began, the ladies who were present threw down their fans upon a table. A gentleman then advanced, took up a fan, and invited the lady to whom it belonged to become his partner.[2] All festive occasions—such for instance as the anniversaries of birthdays, weddings, &c.—were usually celebrated in aristocratic circles with a ball. Here is an account of one given by the Earl of Northumberland in 1764, 'as a compliment to his Majesty's birthday.'

The garden was decorated with ten thousand lamps, and four hundred were fixed to the balustrades descending by the steps, which had a most beautiful effect. Two bands of music were provided—one in the great gallery, which was illuminated with an extraordinary degree of splendour, the other in the garden ; each answered the other alternately. The company consisted of fifteen hundred persons of the first distinction.

---

[1] *Diary*, pp. 46, 47 ; see also *Correspondence of 1st Earl of Malmesbury* ; Miss Burney's *Evelina*, c. xiii. ; *Cecilia*, i. viii.

[2] It appears from Miss Burney's novel, *Evelina*, that at a private ball in 1778, it was not only permissible for the gentlemen to ask the ladies to be their partners without any introduction, but to change their partners at the conclusion of every second dance. The same couples, however, at other times, danced in company during the whole of the evening.

Walpole, writing during the course of the same year to the Earl of Hertford, says :—

We had last night a magnificent ball at Lady Cardigan's ; three sumptuous suppers in three rooms. The house, you know, is crammed with fine things—pictures, china, japan, vases, and every species of curiosity.

The playhouses, of which more will be said anon, were very well patronised, and so was the Italian Opera (an exotic in England until the reign of Queen Anne), judging from this extract from the 'Annual Register' for the month of March 1765 :—

Signor Manzoli, the Italian singer at the Haymarket, got no less, after paying all charges of every kind, by his benefit last week than 1,000 guineas. This added to a sum of 1,500*l.* which he had already saved, and the remaining profits of the season, is surely an undoubted proof of British generosity. One particular lady complimented the singer with a 200*l.* bill for a single ticket on that occasion.

In the same record we are told that when in the previous year the royal family visited the opera, there assembled

a crowd not to be described ; the Duchess of Leeds, Lady Scarborough, and others, sat on chairs between the scenes, the doors of the front boxes were thrown open, and the passages were all filled to the back of the stairs ; nay, women of fashion stood on the very stairs till eight at night.[1]

But if there was one amusement more than another which the English public enjoyed with keener relish, or from which they derived greater pleasure than any other in the last century, that amusement was undoubtedly theatrical representations in general. Like Don Quixote, the English were, from their youth up, great admirers of masques and stage plays. To the metropolitan population, the kind of entertainment which was provided in the theatres, which were then not half so numerous as they are at the present day, was almost a necessity of their very existence. It appealed to the mind through the medium

---

[1] In 1776, concerts of ancient music (music not less than a quarter of a century old) were first held at Tottenham Street Rooms, and subsequently at the King's Theatre in the Haymarket. About the same period Charles Frederick Abel, 'Chamber Musician to the Queen,' began a series of concerts at the Hanover Square Rooms.

of the senses, and in days when books were scarce and expensive and when newspapers were not what they are now, the stage constituted a sort of fourth estate, which became still more so when David Garrick buckled himself to the task of interpreting the leading characters of Shakespeare, and of restoring him to his rightful supremacy over the English stage. Notwithstanding the severe castigation plays had received from the sturdy non-juror Jeremy Collier, in the closing years of the preceding century, and notwithstanding the retrenchments of the Master of the Revels, they continued until long after the accession of George III. to be pervaded to a greater or lesser degree with indecency and indecorum, still obliging ladies frequenting the theatres to wear masks, which, according to Colley Cibber, they usually did during the first few days on which a new play was represented. Addison, writing in the 'Spectator' of 1712, confesses that it was

one of the most unaccountable things in that age, that the lewdness of the theatre should be so much complained of, so well exposed, and so little redressed. . . . As matters stand at present (he continues) multitudes are shut out from this noble diversion by reason of those abuses and corruptions that accompany it. A father is often afraid that his daughter should be ruined by those entertainments which were invented for the accomplishment and refining of human nature. . . . The accomplished gentleman upon the English stage is the person that is familiar with other men's wives and indifferent to his own, as the fine woman is generally a composition of sprightliness and falsehood.

It was in this way that matters stood until the rise of Garrick. Nothing is more noticeable than the extremely low estimate of the female character which the dramatists sought to give. In the witty and artificial comedies of Dryden, of Farquhar, of Wycherley, of Vanbrugh, and of Congreve, women are made to 'have no character at all.' Steele, writing in No. 1 of the 'Tatler,' comments on two plays the production of which was then fresh on everybody's lips—Congreve's 'Love for Love,' and Wycherley's 'Country Wife.' The former had been acted for the benefit of Betterton, and there had not been known so great a concourse of persons of distinction. The stage itself was covered with ladies and gentlemen. In

No. 8 of the same periodical the censor informs his readers that an objectionable comedy composed by Edward Ravens-croft, and first acted in 1682, had been performed 'before a suitable audience, who were extremely well diverted with that heap of vice and absurdity,' although he causes a corre-spondent—'a gentleman òf just taste'—to give expression to his sorrow upon occasion of seeing human nature fall so low in their delights.

I had seen it once (wrote a lady of title in her Diary under date of the year 1715), and I believe there were few in town who had seen it so seldom, for it used to be a favourite play and often bespoke by the ladies.   Went to the play with my mistress : and to my great satisfaction she liked it as well as any play she had seen : and it certainly is not more obscene than old comedies are.   It were to be wished our stage was chaster.

The writer of this passage was Lady Cowper.   Her mistress was the Princess of Wales.   The comedy was the 'Wanton Wife.' Samuel Richardson, in writing to his friend Lady Brad-shaigh under date of June 1748, while frankly acknowledging that a good comedy is a fine performance, felt bound to say that there were then few which could be called good.

Even those that are tolerable (he says) are so mixed with in-decent levities (at which footmen have a right to insult by their roars their ladies in their boxes), that a modest young creature hardly knows how to bear the offence to her ears in the representa-tion, joined with the insults given by the eyes of the young fellows she is surrounded by.

Fielding, in his novel of 'Joseph Andrews,' causes Parson Abraham Adams to observe that he had never heard of any plays which were fit for the perusal of Christians save 'Cato' and the 'Conscious Lovers,' in which latter he owned that there were 'some things almost solemn enough for a sermon.'   The comedy of the 'Conscious Lovers,' which Fielding rightly con-demns for its insipid and languid character, was the composition of Sir Richard Steele, who produced it in 1722.   In many respects it was an admirable comedy, and drew crowded houses.

The great, the appropriate praise of Steele (wrote Dr. Nathaniel Drake), is to have been the first who after the licentious age of

Charles II. endeavoured to introduce the virtues on the stage. He clothed them with the brilliancy of genius; he placed them in situations the most interesting to the human heart; and he taught his audience not to laugh at, but to execrate vice, to despise the lewd fool and the witty rake, to applaud the efforts of the good, and to rejoice in the punishment of the wicked.[1]

Frances Burney, in her first and most successful novel, 'Evelina,' published in 1778, causes the heroine to attend the performance at Drury Lane Theatre of Congreve's 'Love for Love' originally produced in 1695. Evelina in writing to her friend expresses a hope that, abounding in witty dialogue and lively incident as it does, she may never behold it more. 'It is so extremely indelicate—to use the softest word I can—that Miss Mirvan and I were perpetually out of countenance, and could neither make any observations ourselves nor venture to listen to those of others.'[2] Indecorum and licentiousness can scarcely be said to have vanished from the English stage before the appearance of Oliver Goldsmith's comedy, 'She Stoops to Conquer,' and Sheridan's 'School for Scandal.'

In speaking of stage plays, the writer of an entertaining little volume entitled 'The Taste of the Town, or a Guide to all Public Diversions,' published in London in 1731, says:—'All our tragedies are filled with the flagrant crimes of Grecian, Roman, or Turkish tyrants, and our comedies very decently deck'd out with our own boldface follies and nasty vices.' In the next place he confesses that the tragedians of that day put rather too much trust in tedious narration, to the neglect of action; or as Dr. Johnson aptly observed many years afterwards, 'Declamation roar'd whilst passion slept.' A serious indictment is then preferred against the sins of commission and omission on the part of stage managers:—

They don't consider a play (he remarks) as to its merits, the reputation it would bring to their art, or the pleasure or instruction it would give the town. . . . They are less solicitous about this true use of the stage to the world and the dignity of their profession, than they are about filling their pockets, to enable them to rake, and drink, and gamble, as if they had as much right to those vices as the first men of quality in the kingdom.

---

[1] *Essays illustrative of the Tatler*, &c., i. 57.   [2] *Evelina*, c. xx.

The multiplicity of characters on the stage is not allowed to go by uncensured :—

> When the stage is crowded, the greatness of the show casts a mist, as it were, over the eyes of the spectators, and makes the thinnest plot appear full of business. Keep the stage filled thus, you'd instil life and spirit into the dullest play ; the passions will never flag nor the action cool. I have known a tragedy succeed by the irresistible force of a squadron of Turkish turbans and scimitars, and another owe the whole of its merit to the graceful procession of a Mufti and a tribe of priests. A poet who fights cunning will judiciously throw into every act a triumph, a wedding, a funeral, a christening, a feast, or some such spectacle, which must be managed by a multitude. Thus by a well-disposed succession of crowds in every scene he lies, as it were, safe under cover from all criticism.

From the so-called Augustan era to that of the French Revolution, national distinction on the English stage was entirely obliterated, and every hero or heroine of antiquity or of Shakespeare wore the fashionable dress of the passing hour. It never seems to have dawned upon those responsible for the accessories which in theatrical language are known as ' properties,' that actors should be dressed in accordance with the era in which the characters they personated actually lived, or that there was any necessity for consulting authorities on the history of costume. Whenever they did so the result was complete absurdity. The biographer of the celebrated actor Barton Booth, who flourished in the first part of the eighteenth century, records of him that he never omitted to bestow particular attention upon the dress he wore in the several characters he sustained—that for instance, when personating the ' Ghost ' in ' Hamlet,' he was careful to encase the soles of his shoes in felt, not only in order that the sound of his footsteps might be deadened as he stalked along the boards, but that the effect of his supernatural appearance might be heightened. It is a matter for regret that this regard did not extend itself to his impersonation of other characters—the hero, for instance, of Addison's famous tragedy produced in 1712. As to what he did wear on that memorable occasion, Pope says plainly enough in the second book of his ' Imitations of Horace ' :—

Booth enters : hark the universal peal :
But has he spoken ?   Not a syllable.
What shook the stage and made the people stare ?
Cato's long wig, flower'd gown, and lacquer'd chair.

Absurdities equally glaring as these continued for more than eighty years afterwards—the one thing which did not feel the effect of Garrick's chastening hand being stage costume. Theatrical costume fell a sacrifice to what constituted in the eyes of both the public and stage managers, effect.   In 1757 there was published a work entitled Jeffery's 'Collection of Dresses,' in the preface to which the editor writes complacently thus on the subject of dramatic attire, as it then was :—

As to the stage dresses it is only necessary to remark that they are at once elegant and characteristic ; and amongst many other regulations of more importance for which the public is obliged to the genius and judgment of the present manager of our principal theatre [he alludes to David Garrick] is that of the dresses, which are no longer the heterogeneous and absurd mixtures of foreign and ancient modes which formerly debased our tragedies by representing a Roman general in a full-bottomed peruke, and the sovereign of an Eastern empire in trunk hose.[1]

Thus far the writer.   Now let us see what the dresses actually were which he characterises as 'elegant and characteristic,' and which owed their introduction to Garrick's 'genius and judgment.'   In the second volume there appears a representation of Perdita in the 'Winter's Tale.'   What does she wear ?   She wears a pink lutestring dress covered with a white mignonet, a long stomacher, and a hoop festooned with flowers !   Anon, in the same volume, comes a representation of some nameless gentleman as the hero in the masque of 'Comus.'   Of what does his attire consist?   His attire consists of a stiff-skirted coat, over which is thrown a robe of ' pink satin, puft with silver gauze, fastened over the shoulder with a black velvet sash adorned with jewels.   The jacket is of curtained satin ; the collar is black velvet set with jewels, and the boots are blue satin.'   Strange—passing strange—that the 'genius and judgment ' with which the writer just quoted credited the

---

[1] Jeffery's *Collection*, i. 13.

patentee of Drury Lane, did not prevent him from committing the ludicrous mistake of playing Richard III. in a fancy dress, which the pencil of William Hogarth has limned for all time, as well as from personating Macbeth till his retirement from the garish lights in 'a court suit of sky-blue and scarlet.' But if Garrick's eye was slow to note his own deficiencies, the pamphleteers were not backward in directing his attention to it. In the performance of one such, entitled 'The Dramatic Execution of Agis,' published in 1758 on the production of John Home's tragedy of 'Douglas,' he is taken severely to task in that he 'disguised himself for a Grecian chief in the dress of a modern Venetian gondolier,' and that he introduced 'a popish procession made up of white friars, with some other moveables, like a bishop, *des enfans de chœur*, nuns, &c.,' into a play of which the scene was to be laid in ancient Sparta! After this it is not altogether surprising to find Frederick Reynolds stating in his 'Memoirs,' that when a child, in 1765, he saw Barry act Othello in a full suit of gold laced scarlet, a small cocked hat, knee breeches, and silk stockings which conspicuously displayed a pair of gouty legs. John Forster states in his biography of Foote, doubtless on good authority, that Garrick appeared as Othello in a regimental suit of King George II.'s body-guard, with a flowing Ramillies wig. Kirkman describes James Quin as accustomed to play the part of Othello in a large powdered major wig, which, with the black face, made such a magpie appearance of his head as tended more to make the people laugh than cry. Female costume on the stage presented similar anachronisms. Jane Shore, for instance, would pace the boards bedecked with a tower head-dress and a hooped petticoat. Mrs. Yates played Lady Macbeth in a hoop eight yards in circumference. Miss Young, when personating Zara, dressed in much the same style.[1] Another lady performer, whose name is not recorded, thought fit to sustain the character of Cleopatra in a hooped petticoat, a stomacher, and a powdered commode, and holding a jewelled fan in her hand. Mrs. Cibber, we read, in 1753, was decked for

[1] Jeffery's *Collection*, ii. ; Boaden's *Memoirs of J. P. Kemble*, ii. 216, 217.

Juliet in a full white satin dress with an enormous hoop.[1] Before it was relieved of these inconsistencies, English stage costume had to wait for the advent of John Kemble, and even he did not display any particular alacrity in effecting reformation, possibly through distrustfulness of the effect it would produce. His biographer relates that when he first introduced himself to the metropolitan play-goer, he made his appearance in the character of Hamlet, and that he dressed ' in a modern court dress of rich black velvet, with a star on his breast, the garter and pendent, riband of an order, mourning sword and buckles, with deep ruffles ; the hair in powder, which in the scenes of feigned distraction flowed dishevelled in front over the shoulders.' The French Revolution of 1789 effected a remarkable change in the costume of England. The contagion also spread to the *dramatis personæ*, and although by the close of the eighteenth century the costume of the English stage left room for abundant improvement, there is no denying that the last state of it was better than the first. Tate Wilkinson, patentee of the York and Hull Theatres, in the ' Mirror,' the fourth volume of his ' Memoirs,' published in 1790, makes some curious remarks on the subject of theatrical wardrobes of his day. He states that actors arrayed themselves in the cast-off habiliments of 'real lords and dukes,' which were 'bought at much less price than now' (1790).[2]

An old petticoat (he says) made for a large hoop, of the Duchess of Northumberland, thirty years ago would have served a queen in the theatre several years, then descended to a Duchess of Suffolk, afterwards made two handsome tragedy shapes for an old rich Spaniard, and ten years after that turn and produce money to purchase thirty yards of lustring for a modern stage lady. Thirty years ago not a Templar, or decent-dressed young man, but wore a rich gold-laced hat and scarlet waistcoat with a broad gold lace ; as the miser says, ' he carried an estate upon his back ; '—also laced frocks for morning dress. . . . But the gentlemen and ladies in modern dressed tragedies, forty years ago, at Covent Garden Theatre, wore the old laced clothes which had done many years' service at Lincoln's Inn Fields, besides having graced the original wearers ; and the ladies were in large hoops, and the velvet petticoats

---

[1] Boaden's *Memoirs of Mrs. Siddons*, i. 347–8, 363.
[2] Wilkinson's *Memoirs*, iv. 86.

heavily embossed proved extremely inconvenient and troublesome, and always a page behind to hear the lovers' secrets, and keep the train in graceful decorum.[1]

The sneers and reproaches that had under the first Georges been heaped by critics upon the merits of the players—some of which were only too well founded—were destined to vanish before the rise of David Garrick—the greatest actor of modern times—although it was long before actors and actresses showed the working of the new leaven. From the very hour almost in which he became connected with the London stage in 1741, to the hour he took his farewell of it in 1776, Garrick, in the words of Kitty Clive, 'was perpetually engaged in contradicting the old proverb that you cannot make bricks without straw, by doing what is infinitely more difficult, making actors and actresses without genius,' in other words, educating the public from the insipid performances to which it had so long been accustomed, and providing it with intellectual entertainment. Believing as he did that it was to the interest of the best actors that they should be together, Garrick succeeded in bringing around him a' brilliant array of histrionic talent, 'the most powerful,' in the words of Tate Wilkinson, 'ever mustered in the century.'[2] At Drury Lane Theatre, of which Garrick became lessee in 1747, some of the most brilliant stars in histrionic annals were his colleagues—Barry, Delane, King, Macklin, Havard, Quin, Shuter, Sparks, Weston, and Woodward, of the male sex; and Mrs. Abington, Mrs. Winstone, Mrs. Clive, Mrs. Cibber, Mrs. Pritchard, Miss Pope, Peg Woffington, Mrs. Yates, Miss Young, Miss Hippesly, some out of the many of the opposite sex. Terribly uphill work Garrick found it drilling his recruits—separating the chaff from the wheat, the gold from the dross. But his conscientious, painstaking efforts were in the end greatly rewarded. Three years before his death Kitty Clive told him in a letter that 'she had seen him with his magical hammer endeavouring to beat his ideas into the heads of creatures who had none of their own.' 'There are people now on the stage,' she continued, 'to whom you gave

---

[1] Wilkinson's *Memoirs*, iv. 88-9.   [2] *Ibid.* iv. 131.

their consequence ; they think themselves very great, now let them go on in their new parts, and they will soon convince the world what their genius is.' How truly gratifying such an unqualified panegyric must have been to the soul of David Garrick ! Fielding made Partridge say in Book XVI. of ' Tom Jones ' on the occasion of his first visit to the play :—' I am sure if I had seen a ghost, I should have looked in the very same manner and done just as he did '—meaning to say that Garrick's impersonations were nothing out of the ordinary run. Charles Churchill spoke differently and more honestly. In his poem entitled the ' Rosciad,' published in 1761, he satirised the defects of players without mercy. No man escaped from his lash except Garrick. For him he had nothing but unqualified praise. 'Garrick,' he exclaimed, ' take the chair.' And he took it, and what is more, he kept it.

Until Garrick's revival of Shakespeare's dramas, the audaciously ribald comedies—lamentable memorials of the age of Congreve, Wycherley, and Vanbrugh—retained possession of the stage. In these comedies decency was not merely ' most grossly insulted in single speeches and frequently in the whole play, but in the character of the rake, the fashionable debauchee, a moral scepticism was indirectly preached, and marriage was the constant subject of ridicule.' Garrick marvellously extended the popularity of the sublime poet of nature, but did not hesitate in so doing to take liberties with the text which could have been pardonable only on the ground of expediency or of adapting them to the public taste of the age.[1]

The theatrical audiences in the last century were constituted on a very different plan from those of the present day. On the production of a new play, front rows of the pit were almost exclusively reserved for the accommodation of the critics who congregated there, and gave the signal for applause or condemnation. The boxes were entirely occupied by people of rank, note, or fashion. The exquisites attended in full dress, and came more for the purpose of seeing and being seen than for that of attending to the progress of the performance. The ladies con-

---

[1] Davies' *Life of Garrick*, i. 311–5.

ducted themselves in the manner described by Fielding in one of his musical farces ('Miss Lucy in Town') wherein a country-bred damsel, Mrs. Thomas, innocently inquires of Mrs. Tawday what fine ladies customarily did when attending the 'what d'ye-call-em, your plays?' 'Why, if they can,' her informant replies, 'they take a stage box, where they let the footman sit the first two acts to show his livery, then they come in to show themselves, spread their fans upon the pikes, make curtsey to their acquaintances, and then talk and laugh as loud as they are able.' 'Oh, delightful!' she exclaims; 'by gole, I find there is nothing in a fine lady; any one may be a fine lady if that be all.'[1] So much for the deportment of fashionable ladies in an eighteenth-century playhouse. In the fifty-fifth chapter of that veracious autobiography of his, Roderick Random describes the manner in which he conducted himself in a front box at the play, under the misapprehension that the audience regarded him as a beau of the first magnitude. 'I rose and sat down,' he observes, 'covered and uncovered my head, twenty times between the acts, pulled out my watch, wound it up, set it, gave it the hearing again, displayed my snuffbox, affected to take snuff, that I might have an opportunity of showing my brilliant, and wiped my nose with a perfumed handkerchief, then dangled my cane and adjusted my sword-knot, and acted many more fooleries of the same kind, in hopes of obtaining the character of a pretty fellow, in the acquiring of which I found two considerable obstructions in my disposition, namely, a natural reserve and jealous sensibility.'[2] The vulgar and indifferent part of the audience being excluded from the pit

[1] *Fielding's Works*, ed. Murphy, ii. p. 167; Boaden's *Memoirs of Mrs. Jordan*, i. 251.

[2] The reader would err, and that very considerably, were he to suppose that it was the attractions of the stage that induced the majority of fine gentlemen in the last century to resort to the three principal theatres of London. Contemporary light literature bears its emphatic testimony to the fact that it was the attractions presented by the saloons of the playhouses (establishments which partook as much of the nature of brothels as they did of taverns) which filled the benches of the theatres with visitors, and the purses of those who kept them with coin of the realm. The existence of these resorts was the chief inducement for hundreds of men, old and young, to resort to Drury Lane, Covent Garden, and the Haymarket Theatres.

took refuge in the lower gallery, where between the acts they amused themselves with catcalls and other discordant noises.

One of the most absurd customs which prevailed in the theatres during the first half of the last century (one which must have sadly impeded and obstructed every movement on the part of the performers) was that of furnishing people of quality with chairs or stools upon the stage. In this way the theatres often contained two audiences, one on the stage, and another just before the curtain. The consequence was, that on special occasions, when a large audience assembled, the stage was almost covered, and a scene such as the battle of Bosworth Field, for example, was fought in less space than that which was commonly allotted to a cock-fight. It was not until long after 1760 that this absurdity, which had occasioned general complaint, was abolished. Footmen were another source of annoyance at the play. As the reader will have gathered from a passage in one of Fielding's plays which has been cited, they were usually deputed to proceed to the theatres to 'keep places' for their masters and mistresses, and in the discharge of this duty they rendered themselves perfect nuisances. A writer commenting on this system in the columns of the 'Weekly Register' for March 25, 1732, observes :—

The theatre should be esteemed the centre of politeness and good manners, yet numbers of them every evening are lolling over the boxes while they keep places for their masters, with their hats on, play over their airs, take snuff, laugh aloud, adjust their cocks-combs, or hold dialogues with their brethren from one side of the house to the other.

The rule at the theatres was to allow footmen to enter into the gallery when their masters and mistresses had taken their places, a privilege which, as Cibber says, became eventually the most disgraceful nuisance that ever depreciated the theatre. In 1737, Charles Fleetwood, the then manager of Drury Lane Theatre, opposed this objectionable privilege, and caused such occupants of the gallery to be ejected. His action, however, gave rise to a most alarming 'footman riot,' which required no small amount of exertion on the part of the authorities to quell.

Another ridiculous custom was that of stationing two sentinels upon the stage during the representation of a play. Malcolm relates that one night in the month of October 1763, one of the soldiers engaged for this purpose at Drury Lane was so overcome with laughter at the impersonation of Sir Andrew Aguecheek in 'Twelfth Night,' that he actually fell convulsed upon the boards, to the no small amusement of the house.[1] The hour at which the performances in the playhouses began appears to have varied throughout the century. The unfortunate Dr. Dodd, in the first volume of his novel entitled 'The Sisters,' which was published during the course of the year 1754, writes : 'They were at the doors of the theatre before three, and had the high satisfaction to stand there an hour before the doors were opened.' In 1756 the performances at the King's Theatre in the Haymarket commenced at half-past seven o'clock, a time which was then considered very late, as it was fully half an hour behind the two principal theatres. Fourteen years later most of the theatres opened at five o'clock in the afternoon. What were the prices of admission ? At Drury Lane and Covent Garden playhouses, five shillings was charged for admission to the boxes ; two shillings to the pit, and a like sum for admission to the first gallery ; and half that sum for a seat in the second gallery.[2] The main object of such as wished to pose as fine gentlemen was to get behind the scenes ; 'bloods' stepped into the boxes, generally in a half-tipsy condition, and of course attracted all eyes to the spot where they sat, or rather sprawled, by reason of their indecorous behaviour. The pit, as we have seen, was occupied chiefly by the critics, who to denote that capacity smeared their upper lips with snuff. Macklin, referring to the audiences of his time, says that

no indifferent or vulgar person scarcely ever frequented the pit, and very few women. It was composed of young merchants of rising

---

[1] *Anecdotes of London*, ii. 246.
[2] According to Theophilus Cibber's *Life of Barton Booth*, the common prices at Drury Lane Theatre in 1724 were : Boxes 4s., pit 2s. 6d., first gallery 1s. 6d., upper gallery 1s. In 1789, according to Reynolds, the prices at Covent Garden, a small house, were 5s. to the boxes and 3s. to the pit.

eminence, barristers, and students of the Inns of Court, who were mostly well read in plays, and whose judgment was in general worth attending to. The gravity and good sense of the pit not only kept the house in order but the players likewise. Look at your prologues, sir, in those days, and in times long before them, and they all deprecate the judgment of the pit, where the critics lay in knots, and whose favourable opinion was constantly courted.[1]

Angelo mentions that in the latter part of the century it was fashionable to go behind the scenes between the acts and talk to the performers, at the three principal theatres of the metropolis.

The middle-class people, who were those who really paid the most attention to the play, filled the shilling and two-shilling galleries. The ' gods ' crowded into the upper gallery, where they deemed it incumbent upon them to create as much uproar and noise as possible, and to manifest their resentment by ' an occasional shower of oranges and half-eaten pippins, to the infinite terror of the ladies of fashion seated in the pit, where they were so closely wedged as to preclude all possibility of securing a retreat.'[2] The rancour of political feeling which at this time saturated everything, pervaded the theatres. On one side of the house sat ladies who openly proclaimed themselves in sympathy with Tory principles. On the other side of the house dames who considered the interests of the country bound up in Whiggism glared fiercely at them. Every sentence falling from the lips of the performers from which any political significance could possibly be extracted elicited thunders of applause or vehement hisses, just as it chanced to commend itself to the various representatives of political opinions assembled. The lengths to which political sentiment and party clap-trap were carried on the metropolitan stage furnished Sir Robert Walpole with a pretext for passing the famous Licensing Act in 1737, which insisted on the manuscript of every new play being submitted to the scrutiny and censorship of the Lord Chamberlain before it was represented in public.

Some idea of the taste for plays prevalent among our

[1] *Memoirs*, p. 73.
[2] Tate Wilkinson's *Memoirs*, iv. ; Lawrence's *Life of Fielding.*

eighteenth-century forefathers may be conveyed by an enumeration of the dramatic performances which were produced within
the walls of the two chief theatres during a given period of
time—one month for example. Thus an examination of the
theatrical registers for the month of January 1782 shows that
at Drury Lane 'The Beggar's Opera' was represented once,
'The Fair Circassian' four times, 'The Carnival of Venice'
five times, 'The Way of the World' once, 'The Clandestine
Marriage' once, 'Hamlet' once, 'The Maid of the Oaks' four
times. In the same month, at Covent Garden Theatre, 'The
Fair Penitent,' 'The Gamester,' 'Macbeth,' 'As You Like It,'
and 'Henry IV.' were each performed once ; 'Jane Shore'
was represented thrice, and 'The Merry Wives of Windsor'
once. In June of the same year 'The Beggar's Opera'
was performed at the Haymarket Theatre no fewer than six
times, 'The Suicide' four times, 'Jason and Medea' seven
times, 'The Separate Maintenance' three times, and the
'Agreeable Surprise' six times.[1] With regard to the character
of the plays, this much only needs be said, that, although
Garrick and others worked hard during the second half of the
century to eliminate the coarse, obscene, and scandalous
elements which entered only too largely into the composition
of many of them, the state of the stage was very far from satisfactory even in the closing decades of the century, although by
that time the stream of public opinion was being fairly directed
against the coarseness by which it had been so long disfigured.
Foote and other playwrights had introduced a class of dramatic
compositions which, although often of a humble and unpre-
tending character, exercised great influence in developing a
taste for more natural portraiture and language, and these in
turn led the way to those higher productions which are now
venerated as the legitimate comedies of England.

Few of the many popular amusements played a more
important part in the social life of the metropolis in the last
century than the three great fairs—Bartholomew, Southwark,
and May. Bartholomew fair, which had been held in Smith-

field as early as the reign of King Edward I., expressly for the sale of cloth, became under the sway of Queen Anne and the Georges a haunt of pleasure pure and simple, and the centre of appeals to an idle curiosity which suited the taste of a certain class of metropolitan denizens so completely that the civic authorities, scandalised at the 'great profaneness, vice, and debauchery' of which it was the scene, made at different times vigorous, though unsuccessful, efforts to abolish it. This fair annually began on the anniversary of St. Bartholomew's day, August 24, and lasted fourteen days, lovers of the marvellous of course being enabled, meanwhile, to indulge their passion to the full at the innumerable booths, sheds, and stalls which were temporarily pitched in the neighbourhood.

From the subjoined copy of a handbill, dating presumably about 1714, too long for quotation in entirety, it would appear as if our eighteenth-century ancestors had returned to the Mystery plays of their mediæval forefathers :—

At Crawley's Booth, over against the Crown Tavern, in Smithfield, during the time of Bartholomew Fair, will be presented a little opera call'd 'The Old Creation of the World,' yet newly reviv'd, with the addition of Noah's Flood, also, several Fountains playing Water during the time of the Play. The last scene does present Noah and his family coming out of the Ark, with all the Beasts two by two, and all the Fowls of the Air seen in a prospect sitting upon the Trees. Likewise over the Ark is seen the Sun rising in a most glorious manner ; moreover a multitude of Angels will be seen in a double rank, which presents a double prospect, one for the Sun, the other for a Palace, where will be seen six Angels ringing six bells. Likewise, Machines descend from above, double and treble, with Dives rising out of Hell, and Lazarus seen in Abraham's bosom, besides several Figures dancing Jiggs [*sic*], Sarabands, and Country Dances, to the admiration of all spectators ; with the merry conceit of Squire Punch and Sir John Spendall.

However little the 'merry conceit' of Squire Punch might have been in keeping with the subject of these mysteries, certain it is that he was but rarely absent from such performances. An occasional attraction at Bartholomew fair was the firing of a gun by an elephant, as mentioned in some lines of verse printed in the 'Medley' for October 16, 1710, which run thus : —

So have I seen at Smithfield's wondrous fair,
When all his brother monsters flourished there,
A lubberd elephant divert the town
With making legs and shooting off a gun.

As time went on, the occasional attendance of royalty and
the nobility tended in some degree to soften the manners of
'Bartlemy,' and became instrumental in paving the way for
the introduction of exhibitions and entertainments of a superior
character. Among the miscellaneous announcements in
'Dawks's News Letter' for August 27, 1715, appears one announcing that 'there is one great booth erected for the king's
players in the middle of Smithfield,' an allusion to an important
feature, not only of St. Bartholomew's, but of all London fairs
in the days of which we are speaking, namely the erection of
theatrical booths, wherein many of the stars (doubtless attracted
thereto by the high salaries) from the leading metropolitan
theatres performed. Penkethman the elder, who earned the
sobriquet of 'the flower of Bartholomew fair,' was, it is said,
the first actor of repute who performed on the boards of
a temporary playhouse in the fairs. Many other celebrated
actors of the time followed his lead. Quin, Cibber, Macklin,
Edward Shuter (who 'never cared a single pin whether he left
out nonsense or put in'), and others equally renowned in
the annals of the stage, considered it by no means derogatory
to display their histrionic talents to the admiring gaze of a
'Bartlemy' or Mayfair rabble. Indeed, one very sufficient
reason why the fairs in after days fell so terribly low in the scale
lay in the circumstance of the disappearance of the more popular
actors from the theatrical booths, for the middle and upper
ranks of society soon transferred their patronage from the fairs
to other directions, when they found that they were no longer
frequented by the chief actors at Drury Lane and Covent
Garden. For quite nine years of his life, Fielding the novelist
assisted in the management of a theatrical booth in Bartholomew
fair. The 'Daily Post' for August 30, 1732, records that,
'Yesterday the Prince and Princess went to Bartholomew fair,
and saw Mr. Fielding's celebrated droll called the "Earl of
Sussex" and the "Forced Physician," and were so well pleased

as to stay and see it twice performed.' The following is a copy of one of the advertisements relating to the same entertainment :—

> At Mr. Fielding's Great Theatrical Booth in the George Inn Yard in Smithfield, during the time of Bartholomew Fair, will be acted a diverting Dramatic Opera called 'Hunter, or the Beggar's Wedding,' with Alterations, consisting of variety of English, Scots, and Irish Ballad Tunes, with additional Songs never perform'd therein before. N.B. the Booth is very commodious, and the Inn Yard has all the conveniences of Coach room, Lights, &c., for quality and others, and shall perform this evening, at Four, and every day during the time of the Fair ; beginning exactly at Two o'clock, and continuing every hour till Eleven at Night.[1]

A large theatrical booth was supported by three other members of the Drury Lane Company of Comedians (Messrs. Miller, Mills, and Oates), who acted 'The True and Tragic Story of Jane Shore, with the Comical and Diverting Humours of Sir Anthony Noodle and his Man Weazle.' All this time, however, the fair was becoming an eyesore to peace-loving citizens. Protests were set on foot, and in the year 1735 the Court of Aldermen finally resolved, 'touching Bartholomew Fair, that the same shall not exceed Bartholomew's Eve, Bartholomew's Day, and the Day after ; and that during that time nothing but stalls and booths shall be erected for the sale of goods, wares, and merchandise, and no acting be permitted.' As a consequence of this resolution, Bartholomew fair was restricted to its original limit of three days. Within a short time, however, it overstepped its bounds, and had again to be restrained in 1750. Great resistance was always offered to municipal restrictions. In 1760 a man named Buck, acting as 'deputy city marshal,' lost his life in an attempt to quell a disturbance at Bartholomew fair. The following humorous, though undoubtedly strictly accurate, description of this fair was written by the facetious George Alexander Stevens in 1762, just about the time when it was basking in the full sunshine of public favour :—

> Here was first of all crowds against other crowds driving,
> Like wind and tide meeting, each contrary striving ;

---

[1] *Daily Post*, Aug. 23, 1729.

Shrill fiddling, sharp fighting, and shouting and shrieking,
Fifes, trumpets, drums, bagpipes, and barrow girls squeaking,
There was dolls, hornpipe dancing, and showing of postures,
With frying black puddings and opening of oysters,
With saltboxes, solos, and gallery folks squalling,
The taphouse guests roaring and mouthpieces bawling.
Pimps, pawnbrokers, strollers, fat landladies, sailors,
Bailies, jilts, jockies, thieves, tumblers, and tailors.
Here's Punch's whole play of the Gunpowder Plot,
Wild beasts all alive, and pease pudding all hot;
Here's Whittington's cat and the tall dromedary,
The chaise without horses, and Queen of Hungary.
Here's the merry-go-rounds, Come, who rides? Come, who
    rides, sir?
Wine, beer, ale, and cakes, fire-eating besides, sir;
The fam'd learned dog that can tell all his letters,
And some men as scholars are not much his betters.

The pick and flower of London and provincial society came in crowds to enjoy 'the broad laugh,' the varieties of life, and to applaud the 'buds of genius' who were to be found in Bartholomew fair. It is on record that Sir Robert Walpole when premier visited Smithfield, and that in 1740 Prince Frederick of Wales visited the fair, attended by a party of yeomen of the guard bearing lighted torches. Certain 'ill-favoured' persons having openly manifested their aversion to the theatrical booths and puppet shows which had been smuggled into 'Bartlemy,' dramatic performances were once again forbidden in 1763, and for some considerable time afterwards, giants and dwarfs, learned pigs, performing ponies, 'bovine monstrosities,' jugglers, tight-rope dancers, and acrobats, had the entire place to themselves. Puppet-shows, however, contrived to lift up their heads for a short space during 1778. The extracts which have been quoted will sufficiently indicate the character of the amusements that found the most favour in the eyes of those by whom this fair was frequented in the last century. Did time do anything in the way of elevating and purifying their tone? Not in the least. A New England judge who took refuge in this country during the progress of the American War has left in his journal the following record of a visit to Bartholomew fair in 1780 :—

Sept. 2.—Circuited to Smithfield, in order to see the ceremony of opening Bartholomew fair by the lord mayor. Just finished. The whole is a mere rabble rout, relishable only by 'mene peuple ;' conducted by men, women, and children, in painted masks and merry andrew tawdry dresses. The amusements consist in jumping, dancing, riding on round-about horses with legs, speech-making, &c., performed on scaffolds ; together with sleight of hand tricks in front rooms hired for that purpose ; the ascent whereto is by a kind of rough ladder stairs, actors and performers inviting by a thousand antic postures and gestures. Passages round lined with booths and tents, crammed with gingerbread, pastry, and all kinds and varieties of baubles.[1]

The writer of the account of the inauguration of the fair printed in the ' Public Advertiser ' for September 5, 1784, began by saying that ' Saturday being Bartholomew fair day, it was according to annual custom ushered in by Lady Holland's mob.' This mob consisted of a gang of roughs numbering some twenty thousand strong, who systematically anticipated the official proclamation of the fair by parading the streets of Smithfield the day and evening previous, literally making night hideous with their shouting, singing, hooting, bell-ringing, lamp smashing, and other little diversions. Very frequently they broke out into more violent excesses, spreading consternation and terror in every direction they went. The account then goes on to say that they were accompanied by a charming band of music, consisting of marrowbones and cleavers, tin kettles, &c., much to the gratification of the inhabitants of Smithfield. Great preparations were made for the reception of the lord mayor, the sheriffs, and the city officers, who after ' regaling themselves '—a very important part of the programme, according to all accounts—and quaffing ' a cool tankard ' at Mr. Akerman's, made their appearance in the fair about one o'clock, to authorise mimic fools to make real ones of the gaping spectators. ' The proclamation being read, and the lord mayor retiring, he was saluted by a flourish of trumpets, drums, rattles, saltboxes, and other delightful musical instruments. The noted Flockton and the notorious Jobson, with many new managers, exhibited their tragic and comic performers, as did Penley his dolls. There

[1] *Journal and Letters of S. Curwen,* p. 276.

were wild beasts from all parts of the world roaring, puppets squeaking, sausages frying, kings and queens raving, pickpockets diving their hands into everybody's pockets, roundabouts twirling, hackney coaches and poor horses driving, and all Smithfield alive O !' More than enough has perhaps been written of Bartholomew fair, which survived until a date within living memory.

The London newspapers for April 27, 1700, announced that,

> In Brookfield Market Place, at the east corner of Hyde Park, is a fair to be kept for the space of sixteen days, beginning with the 1st of May ; the first three days for live cattle and leather, with the same entertainments as at Bartholomew fair ; where there are shops to be let ready built for all manner of tradesmen that usually keep fairs, and so to continue yearly at the same place.

Mayfair was held annually at the extreme end of Piccadilly, on a plot of land situated on the east side of Hyde Park, which is now covered with mansions. Its duration was sixteen days, and it appears to have yearly attracted large crowds from all quarters of the metropolis down to 1756, notwithstanding two 'presentments' of it as a public nuisance, first in 1708 by the grand jury of Westminster, and subsequently in 1744, by the grand jury of Middlesex. The diary of George Bubb Dodington, Lord Melcombe, contains the following entry under date of October 20, 1749. 'We all went to Ouborn fair ; Prince George in our coach.' One of the chief attractions at Mayfair, as indeed at all others, was 'ducking,' an 'amusing sport,' which will be found described in the subjoined copy of a handbill dated 1748 :—

> At Mayfair ducking pond, on Monday next, the 27th of June, Mr. Hooton's dog (with hardly a tooth in his head to hold a duck, but well known by his goodness to all that have seen him hunt), hunts six ducks for a guinea against the bitch called the Flying Spaniel, from the ducking pond on the other side of the water, who has beaten all she has hunted against excepting Mr. Hooton's Good Blood. To begin at two o'clock. Mr. Hooton begs his customers won't take it amiss to pay twopence admittance at the gate, and take a ticket, which will be allowed as cash in their reckoning. None are admitted without a ticket, that such as are not liked may be kept out. Note.--Right Lincoln ale.

Of the humours and diversions of Southwark fair, an excellent representation may be seen among the works of Hogarth, which, as Samuel Ireland once observed, 'can never fail to excite risibility while the English character lasts, since most of the enterprising heroes of the day, from the monarch of the theatres to the famed Icarus of the rope,' are introduced into it. The figure which is vaulting on the rope was designed by Hogarth for an adventurous Italian named Volante, who achieved considerable notoriety during the reign of George I. ; the tall man who is exhibited on a show-cloth was a giant named Maximilian who was brought over to England from Saxony ; while the individual who is depicted in the act of flying from the church tower represents an acrobat named Cadman, who eventually broke his neck in 1740, while performing one of his feats at Shrewsbury—a mournful event which was commemorated in 'a copy of verses' printed in the February number of the 'Gentleman's Magazine' for that year.

Before dismissing the subject of the London fairs, it may be mentioned that the freezing of the river Thames during the winters of 1715-6, 1739-40, 1788-9 caused a temporary increase in their number. How and what people did at such times is faithfully recorded by those brief and abstract chronicles of the times, the newspapers.

The Thames (remarked the compiler of ' Dawks's News Letter' for January 14, 1716) seems now a solid rock of ice ; and booths for the sale of brandy, wine, ale, and other exhilarating liquors have been fixed there for some time. But now it is in a manner like town : thousands of people cross it, and with wonder view the mountainous heaps of water that now be congealed into ice. On Thursday a great cook's shop was erected there, and gentlemen met as frequently to dine as at an ordinary. Over against Westminster, Whitehall, and White Friars printing presses are kept upon the ice, where many persons have their names printed to transmit the wonders of the season to their posterity.

Numbers of coaches, waggons, and carts were driven over the ice ; and, according to one authority, an enthusiastic preacher saw fit to improve the occasion, and harangued most eloquently a motley congregation which assembled together on the Thames.[1] The historian who has preserved this story gravely adds, that the zeal with which the preacher discoursed was 'fiery enough to have thawed himself through the ice,' had it been at all susceptible to the warmth of religious fervour. In the winter of 1739-40 the Thames was completely frozen over and a fair was held. The same thing happened in the winter of 1788-89. The writer of the 'Common Place Notes' for February 1789 says that 'there were all kinds of diversions ; bear-baiting, festivals, pigs and sheep roasted, booths and turnabouts, and all the various amusements of Bartholomew fair multiplied and improved. From Putney Bridge in Middlesex down to Redriff was one continued scene of merriment and jollity.'

It must not, however, be supposed that the fairs entirely monopolised the whole of the leisure time and attention of the London public in the last century. Quite the reverse, as the newspaper advertisements and press notices relating to all sorts of wonders abundantly testify. Among the announcements, for example, in the issue of the 'English Post' for March 23, 1702, is the one following :—

The effigies of his late Majesty King William III., of glorious memory, is curiously done in wax to the life, richly drest in coronation robes, standing by the effigies of his late Royal Consort, Queen Mary, in the like dress ; likewise the late Duke of Gloucester in his garter robes, together with the effigies of several persons of quality and others, all which are alive or have been so of late years, whereby the spectators may judge of likeness. They are to be seen every day at Mr. Goldsmith's, in Green Court, in the Old Jewry.

Another very popular place of exhibition was Punch's Theatre, situated in the Little Piazza, Covent Garden. This exhibition was opened in 1710 by Robert Powell, a dwarf, who entertained large audiences with 'The History of Susannah,' 'The Diverting Story of Dick Whittington and his Cat,' 'The Destruction of Troy, adorned with Highland dances,' and divers other performances, ranging 'from grave to gay, from lively to severe.' This temple of folly drew such numbers of fashionable votaries away from attendance at divine worship, that the exasperated under-sexton of the neighbouring church

[1] Malcolm's *Anecdotes of London in the Eighteenth Century*, ii. 140, 141.

of St. Paul was obliged to ventilate his grievances in the pages of the 'Tatler.'

Sir (ran his indignant letter to the editor), I have been for twenty years under-sexton of this parish of St. Paul's, Covent Garden, and have not missed tolling into prayers six times in all those years ; which office I have performed to my great satisfaction, until this fortnight past last, during which I find my congregation take the warning of my bell morning and evening to go to a puppet-show, set forth by one Powell, under the Piazzas. By this means I have not only lost my two customers whom I used to place for sixpence apiece over against Mrs. Rachel Eyebright, but Mrs. Rachel herself is gone thither also. There now appears among us none but a few ordinary people, who come to church *only* to say their prayers, so that I have no work worth speaking of but on Sundays. I have placed my son at the Piazzas to acquaint the ladies that the bell rings for church, and that it stands on the other side of the garden ; but they only laugh at the child.

The poor sexton's touching epistle concluded with a request that Mr. Bickerstaff would do whatever lay in his power to remedy so sad a state of affairs. These amusements were diversified by numerous posing exhibitions which abounded in the metropolis. The subjoined is a transcript of a handbill printed about 1711.

At the Duke of Marlborough's Head in Fleet Street, is to be seen the famous posture-master who far exceeds Clarke and Higgins. He twists his body into all deformed shapes, makes his hip and shoulder bones meet together, lays his head upon the ground, and turns his body round twice or thrice without stirring his head from the place.

Punch and Judy shows, and raree shows, were also very numerous about the streets ; and that there were indeed giants in those days will be apparent to all who have dipped into the newspapers of the period.

At the Rummer, in Three Kings Court, Fleet Street, a wonderful tall Essex woman, that had the honour to show herself before their Royal Highnesses the Prince and Princess of Wales, and the rest of the royal family, last Bartholomew Fair, with great applause. She is near seven feet high, and proportionable to her height; though not nineteen years of age. To be seen at any hour from eleven in the morning till eight at night. Any family may see her at their own residences by giving timely notice. Notice, her stay will be but short. *Vivant Rex et Regina.*

Here are other advertisements of other exhibitions of persons of exceptional stature, the first relating to the famous Swedish giant Cajanus, who, according to the generally received accounts, measured eight feet four inches (Swedish) in height.

This is to acquaint all gentlemen and ladies that the Living Colossus, or Wonderful Giant (who has been these five weeks very ill of a fever, which has occasioned a report of his death) is now so well recovered as to be able to show himself to all gentlemen and ladies who will be pleased to honour him with their company, at the same place, at the sign of the Mansion House and French Horn, between the Poultry and the Royal Exchange, at the usual price of 6*d.* each person, from the hour of nine in the morning till eight at night.[1]

The modern Living Colossus, or Wonderful Giant, is to be seen at Mr. Squire's, peruke maker, facing the Mews Walk, within two doors of the Panopticon, Charing Cross, from ten o'clock in the morning till eight at night, at 1*s.* each person.[2]

This is to acquaint the curious that Mr. Blacker, the Modern Living Colossus, or Wonderful Giant, who has given universal satisfaction, is to be seen in a commodious room in Half Moon Court, joining to Ludgate. This phenomenon in nature hath already had the honour of being inspected by great numbers of the nobility and gentry, by many of the Royal Society, and several ladies and gentlemen who are lovers of natural curiosities ; who allow him to be of a stupendous height, and affirm him to be the best proportioned of his size they ever saw. He is to be seen by any number of persons from nine in the morning till nine at night without loss of time.[3]

The number of advertisements relating to 'Young Colossuses,' 'Wonderful Giants,' 'Irish Giants,' and 'Tall Saxon Women,' all fresh from the lands which gave them birth, is well nigh incalculable. Dwarfs and Corsican fairies were quite drugs in the wonder market, and, as in the case of giants, advertisements respecting them may be culled in any number from the files of eighteenth-century magazines and newspapers. The Monthly Intelligence of the 'Gentleman's Magazine' for 1732 records, under date of May 2, that 'a man dwarf, brought from Denmark, not quite three feet high, was presented to their Majesties. He stood under the Duke of Cumberland's arm,

[1] *Daily Adv.* Sept. 27, 1742.
[2] *Ibid.* March 4, 1751.
[3] *Ibid.* Dec. 9, 1752.

which mightily pleased his Highness.' In Ralph Rhymer's Chronicle, contained in the same periodical, under date of December 20, 1735, the public are informed that :

> A dwarf from France arriv'd in town
> Measuring but inches twenty-one,
> At court a wonder great was shown,
> Where he, though aged forty-six,
> Performed twenty childish tricks.

In the 'London Gazette' for January 10, 1752, it is stated that

On Wednesday evening Mr. John Coan, the Norfolk dwarf, was sent for to Leicester House by Her Royal Highness the Princess Dowager of Wales, and was immediately introduced before her, His Royal Highness the Prince of Wales, and all the other Princes and Princesses, where he stayed upwards of two hours.

The 'Daily Advertiser' for Thursday, June 4, 1778, announces that

This Day will be offered to public Inspection, at a commodius Room, opposite the New Inn, Surrey Side of Westminster Bridge, at 1s. each, the Ethiopian Savage. This astonishing Animal is of a different Species from any ever seen in Europe, and seems to be a link between the Rational and Brute Creation, as he is a striking Resemblance of the Human Species, and is allowed to be the greatest Curiosity ever exhibited in England. Just arrived from Abroad, and to be seen in a large commodious Room at a Cheese-monger's, No. 399, opposite Salisbury Street, in the Strand, the grand modle of King Solomon's Temple in curious shellwork, which is allowed to be as fine a Piece of Workmanship as ever was exposed to Public View. Also the Oran Outang, or real Wild Man of the Woods, the surprising Sawfish, with a saw growing out of the Head a yard long, and ten inches broad ; a remarkable large Land Tortoise from the West Indies ; a Calf with eight legs, two tails, two heads, and only one body ; a very remarkable foreign Cat, and an extra-ordinary Exploit done by a White Mouse ; together with many other curiosities.

It would be unprofitable to swell the limits of this chapter by citing more instances of the amusements of the time ; but the reader will have gathered some idea of the immense attractions which such exhibitions possessed for the London citizens in the last century. And from such sports and pastimes as these we must now descend to those of cock-fighting, prize-fighting, boxing, bull and bear baiting, duck-hunting, and the like.

At the New Red Lion Cockpit, near the London Spa, Clerkenwell, this present Monday, being the 12th July, 1731, will be seen the royal sport of cock-fighting for two guineas a battle. To-morrow begins the match for four guineas a battle and 20 guineas the odd battle, and continues all the week, beginning at four o'clock.

The Chronicle of the 'Annual Register' for June of the year 1761 records as follows :—

Thomas Higginson was tried before his Majesty's justices of the peace for the city and liberty of Westminster, on an indictment for a nuisance, to wit, for keeping a place in James Street, near the Haymarket, for his lucre and gain, for boxing, cudgel-playing, cock-fighting, and other disorders, to the great nuisance of that neighbourhood ; of which offence he being convicted, the court set a fine on him, and bound him to his good behaviour for five years.

One of the most notable establishments for these matches was the Royal Cockpit, Birdcage Walk, St. James' Park, the very same which afforded Hogarth characters for his plate, 'The Cockpit.' Cock-fighting continued in the metropolis until the close of the century. So also did duck-hunting, at all the ponds, which were then very numerous around London.

A newspaper paragraph of June 22, 1768, narrates that

On Wednesday last two women fought for a new shift valued at half a guinea, in the Spa Fields near Islington. The battle was won by a woman called 'Bruising Peg,' who beat her antagonist in a terrible manner.

Oct. 8, 1777.—Monday afternoon a terrible battle was fought for 25 guineas in the Hollow by the City Road between one Forrester, a smith, and a butcher from Newport Market, which was won by the latter. The bets depending were many hundred pounds, and the crowds attending incredible, estimated at 12,000, who were continually going from nine till three o'clock.

The 'Weekly Journal' of June 9, 1716, advertises that

At the Bear Garden, at Hockley-in-the-Hole, at the request of several persons of quality, on Monday, the 11th of this instant of June, is one of the largest and most mischievous bears that was ever seen in England to be baited to death, with other variety of Bull-baiting and Bear-baiting ; as also a Wild Bull to be turned loose in the Game Place, with Fireworks all over him. To begin exactly at three o'clock in the afternoon, because the sport continues long.

In 1724 some steps were taken for the suppression of these disgusting spectacles at Hockley, but it is fully evident from the newspapers that they proved absolutely futile until quite twenty years later.

The columns of the newspapers were perpetually studded with challenges from both amateur and professional boxers and prize-fighters, male as well as female. The following are samples of them selected from the 'London Journal' for June 1722 :—

> I, Elizabeth Wilkinson, of Clerkenwell, having had some words with Hannah Highfield and requiring satisfaction, do invite her to meet me on the stage and box with me for three guineas, each woman holding half-a-crown in each hand, and the first woman that drops her money to lose the battle.

Mrs. Highfield signified her acceptance of this challenge in the following terms :—

> I, Hannah Highfield, of Newgate Market, hearing of the resolution of Elizabeth, will not fail to give her more blows than words, desiring home blows and from her no favour ;

and it is satisfactory to learn, on the unimpeachable testimony of the press, that these two Amazons 'maintained the battle with great valour for a long time.' The following advertisement, which is very similar in character, is extracted from the issue of the ' Daily Post ' for October 7, 1728 :—

> At Mr. Stokes's Amphitheatre in Islington Road, this present Monday, being the 7th of October, will be a complete boxing match by the two following championesses :—' Whereas I, Ann Field, of Stoke Newington, ass driver, well-known for my abilities in boxing in my own defence wherever it happened in my way, having been affronted by Mrs. Stokes, styled the European championess, do fairly invite her to a trial of her best skill in boxing for ten pounds, fair rise and fall ; and question not but to give her such proofs of my judgment that shall oblige her to acknowledge me championess of the stage, to the satisfaction of all my friends.'

Answer to the foregoing :—

> I, Elizabeth Stokes, of the City of London, have not fought in this way since I fought the famous boxing woman of Billingsgate 9 minutes, and gained a complete victory, which is six years ago ;

but as the famous Stoke Newington ass woman dares me to fight her for ten pounds, I do assure her I will not fail meeting her for the said sum, and doubt not that the blows which I shall present her with will be more difficult for her to digest than any she ever gave her asses.

Prize-fighting was a recognised sport, and so far from being regarded as brutal, was held to be conducive to manliness. The Right Hon. William Windham, M.P. for Norwich, was an enthusiastic advocate of this as of other so-called manly sports, both in the legislative assembly and out of it ; and many of his contemporaries regarded the national character and the constitutional liberties of the country to be far too closely bound up with them for the connection to be severed. Professors of the noble science of self-defence swarmed all over London. One famous prize-fighter in his own day and generation, who instructed fashionable gentlemen in the use of the small-sword and single-stick, maintained an establishment near the Adam and Eve Court in Oxford Street Road, and figures in one of Hogarth's series of pictures depicting the ' Rake's Progress.'

The following advertisement is extracted from the issue of the ' Daily Advertiser ' for April 26, 1742 :—

Whereas I, William Willis, commonly called by the name of the Fighting Quaker, have fought Mr. Smallwood about twelve months since, and held him the tightest to it, and bruised and battered more than anyone he ever encountered, though I had the ill-fortune to be beat by an accidental fall ; the said Smallwood, flushed with the success blind Fortune then gave him, and the weak attempts of a few vain Irishmen and boys that of late fought him for a minute or two, makes him think himself unconquerable ; to convince him of the falsity of which I invite him to fight me for one hundred pounds at the time and place above mentioned, when I doubt not I shall prove the truth of what I have asserted by pegs, darts, hard blows, and falls.

In the ' Daily Advertiser ' of January 9, 1745, the public are informed that

At Broughton's New Amphitheatre in Oxford Road, the back of the late Mr. Figg's, on Wednesday the 23rd instant, will be exhibited a severe trial of manhood between the following champions, viz. ' I, Edward Morgan, commonly called the Welsh Boy, which same about ten years ago was a terror to the most celebrated boxers now in vogue, especially to the famous Thomas Smallwood and the noted Bellows, both which I beat with ease in one day, being lately returned from ——, hearing of the gallant behaviour of the illustrious Mr. John James, in order to revive my reputation, and increase my honour, do invoke him to fight me for ten pounds, when I doubt not but to put a stop to his conquests, and convince the spectators that the superiority of mankind belongs to Edward Morgan.'

' I, John James, accept the above challenge, and will not fail to meet and fight him for his sum, hoping to continue the character gentlemen have been pleased hitherto to favour me with.—John James.' There will be several bye battles as usual. The doors will be open'd at ten, and the champions mount at twelve.

At the time the poet Gay flourished, bear-baiting spectacles were exhibited so often, that the poet felt constrained to write in his 'Trivia' :—

> Experienc'd men inur'd to city ways
> Need not the calendar to count their days.
> When through the town with slow and solemn air,
> Led by the nostril walks the muzzled bear ;
> Behind him moves majestically dull,
> The pride of Hockley Hole, the surly bull ;
> Learn hence the periods of the week to name,
> Mondays and Thursdays are the days of game.

At Hockley-in-the-Hole there existed an establishment known as the King's Bear Garden, where such exhibitions as the following took place :—

At His Majesty's Bear Garden at Hockley-in-the-Hole, on Monday, 14th of September, 1730, a mad bull is to be dressed up with fireworks over him, and turned loose with the man in the ground. Also a bull to be let loose at the same time, and a cat to be tied to the bull's tail. Note.—The doors will be opened at four, as the sports begin at five exactly, because the diversion will last long, and the days grow short.

In the issue of the ' Daily Advertiser ' of January 29, 1747, it is advertised that,

At the particular request of several persons of distinction, the celebrated white sea-bear which has been seen and admired by the curious in most parts of England, will be baited at Mr. Broughton's amphitheatre this day, being the 29th instant. This creature is now supposed to be arrived at his utmost strength and perfection ; and though there never yet was anyone of this kind baited in Europe, it is not doubted from his uncommon size, excessive weight, and more than savage fierceness, but he will afford extraordinary entertainment ; and behave himself in such a manner as to fill those who are lovers of diversion of this kind with delight and astonishment. Any person who brings a dog will be admitted gratis.

In the columns of the same journal, in the same year, of November 28, the following paragraph makes its appearance :—

We hear there will be a large he-tiger baited on Wednesday next at Mr. Broughton's amphitheatre, in Oxford Road, being the first that ever was baited in England. He is the largest that ever was seen here, being eight feet in length. He is one of the fiercest and swiftest of savage beasts, and it is thought will afford good sport. The doors to be opened at nine and the diversion to begin at eleven.

In a copy of the same journal issued three years later, viz., December 27, 1750, it is announced that ' this day will be baited at the great booth in Tottenham Court, a large Norway bear by two large dogs at a time. None to be admitted under 6*d.* or 3*d.* each.'

The rise of the game of cricket in the national estimation dates from the early part of the eighteenth century. Horace Walpole, in writing on May 6, 1736, of his sojourn at Eton, says :—' An expedition against barge-men or a match at *cricket*, may be very pretty things to recollect ; but thank my stars I can remember things that are very near as pretty.' Thirteen years later (1749) the same writer observes, ' I could tell you of Lord Montford's making cricket matches and fetching up parsons by express from different parts of England to play on Richmond Green.' A very cursory inspection of the history of this game proves that its evolution has been very considerable. Not until the eighteenth century was drawing towards its close did it succeed in establishing itself in the affections of London men. The White Conduit Club was formed in 1780 by Lord Winchelsea, Lord Strathaven, Sir Horace Mann, Thomas Lord, and other well-known personages, who played regularly in the White Conduit Fields, Islington, and in the Artillery Ground, Finsbury Square, until 1789, when for certain reasons they shifted the scene of their operations to a large ground on the site now partly covered by Baker Street and Dorset Square. The Marylebone Cricket Club was formed in 1787.[1]

Among other outdoor sports and pastimes, the useful and charming exercise of football seems to have been the favourite one of the lower orders in the winter months. In the early part of the century it was by no means uncommon to behold the furies of the football war in the porches of Covent Garden or even in the Strand ; and at a time when the sole protection to the lower limbs of gentlemen was afforded by silk stockings, the feelings of nervous pedestrians as they passed that classic thoroughfare may be better imagined than described. Gay has thus depicted a football scene in the second book of his ' Trivia ' :—

> The 'prentice quits his shop to join the crew,
> Increasing crowds the flying game pursue ;
> Thus as you roll the ball o'er snowy ground
> The gathering globe augments with every round.
> But whither shall I run ? The throng draws nigh,
> The ball now skims the street, now soars on high ;
> The dext'rous glazier strong returns the bound
> And jingling sashes on the penthouse sound.

Bowling alleys flourished all over the metropolis, and bowling itself with skittles then constituted the chief pastime of quiet and peace-loving citizens. There were two famous bowling greens in the vicinity of the metropolis, one at Putney, and the other, which stood behind the Manor House of Marylebone ; the latter much resorted to by John Sheffield, Duke of Buckingham. Skittles, too, found much favour, especially among the upper classes.

The noble science of self-defence was greatly patronised during the last century, the chief professor of it being James Figg, who kept an academy (as his business card, drawn by Hogarth, sets forth) ' on ye right hand in Oxford Road near Adam and Eve,' where he instructed gentlemen in 'ye use of ye small backsword and quarterstaff, at home and abroad.' Considering how dangerous the streets were at this time, by night and day, a knowledge of this art was a desideratum. Figg's successor was the celebrated Henry Angelo the elder,

[1] Daniel's *Rural Sports*; Reynolds's *Life and Times*, ii. 275-80; Croly's *Life and Times of George IV.*, i. 172 ; Smith's *Recollections*, p. 179.

author of ' L'Ecole des Armes,' who instructed half the nobility in the art, at his rooms, first in a house in Carlisle Street, and afterwards in the Opera House Buildings, Haymarket. There he remained till 1789, when his establishment being destroyed by fire, he removed to Bond Street, where he continued to give lessons until the time of his death.[1]

Archery, shooting, and rowing were all popular forms of amusement in that age. Proficiency in the last-mentioned was encouraged by Thomas Doggett, a comedian of the early part of the eighteenth century, and one who, as Hone says, was ' so attached to the Brunswick family that Sir Richard Steele called him a Whig up to the head and ears.' Doggett instituted a waterman's orange-coloured coat and a silver badge, to be rowed for by six watermen on the first day of August, the anniversary of the accession of the Hanoverian dynasty, and this has been continued ever since his death, by means of a legacy which he left for the purpose.[2] Strutt says that the legacy provided three prizes to be claimed by three young watermen on condition that they proved victorious in rowing from the Old Swan stairs, near London Bridge, to the White Swan at Chelsea when the current was strongest against them. Eventually the number of competitors was reduced to six, who had not been more than a year out of their apprenticeship. The first English regatta was exhibited on the Thames, between the Ship Tavern, Millbank, and London Bridge, on June 23, 1775. It was very successful, though terminating in a scene of drunkenness and riot.

During the last quarter of the century a mania for ballooning suddenly burst forth. Writing to his friend Sir Horace Mann under date of December 2, 1783, Walpole said :—'Balloons occupy senators, philosophers, ladies, everybody. France gave us the *ton*, and as yet we have not come up to our model.' These words were penned but a very little while after Blanchard's first balloon ascent in France (November 21, 1783) and several spirits in England were ambitious of following his example. We find the Right Hon. W. Windham, M.P. for Norwich, recording in his diary under date of February 8, 1784, that he

[1] Egerton Castle's *Schools and Masters of Fence*, pp. 209-18.
[2] Smith, *Book for Rainy Day*, p. 210-13, ed. 1861.

'did not rise till past nine, and from that time till eleven did little more than indulge in idle reveries about balloons'; and again, under date of 17th of the same month, that he had conversed upon the subject when dining with Sir Joseph Banks at his club. The opportunity of emulating their continental neighbours was not long in coming to Englishmen, for we read that at a quarter before two o'clock on Wednesday, September 15, 1784, Vincent Lunardi, secretary to the Neapolitan embassy, accompanied by a dog, a cat, and a pigeon, ascended in a balloon from the Artillery Ground in London, in the presence of the Prince of Wales, Edmund Burke, Charles James Fox, and a prodigious concourse of spectators, and descended in a field at Standon, near Ware, in Hertfordshire, shortly before six o'clock the same evening. To him belongs the credit of having been the first to make an aerial ascent in this country. On October 16, in the year following, two Englishmen named respectively Blanchard and Shellon ascended in a balloon from Chelsea, and in the following month Sadler started from Oxford on the first of his aerial voyages. On July 7, 1785, Dr. Jefferies and Mr. Blanchard embarked in a balloon from the heights of Dover Castle, and having crossed the Channel in safety, descended in the forest of Guisnes, in France. In the course of the same year no fewer than twenty successful voyages were made; and as Walpole, who was then sojourning in London, in writing to Sir Horace Mann, on May 7, observed :—
'Of conversation the chief topic is air balloons. A French girl, daughter of a dancer, has made a voyage into the clouds and nobody has yet broken a neck; so neither good nor harm has hitherto been produced by these enterprises.' The harm however was to come. In July 1785 two Frenchmen ascended in a balloon from Boulogne. While yet at a vast height, the machine suddenly caught fire, and the occupants being thrown out, were dashed to pieces. After the news of this shocking disaster reached England the ballooning craze began to subside and speedily to give way to some other new thing.[1]

[1] Lunardi's *First Aerial Voyage*, 1784; Turner's *Astra Castra*; Reynolds's *Life and Times*, i. 254–259; Walpole's *Letters*, ed. Cunningham, viii. 451, 493, 505, 511, 512, 550.

CHAPTER VI.

LONDON COFFEE-HOUSES, TAVERNS, AND CLUBS.

Important position held by coffee-houses, taverns, and clubs—Uses of the coffee-houses—Taverns and their votaries—Taverns frequented by Dr. Johnson—Clubs—The spirit of conviviality—The clubs of Queen Anne's time—The October, Scriblerus, and Mug House Clubs—Clubs founded by Dr. Johnson—Cowper and his contribution to the Nonsense Club—Eccentric clubs—The Humbugs' Club—Club-night—Mrs. Elizabeth Montagu and the blue-stockings—Blasphemous clubs—Medmenham Abbey and its monks—The Society of Mohawks.

THE trio which has been placed at the head of this chapter played a part by no means unimportant in the social life of the capital in the last century. To the first of these resorts, although there was nothing remarkable about them, either externally or internally, people of all ranks and conditions repaired daily at stated hours, not so much with the object of sipping 'the black and bitter drink called coffee,' or the waters of the great mineral springs, as with that of lounging, perusing the news-sheets, writing letters, transcribing verbatim the news of the day, discussing politics, concluding bargains, transacting business, and playing cards. The London coffee-houses may be said to have stood, to a very great extent, in the same relation to the general public of those days as the clubs do to us of modern times ; so that a man was sooner asked about the coffee-house he was in the habit of frequenting than his lodging. Appropriately might Juvenal's line, *Quicquid agunt homines*, have been inscribed above their portals. It was ascertained by a competent authority that before the eighteenth century had completed fifteen years of its course the coffee-houses of the capital numbered nearly two thousand, and that by them and in them, every class, profession, trade, calling, occupation, and shade of political opinion was fully represented.[1]

The London clergy discussed the latest items of ecclesiastical and university intelligence either at Truby's or at Child's Coffee House, both of which were situated in St. Paul's Churchyard. Army men took counsel together at Old Man's Coffee House, in the vicinity of Charing Cross. Ardent Whig politicians mustered in great force at the St. James's Coffee House, in St. James's Street, or at the Smyrna in Pall Mall. Tory politicians resorted to the Cocoa Tree in St. James's Street or to Ozinda's (touching which John Macky, in an account he wrote of his ' Journey through England,' observes, ' a Whig will no more go to the Cocoa Tree or Ozinda's, than a Tory will be seen at the Coffee House of St. James's '). Lawyers conversed upon legal technicalities at Nando's Coffee House, situated at the eastern corner of Inner Temple Lane. Artists resorted to Old Slaughter's Coffee House in St. Martin's Lane. The richer citizens and merchants chatted over the rise and fall of stocks at Lloyd's, Garraway's, or Jonathan's, situated in Change Alley ; the former immortalised (in lines sufficiently indicative of the reputation borne by those by whom it was frequented) in Dean Swift's ballad on the infamous South Sea scheme of 1720. Sojourners in London from Scotland generally frequented the British Coffee House. Frenchmen repaired to Giles's. Paymasters, courtiers, and stockjobbers of an inferior class congregated in Old Man's, White's, Tom's, and Littleman's, at which (despite the presence of sharpers and pickpockets) there was playing at piquet and the best of conversation till midnight. At Robins's and Mrs. Rochford's the foreign ambassadors and bankers took financial counsel together. Wits and literary men met either at John's, Child's, Button's, Will's (at the corner of Bow Street), and at a later period at Dolly's Chop House, the Chapter Coffee House in St. Paul's Churchyard, and the Rose by Temple Bar. The

---

[1] Archenholz states that in 1797 there existed several hundred coffeehouses in the neighbourhood of the Royal Exchange alone, and that in them more business was transacted than in the Exchange itself.

virtuosi favoured with their presence Don Saltero's Coffee House in Cheyne Walk, Chelsea.[1]

Several of the coffee-houses just mentioned were immortalised by Steele in the first number of the 'Tatler.' 'All accounts of gallantry,' wrote he in the prefatory note indicative of the scope and intent of that journal, 'shall be under the article of White's Chocolate House,' poetry was to emanate 'from Will's Coffee House,' learning centred at the Grecian in Devereux Court, while the foreign and domestic news was to be dated from 'St. James's Coffee House.' Addison, too, as he himself has told us, might often have been seen thrusting his head into a round of politicians at Will's, or at other times smoking a pipe at Child's Coffee House in St. Paul's Churchyard, and on Sundays at the St. James's. He also mentions that his face was familiar at the parlour of the Grecian, at the Cocoa Tree, and at Jonathan's; Button's Coffee House he renders memorable as the rendezvous of the Spectator's Club.

The modest sum of one penny deposited at the bar of a coffee-house admitted to a long room, generally on the ground floor, though sometimes upstairs, as in the case of Jonathan's, for example, partitioned off into rows and rows of boxes, separated by a central walk, which were filled from early morning till late at night with men of different sorts and conditions. The regulation price of a dish of coffee or tea was twopence, and this also franked the perusal of the daily journals and the chief periodical publications. Smoking was permitted at all except the aristocratic coffee-houses; regular customers had their own seats, and were of course the objects of special attention from the lady superintendent at the bar and her attendant satellites. Letters could be written at the coffee-houses, and addressed to correspondents at them; indeed most of the letters printed in the newspapers will be found to bear the name of one. When Moritz, a Prussian traveller, was sojourning here, in 1782, he relates that he saw a divine hastily pen his Sunday afternoon discourse in a coffee-house.[2] But over and above all else the coffee-house was from first to last the great arena of politics.

[1] De Archenholz, *Picture of England*, 1797, pp. 311–5.
[2] *Travels*, p. 50.

An Englishman (said Goldsmith, writing about the middle of last century), not satisfied with finding by his own prosperity the contending Powers of Europe properly balanced, desires also to know the precise value of every weight in either scale. To gratify this curiosity a leaf of political instruction is served up every morning with his tea. When our politician has feasted upon this he repairs to a coffee-house in order to ruminate upon what he has read and increase his collection.

This fully bears out Addison's humorous testimony of nearly forty years previously, when he gave an account, in the pages of the 'Spectator,' of his ramble through the parishes of London and Westminster, visiting the coffee-houses situated in each, with the object of making himself acquainted with the opinions of 'their particular statesmen' on the current report of the French king's death. Addison's special coffee-house was 'Button's,' which was situated in Russell Street, Covent Garden, whereunto was affixed a letter-box, in form resembling 'a most wide and voracious mouth of a lion's head, in imitation of those in Venice,' through which he requested that all contributions intended for publication in the pages of the 'Guardian' might be dropped. The proprietor of this coffee-house had been at one period of his life in the service of the Dowager Countess of Warwick, whom Addison married in 1716, and after Button had succeeded in establishing himself in 1712 (mainly through the generosity of Addison), the 'Spectator' transferred his patronage thither in company with Steele, Tickell, Swift, Ambrose Philips, and other kindred spirits. In No. 269 of the 'Spectator,' the author of the amusing De Coverley papers states that he accepted the invitation of Sir Roger de Coverley to smoke a pipe with him over a dish of coffee at 'Squire's,' a coffee-house kept by a certain individual of that name in the neighbourhood of Gray's Inn Gate. This furnishes him with an opportunity for supplying one or two particulars of the interior of a coffee-house :—

I waited on him (he writes) to the coffee-house, where his venerable figure drew upon us the eyes of the whole room. He had no sooner seated himself at the upper end of the high table but he called for a clean pipe, a paper of tobacco, a wax candle, and the Supplement, with such an air of cheerfulness and good-humour that all the boys in the coffee-room (who seemed to take a pleasure in serving him) were at once employed on his several errands, insomuch that nobody else could come at a dish of tea until the knight had got all his convenience about him.

In an earlier number of the 'Spectator,'[1] mention is made of Serle's Coffee House, which was situated at the corner of Serle Street, near Lincoln's Inn Square.

I do not know in any of my walks (wrote this great censor of men) objects which move both my spleen and laughter so effectually as those young fellows at the Grecian, Squire's, Serle's, and all other coffee-houses adjacent to the law, who rise for no other purpose but to publish their laziness.

It may be observed that the 'Grecian' herein mentioned stood in Devereux Court, Strand, and was one of the coffee-houses which found favour in the eyes of 'Mr. Bickerstaff' of the 'Tatler' before his creditors compelled him to retire into Wales. The reputation which it enjoyed was so great that Fellows of the Royal Society deemed it no detraction from their dignity to be seen within its walls, since Ralph Thoresby records in his 'Diary,' under date of May 22, 1712, that he 'walked to meet Dr. Sloane, the Secretary of the Royal Society, at the Grecian Coffee House by the Temple'; and again, under date of the 12th of the following month, that he 'attended the Royal Society, where were present, the President (Sir Isaac Newton), both the secretaries, the two professors from Oxford, Drs. Halley and Kell, whose company we often enjoyed at the Grecian Coffee House.' Dear, too, was this notable establishment to the soul of the author of the 'Vicar of Wakefield,' during that period of his eventful career when he was supposed to be prosecuting the study of 'Coke upon Littleton' in the Temple, seeing that it had become the favourite resort of the Irish and Lancashire Templars, whom he delighted to collect around him and to entertain with a cordial and unostentatious hospitality, and occasionally with his flute or with whist.

Another notable London coffee-house which was much patronised in those times was the Turk's Head Coffee House, No. 142, Strand. It was there that Dr. Johnson was in the

[1] No. 49.

habit of supping, 'on purpose,' as he used to say, 'to encourage the hostess, who was a good civil woman, and had not too much business.' Equally celebrated was the Bedford Coffee House, which stood beneath the Piazza in Covent Garden, and was signalised according to 'Genius,' the anonymous author of the interesting 'Memoirs' of it published in 1763, for many years, as 'the emporium of wit, the seat of criticism, and the standard of taste' :—

The situation of this place (wrote the Genius) necessarily makes it a convenient assembly for those who frequent the theatres, as well as those who exert their talents to please the public in dramatic performances ; and for the same reason it may be looked upon as the centre of gravitation between the court and the city ; the noxious effluvia of St. Bride's is here corrected by the genuine eau-de-luce from Pall Mall, and the predominance of ambergris at St. James's is qualified by the wholesome tar of Thames Street. Nor does the conversation receive a less happy effect from this junction ; the price of stock and the lie of the day from the Alley are softened by the *bon mot* of Lady Dolabella which set every soul at the Duchess Trifle's rout in a titter, or the duel that was fought this morning between Captain Terrible and Lord Puncto, when both of them were mortally wounded in the coat.[1]

Samuel Foote, Henry Fielding, Arthur Murphy, and Dr. Arne frequented the Bedford. Another contemporary writer states that this coffee-house

was every night crowded with men of parts. Almost everyone you meet is a polite scholar and a wit. Jokes and *bon mots* are echoed from box to box ; every branch of literature is critically examined, and the merit of every production of the press or perform-ance of the theatres weighed and determined.

The 'Lion's Head at Button's,' which had been removed to the Shakespeare Tavern, under the Piazza in Covent Garden, was in 1751 placed in the Bedford Coffee House as the letter-box for contributions to the 'Inspector,' a journal con-ducted by the notorious quack, Dr. Hill.

For many years a rude shed underneath the portico of St. Paul's Church in Covent Garden did duty as Tom King's Coffee House, 'well-known,' as was remarked by a wit of the time, 'to all gentlemen to whom beds are unknown.' On the death

[1] *Memoirs*, pp. 2–3.

of Tom King his establishment passed into the hands of a certain 'witty woman' named Moll King, under whose management it was frequented night after night by fashionable fops and noblemen 'attired in swords and bags and rich brocaded silks,' after they had quitted the court.

Great numbers of country visitants to the metropolis at the time frequented George's Coffee House, which stood in the Strand, within a stone's throw of Temple Bar. William Shenstone, 'the poet of the Leasowes,' he who once expressed his conviction in lines which have often been quoted to the effect that

Whoe'er has travelled life's dull round,
  Where'er his changeful course has been,
Will sigh to think how oft he found
  His warmest welcome at an inn ;

and who, being a bachelor, passed in consequence much of his time in coffee-houses on his occasional visits to the metropolis, has left on record that, in point of economy, George's Coffee House left nothing to be desired :

What do you think (inquires he, writing from town in 1739, of one of his correspondents) must be my expense, who love to pry into everything of this kind ? Why truly, one shilling. My company goes to George's Coffee House, where for that small subscription I read all pamphlets under a three-shillings dimension, and indeed any larger ones would not be fit for coffee-house perusal.[1]

Last, but by no means least, on the list of the most famous coffee-houses that London had to boast in that age, should be mentioned the St. James's, which among other things is notable as having provoked Goldsmith's celebrated poem, 'Retaliation.' The poet and some of his friends, Edmund Burke, David Garrick, and Sir Joshua Reynolds, frequently dined together at the St. James's Coffee House. There one day it was proposed to compose epigrams upon him, his nationality, his dialect, and peculiarities furnishing a rich theme for witticism. Goldsmith was called upon to retaliate, and when the company next met, he read to them a poem bearing the name of 'Retaliation,' which contains much of that shrewd observation.

[1] *Works,* ed. 1769, iii. 13 ; Foote's *Life of Murphy.*

wit, and sprightliness which so remarkably distinguish his prose writings.

About the latter quarter of the eighteenth century, the coffee-house, which had always been more or less infested with infamous characters, became completely overrun with them. In 1776 Sir John Fielding (a brother of the celebrated novelist of that name), who was at that time a presiding magistrate at Bow Street, in writing a handy guide for the use of strangers to the metropolis, devoted a section to a series of 'necessary precautions to all strangers' to be on their guard against pickpockets and sharpers when frequenting the coffee-houses [1] :

Having been equally profuse of their own substance and character (he remarks), and learned, by having been undone, the ways of undoing, they lie in wait for those who have more wealth and less knowledge of the town. By joining you in discourse, by admiring what you say, by an officiousness to wait on you and assist you in anything you want to have or know, they insinuate themselves into the company and acquaintance of strangers, whom they watch every opportunity of fleecing. And if he finds in you the least inclination to cards, dice, the billiard table, bowling-green, or any other sort of gaming, you are morally sure of being taken in. For this sort of gentry are adepts in all the arts of knavery and tricking. If, therefore, you should observe a person, without any previous acquaintance, paying you extraordinary marks of civility; if he puts in for a share of your conversation with a pretended air of deference; if he tenders his assistance, courts your acquaintance, and would be suddenly thought your friend, avoid him as a pest ; for these are the usual baits which they set to catch the unwary.[2]

From the London coffee-houses it is but fitting that we should proceed to the London taverns, which greatly abounded and were frequented by men in every rank of life above that of the common workman. Dr. Johnson often asserted, in the hearing of Sir John Hawkins, that 'a tavern chair was the throne of human felicity.' 'There is nothing,' said he, 'which

---

[1] It is worthy of note that in the closing years of the eighteenth century the London coffee-houses declined greatly in number. Boaden, in his *Memoirs of Mrs. Siddons,* mentions that actors no longer frequented them. Foote, who died in 1777, deplores, in his *Life of Arthur Murphy,* 'the disappearance of the coffee-houses where the town wits met of an evening.' Dr. Johnson died in 1784, and if there was any foundation for Foote's regrets, the sage must have survived nearly the last of the coffee-houses of what may be termed the Johnsonian period.

[2] *Guide to London,* 1776, p. xxvi.

has been yet contrived by man by which so much happiness is produced as by a good tavern or inn.' Taverns were very numerous, and were known by the signs of Blue Boars, Red Lions, and other nondescript animals. Horace Walpole declares that in the early part of the century women customarily resorted to taverns, but this custom must have been one which soon died out, as there is no mention of it by anyone else. Several of the most famous taverns of eighteenth-century London are associated with the name of Dr. Johnson. There was the famous Mitre Tavern, 'where he loved to sit up late;' the still more famous Boar's Head Tavern in Eastcheap, within the walls of which Oliver Goldsmith penned his well-known 'Reverie;' the Queen's Arms in St. Paul's Churchyard; and probably Pontack's, where the perfection of culinary delicacies might be procured at prices ranging from four or five to twenty-one shillings per head. Smith, in his 'Antiquarian Ramble,' says that this famous establishment, 'probably the first house for genteel accommodation in eating known in the metropolis,' stood in Christ Church passage, leading from Newgate Street to Christ Church, nearest to Bagnio Court. It was opened by a Monsieur Pontack, who had acted in the capacity of president of the parliament of Bordeaux, not long after the accession of King William III., and flourished till the last quarter of the eighteenth century, when the house was pulled down. Dean Swift constantly frequented Pontack's ordinary, and Mrs. Pendarves, writing to her friend Mrs. Anne Granville on April 22, 1740, of a day's sight-seeing in the metropolis, mentions that from the Tower and the Mint she proceeded 'to Pontack's to a very good dinner;'[1] while among the curious memoranda contained in a pocket-book belonging to Thomas Wale, Esq., of Little Shelford in Cambridgeshire, is one to the effect that, being in London in July 1742, he disbursed for a 'dinner at Pontack's 4s. 6d.'[2]

The Pope's Head, in Pope's Head Alley, leading from Cornhill to Lombard Street, was much resorted to until the

---

[1] *Autob. and Corr. of Mrs. Delany*, 1st series, ii. p. 82.
[2] H. J. Wale's *My Grandfather's Pocket Book*, p. 91.

latter end of the reign of George II. So were the Cock
Tavern in Threadneedle Street, and the Crown Tavern behind
Change ; the Salutation and Cat in Newgate Street, Dolly's
Chop House in Paternoster Row, and the Fountain, commonly
called the Mourning Bush,[1] 'which had a back door into
St. Anne's Lane, and was situated near unto Ludgate.'[2]
Other well-known taverns in London during this period were
the Old Black Jack Tavern, or the Jump, in Portsmouth Street,
Lincoln's Inn Fields, where actors and dramatists assembled ;
the King's Head in Fenchurch Street ; the Globe Tavern in
Fleet Street ; the Devil Tavern, mentioned by Swift and Steele
(which stood in the same locality, not far from the Mitre, the
favourite supper-house of Johnson and his friends) ; the
Crown and Anchor in the Strand, described as 'a large and
curious house, with good rooms and other conveniences fit for
entertainments ;' the Fountain Tavern, also in the Strand,
described as 'a very fine tavern, with excellent vaults, good
rooms for entertainments, and a curious kitchen for dressing
of meat, which with the good wine sold there, made it well
resorted to ;'[3] the notorious Cock Tavern in Bow Street ; the
Rose in Covent Garden, the haunt of dramatic authors, the
principal room of which was depicted by Hogarth in the
third picture of the series representing the 'Rake's Progress'
(Leathercoat, the man holding a candle and a bright pewter
dish, represents one of the porters attached to the house) ; the
Salutation, in Tavistock Street, Covent Garden, the Rummer
Tavern near Charing Cross, the Star and Garter in Pall Mall,
whither people of quality drove 'to regale on macaroni ;'[4] the
Thatched House in St. James's Street, besides numerous
others which were established in the suburbs and outskirts of
the capital.[5]

---

[1] Maitland's *Hist. of Lond.*
[2] *Strype, Survey of London and Westminster.*
[3] *Ibid.* [4] *Conn.* 1754.
[5] Sir John Hawkins, in his *Life of Johnson* (1787) says, that in the space
near the Royal Exchange which was encompassed by Lombard Street,
Gracechurch Street, part of Bishopsgate and Threadneedle Streets, the
number of taverns was not so few as twenty. He further states that on
the site of the Bank of England, there stood within his recollection four
taverns, and at the Crown, which was one of them, it was not unusual to.

According to the 'Memoirs' of his own life, Charles Macklin, the celebrated actor, was induced to take his final leave of the stage in 1753, by reason of a scheme upon which he had been long previously cogitating, of suddenly making his fortune by the establishment of a tavern and coffee-house, combined with a school of oratory in the Piazza, Covent Garden.[1] It appears that he started a three-shilling ordinary, at which he presided and carved. It must have speedily acquired celebrity, since Fielding in his 'Voyage to Lisbon' (1753) remarked that 'unfortunately for the fishmongers of London, the dory only resides in the Devonshire sea, for could any of this company only convey one to the temple of luxury under the Piazza, where Macklin the high priest duly serves up his rich offerings, great would be the reward of that fisherman.' In connection with taverns, it may be mentioned that a pamphleteer, writing in or about 1735, stated that it was then by no means an uncommon practice for tavern-keepers to enlist the services of certain individuals commonly called 'decoy ducks' for the purpose of inveigling the passers-by into their establishments.

They are for ever (he wrote) establishing clubs and friendly societies at taverns, and drawing to them every soul they have any dealings or acquaintance with. The young fellows are mostly sure to be their followers and admirers, as esteeming it a great favour to be admitted amongst their seniors and betters, thinking to learn to know the world and themselves. . . . In a morning there is no passing through any part of the town without being hemmed and yelped after by these locusts from the windows of taverns, where they post themselves at the most convenient views to observe such passengers as they have but the least knowledge of ; and if a person be in the greatest haste, going upon extraordinary occasions, or not caring to vitiate his palate before dinner, and so attempts an escape, then, like a pack of hounds, they join in full cry after him, and the landlord is detached upon his dropsical pedestals, or else a more nimble-footed drawer is at your heels bawling out 'Sir ! Sir ! it is your old friend Mr. Swallow who wants you upon particular business.'

---

draw a butt of mountain, 120 gallons, in gills, in a morning. It was then a common practice for tradesmen to muddle away their time at taverns (nearly all of which were brothels) or to get uproariously drunk at them, being sent for thither to their counting-houses or shops when business could not be transacted without them.

[1] *Memoirs*, p. 199.

The resort to taverns declined in the latter quarter of the eighteenth century. 'It is worthy of remark,' said Sir John Hawkins, writing in 1787, 'by those who are curious in observing customs and modes of living, how little these houses of entertainment are now frequented, and what a diminution in their number has been experienced in London and Westminster in a period of about forty years backward.'[1]

The spirit of conviviality was never more widely diffused among Englishmen than it was in the last century, and if any decisive proof as to this were needed, it would be unnecessary to do more than point to the many societies of men of like tastes who met at stated intervals at some chosen coffee-house or tavern in the capital for social intercourse and amusement ; societies which were popularly known under the designation of clubs. One of the many epithets which might be not inaptly bestowed upon the age is 'era of clubs,' for it is certain that never before and never since were such 'little nocturnal assemblies' as Addison styled them established in greater number than they were then. The increase in their number may be dated from the opening years of the century, and the essayists of the reign of Anne did much towards making them both fashionable and popular, and to elevate them to an eminence in public estimation which, it may be confidently affirmed, they are destined never to resume. The chronicles of many of the clubs that were in existence up to that date are contained in a very scarce and curious volume entitled 'The Secret History of Clubs,' which is generally admitted to have been the composition of the eccentric poet Ned Ward, author of 'The London Spy,' who died in 1731. This book, in common with

---

[1] *Life of Johnson,* p. 87. As Sir John Hawkins was a justice of the peace and chairman of the Middlesex Quarter Sessions, he had the means of being correctly informed on this subject, but as he was also a man of the world, it is likely that he derived his knowledge from personal observation. Yet the decline of the habit of resorting to taverns to which he alludes must have been limited only to the upper ranks of society. Place bears his testimony to the fact that long after 1787 every sort of business was still transacted in taverns, that sales were held in them, that goods and merchandise were still bought and sold within them, and that attorneys resorted to them to transact their avocations at all hours of the day over the bottle.

all Ward's writings, while containing much that is coarse, contains also not a little that is amusing, instructive, and perfectly true. One of the first nocturnal assemblies of which Ward's book furnishes an account is the Virtuoso's Club, which, he says, owed its establishment to some of the leading spirits of the Royal Society, and held its meetings every Thursday at a certain tavern in Cornhill.

Its chief design was to propagate New Whims, advance Mechanic Exercises, and to promote useless as well as Useful Experiments ; and in order to carry on this commendable undertaking any Frantic Artist, Chemical Operator, or Whimsical Projector that had but a crotchet in their heads, or but dreamed themselves into some strange fanciful discovery, might be kindly admitted as welcome brethren into this teeming society.

The author then proceeds to give an account of the sayings and doings of a 'rattle-brained society of mechanic worthies,' who dubbed themselves Knights of the Order of the Golden Fleece in Cornhill ; of the No-Nose Club which met at the Dog Tavern in Drury Lane ; the Surly Club, ' chiefly composed of master carmen, lightermen, and old Billingsgate porters, which met at a tavern in Billingsgate ;' the Atheistical Club, held for several years at 'an eminent tavern in Westminster,' the members of which were 'whimsical physicians, half-learned gentlemen, crack-brained philosophers, and conceited libertines ;' the Club of Ugly Faces, consisting of those to whom nature had been exceedingly unkind ; the Split-Farthing Club, 'a parsimonious society of canary-bibbing citizens, who held their weekly meeting at the Old Queen's Head in Bishopsgate ; the club of Broken Shopkeepers, who met at the sign of Tumbledown Dick, near the Mint, and by turns anathematised their creditors and bewailed their misfortunes ; the Man Hunter's Club, the members of which frequented a tavern near the Tennis Court Playhouse, at the back of Lincoln's Inn Fields, and who were accustomed to 'hunt' for amusement all the benighted pedestrians they chanced to meet ; the Yorkshire Club, held at a house in the Rounds, in Smithfield, upon every market day, 'where Northerners, by consulting one another, might be the better able to exercise their cunning in this southern air, and maintain that character they have justly deserved;' the Mock Heroes' Club, 'a heroic society of fantastical bravadoes,' which was held at an alehouse in Baldwin's Gardens, and composed chiefly of 'attorneys' clerks and young shopkeepers whose juvenile prodigality had infected them with being thought brave fellows;' the Beau's Club, 'a finikin society, or Lady's lap-dog Club, kept at a certain tavern near Covent Garden, where every afternoon the fantastical idols so much worshipped and admired by female beauties assembled themselves into a body to compare dresses and invent new fashions; the Wrangling or Hustle Farthing Club, 'a promiscuous society of contentious mortals' who met every night at a tavern in Shovel Money Street, 'where they wrangled over their claret about the Grand Preliminaries and their several Politicks;' the Quacks' Club, held at a certain tavern near the Change, 'where the Emperials (*sic*) of the Town might not only be of mutual service to each other, but defend their Pretensions to Physic, Chemistry, and Pharmacy against the clamorous Insults of the regular Physicians, Chemists, and Apothecaries;' the Bird Fanciers' Club, which held its meetings weekly at a little alehouse in Rosemary Lane, none being admitted members thereof but such whose affection to the feathered kind rendered them fitter company for jackdaws and magpies than for their own fellow-creatures;' the Lying Club, the local habitation of which was fixed at the Bell Tavern, in Westminster, one rule of which was 'that whoever shall presume to speak a word of truth between the established hours of six and seven within the worshipful society without first saying with an audible voice, "by your leave, Sir Harry," shall for every such offence forfeit one gallon of such wine as Mr. Chairman shall think fit;' and the Beggars' Club, 'a mendicant society of old bearded hypocrites, wooden-legged implorers of good Christian charity, strolling clapper dudgeons, limping dissemblers, sham disabled seamen, blind men, and old broken labourers,' who were in the habit of meeting at 'a famous tavern in the middle of Old Street.' Here it may be well to pause, although the list has not by any means been exhausted. According to Ward, 'a parcel of young gentlemen who were pretenders to wit and great adorers of the Muses, formed themselves into a society which they kept at the Rose Tavern in Covent Garden,' styling themselves the Scatterwit Club. Then there was an odoriferous society, 'called the Florists' Club, consisting of pink and tulip worshippers who would walk ten miles to see a new stripe in a clove gilliflower, or gaze away whole hours upon an odd-coloured daisy.' This club, states the 'London Spy,' 'preserved an amicable conversation at the sign of the Four-legged Emperor, near Hoxton Hospital.' Completing Ward's list we have the Cellar Club, the members of which were improvident people who held their meetings every evening 'in a little cellar about six foot under ground,' at the sign of the Still, in the Strand ; the Smoking Club, which received none but devotees of the weed, held at a music shop at the Temple Gate ; the Thieves' Club, 'a society of audacious desperadoes who kept their daily rendezvous at the sign of the Half Moon in Old Bailey ; ' and the Small Coalman's Music Club, held at a tavern in Clerkenwell.

In addition to those which have been enumerated, there were four famous political clubs established during the reign of Anne, concerning which several interesting facts are supplied in the pages of the diary kept by Jonathan Swift, Dean of St. Patrick's, Dublin, more commonly known, perhaps, as his 'Journal to Stella.' The titles of these four societies were the October, the March, the Saturday, and the Brothers. Writing under date of February 18, 1710–11, Swift says :—

We are plagued here with an October Club ; that is, a set of above a hundred parliament men of the country, who drink October beer at home, and meet every evening at a tavern near the parliament, to consult affairs, and to drive things on to extremes against the Whigs, to call the old ministry to account, and get off five or six heads.

Sir Walter Scott aptly remarks in his edition of Swift's works, that this club of country gentlemen, swayed by their prepossessions and totally unable to discover through the mist of prejudice the true road either to the interest of their party or to that of their country, nearly ruined by their embarrassing violence the administration which as Tories it was their chief business to support.[1]

It was upon Dean Swift that the duty devolved, in 1711, of framing the rules of the Brothers' Club, the end of which was to advance conversation and friendship, and to reward learning without interest or recommendation, 'none being admitted but men of wit or men of interest.' Three years later the dean, in conjunction with Pope, Gay, and Arbuthnot, succeeded in founding the renowned Scriblerus Club as a rendezvous for men of letters in general. The Scriblerus Club might have existed longer than it did had it not been for the violence of party faction, which, as Sir Walter Scott truly observes in his memoir of Swift, 'like a storm that spares the laurel no more than the cedar, dispersed the little band of literary brethren, and prevented the accomplishment of a task for which talents so extended and so brilliant can never again be united.'

The most famous club which was instituted in the reign of Queen Anne remains to be mentioned. This was the Kitcat Club, which comprised a perfect galaxy of wits and distinguished Whig statesmen. If the testimony of Ward counts for any value, the Kitcat Club 'had first the honour to be founded by an amphibious mortal, chief servant to the Muses; and in these times of piracy both bookseller and printer.' It has been supposed that the individual who is here darkly alluded to was none other than Jacob Tonson, a famous London bookseller of the day. This may or may not be correct, but the supposition that the Kitcat Club owed its institution to him is, to say the least of it, improbable. The assertion that it held its meetings at a house in Shire Lane belonging to a famous mutton-pie-man named Christopher Katt (from whom both the club and the pies that formed a standing dish at its suppers derived their name of 'Kitcat') is one which lends itself much more readily to acceptance. But whoever may have founded the club, the celebrated and eccentric actress Peg Woffington long acted as its president, while Halifax, Somers,

[1] Swift's *Works*, ed. Scott, ii. 183.

Addison, Congreve, Vanbrugh, Garth, the Dukes of Somerset, Richmond, Grafton, Devonshire, Marlborough, and Newcastle, the Earls of Dorset, Sunderland, and Manchester, Sir Robert Walpole, Granville, Maynwaring, Stepney, and Walsh were some among its eminent members. Though entertaining strong political views, the Kitcats nevertheless prided themselves on being both literary and gallant. Thus it is recorded that in 1709 they subscribed the sum of 400 guineas towards a fund for the encouragement of the production of good comedies. Toasting glasses, each inscribed with some appropriate lines of verse addressed to certain toasts or reigning beauties of the Augustan era, were used by the members of the Kitcat Club at their weekly meetings, and among those who were thus honoured were the four daughters of the Duke of Marlborough, Lady Godolphin, Lady Sunderland, Lady Bridgwater, Lady Monthermer ; and the Duchess of Bolton, Mrs. Brudenell, Lady Carlisle, Mrs. Long, Mrs. Burton, and Lady Wharton.

Queen Anne died on August 1, 1714, and within two months after her decease the Elector of Hanover ascended the throne of this realm under the style and title of George I. His accession was accepted only partially by the nation, in particular by the London citizens, who were strongly leavened with Toryism. Hence arose explosions. Whig loyalty found expression in the establishment of the Mug House Club, the members of which, who were recruited from the upper ranks of society, held their meetings twice a week during the winter months in Long Acre. There were several other clubs, however, in existence about this period which bore the same name. One such was held at the Ship Tavern, which was situated in Tavistock Street, Covent Garden, and was frequented mostly by army officers. Another found a local habitation and a name at the Black Horse in Queen Street, Lincoln's Inn Fields ; a third fixed its abode at the Nag's Head in James Street, Covent Garden ; a fourth at the Fleece in Burleigh Street, near Exeter Change, and so on. The members of these clubs were all avowedly hostile to the claims which the Chevalier St. George, the direct heir of the Stuarts, asserted to the crown, and they contributed greatly by their repression of tumultuous assemblies in his favour to secure the establishment of the Hanoverian dynasty on the throne. On several occasions the members of the Loyal Society, the head-quarters of which were located at the Roebuck Tavern in Cheapside, sallied forth into the streets at night and succeeded in dispersing the bands of Jacobite rioters who figure so prominently in the pages of English history between the years 1715 and 1722.

Let us now glance briefly at some of the most notable clubs that figured in London from the date of their establishment until that which marked the era of their declension. In 1735 there was formed in the capital the celebrated Beef Steak Club, or 'Sublime Society of Beef Steaks,' as its members always desired it to be designated. The origin of this club is sin-gular, and was on this wise. Rich, a celebrated harlequin, and patentee of Covent Garden Theatre in the time of George II., while engaged during the daytime in directing and controlling the arrangements of the stage scenery was often visited by his friends, of whom he had a very numerous circle. One day, while the Earl of Peterborough was present, Rich felt the pangs of hunger so keenly that he cooked a beef-steak and invited the earl to partake of it, which he did, relishing it so greatly that he came again, bringing some friends with him on purpose to taste the same fare. In process of time the beef-steak dinner became an institution. Some of the chief wits and greatest men of the nation, to the number of twenty-four, formed themselves into a society, and took as their motto 'Steaks and Liberty.' Among its early celebrities were Bubb Dodington, Aaron Hill, Dr. Hoadley, Richard Glover, the two Colmans, Garrick, and John Beard. The number of the 'steaks' remained at its original limit until 1785, when it was augmented by one, in order to secure the admission of the Heir-Apparent.[1]

Eight years after the institution of the 'Sublime Society of Beef Steaks,' the Royal Society Club was founded. The members of this club (which subsequently came to be styled the

---

[1] Peake, *Memoirs of the Colmans*, i. 174.

Thursday's Club of Royal Philosophers) met at first in the Mitre Tavern in Fleet Street, over against Fetter Lane, and subsequently at the Crown and Anchor Tavern in the Strand. This club was established primarily for the convenience of certain Fellows of the Royal Society who resided at a distance, in order that they might assemble and dine together on such days as that Society held its meetings.

When the Pandemonium Club was first established, or to whom it was indebted for its initiation, are points upon which the annals of clubs preserve a solemn silence, but a society dignified with this title held its meetings at a house in Clarges Street, Mayfair, while a similar gathering took place at the Blenheim Tavern-in Bond Street.

Any notice of the London clubs of the eighteenth century would be necessarily imperfect if it omitted to say anything about those with which Dr. Samuel Johnson had connections. Of all the many denizens of London in the Georgian era, none exceeded in his partiality for nocturnal assemblies the venerable sage of Fleet Street. Johnson was essentially what Boswell once termed him, 'a clubbable man,' and it is worth noting that every such society in which he bore lot or part seems to have fulfilled to the letter the Johnsonian definition of one, which the reader at all familiar with the 'Dictionary' will remember was, 'an assembly of good fellows meeting under certain conditions;' a definition which, however appropriate then, would scarcely apply at the present time. During his literary career Dr. Johnson assisted in the foundation of no fewer than three clubs, each of which was fully deserving of the name. In 1749 he established a club at a house in Ivy Lane, Paternoster Row, and only the year before he died he drafted a code of rules for a club, of which the members should hold their meetings, thrice in each week, at the Essex Head in the Strand; an establishment which was then kept by a former servant of his old friends the Thrales. Those members who failed to put in an appearance at the club were required to forfeit the sum of twopence. There is an interesting account of one of the meetings of the Ivy Lane Club, at which Johnson presided, in Sir John Hawkins's biography of him.

One evening at the club (he says) Johnson proposed to us the cele·brating of the birth of Mrs. Lennox's first literary child,[1] as he called her book, by a whole night spent in festivity.   Upon his mentioning it to me I told him I never sat up a whole night in my life ; but he continuing to press me, and saying that I should find great delight in it, I, as did all the rest of our company, consented.   The place appointed was the Devil Tavern, and there, about the hour of eight, Mrs. Lennox, and her husband, and a lady of her acquaintance, as also the club, and friends to the number of near twenty, assembled. The supper was elegant, and Johnson had directed that a hot apple-pie should make a part of it, and this he would have stuck with bay-leaves, because, forsooth, Mrs. Lennox was an authoress, and had written verses ; and further he had prepared for her a crown of laurel, with which, but not till he had invoked the Muses by some ceremonies of his own invention, he encircled her brows. The night passed, as must be imagined, in pleasant conversation and harmless mirth, intermingled at different periods with the refresh-ments of coffee and tea.   About five Johnson's face shone with meridian splendour, though his drink had been only lemonade ; but the greater part of the company had deserted the colours of Bacchus, and were with difficulty rallied to partake of a second refreshment of coffee, which was scarcely ended when the day began to dawn. This phenomenon began to put us in mind of our reckon-ing ; but the waiters were all so overcome with sleep that it was two hours before a bill could be had, and it was not till near eight that the creaking of the street door gave signal for our departure.[2]

The next club with which Johnson became acquainted was the most influential of them all, and was the one which is now chiefly remembered in connection with his name.   It was, how-ever, a plant of slow and gradual growth.   The first meeting of its members, who exulted in the designation of 'The Club,' was held in 1763 at a hostelry called the Turk's Head, situated in Gerrard Street, Soho.   'The Club' retained that title until after the funeral of Garrick, when it was always known as 'The Literary Club.' As its numbers were small and limited, the admission to it was an honour greatly coveted in political, legal, and literary circles.[3]

The Club originated with Sir Joshua Reynolds, then Presi-dent of the Royal Academy, who at first restricted its numbers to nine, these being Reynolds himself, Samuel Johnson,

---

[1] This was *The Female Quixote*, published anonymously in 1752.
[2] *Life of Johnson*, p. 287.
[3] Teignmouth, *Life and Corr. of Sir William Jones*, i. 357 ; Hardy's *Memoirs of Earl Charlemont.*

Edmund Burke, Dr. Christopher Nugent (an accomplished Roman Catholic physician), Bennet Langton, Topham Beauclerk, Sir John Hawkins, Oliver Goldsmith, and M. Chamier, secretary in the War Office. The members assembled every Monday evening punctually at seven o'clock, and having partaken of an inexpensive supper, conversed on literary, scientific, and artistic topics till the clock indicated the hour for retiring. The numbers of the Literary Club were subsequently augmented by the enrolment of Garrick, Edward Gibbon, Lord Charlemont, Sir William Jones, the eminent Oriental linguist, and James Boswell of biographical fame. Others were admitted from time to time, until in 1791 it numbered thirty-five. In December 1772 the day of meeting was altered to Friday, and the weekly suppers were commuted to fortnightly dinners during the sitting of Parliament. Owing to the conversion of the original tavern into a private house, the club moved, in 1783, first, to Prince's in Sackville Street ; next to Le Telier's in Dover Street; then, in 1792, to Parsloe's in St. James's Street ; and lastly, in February 1799, to the Thatched House Tavern in St. James's Street, where it remained until long after 1848. It is singular that Boswell, who must frequently have been present at the gatherings of the Literary Club, never but once records any of the conversations which passed between its members. It is possible, however, that he would have regarded it as a breach of confidence to have done so. It is very clear that the object of his idolatry entertained very strong views on the advantages that were to be derived from the membership of a good club. Boswell mentions that once during their tour in the Hebrides he happened to mention 'a club in London at the Boar's Head in Eastcheap, the members of which all assumed Shakespeare's characters.' ' Don't be of it, Sir !' retorted the Doctor. ' Now that you have a name, you must be careful to avoid many things, not bad in themselves, but which will lessen your character.'

The mania for clubbing raged so strongly in the breasts of the fine gentlemen of the days of the Georges that they could seldom rest content with the membership of one. They sought admission to half a dozen. Goldsmith, for instance, besides enjoying the membership of The Literary Club, must needs be admitted a member of the very unintellectual Moderate Whist Club, held at the Devil Tavern near Temple Bar, and the Free and Easy Wednesday Club, at the Globe Tavern in Fleet Street, where his favourite song, 'An Old Woman Tossed in a Blanket seventeen times as high as the Moon,' never failed to evoke uproarious applause. His biographer believes that in 1767, during a summer's sojourn which the vigilance of the bailiffs compelled him to take at Canonbury Tower, he was in the habit of resorting to a temporary club, the members of which met round the festive board of the Crown Tavern, in the Lower Road, Islington, at that time a country village.[1]

The last century witnessed the rise and fall of many so-called 'play' clubs, but these will be noticed in the course of the chapter devoted to an account of gambling.

The late George Daniel, in his amusing work entitled 'Merrie England in the Olden Time,' quotes the titles of a number of clubs (chiefly resorted to by the devotees of Bacchus and eccentricity) which were in existence in London about 1790. The list is here subjoined, but as no clue is given to the source or sources whence it was derived, it is impossible to vouch for its accuracy in every particular. According to Daniel there were the Oddfellows' Club, the Humbugs' Club, which held its meetings at the Blue Posts in Covent Garden, the Samsonic Society, the Society of Bucks, the Purl Drinkers, the Society of Pilgrims, the Thespian Club, the great Bottle Club, the *Je ne sçai quoi* Club (which was held at the Star and Garter in Pall Mall, numbering among its members the Prince of Wales, and the Dukes of York, Clarence, Orleans, Norfolk, and Bedford) ; the Sons of the Thames Society, the Blue Stocking Club, and the No Pay No Liquor Club, held at the Queen and Artichoke, in the Hampstead Road, every new member of which, after first paying his fee, was required to wear throughout the first evening upon which he made his appearance, a hat made in the shape of a quart pot, and to drink to the health of his brother members in a goblet of ale.[2] To these may be added

---

[1] Forster's *Life of Goldsmith*, iii. c. xvii ; Hone's *Every Day Book*, i. 638.
[2] *Merrie England*, ii. 38.

the Anonymous Club, which held its meetings monthly at the British Tavern in Cockspur Street, of which Professor Porson, John Kemble, and others were members, and the Nonsense Club, of which Cowper when a Templar, Bonnel Thornton, Lloyd, and George Colman the elder, enjoyed the associate-ship.[1] As this chapter is principally concerned with recitals of a not particularly enlivening nature, it may not be unpardonable to transcribe for the amusement of the reader one of Cowper's *jeux d'esprit* written as a contribution to the proceedings of the Nonsense Club. It is entitled 'A Letter from an Owl to a Bird of Paradise,' and is as follows :—

Sir,—I have lately been under some uneasiness at your silence, and began to fear that our friends in Paradise were not so well as I could wish ; but I was told yesterday that the pigeon you em-ployed as a carrier, after having been long pursued by a hawk, found it necessary to drop your letter in order to facilitate her escape. I send you this by the claws of a distant relation of mine, an eagle who lives on the top of a neighbouring mountain. The nights being short at this time of the year my epistle will probably be so too ; and it strains my eyes not a little to write when it is not as dark as pitch. I am likewise much distressed for ink ; the blackberry juice which I had bottled up having been all exhausted, I am forced to dip my beak in the blood of a mouse which I have just caught, and is so savoury that I think in my heart I swallow more than I expend in writing. A monkey who lately arrived in these parts is teaching me and my eldest daughter to dance. The motion was a little uneasy to us at first, as he taught us to stretch our wings wide and to turn out our toes ; but it is easier now. I am a tolerable proficient at a hornpipe and can foot it very nimbly with a switch tucked under my left wing, considering my years and in-firmities.

We have had a miserable dry season, and my ivy-bush is sadly

---

[1] Another eccentric club sprang into existence in London about the 'Reign of Terror' epoch. Frederick Reynolds, who mentions it in his auto-biography, says that it was called the Keep the Line Club, and that the members of it, who were chiefly actors, playwrights, and authors, met at the Turk's Head Coffee House in the Strand. Reynolds cites two absurd rules of this club. One ordered, that if any member insulted another by giving him the lie, or by otherwise grossly provoking him, the member so insulted should immediately rise and satisfy the aggressor by immediately *asking his pardon*. This rule was to extend to visitors. By another rule, equally absurd, every member on publishing a literary composition was bound to give a dozen of claret to the club. Reynolds was also a member of the Lion Club, which existed nearly a hundred years, and consisted of the ominous number of members, thirteen.

out of repair. I shall be obliged to you if you will favour me with a shower, which you can easily do by drawing a few clouds together over the wood, and beating them about with your wings till they fall to pieces. I send you some of the largest berries the bush has produced for your children to play withal. A neighbouring physician, who is a goat of great experience, says if they should chance to swallow them you need not be frightened. I have lately had a violent fit of the pip, I have shed almost every feather in my tail ; and so shall think myself happy if I escape the chin-cough, which is generally rife in moulting season. I am, Dear Sir, yours, &c.,—Madge.[1]

Doubts have not infrequently been expressed as to the existence of the second club which appears in the list cited from Daniel's work. But that such a club as the 'Humbugs' did actually exist, and about the time that he asserts that it did, is very evident from the long notice of it which is contained in the curious 'Memoirs' of Pryse Lockhart Gordon, who states that it was founded by a man named Perry who was editor of the 'Morning Chronicle' in the last decade of the century. Pryse Gordon, who was himself a member of the club, states that it was a sort of quiz on all institutions, and that it was composed of many town wits of that time. There were a president and twelve judges, and the meetings were held at a tavern week by week, during two or three of the winter months. The Humbugs' Club was assembled by means of a proclamation which was published in the columns of the 'Chronicle' on the first day of the New Year. These proclamations, which were indited by the president, Perry, who called himself 'Humbugallo Rex,' and countersigned by his secretary 'Screech,' were of a very humorous character, as samples of them which may be discovered by searching the volumes of the 'Morning Chronicle' from 1790 onwards will testify.

When a new member was proposed (says Gordon), he was admitted blind-folded with great ceremony. He was then conducted by a member to the bottom of a large apartment, where he mounted a dozen of almost perpendicular steps, being warned that if he slipped he would probably break his neck. When the candidate had ascended to the top of this rostrum and the bandage was removed from his eyes, he found himself elevated some ten feet above

---

[1] Cowper's *Corr.* ed. Johnson.

the rest of the company, near the ceiling, and standing on a platform of four feet square, looking on a table round which were seated
the president, his secretary, and twelve judges, all masked, with long
beards and black gowns ; and in the centre of the table was a
cauldron of spirits of wine, which threw a most lugubrious light on
these hideous *dramatis personæ.* It required a man of good nerves
to look on this *coup d'œil* without being a little agitated. Behind
the president's chair was placed on a perch a live owl, whom he
consulted in all difficult cases. The secretary 'Screech' was
ordered to examine the candidate, and the queries were so extremely
absurd that answering them gravely was out of the question. ' Pray,
Sir, were you present at your birth ?' was the first question put to
me. ' I do not remember,' said I. ' Are you a sportsman ?' ' Yes.'
' Well, suppose you are in a stubble field—the wind being easterly,
your dog Nero points, and your bitch Juno backs—a covey of
partridges take flight—there are thirteen in it : you kill two birds
with the first barrel, and one with the second, how many remain ?
—take care what you reply, Sir—think well before you speak.' I
did not hesitate, boldly exclaiming ' Ten remained !' ' You may
be a good shot, Sir,' rejoined my examiner, ' but you have made a
bad *hit* there—why three only remained, the ten flew away !' After
having been badgered in this way for ten minutes, I was admitted
a member on paying a bottle of claret—the usual fine.

The character of the clubs of the eighteenth century was
convivial. Each party and each section of a party had its own
club.

Many of the coffee-houses were changed into clubs and
gambling hells, as for instance White's, the fashionable coffee-
house for the Court end of the metropolis in 1736 ; ' the
New Club at Almack's,' established in Pall Mall in the course
of the same year ; and Tom's, nearly thirty years later (1764).
Among the original rules of White's was one to the effect that
every member was to pay one guinea a year towards having a
good cook ; another that supper was to be upon the table at ten
o'clock, and the bill at twelve ; and a third, that every member
who was in the room after twelve o'clock and played, should
pay half-a-crown. During the latter half of the century
political clubs became very strong. The Opposition Club
met at Wildman's in Albemarle Street ; the Ministerial Club
at the Cocoa Tree in St. James's.

That respectable body (wrote Gibbon with reference to the
latter), of which I have the honour of being a member, affords
every evening a sight truly English. Twenty or thirty, perhaps,

of the first men of the kingdom in point of fashion and fortune supping at little tables covered with a napkin, in the middle of a coffee-room, upon a bit of cold meat or a sandwich, and drinking a glass of punch.

Horne Tooke relates that in his younger days it was no uncommon thing for the 'club night' to end by the members burning their wigs. It may be well believed, not only that such was the case, but that the practical joking did not stop there, more especially when it is substantiated by testimony such as the following, extracted from the 'London Magazine' for February 1735 :—

On the 30th of last month, in the evening, a disorder of a particular nature happened in Suffolk Street. Several young gentlemen of distinction having met at a house there called themselves the Calf's Head Club, and about seven o'clock, a bonfire being lit up before the door, just when it was in its height they brought a calf's head to the window, dressed in a napkin cap, as some say, or as others, showed a bloody napkin at the window, or one that, being stained with claret, appeared so ; and after some huzzas threw it into the fire. The mob having been entertained with strong beer for some time, huzza'd with them ; but taking a disgust at some healths which were proposed, and bethinking themselves of the day, grew so outrageous that they broke all the windows, forced themselves into the house, and would probably have pulled it down and destroyed the impudent aggressors, had not the Guards been sent for to prevent further mischief.

According to another account, which appeared in the 'Weekly Chronicle' of February 1, 1735, the damage was estimated at several hundred pounds, and it adds that the Guards were posted all night in the street for the security of the neighbourhood. Many of the accounts which abound of the disreputable and atrocious conduct of club members are such that if they were not proved by collateral evidence would not now be credited.

Did the ladies of the eighteenth century ever succeed in establishing a club for themselves? Not exactly, and as it is sometimes possible to hear and to read of a Blue Stocking Club, it may not be amiss to observe that such a society never existed. The truth is that in the second half of the last century certain ladies set themselves to the commendable task of endeavouring to soften a little the manners of the society in which they customarily moved. To this end Mrs. Elizabeth Montagu, aided by Mrs. Vesey, Mrs. Carter, the learned translator of Epictetus, and Mrs. Ord, Miss Mulso (afterwards Mrs. Chapone), four bright particular stars, organised a series of breakfast parties at which the company should have some better topic upon which to converse than the knave of spades and the king of clubs, which were usually the main topics of conversation of belles when they were not otherwise engaged. Of the mode in which these breakfast parties were conducted, a highly accomplished French lady, Madame du Bocage, who was present at them, thus speaks in writing to her sister under date of April 8, 1750 :—

We breakfasted to-day at Lady [a slip for Mrs.] Montagu's, in a closet lined with painted paper of Pekin, and furnished with the choicest moveables of China. A long table covered with the finest linen presented to the view a thousand glittering cups, which contained coffee, chocolate, biscuits, cream, butter, toasts, and exquisite tea. You must understand that there is no good tea to be had anywhere but at London. The Mistress, who deserves to be served at the table of the gods, poured it out herself (this is the custom), and in order to conform to it the dress of the English ladies, which suits exactly to their stature, the white apron, and the pretty straw hat, become them with the greatest propriety.[1]

As time went on these breakfasts gave place to evening coteries, sometimes at Mrs. Vesey's, sometimes at Mrs. Montagu's, sometimes at the houses of other ladies. To all these assemblies the term of *Bas Bleu* or 'blue stocking' was applied. And why? Mrs. Montagu had early distinguished herself as an authoress. The society consisted originally, according to Sir William Forbes (who devoted some space to an account of it in the first volume of his 'Life of Dr. Beattie'), of Mrs. Montagu herself, Mrs. Vesey, Mrs. Boscawen, Mrs. Elizabeth Carter,[2] Lord Lyttelton, the Earl of Bath (better known as

---

[1] *Letters concerning England, &c.*, i. 8; Pennington's *Memoirs of Mrs. Carter*, i. 469.

[2] This lady is often called Mrs. Carter, but in reality she was never married. With advancing years the title of ' Mrs ' gradually took the place of ' Miss,' an alteration very common during the century, as in the case for example of Mrs. Hannah More.

Pulteney), Horace Walpole, afterwards Earl of Orford, and Mr. Benjamin Stillingfleet. The latter was a man of great piety and worth, the author of several works bearing on natural history, and of some poetical pieces in ' Dodsley's Collection.' He being somewhat of a humourist in his habits and manners, and a little negligent in his dress, literally wore grey stockings, from which circumstance Admiral Boscawen used by way of pleasantry to call them the Blue Stocking Society, as if to indicate that when these brilliant friends met it was not for the purpose of forming a dressed assembly. A foreigner of distinction hearing the expression, translated it literally *Bas Bleu*, by which these meetings came afterwards to be distinguished. Mrs. Hannah More, who was herself a distinguished member of the society, subsequently wrote a poem, entitled *Bas Bleu*, in which she characterised several of the most eminent of the brethren.

They who are acquainted with Addison's contributions to the 'Spectator' will remember the allusions which he makes in some of his papers to the savage proceedings of an extraordinary club established in the metropolis early in the eighteenth century, with the express object of subjecting defenceless passengers in the streets at night-time to terror and brutal usage. Into such a state of fear and alarm did the atrocities and audacities of the Society of Mohocks plunge the capital, that were it not for the plain and unmistakable seriousness with which the literature of the time treats them, it might be doubted whether the story of them is not apocryphal, or at least the wanderings of a disordered brain. Maitland when referring to them in his ' History of London ' expressed great doubts as to whether they ever existed ; but their personality is treated so gravely by their contemporaries that it is almost impossible for posterity to doubt that they did exist, although it may not unreasonably indulge in a certain amount of scepticism with reference to some of the stories which were circulated of their doings. It has been supposed that the members of this infamous society called themselves Mohocks after the Mohawks, a name borne by one of the most ferocious tribes of Red Indians, and if report be true, they went far to rival them as regards the enormities in which they indulged. 'The great cement of their assembly, and the only qualification required in the members, was an outrageous ambition of doing all possible hurt to their fellow creatures.' In order that they might be enabled to act fully upon this principle they first imbibed liquor to an extent that placed them 'beyond the possibility of attending to any notions of reason or humanity.' This done, they patrolled the streets, knocking down, stabbing, wounding, or carbonadoing all who had the misfortune to come in their path. The worthy Sir Roger de Coverley was so terribly apprehensive of an attack from these devils incarnate, that before setting out to witness the performance of the new tragedy at Drury Lane playhouse, he took the precaution of organising a stalwart body-guard, consisting of Captain Sentry, who bore 'the same sword which he had made use of at the battle of Steenkirk,' and a whole posse of servants, 'including the butler,' provided with 'good oaken plants.' That the estimable knight's apprehensions were not altogether groundless is conclusively proved by the following lines transcribed from Gay's poem entitled 'Trivia, or the Art of Walking the Streets,' published in 1712 :—

> Who has not trembled at the Mohock's name?
> Was there a watchman took his hourly rounds
> Safe from their blows or new invented wounds?
> I pass their desperate deeds and mischief done,
> When from Snow Hill black steepy torrents run,
> How matrons hoop'd within the hogshead's womb,
> Were tumbled furious thence ; the rolling tomb
> O'er the stones thunders, bounds from side to side,
> So Regulus, to save his country, died.[1]

The presiding genius of the 'Society of Mohocks' was known as the 'Emperor,' and each member of the club belonged to a different department. One division was known as the 'sweaters,' who having selected their victim, quickly formed a circle, and capered round him with fiendish glee, pricking him meanwhile with their swords, until he fell exhausted to the ground. Another section, styling themselves 'dancing masters,' kept their unfortunate victims in perpetual motion by thrusting swords through their legs. The special

---

[1] *Trivia*, iii. 326.

delight of a third party consisted in 'tipping the lion' upon
their victims, in other words, of violently flattening their noses
and boring out their eyes with their fingers. 'Tumblers' was
the designation borne by a fourth set of wretches who primarily
devoted themselves to setting women upon their heads or
thrusting them into tar barrels and rolling them down hill.[1]

Swift, who during his tenure of the deanery of St. Patrick's,
Dublin, made the metropolis his home for the greater part of
the year, was greatly alarmed during the year 1711–12 at what
he heard of the deeds of the Mohocks, as is evident from the
repeated allusions to them which are interspersed in the
pages of his 'Journal to Stella.' 'Did I tell you of a race
of rakes called the Mohocks?' he inquires under date of
March 8, 1711–12—'that play the devil about this town every
night, slit people's noses and bid them, &c.?' In the next
entry (March 9) he writes as follows :—

> Young Davenant was telling us at Court how he was set upon
> by the Mohocks, and how they ran his chair through with a sword.
> It is not safe being in the streets at night for them. The Bishop
> of Salisbury's son ('Thomas Burnet) is said to be of the gang. They
> are all Whigs ; and a great lady sent to me to speak to her father
> and to lord-treasurer to have a care of them, and to be care-
> ful likewise of myself; for she heard they had malicious intentions
> against the ministers and their friends. I know not whether there
> be anything in this, though others are of the same opinion. I
> walked in the park this evening and came home early to avoid the
> Mohocks.

Four days later he writes :—

> My man tells me that one of the lodgers heard in a coffee-house,
> publicly, that one design of the Mohocks was upon me if they
> could catch me ; and though I believe nothing of it I forbear walk-
> ing late, and they have put me to the charge of some shillings
> already.

Under date of March 15 the journal contains this entry :—

> I came a-foot, but had my man with me. Lord-treasurer ad-
> vised me not to go in a chair because the Mohocks insult chairs
> more than they do those on foot. They think there is some mis-

---

[1] *Spectator*, No. 324.

chievous design in those villains. Several of them, lord-treasurer told me, are actually taken up. I heard, at dinner, that one of them was killed last night. We shall know more in a little time. I do not like them as to men.

On March 16 the Dean writes to this effect :—

Lord Winchelsea told me to-day at court that two of the Mohocks caught a maid of old Lady Winchelsea's at the door of their house in the park with a candle, and had just lighted out somebody. They cut all her face and beat her without any provocation. I hear my friend Lewis has got a Mohock in one of the messengers' hands.

On the 18th he informs Stella that ' There is a proclamation out against the Mohocks. One of those that are taken is a baronet ;' and on the 26th he records that ' Our Mohocks go on still, and cut people's faces every night, but they shan't cut mine.'[1] The reader must take the Dean's allusion to the Whigs with the proverbial grain of salt. It should be borne in mind that the very reverend gentleman was then a staunch adherent of the Tory party, and this snarl is only another way of impressing the unhappy Stella with the fact that he was a person of no small importance in the sphere in which he moved. The foregoing excerpts extend over a period of about three weeks. During all this time the lives of the London citizens had been at the mercy of the Society of Mohocks, which if their existence was not mythical, it must be confessed stands out in the metropolitan annals as one of the most extraordinary combinations which ever pestered society or set the law at defiance. Swift does not hesitate to record in the first book of his ' History of the Four Last Years of the reign of Queen Anne,' that the proceedings of the Mohocks were instigated by Prince Eugene of Savoy during his stay in England as a 'part of an extensive plan to create riot and disturbance in the night,' under cover of which the assassination of the then treasurer might be accomplished. For such an assertion, however, there is absolutely no foundation.[2]

The outrages and iniquities perpetrated by similar clubs led

[1] *Journal to Stella ;* Swift's *Works*, ed. Scott, iii. pp. 4–30.
[2] *Hist. of Queen Anne*, v. p. 53; *Works*, ed. Scott.

to the issue of a royal proclamation in the month of April 1721, for the suppression of 'certain scandalous clubs or societies of young persons' whose proceedings had long been a source of terror to the city. Two of these bore the names respectively of 'The Bold Bucks' and 'Hell-Fire.' It is unnecessary to notice the former ; their 'Blind and Bold Love,' a motto upon which its members acted to the letter, needs no comment. The latter, which was formed at a much later date, were equally as bad. This society was one composed of twelve gentlemen who called themselves Franciscans, from their founder, Sir Francis Dashwood, subsequently Lord De Spencer. The names of the members were as follows : Sir Francis Dashwood, Charles Churchill, John Wilkes (member for Middlesex), George Bubb Dodington (Lord Melcombe), Robert Lloyd, Sir John Dashwood King, Henry Lovibond Collins, Paul Whitehead, Sir William Stanhope, Sir Benjamin Bates (the owner of Medmenham), Francis Duffield, and another whose name does not appear. Secluded in a delightful situation on the banks of the Thames, about three miles and a half from Marlow, there stood a ruined Cistercian abbey, known as Medmenham, which about the middle of the century was rented by these choice spirits as a convivial retreat for the summer months, and subsequently earned a most unenviable notoriety. For a full account of some of the profane orgies there enacted the curious reader may be referred to 'Chrysal, or the Adventures of a Guinea,' a novel written by Charles Johnstone. It needs only here be said that demon worship, mock celebrations of the rites and ceremonies peculiar to the continental monastic orders, and the pouring of libations to the *bona dea*, with much pomp in the chapter house, were the mildest of their ceremonies. Over the grand entrance to the abbey, the Medmenham club caused to be inscribed the motto from Rabelais' abbey of Theleme, *Fay ce que voudras,* and at the end of the passage over the door *Aude hospes contemnere opes.* At one end of the refectory stood the figure of Harpocrates, the Egyptian god of silence, and that of the goddess Angerona stood at the other. In close proximity to the abbey a small temple was erected to Cloacine, with the inscription 'This Chapel of Ease was founded in the year 1760.' Facing the door within was a tablet bearing the inscription appended :

> Æquè pauperibus prodest, locupletibus æquè ;
> Æquè, neglectum, pueris senibusque nocebit.

The gardens, the grove, the orchard, and the neighbouring woods were studded with statues and columns.

Several writers have stated that these debauchees were in the habit of sleeping in cradles, and, according to Sheahan, the historian of Buckinghamshire, a fragment of the particular cradle in which the member for Middlesex was wont to seek repose was preserved in an apartment of the abbey so late as 1862. It is conjectured that this infamous society was dissolved about four years after the accession of George III., though its unhallowed memories were long afterwards kept green by certain pictures purporting to represent the orgies of its members, preserved at the Thatched House Tavern in St. James's Street.[1] Whether, as some have supposed, the Medmenham Franciscans were identical with the Society of Bold Bucks, or whether they were their legitimate descendants, as others have supposed, it is impossible to say, nor is it necessary to pause to inquire. Be that as it may, the primary qualification for admission to the latter society was a denial of the existence of a Supreme Being. The members contented themselves with murdering, or attempting to murder, every watchman and defenceless person, man, woman, and child, whom they met in the streets at night, an exploit which they varied on Sunday by dining in company with each other at a certain tavern in the Strand, when a 'Holy Ghost pie' constituted the principal item on the bill of fare. Some accounts say that the leading spirit among this abandoned crew was the profligate Duke of Wharton, upon whose head Pope poured forth his well-known torrent of versified invective, in the first of his 'Moral Essays.'

It must not be supposed that clubs were institutions peculiar only to the upper grades of society. It was not so. The working classes had their clubs. There was scarcely a public-

---

[1] Almon's *Correspondence of Wilkes*, iii. pp. 61-3. See also *New Foundling Hospital for Wit*, iii. pp. 71-5; Sheahan's *Hist. of Buckinghamshire; Life and Times of Reynolds.*

house in any respectable neighbourhood of the capital which had not its friends' club, its lottery club, its smoking club, charity club, or choir club, in the parlour, where the neighbouring shopkeepers regularly spent their evenings, and where they frequently got drunk, and always drank to some excess.[1] 'Cock and hen' clubs were to be found in any number from Mile End to Westminster, and these were frequented chiefly by small tradesmen and their wives, by working men and apprentices. Place says that the members of many of these clubs, notably of one which met at the Bull-in-Pound between 1780 and 1792, wore a peculiar style of dress, striped silk stockings, numerous knee-strings, and long-quartered shoes.

[1] For much evidence of this see the curious autobiography of a London silversmith of that age entitled *Fruits of Experience*, by Joseph Brasbridge. London, 8vo. 1824, pp. 16-59.

CHAPTER VII.

GAMBLING AND DUELLING.

National mania for gambling in the last century—Whist—The South Sea Bubble—State lotteries—Gambling clubs—Notorious gamesters—The Selwyn correspondence—Charles James Fox—Wagers—Female gamesters—Frequency of duelling—Its causes—Notable English duels of the eighteenth century—Lord Byron and Mr. Chaworth—Sheridan and Captain Mathews—Pitt and Tierney.

THAT the passion for gambling has exercised a potent influence over the human race from time out of mind is an indisputable fact, but it may be fairly questioned whether it ever wielded such absolute sway in any country as it did in England during the whole of the eighteenth century. Gambling seemed indigenous to our soil, and the demon of play never ran his course more smoothly. People turned to it as they did to an ordinary recreation. It was not regarded as a vice. It was at worst regarded as an indiscretion. Few appear to have escaped the infection. Most, if not all, from the highest to the lowest, carried with them some traces of it. People of quality, lawyers, physicians, army and navy men, actors, politicians, even the clergy, gambled prodigiously and systematically.

Society was one vast casino. On whatever pretext and under whatever circumstances half a dozen people of fashion found themselves together—whether for music, or dancing, or politics, or for drinking the waters or each other's wine,—the box was sure to be rattling, and the cards were being cut and shuffled.[1]

As gambling led to ruin, so ruin led to the perpetration of crime, which again led to detection, and thence to the gallows, so that it is not at all surprising to learn from a contemporary

[1] Trevelyan's *Early Life of C. J. Fox*, p. 89.

writer that he had himself seen hanging in chains a man whom but a short time before he had seen sitting at a hazard table. Like Roderick Random, many persons regarded the gaming tables as a certain resource for a gentleman in want. It has already been mentioned, that the most fruitful sources of this unmitigated evil were the coffee-houses, in which it was possible for men to gamble to almost any extent. Rife as had been the gambling within them while Queen Anne occupied the throne, it assumed gigantic proportions in the reigns of her successors, although it received but little countenance from any of them.[1] None of the London coffee-houses was so completely given over to gamesters as White's. Swift was not far wrong when he called it the bane of half the English nobility. That the company who frequented this coffee-house was a decidedly mixed one is broadly hinted at by George Farquhar in the third scene of his comedy of the 'Beaux Stratagem,' when he makes Aimwell, a gentleman of broken fortune, inquire of Gibbet, 'Han't I seen your face at Will's coffee-house?' 'Ay,' replies the highwayman, 'and at White's too !' Will's Coffee House, together with White's, Tom's, Old Man's, and Jonathan's, being the notorious seats of loo, ombre, and piquet. Every student of Hogarth's pictures is familiar with the figure of the highwayman who is depicted in the gambling scene at White's, as waiting in readiness by the fireside until the heaviest winner at piquet or basset prepares to take his departure in order to replenish his empty purse by the aid of the pistols of which the muzzles peer forth from one of the pockets of his great-coat. In 1750, after the capture of Maclean and Plunket, two notorious highwaymen, Walpole informed his friend Mann that their faces were as well known in St. James's as those of any gentlemen 'who lived in that quarter, and who perhaps went upon the road too.'

By some of those who haunted White's, six days' gambling a week was considered insufficient.

As I passed over Richmond Green (so runs one of Walpole's epistles, dated June 4, 1749), I saw Lord Bath, Lord Lonsdale,

---

[1] Chesterfield's *Letters.* June 26, 1752.

and half a dozen more of the White's Club, sauntering at the door of a house which they have taken there and come to every Saturday and Sunday.

It seems that between the years 1710 and 1714, ombre was the game which found the most favour in the eyes of professional gamblers, as it is alluded to more than once in Pope's 'Rape of the Lock' and in Swift's 'Journal to Stella.' Shortly before the accession of George I., crimp, according to Steele, became the idol of the ladies. In 1726 the poet Gay wrote to Swift about the high estimation in which the game of quadrille was held, declaring it to be the universal employment of life in fashionable circles. During the next ten years polite society went crazy over whist, a game which had up to that time been chiefly confined to the clergy. The poet Thomson, in 'Autumn,' the third book of his 'Seasons,' published in 1730, mentions that in sporting circles in the interval between dinner and hard drinking, 'whist awhile walked his dull round, beneath a cloud of smoke wreath'd fragrant from the pipe.'

The girls and boys (wrote the Countess of Hertford to her friend the Countess of Pomfret, under date of March 26, 1741), sit down as gravely to whist-tables as fellows of colleges used to do formerly. It is actually a ridiculous, though I think a mortifying sight, that play should become the business of the nation from the age of fifteen to fourscore.[1]

'Whist,' wrote Walpole to Sir Horace Mann under date of December 2, 1742, 'has spread an universal opium over the whole nation ; it makes courtiers and patriots sit down to the same pack of cards.' In another place he observes : ' The kingdom of the dull is come upon the earth. The only token of this new kingdom is a woman riding on a beast, which is a mother of abominations, and the name on the forehead is whist ; and the four and twenty elders, and the woman, and the whole town do nothing but play with the beast.' This game was now beginning to be taught professionally by the renowned Edmund Hoyle, who wrote a treatise on the subject which

---

[1] *Corr.* iii. p. 103.

passed through no fewer than seven editions in the space of twelve months.

There never was so excellent a book printed. I'm quite in raptures with it; I will eat with it, sleep with it, go to Parliament with it, go to Church with it. I pronounce it the gospel of whist players. I want words to express the author, and can look on him in no other light than as a second Newton. I have joined twelve companies in the Mall, and eleven of them were talking of it. It's the subject of all conversation, and has had the honour to be introduced into the cabinet.

It is in this strain that a character is made to talk in 'The Humours of Whist, as acted every day at White's, and other Coffee Houses and assemblies,' a comedy which appeared in 1743, and it is really far from exaggerated. The rage for whist spread from the palace downwards to the club. It even extended to Granta's bowers, as in 1758 the senior fellow of one of the colleges at Cambridge speaks of himself and his friends, in the ' Idler' No. 33, as sitting 'late at whist' during the evening.

As for play (wrote a fair correspondent in the 'Rambler' for May 8, 1750), I do think I may, indeed, indulge in that now I am my own mistress. Papa made me drudge at whist till I was tired of it; and, far from wanting a head, Mr. Hoyle, when he had not given me above forty lessons, said I was one of his best scholars.

A member of the medical profession, detailing his early experiences in the February number of the 'Gentleman's Magazine' 1755, says that Hoyle tutored him in several games at cards, and under the name of guarding him from being cheated, insensibly gave him a 'taste for sharping'—a state of affairs which was no doubt strictly true in the majority of cases.

It can hardly be a matter for surprise that the spirit of gambling animated the lives of English men and women of all grades to the extent it did in the last century, when it is borne in mind that gambling had to a certain extent received the sanction of authority. The State, it must not be forgotten, patronised gambling in the form of lotteries, which of course yielded no inconsiderable revenue to the Crown. It was in 1720 that the South Sea Company, a trading company established ostensibly for the purpose of whaling, and for trading with the Spanish American possessions, sprang into existence.

The directors proposed to the Ministry, that in return for a charter of exclusive privileges, they would relieve them of divers enormous irredeemable annuities which their necessities had at sundry times compelled them to grant at ruinous rates. Their proposal was accepted, and after much opposition an act was passed endowing them with the requisite powers. What was the result? This: that

the whole nation was infected with the spirit of stock-jobbing to an astonishing degree. All distinctions of party, religion, sex, character, and circumstances were swallowed up. Exchange Alley was filled with a strange concourse of statesmen and clergymen, churchmen and dissenters, Whigs and Tories, physicians, lawyers. tradesmen, and even with females ; all other professions and employments were utterly neglected.

These are the words of Smollett. There is no necessity to dwell upon the awful state of panic into which the bursting of the South Sea Bubble threw the nation in 1720. It is a thrice-told tale. But it is difficult at this distance of time to conceive how so momentous a crisis could have failed to produce any visible effect upon the English people of that day, or how it was that there flourished such extraordinary 'Companies' as those established

for carrying on the undertaking business and furnishing funerals, capital 1,200,000*l.*, at the Fleece, in Cornhill ; for discounting pensions, 2,000 shares, at the Globe Tavern; for preventing and suppressing thieves and insuring all persons' goods from the same, capital 2,000,000*l.*, at Cooper's ; for making of Joppa and Castile soap, at the Castle Tavern ; for sweeping the streets; for improving gardens and raising fruit trees, at Garraway's ; for insuring horses against natural death, accident, or theft, at the Crown Tavern, Smithfield ; for introducing the breed of asses ; an insurance company against the thefts of servants, 3,000 shares of 1,000*l.* each, at the Devil Tavern ; for a perpetual motion by means of a wheel moving by force of its own weight, capital 1,000,000*l.*, at the Ship Tavern ; for assurance of seaman's wages ; for insuring and increasing children's fortunes; for making looking glasses ; for improving malt liquors ; for planting of mulberry trees and breeding of silkworms in Chelsea Park ; for fattening of hogs ; for discovering the Land of Ophir.[1]

---

[1] Malcolm's *Anecdotes of London in the Eighteenth Century*, ii. 111–8.

and scores of others equally delusive and absurd.   One of the most ludicrous examples of the blindness of popular credulity at this time is furnished in the success which attended the scheme of one wily impostor who knew full well the effect which a mysterious announcement will often be found to produce upon simple and unwary people.   Dr. Hughson, who narrates the story in his 'History of London,' says that this rascal issued the following proposal :—'This day, the 8th inst., at Sam's Coffee House, behind the Royal Exchange, at three in the afternoon, a book will be opened for entering into a joint-copartnership for carrying on a thing that will turn to the advantage of all concerned.'   No particulars of this 'thing' were to be revealed for a month, and he intimated that in the meantime 'every person paying two guineas should be entitled to a subscription of one hundred pounds, which would produce that sum yearly.'   In the forenoon he received no fewer than a thousand subscriptions.   In the evening he complacently set out for another kingdom.

The State patronage of lotteries continued until quite the latter end of the eighteenth century, and of all the baneful things that the evil propensities of Government ever induced it to patronize, assuredly they were the worst.   By the schemes of the lotteries, the drawing continued for several weeks, and although it was illegal either to insure or to take insurances, the law produced little or no effect until 1791, when the Stamp Act began to set the acts in operation, as far as it was possible to do so.   In 1797 Dr. Patrick Colquhoun, in his remarkable treatise on the metropolitan police, complained that the evil had increased notwithstanding.   Place, however, thought that there was reason to believe that it had materially diminished.   It was a moot point for some considerable length of time as to how far the law really forbade insurance, and it was not until this point had been decided in the Court of King's Bench in Michaelmas term 1791, that recourse was had to any active measures for the suppression of the evil.   In 1792, Wood, the Stamp Office Inspector, stated before a Committee of the House of Commons, that although the magistrates generally convicted persons who were brought before them, they gave no assistance whatever to the Stamp Office officials in putting down illegal insurance offices. In 1778 an Act had been passed to compel keepers of lottery offices to take out licences for the sale of tickets and shares. The licence in London cost 50*l*. In the country it cost 10*l*. Before this act was passed everyone who chose to do so sold both lottery tickets and shares. All who sold tickets took in insurances. Prior to 1778 no fewer than four hundred lottery offices existed in London alone ; but the whole number which took out licences amounted to no more than fifty-one for the whole of England. So late as the autumn of 1791 every licensed lottery office keeper took in insurances publicly. The number of tickets that were drawn in each day was a proportionate number according to the number of days during which the lottery continued to be drawn. Hence the rate at which insurances might be effected at any time during the lottery could be calculated with accuracy. The sum of eightpence was commonly paid at the commencement of the lottery to insure for a guinea, and the sum increased day by day as the number of tickets decreased and the chances of winning increased. Books for insurance and inspection were kept openly at every licensed office, and privately at any unlicensed place where insurances were effected. They were large folio books ruled in squares, having the leading numbers, such as 100—1000, &c., printed in colours, the squares of which were filled in as the numbers were drawn. These books were open to the inspection of anyone who chose to disburse the sum of fivepence for the privilege. A single glance sufficed to show those numbers which were drawn and those numbers that were undrawn. It would be difficult, if not impossible, to describe the mischief which the practice of insuring in that age occasioned, or to convey an idea of the extent to which it spread. Hundreds of thousands of people were totally ruined by it both in mind and body. The evils were complicated and enormous. The degradation among the small tradesmen and working people was terrible, and their demoralisation was greater than can now be imagined. Such insurances were the cause of every vice that could be practised, the cause of every crime that could be committed. They sowed the seeds of disunion among families, they

separated husbands and wives ; in short, they carried devasta-
tion from one end of the metropolis to the other and ruined in
masses people of every rank and station. From the best information that could be collected in 1796, after great pains had
been taken to suppress the practice, it appeared that the lottery
insurance offices afforded employment to about 2,000 agents
and clerks, to about 7,500 'morocco men,' or fellows who went
from house to house taking insurances for others clandestinely,
in addition to dozens of ruffians, commonly known as 'bludgeon-
men,' who were employed for the protection of the unlicensed
places.   These flagrant evils were at length nearly eradicated
by an alteration which was effected in the mode of drawing the
lottery.   That alteration, in causing all the tickets to be drawn
on one day, put an end to all speculation.   By the removal of this
demoralising influence, the working classes reaped immediate
benefit, and as it happened at a time when a right impulse had
been given to the people, the money, which would otherwise
have been spent in lottery gambling, was to a considerable
extent applied to good purposes.   This in itself was a great and
remarkable change for the better.   That the lottery contractors
were notoriously the most active and indefatigable promoters
of their own interests needs scarcely be said.   Never was a
mission carried out with more industry or greater perseverance
than that which called upon all sorts and conditions of men
to get rich at the expense of their fellows.   From the commencement of the lottery, or from a few days previous to the
drawing of it, until its conclusion, the lottery offices were
illuminated with variegated lamps.   Large flaming pictures or
paintings, depicting Dame Fortune in the act of showering
guineas from a cornucopia into the laps of her votaries, were
exhibited in all the shop-windows.   Before the lottery commenced, the price for insuring only a prize was sixpence.
Twenty guineas would be spread on a board within the shop-
windows at the lottery offices, with a large printed label
inscribed, 'All this may be had for ten shillings.'   More guineas
were placed in another part of the window—'All this may be
had for five shillings.'   Within Guildhall and overlooking the
platform on which the numbers were drawn, were galleries for

people to see the drawing. For admission to these galleries sixpence was charged to each person, and hundreds, after having spent all their money, would 'rake hell with a nail,' to use an expression common at that time, to secure another sixpence, in order that they might ascend to the galleries, and waste the day in idleness, watching the progress of the drawing. Besides the crowds in the galleries, there was always a large mob in the hall. At some of the offices, the people used to assemble in the evening in hundreds, and contend for admission by quarrelling and fighting. Some offices employed as many as eight or ten clerks, and yet the crowds at their doors continued all the evening and until a late hour at night. In the morning there were also numbers of people in and at the doors of the offices. The drawing of the lottery commenced at Guildhall precisely at nine o'clock, an hour at which all the offices closed their doors. They who were shut in were permitted to insure those who could not get in before the clock struck nine ; but as the office-keepers were eager to obtain all the customers they could, they never closed their doors until the last moment. Men with carrier pigeons waited in the hall to obtain the numbers. Often as many as a dozen were engaged on this errand. Generally the pigeon took a turn or two, and flew off home. Sometimes, however, it happened that one alighted upon a house, or on some part of the Guildhall, and when this occurred the bystanders raised loud shouts, and flung stones in all directions, to cause it to wing its flight. Men on horseback used also to await the drawing of the lottery, and then gallop off to their confederates. The numbers drawn every day were sent by express on horseback to Holyhead for the purpose of being despatched thence to Dublin. Yet to such an extent did this sort of gaming extend, that even the expresses were occasionally beaten, and in spite of all the precautions that could be taken the lottery office keepers were cheated.[1] An

---

[1] *Place MSS., Add. MSS., Brit. Mus.* 27,825, pp. 268–73. These manuscripts, which form part of a very voluminous collection of documents relating to the history of English manners and morals from the close of the seventeenth century down to a period within the memory of thousands who are still living, constitute one of the most valuable contributions to the social history of our country. The collection, which is very carefully preserved

American loyalist who took refuge in England in 1780, thus describes a lottery that was drawn in the Guildhall, London, in the month of November in that year :—

A gallery for spectators is erected with seats, one of which I obtained for sixpence. The first object that struck me was a great number of clerks writing down the numbers of tickets and quality, as they were proclaimed. The wheels were placed on either hand upon a stage raised about six feet from the floor, at the bottom of the hall, under Beckford's statue ; between were seated the commissioners at a long table, and a boy at each wheel. After delivering the ticket the boy raises his hand above his head with fingers displayed open, and after two flourishes thrusts it into the wheel, delivering the tickets severally to the man on either side, who on cutting the tickets open, being tied and sealed, declares the number. To prevent future pranks from boys employed to draw out the numbers a commissioner sits in a box directly opposite each boy and near him ; who besides is obliged on taking out each number to raise up his hand, holding the ticket between his forefinger and thumb, delivering it to the man, who after cutting it open announces its fate or fortune.[1]

It may not be without interest to mention that Francis Place was told late in life by an old tradesman of his acquaintance,

that he had been in a lottery office with a large number of others in the evening, when, all their money being gone, and none of them being able to raise the three or four shillings to insure for a guinea when the price had been raised to that sum, he had pulled off his waistcoat and buttoned up his coat ; that other men did the same ; that women pulled off their petticoats, and even their stockings, to make a lot for the pawnbroker to raise money, which, when obtained, was invariably clubbed for the purpose of insuring.

It is possible, if not probable, that the crimes which the

---

in the library of the British Museum, was made during the course of a long life by Francis Place, a warm adherent of the Benthamite school, who for many years carried on the business of a military tailor in Pall Mall, where he seems to have won the respect of all with whom he came into contact. His voluminous accounts of the manners and morals of the middle and lower classes of society are curious and instructive in the highest degree, and deserve consultation at the hands of all those who would fain familiarise themselves with the extraordinary contrast that exists between the state of the English people under Queen Victoria and their ancestors under the House of Brunswick. Place's unpretentious collections may be said to resemble the ancient pyramids of Egypt, which, in spite of their deficiencies in the graces of classical architecture, will endure for ever as monuments of departed worth, and as treasure houses of valuable information respecting the social habits of the times to which they refer, for the generations that are yet to come.

[1] *Journal and Letters of S. Curwen*, pp. 293-5.

lottery caused directly as well as indirectly were as numerous as perhaps two-thirds of all the crimes now committed taken as a whole, *pro ratâ* with the population. Insurance in the lottery was alone sufficient to demoralise and tantalise the people, to make them vicious, base, and degraded, more than all the other evils with which society was affected put together.[1]

Somewhere about the beginning of the year 1731 several attempts appear to have been made to suppress the most notorious gambling hells in the metropolis, but these efforts do not seem to have been rewarded with any measure of success. During the time that the question of their suppression was agitating the public mind, the editor of the ' St. James's Evening Post' printed in the columns of that newspaper, 'for the instruction as well as amusement of his readers,' the following curious ' list of officers' who were attached to the most notorious gaming houses, which is sufficiently indicative of the manner in which such establishments were wont to be conducted. Among these officers there figure :—

1. A ' Director' who superintends the room. 2. An ' Operator,' who deals the cards at a cheating game called faro. 3. Two ' Crowpees' (*i.e.* croupiers), who watch the cards and gather the money for the bank. 4. Two ' Puffs,' who have money given them to decoy others to play. 5. A ' Clerk,' who is a check upon the puffs to see that they sink none of the money given them to play with. 6. A ' Squib,' who is a puff of a lower rank, who serves at half salary while he is learning to deal. 7. A ' Flasher,' to swear how often the bank has been stripped. 8. A ' Dunner,' who goes about to recover money lost at play. 9. A ' Waiter,' to fill out wine, snuff, candles, and attend in the gaming room. 10. An ' Attorney,' a Newgate solicitor. 11. A ' Captain,' who is to fight any gentleman who is peevish for losing his money. 12. An ' Usher,' who lights gentlemen up and down stairs, and gives the word to the porter. 13. A ' Porter,' who is generally a soldier of the foot guards. 14. An ' Orderly Man,' who walks up and down the outside of the door, to give notice to the porter, and alarm the house at the approach of the constables ; and (15) a ' Runner,' who is to get intelligence of the justices' meetings. Link-boys, watchmen, chairmen, drawers, or others who bring the first intelligence of the justices' meetings or of the constables being out, half a guinea reward Common bail, affidavit men, ruffians, bailees, *cum multis aliis.*

---

[1] *Place MSS., Brit. Mus. Add. MSS.,* 27,825, ff. 268-73 ; see also on this subject Adolphus's *History of the Reign of George III.,* iv. pp. 211-2.

Into such veritable Maëlstroms as these drifted the young and old alike, despite the act passed for the prevention of excessive and deceitful gambling. What are more pitiable to read than the awful revelations contained in some of the letters which George Augustus Selwyn received from his amiable friend, Frederick, fifth Earl of Carlisle, whose life it has been truly said was for many years nothing but a constant struggle between the temptations presented by the gaming table on the one hand and the warnings of conscience and affection on the other? One such epistle, which Selwyn, who was thirty years his senior, endorses as having been received 'after the loss of the 10,000*l*.' in July 1776, runs as follows :—

My dear George,—I have undone myself, and it is to no purpose to conceal from you my abominable madness and folly, though perhaps the particulars may not be known to the rest of the world. I never lost so much in five times as I have done to-night, and am in debt to the house for the whole. You may be sure I do not tell you this with an idea that you can be of the least assistance to me ; it is a great deal more than your abilities are equal to. Let me see you, though I shall be ashamed to look at you, after your goodness to me.[1]

Elsewhere he tells his friend :—

I do protest to you that I am so tired of my present manner of passing my time—however I may be kept in countenance by the number of those of my own rank and superior fortune—that I never reflect on it without shame.[2]

Again he writes :—

If the sun shines to-morrow I shall be better ; I fear if I go on much longer you will think that the moon has more influence over me than the sun. Lady Carlisle is very well. You may be sure I shall prevent this man from setting ruin like a bulldog at her. She is very nearly made familiar with it ; and if it is not made to fly at her she will approach it with as little fear as anyone I know. The children are all well.[3]

At twenty-seven years of age, the lord of Castle Howard is found telling his friend, 'Except that the welfare and interest of others depend upon my existence, I should not wish that existence to be of long duration.'[4] It appears, from a letter addressed in 1773 by Lord Carlisle to Lady Holland, mother of

[1] Jesse's *Selwyn and his Contemporaries*, iii. 16.
[2] *Ibid.* p. 138.   [3] *Ibid.* 137.   [4] *Ibid.* 137.

Charles James Fox, that he had become security for the latter to the amount of 15,000*l*.

It is really appalling even to think of the enormous sums of money, the estates, jewels, and other valuables which it is recorded were staked, lost, and won, night after night, at single sittings during the Georgian era. The Duke of Devonshire lost his valuable estate of Leicester Abbey to Manners at basset. Lord Carlisle, in writing to George Selwyn, informed him of a set in which at a certain point in the game a gentleman stood to win 50,000*l*. Walpole mentions that Sir John Bland, of Kippax Park, member for Luggershal, in Wilts, who died suddenly abroad in September 1755, squandered his entire fortune away at hazard. 'He t'other night,' wrote Walpole, 'exceeded what was lost by the late Duke of Bedford, having at one period of the night (though he recovered the greatest part of it) lost two and thirty thousand pounds.'[1] The Earl of March, writing to Selwyn on a certain Sunday morning in 1765, says : 'When I came home last night I found your letter on my table. So you have lost a thousand pounds ; which you have done twenty times before in your lifetime, and won it again as often, and why should not the same thing happen again?' The news of a large sum of money won is announced in one part of a letter from Rigby to George Selwyn, dated March 12, 1745 :—

I held my resolution of not going to the ridotto till past three o'clock ; when finding nobody was to sit any longer, but Boone, who was not able, I took, as I thought, the least of two evils, and so went there rather than to bed, but found it so infinitely dull that I retired in half an hour. The next morning I heard there had been extreme deep play, and that Harry Furness went drunk from White's at six o'clock, and won the dear memorable sum of 1,000 guineas. He won the chief part of Doneraile and Bob Bertie.

Many a man committed suicide through his reverses at the gaming tables. In 1755 Lord Mountford made his *quietus* with a pistol, owing to that cause. Having lost tremendous sums of money at play, and being in mortal dread of beggary, his lordship made application to the Duke of Newcastle for the governorship of Virginia or the Foxhounds, inwardly

---

[1] Walpole's *Letters*, ed. Cunningham, ii. 425.

resolving to stake his existence on the result. Receiving an unfavourable reply, he took counsel with his friends as to the easiest method of committing suicide. On New Year's eve, 1755, Mountford supped at White's chocolate house, and afterwards played whist till the small hours of the following morning. Later in the day he sent for a lawyer and three witnesses, in whose presence he executed a will, which he ordered to be read over thrice, clause by clause. As soon as they had done so, he inquired whether such a will would hold good in the event of his taking his life. On receiving assurance that it would, he politely requested them to excuse his absence, and, stepping into an adjoining apartment, deliberately made away with himself, so quietly that no report of the pistol was audible.[1]

The next recorded suicide of a gamester in high life was the Hon. John Damer (eldest son of the last Baron Milton), who, having become involved in pecuniary difficulties, and seeing no way out of them, blew out his brains at 3 o'clock on the morning of August 15, 1776, at the Bedford Arms in Covent Garden. He had barely attained his twenty-third year.

Still the play went on. Still the play continued to be the canker which corroded the full-blown flower of human felicity, the pestilence which smote at the bright hour of noon. Morning, afternoon, and evening, the sport of chance was to be witnessed in White's, in Brooks's, in Boodle's, reducing thousands to beggary and many hundreds to starvation. There were to be witnessed the clenched fist of passion, the grin of malicious exultation, the fearful oath of desperation, the frantic eagerness of those who had staked their little all upon the chances of some game. Lord Ilchester, a cousin of Charles James Fox, upon one occasion lost thirteen thousand pounds at a single sitting to the Earl of Carlisle. He agreed to accept three thousand pounds down, but never received a farthing of it. Years afterwards, when he pressed for it, he met with no success.

The only way in honour that Lord I. could have accepted my offer (he complained to Selwyn), would have been by taking some steps to pay the 3,000*l.* I remained in a state of uncertainty, I think, for nearly three years, but his taking no notice of it during that time con-

---

[1] Walpole's *Letters*, ed. Cunningham, ii. 417.

vinced me that he had no intention of availing himself of it. Charles Fox was also at a much earlier period clear that he never meant to accept it. There is also great justice in the behaviour of the family in passing by the instantaneous payment of, I believe, five thousand pounds to Charles, won at the same sitting, without any observations. At one period of play, I remember, there was a balance in favour of one of those gentlemen of about fifty thousand.

Poor Lord Lempster is more Cerberus than ever ; he has lost twelve thousand pounds at hazard to an ensign of the Guards.[1]

I won five hundred pounds last night (writes Fitzpatrick), which was immediately appropriated to Mr. Martindale, to whom I still owe three hundred pounds ; and I am in Brooks's books for twice that sum.[2]

A few pages further on occur letters from two noblemen, one of whom states that, in a moment of 'cursed folly,' his little account with Brooks rose from one to five hundred pounds. Mr. Brooks, it may be mentioned, was a wine-merchant, and a money-lender. He succeeded Almack as the proprietor of one of the first-rate gaming clubs, and was so obliging as to give credit on easy terms. In some verses which were written by Tickell, and represented as an 'Epistle from the Hon. Charles James Fox, partridge-shooting, to the Hon. John Townshend, cruising,' he is called :—

> Liberal Brooks, whose speculative skill
> Is hasty credit and a distant bill :
> Who, nurs'd in clubs, disdains a vulgar trade,
> Exults to trust, and blushes to be paid !

'Having lost a very monstrous sum of money last night,' writes one of Selwyn's correspondents, 'if it is not very inconvenient to you, I should be glad of the money you owe me. If it is, I must pay what I can, and desire Brooks to trust me for the remainder.' The gaming and extravagance in which young men of quality indulged at Brooks's was extraordinary, yet there is reason to believe that it must have been greater at Almack's club in Pall Mall. There the gamesters played only for rouleaus of fifty pounds each, and generally there were ten thousand pounds in specie on the table. Lord Holland had paid more than twenty thousand pounds for his two sons. Before gaming began, it was customary for the players to pull

---

[1] Walpole's *Letters*, ed. Cunningham, ii. 234.
[2] *Selwyn Correspondence.*

off their embroidered clothes and to put on frieze great-coats. Occasionally they turned their coats inside out, for luck as they used to say. To prevent his laced ruffles from being soiled, each gamester put on a piece of leather, such as was worn by footmen when cleaning knives ; and in order to shade his eyes from the light, and to prevent him from tumbling his hair, he wore a high-crowned straw hat with broad brim, and adorned with flowers, ribbons, besides a mask to conceal his emotions when he played at quinze. Moreover, each gamester had a small neat stand by him to hold his tea, or a wooden bowl with an edge of ormolu to hold his rouleaus.

The gaming at Almack's (wrote Walpole to Sir Horace Mann, on February 2, 1770), which has taken the *pas* of White's, is worthy the decline of our empire or commonwealth, which you please. The young men of the age lose ten, fifteen, twenty thousand pounds in an evening there. Lord Stavordale, not one and twenty, lost 11,000*l.* there last Tuesday, but recovered it by one great hand at hazard. He swore a great oath—' Now if I had been playing *deep* I might have won millions.' [1]

Hundreds of young men of rank were hopelessly meshed in the webs of the usurers, from whom they borrowed great sums of money at most exorbitant premiums. Charles Fox used to call his outward room, where those Jews waited until he rose from play, his ' Jerusalem chamber.'

Some of the best friends of Charles James Fox, the greatest statesman of his generation, ran in danger of being half ruined in annuities which were given by them as securities for him to the Jews, to whom, long before he had attained his twenty-fourth year, he was indebted to something like 100,000*l.*, the result of his devotion to cards and dice. Walpole, writing to General Conway on June 22, 1771, says : ' I do not think I can find in Patin or Plato, nor in Aristotle, a parallel case to Charles Fox ; there are advertised to be sold more annuities of his and his society, to the amount of five hundred thousand pounds a year.' Walpole wondered what Fox would do when he had succeeded in selling the estates of all his friends. Gibbon, the Roman historian, writing in February 1772, informed his friend Holroyd that Fox strengthened himself for the memorable de-

[1] Walpole's *Letters*, ed. Cunningham, v. 226.

bate in the House of Commons on the relief of the clergy from subscription to the Thirty-nine Articles by indulging in a twenty-two hours' recreation at hazard, at the trifling cost of 500*l.* per hour, eleven thousand pounds in all.

'Charles Fox,' wrote Mrs. Harris to her son at Madrid, under date of February 7, 1772, 'sat down to cards last Tuesday after dinner, played all night and next morning, and in that time lost 12,000*l.*; by five that afternoon he lost 12,000*l.* and 11,000*l.* more.'[1]

There was doubtless a little excuse for Fox, seeing that, when but a lad of fifteen summers, sojourning at Spa, his father, Lord Holland, gave him a rouleau of guineas to stake at the notorious gaming tables of that city. A year later he became a member of Brooks's, the notorious gaming club in St. James's Street, where deep play was the rule rather than the exception, and there displayed his headstrong indulgence in its fatal fascinations to which the principal misfortunes of his life were attributable. It is to this passion that Mason alludes in his 'Heroic Epistle to Sir William Chambers' :—

> But hark the voice of battle shouts from far,
> The Jews and Macaronis are at war,
> The Jews prevail, and thundering from the stocks,
> They seize, they bind Charles Fox.

Fox, however, did not by any means stand alone in his extravagance and profligacy.

John Damer and his two brothers (wrote Walpole to Sir Horace Mann, in 1776), have contracted a debt, one can scarcely expect to be believed out of England, of 70,000*l.* The young men of this age seem to make a law amongst themselves for declaring their fathers superannuated at fifty, and thus dispose of their estates as if already their own.

Under date of August 11 in the same year, the same writer inquired of Mann, 'Can you believe that Lord Foley's two sons have borrowed money so extravagantly, that the interest they have contracted to pay amounts to 18,000*l.* a year?' 'Charles Fox left us this morning,' wrote the Earl of Carlisle to Selwyn on October 10, 1776. 'He has been excellent company, in good spirits, and not the worse for having levanted every

---

[1] 1*st Earl of Malmesbury's Corr.* i. 247.

236 ENGLAND IN THE EIGHTEENTH CENTURY.

soul at Newmarket, after having lost everything he could raise
on Stavordale's bond.'[1] The same to the same on Sunday :—
'Not to keep you in suspense, I was foolish last night to lose
near 400*l.* Brooks was, in the list of debts I made out, a
creditor for 100*l.* He is now, by my cursed folly, 500*l.*' The
Earl of March to G. Selwyn in 1767 :—' There are a great many
people at White's every night. Bully has lost 700*l.* at quinze.'

It was the desperate state to which whist, piquet, faro, and
hazard had reduced him by the summer of 1773 that led to Fox
becoming the dupe of a certain 'sensible woman' who gave
advice on all emergencies for half a guinea'—the Hon. Mrs.
Grieve, who gave herself out as a cousin to Lord North, the
Duke of Grafton, and Mrs. Fitzroy. She persuaded Fox that
she could be instrumental in his contracting a marriage with a
certain Miss Phipps who was on her way from the West Indies
to England with a fortune of 80,000*l.* It was owing to the
Hon. Mrs. Grieve being carried before Justice Fielding by
another of her dupes that her dealings with Fox were dis-
closed.[2] Topham Beauclerk, who enjoyed his friendship, was
accustomed to say that it was difficult to form a conception of
the extremities to which he was reduced after having lost his
last guinea at the gaming table. He never appeared despon-
dent. Beauclerk stated that on calling upon him one morning
after he had lost a ruinous amount, he found him to his
amazement deep in the perusal of Herodotus in the
original Greek. Explaining his amazement, Fox replied, 'What
would you have me do when I have lost my last shilling?'[3]

More than half a century ago, Lord Egremont, who remembered well the earlier portion of the reign of George III.,
told Lord Holland that he was convinced by reflection, aided
by his subsequent experience of the world, that there was at
that time some unfair confederacy among some of the players,
and that the great losers, especially C. J. Fox, were actually
duped and cheated. Had he even dared to hint such a thing at
the time, he said, he felt certain that he would have been torn

[1] Jesse's *Selwyn*, iii. 158.
[2] *Correspondence of Fox*, ed. Lord John Russell, i. 94.
[3] Jesse's *Selwyn*, ii. 223.

into pieces and stoned by the losers themselves. He was satisfied, nevertheless, that the immoderate, constant, and unparalleled advantages over Charles Fox and other young men were not to be accounted for only by the difference of passing or holding the box, or the hazard of the dice.

Let it not be supposed that gambling was not to be found outside the metropolis. The fashionable racing towns and the mineral spas were all replete with gaming clubs and subscription rooms, none more so, perhaps, than Bath, whither sharpers bent their steps during the summer season from all parts of the Continent. At Newmarket, distant scarcely eighty miles from London, the rooms in which the hazard tables stood were never empty. Here it was that in 1756 George Selwyn, seeing a number of bank bills tossed about by Ponsonby, the then Speaker of the Irish House of Commons, wittily remarked to a friend who stood by :—'Look how easily the Speaker passes the money bills.' 'The rich people win everything,' wrote the Earl of March from Newmarket ; 'Sir James Lowther has won about 7,000*l.*' [1] It appears from some recently published reminiscences of Sir N. Wraxall, that in the latter part of the century the Prince of Wales was in an evil hour tempted to be initiated into the mysteries of Newmarket—with consequences which 'proved very injurious not only to his purse but in other respects.' [2]

The knights of the industry in that age were indeed masters of their craft.

Considering the combinations of gamesters (says worthy James Puckle when delivering sundry wholesome counsels on this head in his 'Club ; or a Grey Cap for a Green Head,' 1733), their tricks to make their bubbles drunk, and then to put upon them the doctors, the fulloms, loaded dice, flats, bars, cuts, high slipped, low slipped, chain, dice, &c. ; that besides false dice there are several sorts of false boxes ; that supposing both box and dice fair, gamesters have the top peep, eclipse, thumbing, &c. ; that by long practice sharpers can, from conveniences in pockets, caps, sleeves, rolls of stockings, &c.

In the event of everything else failing, the choice of one of

[1] Jesse's *Selwyn and his Contemporaries.*
[2] See *Wraxall's Reminiscences appended to Memoirs,* ed. Wheatley, v. 359.

two alternatives lay open to a gambling gentleman. He might marry a wealthy woman if he got the chance, or importune his friends at court, if haply he had not lost all credit with them, to procure him some snug position under the Government, with plenty to receive and nothing to do.

> You ask me how play uses me this year. I am sorry to say very ill, as it has already since October taken 800*l.* from me ; nor am I in a likely way to reimburse myself soon by the emoluments of any place or military preferment, having voted the other evening in a minority.

This jeremiad was penned by the Hon. Henry St. John, and addressed to his friend George Augustus Selwyn in 1766.[1]

The Earl of Carlisle to George Selwyn, June 5, 1776 :—

> The hazard this evening was very deep. Meynell won 4,000*l.* and Pigot 5,000*l.* I did nothing. As for hazard, the depriving you of so great a pleasure I am sure is very far from my intention ; no one would wish more to contribute to them. We have both been shipwrecked upon that coast, and a very dangerous one it is.[2]

Even in the closing years of the century, the gambling that went on in private houses was very great. People of *ton* commonly met at one another's drawing-rooms to play at commerce with a thousand guineas in the pool. Many a tragedy took place like that of Harrel in Miss Burney's novel of 'Cecilia.' It had long been the custom for young men of gentle birth to start on their careers by being admitted to the best London . clubs. Of these there were many, but the choice was influenced by politics as much as by inclination.

When William Wilberforce journeyed up to the capital in 1780 as the newly elected representative for the seaport of Hull, he was expected, being a man of property and position, to become a member of the clubs which at that time were frequented by fashionable and political society. He did so, and has thus recorded his experiences of them.

> The very first time I went to Boodle's, I won 25 guineas of the Duke of Norfolk. I belonged at that time to five clubs—Miles and Evans's, Brooks's, Boodle's, White's. The first time I was at Brooks's, scarcely knowing anyone, I joined from mere shyness in play at the faro-table, where George Selwyn kept bank. A friend who knew my inexperience, and regarded me as a victim

---

[1] Jesse's *Selwyn*, iii. 129.   [2] *Ibid.* ii. 102.

decked out for sacrifice, called out to me, ' What, Wilberforce, is that you ?' Selwyn quite resented the interference, and turning to him said in his most expressive tone, ' O sir, don't interrupt Mr. Wilberforce ; he could not be better employed.' [1]

George Selwyn during the next eleven years of his life got the better of his propensities for deep play, finding, as he himself confessed, that ' it was too great a consumer of four things —time, health, fortune, and thinking.' Wilberforce also belonged to a more select society, called Goosetree's, at a house in Pall Mall, on the site afterwards occupied by the Shakespeare Gallery, and which, some years previously, had been in the occupation of Almack. ' We played a good deal at Goosetree's,' says Wilberforce, ' and I well remember the intense earnestness which Pitt displayed when joining in those games of chance. He perceived their increasing fascination, and soon after abandoned them for ever.' How it was that the great man came to abandon them is thus recorded by his sons in their biography of him, on the authority of his own private journal. ' " We can have no play to-night," complained some of the party at the club, " for St. Andrew is not here to keep bank." " Wilberforce," said Mr. Bankes, who never joined himself, "if you will keep it I will give you a guinea." The playful challenge was accepted, but as the game grew deep, he rose the winner of 600*l*. Much of this was lost by those who were only heirs to future fortune, and could not therefore meet such a call without inconvenience. The pain he felt at their annoyance cured him of a taste which seemed but too likely to become predominant.' Wilberforce bears testimony to the fascination which play exercised over Pitt at one period of his political life :—

I was one of those who met to spend an evening in memory of Shakespeare at the Boar's Head, Eastcheap. Many professed wits were present, but Pitt was the most amusing of the party, and the readiest and most apt in the required allusion. He entered with the same energy into all our different amusements ; we played a good deal at Goosetree's, and I well remember the intense earnestness which he displayed when joining in those games of chance. He perceived their increasing fascination, and soon after suddenly abandoned them for ever.[2]

---

[1] *Life of Wilberforce,* i. 117.
[2] *Ibid.* i. 18 ; see also Lord Holland's *Memoirs of the Whig Party,* ii. 32.

Towards the close of the American War, the game known as Faro or 'Pharaoh,' as it is jocosely called by Walpole, became the rage. Writing on June 12, 1781, Walpole mentions that Princess Amelia had been at Marlborough House the night before and had played at faro till the clock struck twelve. E.O. came into vogue concurrently with faro, and became so great a favourite that in June 1782 a bill was introduced into Parliament for the suppression of the establishments in which it was played. In the important debate which followed, Mr. Byng, M.P. for the county of Middlesex, who clamoured loudly for state interference like many another misguided senator before and since, stated that E.O. tables were to be found in every part of London. He knew that in one house in the parish of St. Anne, Soho, there were actually five E.O. tables, and he did not doubt but that the electrical bed itself would be turned into an E.O. table. In another speech he urged the necessity of the bill from the circumstance that in two parishes in Westminster alone there were 296 E.O. tables, that there was not a public meeting in the kingdom into which they did not find their way, and that there were instances in which bankrupts had amassed 20,000*l.* by E.O., to the ruin of many unfortunate and unwary persons. George Onslow in the course of his speech asserted that there were 296 E.O. tables in two parishes in Westminster, and he believed that there were at least 500 more on the stocks. Sheridan, who displayed greater wisdom than any of the speakers, observed that it would be no use prohibiting E.O. tables while gaming in lotteries was countenanced by law, and recommended the House, instead of passing the bill, to turn its attention towards a reformation of the police of Westminster.[1]

There was no subject so trivial, no event however unimportant, which did not at this time afford fine gentlemen an excuse to lay a wager. Births, marriages, and deaths, the number of years an individual was likely to live, the duration of a ministry, an infamous character's chances of dying on the gallows instead of in his bed, the results of parliamentary elec-

---

[1] *Parl. Hist.* vol. xxiii. 1782-83, p. 110 *et seq.*

tions, earthquakes, and other remarkable phenomena. Young men of rank, heirs to great estates, would even 'run their fathers,' that is to say, would lay wagers one with another as to which of them survive the other. At several of the coffee-houses where play-clubs were in the habit of meeting, particularly Brooks's and White's, it was customary for large books to be kept for the express purpose of entering the numerous bets which the members were perpetually making and exchanging. Here is a sample from one of the betting books of White's Chocolate House : 'Lord Mountford bets Sir John Bland twenty guineas, that Beau Nash outlives Cibber.' Cibber died in 1757, Nash lived till 1761—six years after the two betters had each departed this life. Here is another speci-men :—

In consideration of 10 guineas received by me, this 2nd day of July, 1771, of Francis Salvador, Esq., I promise for myself, my heirs and executors, to pay unto the said Francis Salvador, Esq., his heirs or assigns, the sum of 100 guineas, that is to say, in case John Wilkes, now alderman of London, shall be hang'd, 105*l.* Tho. Roche.

In the list of wagers laid by Richard Brinsley Sheridan for the year 1793 occur the following :—

May 25, 1793.—Mr. Sheridan bets General Fitzpatrick 100 guineas to 50 guineas that within two years from this date some measure is adopted in Parliament which shall be *bond fide* con-sidered as the adoption of a Parliamentary Reform. January 29, 1793.—Mr. S—— bets Mr. Hardy 100 guineas to 50 guineas that Mr. W. Windham does not represent Norwich at the next general election. March 25, 1793.—Mr. S—— bets Mr. Hardy 100 guineas that the three per cent. consols are as high this day twelvemonth as at the date thereof.[1]

There is a man about town (wrote Walpole to Mann in 1768), a Sir William Burdett, a man of very good family, but most infamous character. In short, to give you his character at once, there is a wager entered in the bet-book at White's (an MS. [*sic*] which I may one day or other give you an account of), that the first baronet that will be hanged is this Sir William Burdett.

Writing to the same individual under date of July 10, 1774, he says that a certain Mr. Blake having betted 1,500*l.* that a

---

[1] Moore's *Life of Sheridan*, chap. xvi.

man could live twelve hours under water, hired a desperate fellow, and by way of experiment sunk him in a ship. Both went to the bottom. 'Another man and ship,' adds Walpole, 'are to be tried for their lives instead of Mr. Blake, the assassin.'

Walpole has preserved what he calls 'a good story made on White's,' indicative of this extraordinary mania for wagering. One morning in 1750 a man was suddenly observed to fall down just outside White's Coffee House. Instantly odds were laid and taken among the bystanders and spectators on the chances of his being alive. Somebody, however, proposed to bleed the poor fellow, whereupon loud protestations arose from a section of the betting men, on the ground that the use of a lancet would affect the fairness of the betting ![1] Elsewhere Walpole tells another good story of a pious divine, who, walking into White's on the morning of the earthquake in 1750, and hearing bets laid as to whether the shock had really been caused by an earthquake or by an explosion at a powder mill, departed horror-stricken from the spot, muttering that they were such an impious set of men, that he believed, 'if the last trump were to sound, they would bet puppet show against judgment.'

In the same year, a noble lord, a minor, lost 11,000*l.* at one sitting, and then won it back again at one chance.

In 1772 Mr. Thynne won only twelve thousand guineas at the same club. There is a tradition that Drummond, a member of the famous banking firm of that name, lost one night at White's to Beau Brummel a sum of 20,000*l.* at whist. There is another tradition, perhaps equally well authenticated, that General Scott won 200,000*l.* in the same place, and at the same game. There is a third tradition, no doubt as well founded as the other two, that Lord Robert Spencer, brother to the second Duke of Marlborough, won 100,000*l.* at Brooks's by joining General Fitzpatrick in keeping a faro bank.

Walpole, in writing to Mann under date of January 10, 1750, tells him a story which, if true, not only sheds a curious light upon the times, but furnishes indubitable evidence of the fearful straits to which gamblers were sometimes reduced ; that

[1] *Walpole's Letters,* ed. Cunningham, ii. p. 225.

General Wade was at a low gaming house, and had a very fine snuffbox, which on a sudden he missed. Everybody denied having taken it ; he insisted on searching the company. He did : there remained only one man who had stood behind him, but refused to be searched unless the general would go into another room alone with him. There the man told him that he was born a gentleman, was reduced, and lived by what little bets he could pick up there, and by fragments which the waiters sometimes gave him. 'At this moment I have half a fowl in my pocket ; I was afraid of being exposed ; here it is ! Now, sir, you may search me.'

Walpole adds that the general was so struck with the man's story that he presented the wretched gamester with a hundred pounds.

Mr. Harris, in a letter to his son at Madrid, dated February 26, 1770, says, 'Gaming, I fear, makes great havoc here ; people win or lose six or seven thousand pounds of a night.'

Were the weaker vessels of the age better able to withstand the manifold temptations which gambling presented than the sterner sex ? It is to be wished that the student of eighteenth-century society could say they were ; but he cannot, at any rate with veracity. If the truth must be told, the ladies were even worse than the gentlemen, for wheresoever a card-table was, there assuredly would they gather together. It was not unusual for a lady of quality to hire a professional gamester, at eight or ten guineas a night, to set up a table for the company. Swift lashed their proclivities in this direction in his 'Journal of a Modern Lady,' and William Hogarth held them up to the scorn and ridicule of posterity, on canvas, in his 'Taste in High Life ;' wherein may be seen lying on the floor a pyramid consisting of a pack of cards, with a scrap of paper by its side, inscribed with the words 'Lady Basto Dr. to John Pip for cards, 300*l*.' Edward Moore endeavoured to point a moral in the characters and incidents of his domestic tragedy called 'The Gamester' produced in 1753. Frederick Reynolds, in his amusing autobiography, says that in his infancy, 1764 to 1774, one of the greatest card-playing places around London was Twickenham, and that his grandmother, a lady of the name of West, who resided in Montpelier Row, reigned queen of all the card players in that locality. He further states that this infatuation was carried to such an extent that the four old maids of Montpelier Row, her principal subjects, were chiefly known in the neighbourhood by the names of *Manille, Spadille, Basto,* and *Punto.* Every night they assembled at one of their houses in succession ; and, on the first of every month, each also took her turn to give a grand party, at which gambling continued till an early hour of the morning.[1]

Lady Cowper records in her 'Diary,' under date of 1715, as follows :—

My mistress (the Princess of Wales) and the Duchess of Montagu went halves at hazard and won 600*l.* Mr. Archer came in great form to offer me a place at the table ; but I laughed, and said he did not know me if he thought I was capable of venturing two hundred guineas at play, for no one sat down to the table with less.

The ladies, it is to be feared, were not only desperately fond of play themselves, but sometimes did all they could to draw into its meshes those who were not fond of it at the social parties and assemblies :—

Madame de Walderen (says Mrs. Harris, writing under date of October 25, 1768) would fain have tempted me to her loo party, but I needed little fortitude to withstand it, as one stake lost would ruin a whole assembly ; I preferred a sober game of quadrilles with Miss Chudleigh (afterwards the celebrated Duchess of Kingston, found guilty in 1776 of bigamy by the House of Lords).[2]

In the reign of George II., Lady Mordington and Lady Cassilis made no secret of keeping gambling establishments, or excusing themselves for so doing on the ground that their privilege of peerage exempted them from any of the statutes then in force for their suppression :—

I, Dame Mary, Baroness of Mordington (runs a manuscript declaration discovered some years ago) do hold a house in the Great Piazza, Covent Garden, for and as an Assembly, where all persons of credit are at liberty to frequent and play at such diversions as are used at other Assemblies. And I have hired Joseph Dewberry, William Horseley, Hans Cropper, and George Sanders as my servants or managers (under me) thereof. I have given them orders to direct the management of the other inferior servants (namely) John Bright, Richard Davies, John Hill, John Vandenvoven, as box-keepers ; Gilbert Richardson, housekeeper, John Chaplin, regu-

[1] *Life and Times,* i. pp. 32-39.
[2] *Corr. 1st Earl of Malmesbury,* i. 161.

lator ; William Stanley and Henry Huggins, servants that wait on the company at the said assembly ; William Penny and Joseph Penny as porters thereof. And all the above-mentioned persons I claim as my domestic servants and demand those privileges that belong to me as a peeress of Great Britain appertaining to my said Assembly. M. MORDINGTON.
Dated January 8, 1744.

What did the Lords do ? They 'resolved and declared that no person is entitled to privilege of peerage against any prosecution or proceeding for keeping any public or common gaming house, or any house, room, or place for playing at any game or games prohibited by any law now in force.'

Time thrown away in the country ! (exclaims Mrs. Blandish in General John Burgoyne's comedy of ' The Heiress,' 1786). As if women of fashion left London to turn freckled shepherdesses ! No, no ; cards, cards, and backgammon are the delights of rural life ; and slightly as you may think of my skill, at the year's end I am no inconsiderable sharer in the pin money of my society.

Old and young, married and single, assembled together and gambled away their nights and days to an extent now quite unknown.

If their passion for gaming (wrote in the ' Connoisseur') continues to increase in the same proportion that it has for some time past, we shall very soon meet with abundance of sharpers in petticoats ; and it will be mentioned as a very familiar incident that a party of female gamblers were seized by the constables at the gaming-table.

With women the habit of gaming was fraught with the direst consequences. A hint thrown out by Lord Townly, a character in the play of ' The Provoked Husband,' will suffice to illustrate this :—

Lord T. :—'Tis not your ill hours that always disturb me, but as often the ill company that occasions those hours. Lady T. :—Sure, I don't understand you now, my lord. What ill company do I keep ? Lord T. :—Why, at best, women that lose their money, and men that win it ; or perhaps men that are voluntary bubbles at one game, in hopes a lady will give them fair play at another.

We are informed (says the Chronicle of the ' Annual Register,' under date of February 9, 1766) that a lady at the west end of the town lost, one night last week, at a sitting, 3,000 guineas at loo.

All through the century the ladies appear to have acquitted themselves at gaming satisfactorily ; so satisfactorily, indeed, that Lord Chief Justice Kenyon in 1797 cautioned them that if any prosecutions of a gambling nature were fairly brought before him, and the parties were 'justly convicted, whatever might be their rank and station, though they should be the first ladies in the land, they should certainly exhibit themselves in the pillory.' His lordship was alluding in particular to four dames of title : Lady Buckinghamshire, Lady Elizabeth Luttrell, Lady Archer, Lady Mount Edgcumbe, familiarly known as ' Faro's daughters,' and Mrs. Concanon. These four were each convicted of keeping a gaming-table. They were, however, let off with a fine.[1]

The following paragraph, transcribed from the Chronicle of the 'Annual Register' for 1797, shows that the star of deep play among the ladies, as late as that year, was still in the ascendent.

At the police office, Marlbro' Street, Lady Buckinghamshire, Lady E. Luttrell, and Mrs. Sturt were convicted before N. Conant and T. Robinson, Esqrs. in the penalty of 50*l.* each for playing at the game of faro ; and Henry Martindale was convicted in the sum of 200*l.* for keeping the faro table at Lady Buckinghamshire's house. The witnesses were two *ci-devant* servants of Lady Buckinghamshire. There were informations against Mrs. Concanon and Mr. O'Brien for similar offences. Both the defendants were found guilty, and paid the penalty.

Play not unfrequently afforded eighteenth-century amazons an opportunity of avenging themselves upon their adversaries in a manner not likely to be readily forgotten :—

Jemmy Lumley last week had a party of whist at his own house: the combatants Lucy Southwell, that curtsies like a bear, Mrs. Prijean, and a Mrs. Mackenzy. They played from six in the evening till twelve next day, Jemmy never winning one rubber, and rising a loser of two thousand pounds. How it happened I know not, nor why his suspicions arrived so late, but he fancied himself cheated, and refused to pay. However the bear had no share in his evil surmises ; on the contrary, a day or two afterwards, he promised a dinner at Hampstead to Lucy and her virtuous sister. As he went to the rendezvous his chaise was stopped by somebody who advised him not to proceed. Yet no whit daunted, he advanced. In the garden he found the gentle conqueress, Mrs. Mackenzy, who accosted him in the most friendly manner. After a few compliments, she asked him if he did not intend to pay her.

[1] See *Annual Register*, March 1797. See also *Life of Kenyon.*

'No, indeed, I shan't; I shan't; your servant, your servant.' 'Shan't you?' said the fair virago, and taking a horsewhip from beneath her hoop, she fell upon him with as much vehemence as the Empress-Queen would upon the King of Prussia if she could catch him alone in the garden at Hampstead.[1]

The Rev. Dr. Dibdin, in his 'Reminiscences of a Literary Life,' speaking of his friends, mentions the sad end which befel one in particular, a young man of gentle birth. Having lost his all at a metropolitan gambling hell, he, after the fashion of the time, played the part of a highwayman on Hounslow Heath at the hazard of life or death. One dark tempestuous evening the masked spendthrift was on horseback with two loaded pistols in his holsters. A postchaise drew near, and the travellers were unceremoniously ordered to 'stop and deliver their moneys.' Both were armed, one drew his pistol, and shot the highwayman through the heart. It was the hand of the highwayman's own father which drew the trigger of that pistol![2]

The seer of Chelsea once gave it as his opinion that duelling was one of the sincerities of human life. It was certainly one of the sincerities of English life in the eighteenth century, and the reasons why it was so are not far to seek. In the first place, the fact must be taken into account that the condition of the London thoroughfares was so disgraceful until the latter end of the century that it rendered all attempts on the part of the poor feeble old watchmen to prevent and quell the daily, nay hourly, disturbances of the public peace inefficacious. In the second place, the strife and rancour of political feeling, the brawls and squabbles of coffee-houses and taverns, *love affairs*, and, beyond everything else, the universal mania for gambling, tended to produce quarrels and irritation; and, at a time when the canons of fashion declared swords to be indispensable articles of male attire, it can hardly be wondered at that duels were of such frequent occurrence as they were. Mrs. Delany has recorded that the practice of duelling was the reigning curse of the age in which she lived. She was perfectly justified in so saying. The ball-room, the masquerade, the open streets, the public walks, the coffee-houses, the pits of the

---

[1] *Walpole to Montagu*, May 14, 1761   [2] I. p. ·94.

theatres, were the scenes of quarrels, which, in ninety-nine cases out of a hundred, ended in duels; and scarcely a week passed without one human victim at least being immolated on the altar of worldly honour. Suppose, for example, that two bewigged and powdered gentlemen of the Georgian era, the one a staunch Whig and the other an equally staunch Tory, chanced to meet after nightfall at the corner of some dimly-lighted street or in the midst of a narrow, miry lane, and both, like the two misguided goats in the old fable, flatly refused to make room for the other to pass. Does the reader imagine that either would have thought twice about drawing his sword, and endeavouring to move his opponent by force? Or suppose again that two coffee-house wiseheads, each professing an entirely different religious and political creed, were seated in White's Chocolate House, warmly engaged in discussing over the steam of the cups which cheer but not inebriate some such knotty problem as, 'Whether, in the case of a religious war, the Protestants would not be too strong for the Papists?'—would it have occasioned much surprise among the company if, in the heat of the discussion, the two wiseheads lost their tempers, and eventually rose to decide so momentous a question at the point of the sword, either in the street, or in an adjoining apartment? Not in the least. Or suppose, again, that Lord Mudler whom Dame Nature had slighted, and Lord Swamp to whom she had been exceedingly kind, were both simultaneously paying their addresses to that comely damsel the Lady Carolina Amelia Wilhelmina Crimp, and that her ladyship resented not the blandishments of Lord Swamp, although not the first to arrive in the field, while she hardly condescended to give ear to the passionate confession of love poured forth by his lordship of Mudler. Would that worthy, finding his suit rejected, have hesitated to call out his rival sooner or later to 'an affair of honour' in the fields at the rear of Montagu House, or in the 'Ring' within Hyde Park? Not for a moment.

Curiously enough, the prevalent idea even among the most orthodox people at this time seems to have been that some knowledge of the art 'of crossing swords' was absolutely essential to all who wished to be included in the category of fine gentlemen. Dr. Johnson was only endorsing with approval the public opinion of the age in which he lived on this particular subject, when he asserted in the hearing of Boswell that ' he who fought a duel did not fight from passion against his antagonist, but out of self-defence, to avert the stigma of the world and to prevent himself from being driven out of society ; ' and when on another occasion he declared that ' its barbarous violence was more justifiable than war, in which thousands went forth without any cause of personal quarrel to massacre each other.' [1] Mrs. Peachum in Gay's ' Beggar's Opera ' counts it a great blessing that no one of the gang of rogues has committed murder for seven months. Wherepon Mr. Peachum answers, ' What a dickens is the woman always whimpering about murder for ? No gentleman is ever looked upon the worse for killing a man in his own defence, and if business cannot be carried on without it, what would you have a gentleman do ? ' The melancholy letter which the poet Moore has preserved, written by a gentleman to his family the night preceding the day on which he was to perish by the hand of his antagonist in a duel, shows in what a serious light the practice was regarded in society :—

London, Wednesday night, September 3, 1783. I commit my soul to Almighty God, in hopes of his mercy and pardon for the irreligious step I now, in compliance with the unwarrantable custom of this wicked world, put myself under the necessity of taking.

Actuated by notions of pride utterly false, men considered it beneath their dignity either to acknowledge, apologise, or retract, and held that all shortcomings should be atoned for either at the point of the sword or the mouth of the pistol. Retired spots were to be found in profusion in the vicinity of the metropolis, and in them ' gentlemanly satisfaction ' might be demanded and received at any hour of the day or night. There were few men of any eminence in the last century who were not in their time ' called out,' to use the phrase in vogue ; but the passion, like that of gambling, was not confined to any one class or rank. It pervaded all without exception.

[1] Croker's *Boswell*, c. xxvii.

Every significant and every insignificant gambling establishment, every coffee-house, tavern, and place of public amusement, produced its brace of duellists.[1] If a 'deep player' became
'peevish at losing his money,' or a desperate sharper sought
the wherewithal to improve the low state of his finances
he would seize the first opportunity of picking a quarrel with
some member of the company, and challenge him to a duel.
If the challenge was accepted, the conflicting parties stepped
into an empty room or walked into the streets to begin operations, and wounded each other with their swords or hangers in
the twinkling of an eye. The thirst for revenge or plunder
maddened and goaded them on, and not unfrequently death
stepped in and relieved both, long before the drowsy watchman
in his box scarcely a hundred yards off had fully persuaded
himself that he was awake. The discovery of dead bodies in the
London streets was very far from uncommon during the century,
and duellists and thieves seem at times to have fairly vied
with one another in furnishing the greater number of victims.

The principal localities which duellists selected for glutting
their passion were Covent Garden, Lincoln's Inn Fields,
the Ring in Hyde Park, the Field of the Forty Footsteps,
Barnes Elms, and Wimbledon Common in Surrey. It was
customary to invite to a duel the friends of the respective
combatants, and it sometimes happened that more than two
parties engaged in it, for the seconds occasionally grew excited
as it proceeded, and ended by wielding their own swords right
lustily in defence of their principals. Very often the challenges
were both written and delivered by personal friends, and it is
to this custom that Foote, the playwright, is alluding, when in
act the second, scene the first, of his play entitled 'The Mayor
of Garrat,' he causes a captain of militia to exclaim, 'I will get
our chaplain to pen me a challenge.'

The English essayists in the reign of Queen Anne, to their
credit be it said, did what they could by means of the pen to
arouse public feeling against duelling. Sir Richard Steele, in
particular, contributed to No. 84 of the 'Spectator' an ably
written essay on that topic, having special reference to a duel

[1] Davies's *Life of Garrick*, i. 23.

which had then been recently fought in Tothill Fields between one Richard Thornhill and Sir Cholmondeley Dering, a Kentish baronet in whose death it had resulted, denouncing the detestable practice. But the public for whom Mr. Bickerstaff catered either could not, or would not, be converted by essays, octavos, or quartos. The number of duels continued to increase notwithstanding, and during the first forty years of the reign of George III. (1760–1800) fifty-three it is recorded were fought in England alone, but this probably does not represent more than half of those which actually took place. It must not be forgotten, however, that in the eyes of the law, duelling was regarded as murder, and as such was often punished, for in 1708 a man named Mawgridge was executed at Tyburn for having two years previously slain in a duel a certain William Cope.[1]

One of the most sensational duels which were fought in this country during the last century was that between the Duke of Hamilton and Lord Mohun. On the morning of Saturday, November 15, 1712, the keepers of Hyde Park heard from afar the loud clashing of swords. Hastening in the direction whence the sounds were proceeding, they found the Duke of Hamilton and Lord Mohun both stretched upon the greensward weltering in their blood. The duke's second, Colonel Hamilton, remaining, was taken into custody ; but Lord Mohun's second, General Macartney, immediately took to his heels and fled. In the explanation which followed, it transpired that for certain reasons the Duke of Hamilton had conceived a deadly hatred against Lord Mohun, described as 'one of the arrantest rakes in the town,' 'a scandal to the peerage,' and one moreover who before he had attained his majority had been thrice tried for murder by the House of Peers. Furthermore it was alleged that at a chance meeting the Duke of Hamilton grossly insulted Lord Mohun, who there and then angrily challenged him to a duel—a challenge which the duke was with great reluctance prevailed upon to accept. According to Bishop Burnet's gossiping 'history' of the times in which he lived,

---

[1] *State Trials.*

both being harried by false points of honour, fatally went out, and fought with so violent an animosity that, neglecting the rules of art, they seemed to run on one another, as if they tried who should kill first, in which they were both so unhappily successful that the Lord Mohun was killed outright, and Duke Hamilton died in a few minutes after.[1]

Dean Swift, writing in the ' Journal to Stella' under date of November 15, 1712, states that 'the duke was helped to the Cake House, by the Ring in Hyde Park, where they fought, and died on the grass before they could reach the house.' Shortly after this disgraceful affair occurred, a bill was introduced into the House of Commons for the imposition of a more effectual restraint upon duelling, but it was lost after the second reading. Affrays very similar to the one just described were of constant occurrence. This is evident from the various newspapers and periodicals of the times. Malcolm is the authority for a story to the effect that on the evening of one of the court drawing-rooms or levées in 1717, a large party of individuals who 'moved in the sphere of gentlemen,' assembled at the Royal Chocolate House in St. James's Street. Very soon disputes at hazard provoked a violent quarrel, which speedily became general throughout the room. By-and-by sword-fighting began ; a fierce encounter ensued, and it was not long before three gentlemen lay mortally wounded on the floor. The affray was at length ended by the arrival of the Royal Guards, who were compelled as a last resource to fell the most pugnacious of the combatants to the ground with the butt ends of their muskets, as all their entreaties and commands were found to be of no avail. Time rolled on, and the mischief multiplied an hundred-fold.

In the month of June 1719 two Doctors of Medicine, one named Mead and the other named Woodward, in consequence of some professional altercation, fought ' like butchers' at the gates of the Gresham College, a circumstance sufficient to have caused the pious founder of that venerable institution to turn in his grave. ' Take your life,' growled Dr. Mead. ' Anything but your physic,' muttered his adversary as he fell wounded to

---

[1] Burnet's *History of the Reign of Queen Anne*, b. vii.

the ground. In further illustration of the lengths to which the practice of sword-drawing ran, the following paragraph, transcribed from the issue of the 'Original Weekly Journal' for May 21, 1720, may be adduced :—

On Wednesday night last, about twelve, there was such a great riot in Windmill Street, near the Haymarket, that near 100 gentlemen and others were all engaged at one time, some with swords and others with sticks and canes, wherein abundance were dangerously wounded ; the watchmen that came to put an end to the affray were knocked down and barbarously used. At last the patrol of Horse Guards came, and, finding them obdurate, rode through them, cutting all the way with their swords ; yet we hear of none that were killed upon the spot, though many, it is thought, cannot recover of their wounds.

A week had scarcely elapsed after this breach of the peace, when a certain Captain Fitzgerald and three of his companions, while passing down the Strand, met a lady returning home from St. James's in a sedan chair, and attempted to arrest her progress ; opposed by the chairmen, the assailants drew their swords, demolished the chair, and ran through the body a watchman who arrived on the scene.

The pits of the playhouses often contributed a brace of duellists, and it not unfrequently happened that as the hour of trial drew near, the valour of the parties, like that of Mr. Robert Acres, oozed out at the ends of their fingers. Thus one evening in 1720, while the celebrated actress Mrs. Oldfield was captivating an audience with her impersonation of the 'Scornful Lady,' Beau Robert Fielding (immortalised by Steele in the 'Tatler' as 'Orlando the Fair') insulted a barrister named Fulwood by pushing rudely against him. Fulwood loudly expostulating, the beau clapped his hand upon his sword. Fulwood drew his, and ran it into the body of his adversary, who walked off exhibiting his bleeding wound to the audience, in order to excite the pity of the fair sex. Greatly to his chagrin the ladies laughed loudly at his misfortune.

In 1730 William Pulteney, who subsequently became Earl of Bath, and Lord John Hervey, unjustly and ungenerously immortalised by Pope in the prologue to his 'Satires' as Sporus, 'that thing of silk, that mere white curd of asses' milk,' fought a duel. Lord Hervey had on several occasions earnestly defended the administration of Sir Robert Walpole, who had been bitterly attacked in the 'Craftsman' newspaper, of which Pulteney was the editor. One of these defences was answered by William Pulteney in a pamphlet which he entitled 'A Proper Reply to a late Scurrilous Libel,' containing several remarks of a decidedly personal nature. Hervey thereupon sent his antagonist a challenge, which was accepted, and the pair fought with swords in St. James's Park during the afternoon of Monday, January 25, 1730, between the hours of three and four o'clock, Charles James Fox and Sir John Rushout acting in the capacity of seconds. As it happened, this particular duel terminated bloodlessly, and without any serious consequences ensuing to either.[1]

Under date of August 7, 1735, a paragraph in the Gentleman's Monthly Intelligencer of the 'London Magazine' sets forth that

> About six this morning a duel was fought near the Horse Guard House at Kennington, between James Lee, of the county of Salop, Esq., and an ensign in Colonel Reed's regiment of foot at Gibraltar, when, after several passes, the former received a slight wound in his left breast, and the other was run through his body and died on the spot. Mr. Andrews gave the challenge, and they fought at first in the Privy Garden ; but Mr. Lee's sword being broke, they were parted, and went home to their lodgings, which was in the same house. Mr. Andrews would not rest, but challenged him again and so met his fate.

Not a word is here said respecting the origin of the quarrel, nor is it even stated upon what grounds, if any, Mr. Andrews deemed it his bounden duty to challenge Mr. Lee again.

The following account of a duel is extracted from a number of the 'Westminster Journal,' 1735, and will serve to indicate the nature of the frivolous quarrels and disputes which too often ended in affairs of honour :—

> Wednesday (it runs) a duel was fought behind Montagu House between two journeymen lace-weavers. The combatants entered the field, accompanied by their seconds, when, the usual cere-

---

[1] *Gent.'s Mag.* January 1731 ; *Lord Hervey's Memoirs,* ed. Croker, i. 24.

monies being gone through, one of the parties discharged his pistol, the ball from which took away part of the sleeve of his antagonist's coat, and then like a man of courage, without waiting for the fire being returned, made the best of his way off the field. The quarrel began at a public house about the mode of cooking a dish of sprats, one insisting on having them fried, and the other on having them boiled. With the assistance of some friends, the sum of 3*s.* was raised to procure the use of pistols to decide this important contest. To such a pitch is the most honourable profession of duelling arrived.

Not the least important topic which engrossed the talk of the fashionable world in the early part of November 1763 was Wilkes's duel with Mr. Martin. Mrs. Harris, writing from Whitehall to her son at Oxford under date of November 22, 1763, gave the following particulars of it :—

Wilkes fought a duel this morning in Hyde Park, with Mr. Martin (member for Camelford) ; he has received two balls in his body, which are extracted, and the wound thought not dangerous. Mr. Martin said yesterday in the House that whoever wrote an anonymous paper so impudent and abusive as the ' North Briton ' was a lying scoundrel, and repeated it again, ' I say he is a lying scoundrel.' I surmise from this that Wilkes must have sent the challenge, but that I only guess.[1]

The worthy lady guessed correctly. Mr. Samuel Martin, M.P., according to other accounts, had stigmatised the great agitator in the House of Commons as ' a cowardly and malignant scoundrel.' This was too much for Wilkes, who greatly prided himself upon his gallantry. He thereupon sent a challenge to Martin, who accepted it. Both repaired to Hyde Park with a couple of pistols apiece, and fired four times, when Wilkes fell wounded to the ground. On one occasion this worthy was unwittingly the cause of a duel. A certain coffee-house wiseacre, while estimating his character, did not scruple to call him a ' coward and a scoundrel in the same breath '— epithets which he further asserted were equally true of all who supported his cause. Thereupon a reverend gentleman named Green came to the defence of Wilkes, and having pulled the wiseacre lustily by the nose, told him, that he for one would be prepared to back John Wilkes against a Scotchman any

---

[1] *Correspondence of 1st Earl of Malmesbury*, i. 101.

day. As this proved to be more than the other could stand, they posted off, although the night was far spent, to the 'Ring' in Hyde Park, where they presently set matters to rights.

After the memorable fracas between Lord Byron and William Chaworth, which took place in 1765, the fashion of beaux wearing swords in public began gradually to fall into desuetude. It would have been well for the peace of society if the passion for duelling had gone with it. But the time for that had not yet arrived. The cause of the duel which has just been mentioned, like that of many others, was frivolous to the last degree. The two combatants both belonged to the Nottinghamshire Club, the members of which were in the habit of dining together in London once a month at the Star and Garter Tavern, in Pall Mall. On January 26, 1765, the club met as usual, and the conversation happening to turn upon the best methods of preserving game, Mr. Chaworth warmly disputed with a gentleman who happened to be sitting next to him. Lord Byron, grand-uncle of the illustrious poet of that name, joining, gave it as his opinion that game was best left to take care of itself. From that opinion Mr. Chaworth, who was his kinsman, expressed his dissent. This drew on an altercation, but as both contrived to keep their tempers, nothing came of it. Later in the evening, however, they had recourse to a duel, which was fought with rapiers in the dining-room of the Star and Garter, by the light of a small tallow candle, with the result that Mr. Chaworth was run through the body. Lord Byron was committed to the Tower, and subsequently tried before the House of Lords. The peers who were present, with the exception of four, found him guilty of manslaughter. His lordship, however, conveniently claimed the benefit of the clergy, under an old statute enacted in the first year of the reign of King Edward VI. The peers assenting to this claim, Lord Byron regained freedom on payment of the customary fees.[1]

On January 29, 1771, Lords Milton and Poulett fought a duel behind Bedford House, for what reason is not recorded.

[1] Howell's *State Trials*, xix. 1178-1235; Walpole's *Memoirs*, ii. 51; *Letters*, iv. 491.

In May 1772, Richard Brinsley Sheridan, the playwright, fought two duels with Captain Mathews on account of Miss Linley, 'the maid of Bath,' a celebrated singer of that day. First, at the Castle Tavern, Henrietta Street, Covent Garden, wherein Sheridan was much wounded. 'Both their swords breaking upon the first lunge, they threw each other down, and with the broken pieces hacked at each other, rolling upon the ground, the seconds standing by, quiet spectators.'[1] The second took place on July 1 following, and is thus alluded to by the 'Bath Chronicle' of July 2 :—

> This morning about three o'clock a second duel was fought with swords between Captain Mathews and Mr. R. Sheridan, on Kingsdown, near this city, in consequence of their former dispute respecting an amiable lady, which Mr. M. considered as improperly adjusted ; Mr. S. having since their first rencontre, declared his sentiments respecting Mr. M. in a manner that the former thought required satisfaction. Mr. Sheridan received three or four wounds in his breast and sides, and now lies very ill. Mr. M. was only slightly wounded, and left the city soon after the affair was over.

In February 1773 Lord Townshend and the Earl of Bellamont settled long-standing differences which had existed between them with small swords and pistols in Marylebone Fields. The duellists embraced before they engaged in conflict, and each exclaimed, 'Long life to your lordship.' The latter recommended his seven natural children to the care of his opponent in the event of his death. Lord Bellamont, however, did not die, although he was wounded in the encounter.[2] During the course of the same year, Whately and Temple fought in Hyde Park, on account of certain confidential letters. Four years later, Captain Stoney and the Rev. Henry Bate (the Fighting Parson), who was then editor of the 'Morning Post,' were embroiled in an affair of honour. Bate (who subsequently assumed the name of Dudley) saw fit to give publication to some paragraphs in the columns of the 'Morning Post' which reflected discreditably upon the character of Lady Strathmore. These paragraphs gave great offence to Captain Robinson Stoney, who forthwith demanded the names of the

[1] Moore's *Life of Sheridan*, c. ii.
[2] *Correspondence of 1st Earl of Malmesbury*, i. 265.

writers. Bate persisting in his refusal to furnish him with them,
the captain sent him a challenge, which was accepted. The
Adelphi Tavern in the Strand was the scene of this duel, which
was fought first with pistols and subsequently with swords, both
combatants wounding each other very severely. The captain
afterwards assumed the name of Bowes, and married the lady.
His opponent became vicar of Bradwell, in Essex, and long
afterwards was created a baronet by the Prince Regent.[1]

At eight o'clock in the morning of November 29, 1779,
in consequence of a disagreement about certain expressions
uttered during the progress of a debate in the House of Commons, Charles James Fox fought a duel with Mr. Adam, receiving a slight wound.[2] In 1780 the Rev. Henry Bate fought
a duel in Hyde Park with a law student, who was wounded.
In March of the year following, Colonel Fullarton, member for
Plympton, and the Earl of Shelburne fought a duel in Hyde
Park in consequence of some altercation. Pistols were the
weapons which they selected, and the earl was wounded. In
April 1780 a gentleman named Donovan was tried at the
Kingston assizes on a charge of having killed Captain James
Hanson in a duel ; was found guilty of manslaughter and fined
ten pounds.

On September 4, 1783, Colonel Cosmo Gordon and Lieut.-
Colonel Thomas fought a duel in Hyde Park in which the
latter received a mortal wound. On the 17th of the next
month two gentlemen, named respectively Monro and Green,
met in a field near Battersea Bridge to settle a dispute. One
ball entered Monro's knee, and another entering Green's body
caused his death. During the same month Lieutenant Harrison,
of the Marines, and Harman Van Berkensham, an officer in
the Dutch service, fought behind the Foundling Hospital.
In August 1784 a naval officer, and a gentleman described as
'in the German service,' combated with swords and pistols
in Bayswater Fields, in which the latter was severely wounded

[1] Croker's *Boswell.*
[2] *Gent.'s Mag.* 1789. See also *Autob. and Corr. of Mrs. Delany,* 1st
series, iii. 317 ; Reynolds's *Life and Times,* i. 49; *Correspondence of 1st
Earl of Malmesbury,* i. 444, 454-5, 482 ; Barrow, *Life of Lord Macartney,*
i. 582.

in the thigh. In the month following, Lord Macartney and Thomas Sadleir contended in combat, the latter being wounded. In January 1786, Lieutenant Gamble and Lieutenant Mollison met as duellists at Chatham ; and in June of the same year, Lord Macartney and Major-General Stewart met for the same purpose near Kensington, in which the former was severely wounded. In September 1787 Sir John Macpherson and Major Browne fought with pistols in Hyde Park, in which the former 'behaved with great gallantry, and much like a man of honour.'

On May 17, 1789, the Duke of York and Colonel Lennox fought a duel on Wimbledon Common. His Royal Highness had chanced to let this expression fall from his lips : 'Colonel Lennox heard words spoken to him at Daubigny's, to which no gentleman ought to have submitted.' A dispute arose in consequence, and one sent the other a challenge, and both met as just stated, on Wimbledon Common, Colonel Lennox firing first, and grazing the duke's curl.[1] During the course of the same year three other duels were fought ; one between Captain Pellew and Lieutenant Northey, at Exeter, in June ; a second between Captain Tongue and Captain Paterson on the 19th of the same month ; and a third, between Lieut.-Colonel Lennox and Theophilus Swift, in a field on the Oxford Road on July 1. Instances enough have been quoted, but it may be worth while to complete the list covered by the next ten years. Captain Aston and Lieutenant Fitzgerald, near Chalk Farm, June 25, 1790 ; Graham and Julius, upon Blackheath, July 19, 1791, the former being killed ; Frizell and Clark, in Hyde Park, June 1792, in which the latter was killed. A dispute between Kemble and Atkin respecting certain arrangements at Drury Lane led to a duelling contest in March 1792, with pistols, in Marylebone Fields.

Early on the morning of June 9, 1792, the Earl of Lonsdale and Captain Cuthbert fought at Hyde Park. The captain had issued orders that no vehicle of any kind or description should pass through Mount Street. Lord Lonsdale attempted to pass, but being foiled in his attempt, addressed Captain Cuthbert in

[1] *Bland Burges Papers*, ed. Hutton.

S 2

this fashion :—' You rascal, do you know that I am a peer of the realm ? ' ' I don't know that you are a peer ; but I know you are a scoundrel for applying such a term to an officer on duty ; and I will make you answer for it,' and a brace of pistols was accordingly fired on either side.

July 2, 1792, witnessed a meeting between Lord Lauderdale and General Arnold, near Kilburn Wells, but nothing came of it, which was quite the reverse in the duel which was fought ir. the vicinity of Cobham in Kent on January 12, 1796, between Major Sweetman and Captain Watson, wherein the former was killed, and the latter severely wounded.

On April 30, 1796, the Duke of Norfolk and Lord Malden were engaged in an affair of honour in a field near Paddington. William Carpenter and John Pridi, both Americans, fought in Hyde Park on August 20, 1796, when Carpenter was killed. On May 4 in the year following Lieutenants Fitzgerald and Warrington quarrelled in the theatre at Plymouth, and subse- quently exchanged shots. In the October following Colonels King and Fitzgerald fought a duel on a spot near the Magazine in Hyde Park. The former had challenged the latter by reason of his elopement with his second cousin, the Hon. Miss King. At the meeting in Hyde Park six shots were fired without effect, but at a second meeting in Ireland, Colonel Fitzgerald received a fatal wound. The last duel on English soil during the eighteenth century of which any record remains was that in May 1798, between the Right Hon. William Pitt, M.P. and Mr. George Tierney, M.P. Briefly it originated thus. On the 25th, Pitt had introduced into Parliament a bill for the repeal of all protections from pressing for six months ; and in bringing forward his motion had justi- fied both the bill and his proposal to pass it through all its stages in one day, by the precedent of 1779, when a similar measure had met with complete success. Tierney's opposition to it arose in consequence of its having been ' brought in with- but previous notice,' and of his inability to see any necessity for celerity. 'After some transactions that have taken place,' he observed, 'I shall be extremely jealous of everything the right honourable gentleman proposes to do, and at present I consider him as calling upon the House to surrender the few remaining liberties of the country.' Pitt, on rising, remarked that 'the honourable gentleman seemed to have something in his mind which it was to be wished that he had spoken out more distinctly, when he said that he entertained a jealousy in consequence of something which had recently taken place.' He then proceeded to assign certain reasons which rendered the speedy passing of the bill a necessity, and before he resumed his seat, remarked that if the honourable gentleman meant to oppose the measure, he should conclude that the only motive which actuated him to do so was that of impeding the service and defence of the country. Tierney on hearing this claimed the protection of the chair, whereupon the Speaker rose and said that 'if Mr. Pitt had made use of the language to which Mr. Tierney had taken exception, it certainly was disorderly and unparliamentary. It was, however, for the House to determine whether such was the language or not ; and the House would wait for the right honourable gentleman's explanation.' Any explanation, however, Pitt declined to give, and maintained that although he had no right to impute any particular motives to any gentleman, he had a right to infer motives from arguments ; and therefore if he were right in saying that no man could be justified in opposing the present measure, and that to oppose it was to impede the defence of the country, it was fair for him to state those arguments, which he believed to be conclusive, and which he would submit to the judgment of the House, but which he would not in the slightest degree retract. Later in the evening, this language was commented on by a member. Pitt declared 'that he would abide by his words and give no explanation.' There was no further interposition on the part of the Speaker. In the course of the following day, however, Tierney sent Pitt a challenge, which he accepted. On the 27th, accompanied each by seconds (Mr. Ryder for Pitt, and Sir G. Walpole for Tierney), they proceeded to Wimbledon Common, where having discharged their pistols they were reconciled.[1] The greatest triumph of civilised man is that of

[1] Lord Colchester's *Diary*, i. pp. 154-5.

reason over impulse. ' Hates any man the thing he would not kill ? ' says Shylock. Hatred is often the cause of murder, and the reason why there are not more duels nowadays is to be found in the fact of the predominance of reason over impulse. That in political as well as in private matters, hatred does visit the breasts of the opponents is, of course, true enough, but reflection in most cases asserts itself, and extinguishes the sparks before they burst into the flames of physical opposition.

CHAPTER VIII.

THE annals of English popular credulity and superstition, so far
as the last century is concerned, will bear favourable comparison
with any of those golden eras by which it had been preceded.
Though the human mind had been stimulated by various con-
curring causes to extraordinary displays of strength and energy,
it was still in a state which disposed it strongly to credulity and
superstition.   Men, to borrow the language of Butler in
'Hudibras,' still 'groped to anticipate the cabinet designs of
fate,' still sought the invaluable aid of astrologers, wizards, wise
women, and fortune-tellers in their eagerness to pierce the thick
veil which concealed the weighty secrets of futurity from their
prying gaze, still continued to swallow with avidity the most
palpable deceptions and the most audacious impostures, still
regarded with a veneration bordering almost upon idolatry,
hundreds of nameless charlatans who made pretensions to
augury, geomancy, hydromancy, oneiromancy, palmistry, and
endless other forms of divination, manifesting their adherence
thereto not only by consulting them

> When brass and pewter pots did stray
> And linen shrank out of the way,

but what was of still more importance, when in doubt as to
the auspiciousness and inauspiciousness of days for the commencement of undertakings, to the possibilities of happiness
or unhappiness in the times which were to come, to their
chances of matrimony, to their prospects of health, wealth,
and prosperity. Belief in what was possible exercised an
influence to an extent which it would now be difficult, if not
impossible, accurately to appraise. Men were still the uncon-
scious slaves of superstition. They yet entertained many of the
fantastic beliefs which had been handed down from a remote
past. They were firmly persuaded that the prince of darkness
made bondservants of humanity, that he entered into alliances
with men, and that he was easily to be propitiated with gifts.
The marvellous properties of the philosopher's stone, at the
touch of which all baser metals changed to gold, and the elixir
of life, which conferred immortality on all who tasted it, had
not even yet been relegated to the limbo of exploded heresies.
As of yore the denizens of the elfin world were vulgarly
supposed, apparelled in celestial light, to pace with printless
feet the dewy green in many a forest glade, and the circles
commonly seen on grassy links and pastures were regarded as
indubitable signs of their revels.

Owing to the spread and increase of knowledge upon the
subject of natural philosophy, the once sublime science of
astrology has lost its savour, and whereas it now numbers its
adherents and believers by tens, it then numbered them by
thousands. The capital and the provinces literally teemed
with men and women who gained a livelihood by telling fortunes and casting nativities, and by the extensive sale of their
ridiculous inventions called 'sigils,' the possession of which
was vulgarly supposed to avert evil and destruction from life
and property. In those days the pretended 'dealers in
Destiny's dark counsel,' whom the slings and arrows of modern
legislative enactments have all but exterminated, were unques-
tionably people of no small importance in their way. Who they
really were, or where they came from, probably few troubled
themselves to ascertain. Nameless they lived, nameless they
died. The broad fact that they were astrologers, men who

professed to be endowed with the power of foretelling what should and what should never be, and of disclosing 'the secrets of the world unknown,' was quite sufficient for the English public in the eighteenth century, who swallowed their oracular utterances with a complacency which throws the age in which we live, credulous as it is in many respects, far into the shade. To all those who had failed to make their way in any other profession, or who had missed their vocation, the field of astrology afforded a welcome refuge ; and it can easily be understood how it was that they came to be regarded with such superstitious awe and respect as it is evident they were, by the ignorant and credulous multitudes who visited them for the purpose of having their fortunes told or their doubts 'resolved,' when the imposing display they were accustomed to make in their dusky dens, which were situated for the most part in Spitalfields and Seven Dials, is taken into account. Nothing was easier of accomplishment at this time to either man or woman gifted with an ordinary amount of self-assurance and plenty of that to which the world usually applies the term of humbug, than to set up as an astrologer.

To engage a convenient lodging, and to suspend a hatch over the door of it—to darken one chamber and to hang it round with mirrors and awe-inspiring pictures—to deposit where they were most likely to arrest attention a number of empty coloured bottles, gallipots, and vials filled with drippings of tar and oil, several skulls, a stuffed animal, a skeleton or two, several musty tomes of Greek, Latin, and Arabic literature to heighten the effect—to place wide open on a table the fourth book of Cornelius Agrippa's 'Occult Philosophy,' for the delectation of visitors, a caduceus, one or two packs of cards, and half-a-dozen gilt shillings on a tray to represent a number of guineas just received by way of fees—this in effect was the sum total of all the requisite preliminary operations. Surrounded by these outward and visible signs of his profession, the astrologer, arrayed in a rusty or threadbare black academical gown or cloak, sat down to wait for customers, who would be brought in by a touter like Cadwallader in 'Peregrine Pickle' who conveyed *à priori* information concerning intending visitors, the questions they were desirous of asking, and the answers they were most desirous of receiving, fees being charged according to the known rank and means of the inquirer.[1]

Taking all this into account, it is not surprising that those who exercised the craft of an astrologer grew rich. Yet now and then the professor of planetary influence was liable to suffer severe reverses of fortune, as the following sad story, extracted from the February number of the 'Universal Magazine,' 1775, sufficiently indicates :—

> January the tenth, Saturday evening.—A woman applied to a resolver of lawful questions in a court in Fleet Street, to be satisfied in relation to some future events ; but while poor Albumazer was consulting the stars in his chamber in order to resolve her doubts, he seems to have been utterly ignorant of his own pleasant fortune, for some thieves (supposed to be the inquirer's confederates) stripped his other apartments of everything that was conveniently portable.

Belief in the potency of astrology penetrated the strata of society. Among people 'of quality' it found, of course, many dupes, among the working classes many more. Its fees, however, were in most cases very high, and often altogether beyond the purses of the poor. This, that quick penetration which would seem to have been one of the most marked characteristics of the fraternity, enabled them to see. But they were equal to the occasion. If the mountain could not go to Mahomet, Mahomet could go to the mountain. They catered for the ignorant simple-minded mortals who could not afford an 'interview' by the publication of almanacs and astrological diaries, widely diffusing and disseminating them through the rural districts. The titles and names of the authors of a few of the most popular of these presumptuous brochures are here subjoined : 'Merlinus Anglicus, junior; or the Starry Messenger,' by Henry Coley, Student in the Mathematicks and Celestial Sciences (printed by T. Read, 1723) ; 'A Diary Astronomical, Astrological, and Meteorological,' by Job Gadbury, Student in Physick and Astrology (printed by J. W., 1723) ; 'Vox Stellarum,' by Francis Moore, Licensed Physician and Student in Astrology (printed by Tho. Wood) ;

[1] Dr. Archenholz, *Picture of England*, pp. 116–7.

'Merlinus Liberatus,' by John Partridge (printed by J. Roberts) ; 'Parker's Ephemeris' (printed by J. Read) ; 'The Celestial Diary,' by Salem Pearse, Student in Physic and Celestial Science (printed by J. Dawkes) ; 'Apollo Anglicanus ; the English Apollo,' by Richard Saunder, Student in the Physical and Mathematical Sciences (printed by A. Wilde) ; 'The Apollo Anglicanus, the English Apollo ; assisting all persons in the right understanding of this year's Revolutions, as also of things past, present, and to come ;' by Richard Saunder, Student in the Physical and Mathematical Sciences (London : printed by J. Wilde for the Company of Stationers), 1715 ; 'Poor Robin,' 1715. An Almanack of the Old and New Fashion, or an Ephemerism Jest and Earnest, being of the best and newest edition, wherein the reader may observe (if he be cunning in observations) many remarkable things worthy his and others' choicest observation. Written by Poor Robin, Knight of the Burnt Island, a well-wisher to the mathematics ; 'Ephemeris Britannica, or an Astronomical State of the Heavens for the year of Our Lord 1715,' by G. Kingsley, Gent. (London, printed by J. D. for the Company of Stationers). It is to be noted that the original compilers of these trashy productions, so contrary to sound doctrine in religion, morals, and the sciences, all lived and died in the preceding century. The only name of eminence among their numerous successors was 'Old Moore,' the pseudonym of Henry Andrews, who was born at a village near Grantham in 1744, and who long acted as astronomical calculator to the Board of Longitude.

The perusal of one of these astrological diaries was doubtless well calculated to make 'the chilled blood shoot cold through every vein.' The prognostications of wars and battles to the day, nay the very hour of their occurrence, the plagues, pestilences, and famines, storms, earthquakes, the downfall of empires, the dark hints at the invasion of the country by foreign powers, the full and trustworthy information respecting the manifold arrangements of the clerk of the weather for twelve months to come ; impending revolutions in Church and State ; the proper months for purging the blood with potions, and for the letting of blood (for it should be borne in mind that in the eighteenth century bleeding at least six times during the year was considered a necessary condition of health) ; the times and seasons for the sowing of herbs and seeds—all this in addition to much other interesting, entertaining, not to say alarming matter, might be ascertained by a diligent perusal of their pages.

Widespread and universal was the belief in these cunning and wily impostors. Nothing could shake it, and one proof of the fact that plebeians were not the only ones who were tainted by it, is afforded by the fact that George I. consulted a certain French astrologer, who among other things confidently assured him that he would not survive the death of his consort above the space of a year, a prediction in which he placed such implicit credence that it is recorded that on the eve of his final departure for his Hanoverian dominions, he took a most affectionate farewell of all the members of his family, telling them with tears in his eyes that they would never behold him in the flesh again. It is really lamentable to reflect upon the amount of injury which the fortune-tellers and their compilations did in their own times, and yet in a certain degree their pernicious absurdities are even yet partially countenanced. But if astrology had its gloomy side, it certainly had its humorous side, since a famous professor of the occult sciences who flourished in the early part of the eighteenth century, 'Doctor' Partridge by name, was held up for ever to the scorn and ridicule of the world through the instrumentality of the Dean of St. Patrick's, Dublin. John Partridge (whose real name was Hewson) was born at East Sheen in 1644. He was a cobbler by trade, but became an assistant to Job Gadbury, an eminent astrologer. It is further stated (though this is on very doubtful authority) that he graduated in the faculty of medicine at the University of Leyden. In the closing years of the seventeenth century, Partridge published an almanack annually from his house at the sign of the Blue Bull in Salisbury Street, Strand. That which he issued in 1707 ('Merlinus Liberatus') tickled the fancy of Swift, and when it appeared in the year following, he wrote one which he entitled Isaac Bickerstaff's 'Predictions for the Year 1708,' of which the first related to Partridge, the almanack-maker. ' I have consulted the star of his nativity,' he writes, 'by my own rules ; and find he will infallibly die upon the 29th of March next, about eleven at night, of a raging fever. Therefore I advise him to consider of it, and settle his affairs in time.' On March 30, Swift, in the character of a Revenue Officer, wrote a letter to a lord, in which he said that Partridge died on March 30, 1708, of a raging fever, not without having confessed himself a fanatic or nonconformist, and repented of his astrological fooleries from the bottom of his heart. Partridge now saw clearly enough that if the public were not speedily informed that he was still in the land of the living, the public would believe that he had crossed the Stygian ferry, so he persuaded Nicholas Rowe, or Dr. Yalden, preacher at Bridewell, to write a pamphlet roundly denying Bickerstaff's assertions. Forthwith appeared ' Squire Bickerstaff detected ; or the Astrological Impostor convicted ; ' by John Partridge, Student in Physic and Astrology. To this Swift replied in a pamphlet which he entitled ' A Vindication of Isaac Bickerstaff, Esq.,' in which among other things he asserted that Mrs. Partridge had gone about for some time to every alley in the neighbourhood in which she lived, swearing to the gossips that her husband 'had neither life nor soul in him.' After this onslaught, Partridge refrained from publishing his almanack. In 1714, he seems to have taken heart again, for his ' Merlinus Redivivus ' appeared in that year, and contained an abusive epistle addressed to Isaac Bickerstaff, Esq., and on the last leaf the subjoined notice :—

This is to give notice to all people, that all those Prophecies, Predictions, Almanacks, and other Pamphlets that had my name, either true or shammed with the want of a letter, I say they are all impudent forgeries, by a breed of villains, and wholly without my knowledge and consent.

Partridge, it is recorded, died in London in June 1715, and was interred at Mortlake in Surrey. That he did not shuffle off the coil of mortality before the annual appearance of his almanack is evident from the following brief prefatory note prefixed to it :—

It is very probable that the beggarly knavish crew will be this year also printing prophecies and predictions in my name, to cheat the country as they used to do. This is, therefore, to give notice that if there is anything of that kind done in my name besides this Almanack printed by the Company of Stationers, you may be certain it is not mine, but a cheat, and therefore refuse it. Those that have occasion for that medicine called Matthews his pill, or Starkey's, they may be furnished at my house with it at 3*s.* 6*d.* the ounce.

Partridge's almanack continued in common with others to be published until the close of the period.

In the first half of the eighteenth century there was a famous soothsayer or fortune-teller in London who lived 'in Exeter Court over against the Savoy in the Strand.' The name of this man was Duncan Campbell, and according to a history of his life and adventures, which was written or rather concocted by Daniel Defoe, and published in 1720, was born in Scotland both deaf and dumb. Duncan Campbell held daily receptions to which people of the highest rank resorted to receive his oracular counsel. 'Visitants,' wrote Steele in No. 14 of the 'Tatler,' 'come to him full of expectations and pay his own rate for the interpretations they put upon his shrugs and nods.' Campbell is also alluded to in the pages of No. 560 of the 'Spectator':—

Everyone has heard of the famous conjuror, who, according to the opinion of the vulgar, has studied himself dumb. Be that as it will, the blind Tiresias was not more famous in Greece than this dumb artist has been for some years last past in the cities of London and Westminster.

Like almost every other impostor at this time, Duncan Campbell wriggled himself into the good graces of royalty, 'The Daily Post ' of Wednesday, May 4, 1720, informing its readers that ' Last Monday Mr. Campbell, the deaf and dumb gentleman (introduced by Colonel Carr) kissed the king's hand and presented to his Majesty "The History of his Life and Adventures," which was by his Majesty most graciously received.' Campbell, in addition to investigating the mysteries of the lights of heaven, sold nostrums ; for in a postscript to a ridiculous pamphlet which he published in 1726, entitled 'The Friendly Demon, or the Generous Apparition, Being a True Narrative of a Miraculous Cure newly performed upon that famous Deaf and Dumb Gentleman Mr. Duncan Campbell, by a familiar spirit that appeared to him in a white surplice like a Cathedral Singing Boy,' the readers were informed that at Dr. Campbell's house in Buckingham Court, over against Old Man's Coffee House, at Charing Cross, they may be readily furnished with his ' Pulvis Miraculosus, and finest sort of Egyptian loadstones.' Death terminated the career of this impostor in 1730.

The subjoined advertisement will show that astrology was a science of the secrets of which the fair sex made themselves thoroughly master : —

Mrs. Williams, from Bath and Bristol Hot Wells, who is universally known to all Ladies who frequent the public watering places, informs her sex that she continues to be consulted, and delivers her astrological opinions as usual, which for their peculiar infallibility have been proved and acknowledged by the most general approbation during an extensive practice to be infinitely superior to anything ever yet attempted by the numerous pretenders to the art or mystery of prescience. She may be spoken with (by Ladies only) from ten in the morning till eight in the evening, at her house, the Artificial Flower Warehouse, Store Street, Bedford Square. Ladies will please to observe it is a small house with green rails.[1]

Why this obliging dame dedicated her knowledge to her own sex she does not say, but it is not difficult to guess.

It is related by the biographer of Bishop Butler, the author of ' The Analogy,' that that excellent prelate was one day observed by his chaplain to be buried in deep meditation above his ordinary wont. Questioned subsequently as to the particular subject or subjects which had occupied his thoughts, Butler replied that he had been engaged in considering whether as individuals went mad, it was not possible for whole nations to go mad. That men have apparently lost their wits *en masse*, at times, is a fact well known to every person even moderately well acquainted with the leading facts in the history of popular progress. A striking illustration of this is afforded in the annals of this country for the year of grace 1750. An earthquake had been foretold in the capital, and on the 8th day of February, according to Dr. Hugson, a shock was experienced in London, in Westminster, and on either side of the river, and of course greatly disconcerted the minds of the supersti-

[1] *Morning Post*, Jan. 12, 1788.

tious. A month later a second shock was felt, much more severely than the first, shaking the houses violently from top to bottom. The hearts of courtiers and citizens alike now began almost to fail them for very fear. Many regarded the earthquake as a sign of the wrath of the Deity at the vices and hideous corruption which surrounded the Church, and which her pastors made little or no attempt to stem—an opinion which was strengthened by the lectures, three in number, which were delivered by William Whiston at the Royal Exchange coffee-house early in March, and by the ravings of a fanatical soldier who called upon the inhabitants of the city to set their houses in order, in view of another shock which would take place on April 8, wherein the cities of London and Westminster would be engulfed. The churches and conventicles, usually deserted, now began to be crowded to overflowing with penitents. George Whitefield delivered eloquent orations to the crowds which had encamped in Hyde Park. The gambling hells were forsaken, and as the destined day drew near, dozens of the aristocracy permitted their fears so far to prevail over their sober judgment, that they quitted their town residences in great haste for their country seats. The highways for miles out of the metropolis were blocked with the array of coaches and carriages. This we learn from the testimony of Horace Walpole, Lady Hervey, and other contemporary writers :—

Several women (said Walpole, in writing to Sir Horace Mann under date of April 2, 1750) have made earthquake gowns, that is, warm gowns to sit out of doors all to-night. These are of the more courageous.

One woman, still more heroic, is come to town on purpose ; she says all her friends are in London, and she will not survive them. But what will you think of Lady Catherine Pelham, Lady Frances Arundel, and Lord and Lady Galway, who go this evening to an inn ten miles out of town, where they are to play at brag till five in the morning, and then come back, I suppose, to look for the bones of their husbands and families under the rubbish.

April 8 came at last, and with it the fears of all London citizens culminated :—

In after ages (wrote Smollett) it will hardly be believed, that on the evening of the eighth day of April, the open fields that skirt the metropolis were filled with an incredible number of people assembled in chairs, chaises, and coaches, as well as on foot, who waited in the most fearful suspense until the morning, and the return of day disproved the truth of the dreaded prophecy.

Another panic equally sudden and absurd occurred in 1756, several days elapsing before the panic subsided.

As an instance of the capriciousness of the popular taste it may be mentioned that some time after the year 1750 many thousands of people afflicted with asthma and other complaints resorted for cure to certain mineral springs, which had then recently been discovered in the neighbourhood of Glastonbury in Somersetshire ; and as his farrago is curious there is no need for any apology for here inserting 'a Copy of the Certificate of Matthew Chancellor's Dream,' whereby the virtues of these waters were discovered, transcribed from the July number of the ' Gentleman's Magazine ' 1751 :—

This is to certify all whom it may concern, that I, Matthew Chancellor, of the parish of North Wotton, in the county of Somerset, yeoman, had been very much afflicted with an asthma and phthisic almost 30 years till some time about the middle of October 1750, when I had a violent fit in the night, and afterwards fell asleep and dream'd that I was at Glastonbury some way above Chain Gate, and that I was in the horse track, and there saw some of the clearest water I ever saw in my life. I kneeled on my knees, and drank of it, and I could plainly perceive the plashing of the horses on both sides. As soon as I stood up, there seem'd to be a person by me, who, pointing with his finger, said unto me, if you will go to that freestone shoot and take a clean glass and drink a glass full (fasting) seven Sunday mornings following, and let no person see you, you will find a perfect cure of your disorder : and then make it public to the world. I asked him why seven Sunday mornings? He said, The world was made in six days, and on the seventh day God Almighty rested from his labour and blessed it above other days. He said likewise This water comes from out the holy ground where a great many saints and martyrs have been buried. He told me something concerning our Saviour being baptised in the river Jordan, but I could not remember it when I awaked. The Sunday morning following I went to Glastonbury, which is about three miles from the place where I live, and found it exactly according to my dream ; but as it was a very dry time, I could scarce see the water run in the shoot, so I dipp'd the glass three times into the hole where the shoot drooped, and took up to the value of a glass full, and drank it, giving God thanks; and so I continued to do seven Sundays, and by the blessing of God it recovered me of my disorder.

The ' Gentleman's Magazine' for 1751 records that

at Glastonbury, Somersetshire, a man, thirty years afflicted with an asthma, dreamed that he saw near the Chain Gate in the horse-track the clearest of water, and that a person told him if he drank a glass of water fasting seven Sunday mornings he should be cured, which proved true, and he attested it on oath ; many since have received great benefit from it.

Ten years later the readers of the same magazine were informed that

A young farmer, being in company at a public house in Petty France, Gloucestershire, on the 7th past, and going out was missed by his companions, who thought he had given them the slip, and was gone home ; but next morning inquiry was made after him by his father, who searched the country round for him in vain. Some time after, a relation of his having dreamt that he was drowned in a well, the well of the public house where he was missing was this day searched and his body found.

That curious superstition respecting the power possessed by the reigning sovereign of curing scrofula, or as it was more commonly known, 'the king's evil,' by touching individuals afflicted with it, was widely prevalent in England during the first half of the eighteenth century. Swift, in his 'Journal to Stella' under date of 1711, mentions that he had made application to the Queen Anne, through the Duchess of Ormond, in order to get a little boy suffering from scrofula 'touched' by her Majesty ; but the queen had been unable to touch, and as the season was then growing warm, the dean feared she would not be able to do so at all. Daines Barrington relates that an old man who was witness in a case that came before him solemnly averred that he was touched for the evil when a child by Queen Anne, at Oxford. Dr. Samuel Johnson as an infant 'had the misfortune to · be much affected with the scrofula or king's evil,' and when he was only thirty months old, his mother, acting on the advice of Sir John Floyer, a celebrated Warwickshire physician, brought him all the way from Lichfield to London to be touched by the same sovereign. Upon him, however, the queen's touch had no power. It was long asserted that the House of Brunswick never made any preten-sions to the possession of this virtue, which was supposed to have expired with the Stuart dynasty. Lord Braybrooke, the editor of 'Pepys' Diary,' asserts that with the view of testing the truth of the assertion, reference was made to the library of the Duke of Sussex, resulting in the discovery of no fewer than four Oxford editions of the Book of Common Prayer, all of which had been printed after the accession of George I., and all of which contained the 'office for the healing of the sick' as an integral part of the book. In the records of the century considerably later, it is not uncommon to meet with accounts of scrofulous children being brought up by their parents to the scaffold after an execution had taken place at Newgate, in order that the hands of the dead criminal when untied by the hangman might be gently stroked to and fro nine times across the affected parts of their bodies, it being regarded as an excellent specific for the cure of 'king's evil.' This revolting practice continued to be observed so late as the year 1758.[1] Another supposed remedy for the effectual cure of the 'king's evil' or scrofula was the dried or baked body of a toad :—

A girl at Gaddesden, Herts (writes William Ellis, in his 'Country Housewife's Family Companion,' 1750), having the evil in her feet from her infancy, at eleven years old lost one of her toes by it, and was so bad that she could hardly walk, therefore was to be sent to a London hospital in a little time ; but a beggar woman coming to the door and hearing of it, said that if they would cut off the hind leg, and the fore leg on the contrary side of that, of a toad, and wear them in a silken bag about her neck, it would certainly cure her ; but it was to be observed that on the toad's losing its legs it was to be turned loose abroad, and as it pined, wasted, and died, the distemper would likewise waste and die ; which happened accordingly, for the girl was intirely (*sic*) cured by it, never having had the evil afterwards.

On the same page this worthy states that he is firmly of opinion that for the cure of 'king's evil' no medicine known by man exceeds that of 'quicksilver water,' more especially if the patient will, while drinking it, 'exercise his body with some labour, and live on a milk diet.'

In a volume of the 'Family Magazine' for 1741 there are printed several prescriptions for the bite of a mad dog. One such, which is here subjoined, is stated to have been taken out of Cathorpe church, in Lincolnshire, in which it is solemnly recorded, for the perpetual memory of the thing, that the whole

[1] *Ann. Reg.* vol. i. 90.

town almost being bitten, not one person miscarried, but was cured :—

> One pound of salt to a quart of water—wash, bathe, and squeeze the wound for an hour, and bind a little salt upon the wound, and keep it on for twelve hours. Be sure as soon as the wound is given make use of the abovesaid medicine.

Here is another prescription, dating about 1754, extracted from the pocket-book of Thomas Wale, a gentleman who resided for many years on his estate at Little Shelford, in the county of Cambridge:—

> Take of the commonest salt and rub it well into the wound, washing it well with brine, squeeze out as much blood as possible from it, pressing or stroking down the veins, so as to expel the venom of the bite ; after which apply a poultice or pledget of salt, tied with a linen rag to the part, renewing it with fresh salt every hour or two for some days.[1]

'The Duchess of Portland's receipt for a whooping or any nervous cough,' says Mrs. Delany, writing to Mrs. Dewes on January 17, 1758, 'is rubbing the palms of the hands, soles of the feet, and pit of the stomach with oil of amber and hartshorn, an equal quantity, night and morning, and the backbone with rum.'[2]

> I am very much concerned for my dear godson (wrote the same amiable lady to her friend Mrs. Dewes on March 1, 1743-4), but hope before this reaches you that his ague will have left him. Two *infallible receipts* I must insert before I proceed further. 1. Pounded ginger, made into a paste with brandy, spread on sheep's leather, and a plaster of it laid over the stomach. 2. A spider put into a goose-quill, well sealed and secured, and hung about the child's neck as low as the pit of the stomach. Either of these I am assured will ease. *Probatum est.*[3]

In another letter, Mrs. Delany strongly recommends the application of rotten-apple water to persons afflicted with sore or weak eyes.[4]

In the 'Connoisseur' may be found particulars of a custom, which, no doubt, was generally observed among a goodly proportion of the fair sex at this time of day :—

---

[1] Wale's *My Grandfather's Pocket-Book*, p. 117.
[2] *Autob. and Corr.* 1st series, iii. p. 475.
[3] *Ibid.* ii. p. 273.   [4] *Ibid.* i. p. 185.

On the eve before Valentine's Day I got five bay-leaves and pinned four of them to the four corners of my pillow, and the fifth to the middle, and then if I dreamt of my sweetheart, Betty said we should be married before the year was out. But to make it more sure I boiled an egg hard and took out the yolk, and filled it with salt ; and when I went to bed, eat it, shell and all, without speaking or drinking after.

Coffee-grounds, as well as bay-leaves, were pressed into the service of divination, a cast of the cup being regarded as the picture of the future. In No. 56 of the 'Connoisseur' a damsel who divines in order to discover the station in life which her husband will occupy, beheld him 'several times in coffee-grounds with a sword by his side ; and once at the bottom of a tea-cup in a coach-and-six with his footmen behind it.'

The upper classes of society were not exempt from superstition, and if their faith in the powers of the family doctor was weak, their faith in the powers of the 'cunning' man or woman was strong, as the following transcript of a charm given by Lady Smith of Newbury to one of her tenants in 1767 proves :—

When our Saviour Christ saw the cross whereon he was to suffer, his body did shake ; the Jews said unto him hast thou an aaga (*sic*) ; he answered and said unto them, whomsoever beareth this in mind or in writing shall not be troubled with an agua nor feaver (*sic*). So Lord help thy servant, and they that put their trust in thee.

This charm was required to be worn round the neck in a small bag.

Sailors, a class of men exposed to dangers which are not to be averted by the exercise of forethought and prudence, placed much faith in whistling for the wind, and in the purchase of children's cauls, which were often advertised in the newspapers. The possession of a caul was regarded as a preservative against shipwreck. So, too, was the possession of a piece of the wicken, or mountain ash, which was also regarded as a counter-spell against witchcraft. Silver rings made of money offered at the altar were reputed to be excellent charms against the recurrence of fits, and a single magpie crossing the path was regarded as an evil omen, the maleficence of which might be averted by placing two straws one across the other, or by describing a cross upon the ground.

Spells or charms made by rustics of blades of oats or wheat were much used as love-knots. The following extraordinary recipe is for 'the Diet Drink' and is one of the items contained in the pocket-book of Thomas Wale, Esquire, of Little Shelford, Cambridgeshire, dating presumably from 1789 :—

Quicksilver ¼ lb. Crude Antimony 6 ounces. Flower of Sulphur 2 ounces. Well lævigated together in a mortar which tye up in a bag. Then take rasping of Ling, Guaugacum, or Lignæ Vitæ 4 oz. Sassafras ¼ lb., boiled in 8 gallons of mead to 6, then strained off and whilst in fermentation add—Yellow Sanders, Cassummary root, Zedrang and Cinnamon each one ounce. Juniper Berries 6 oz. Coriander Seeds 2 oz. Leaves of Agrimony, Ground pine, St. John's Worte, Hore Hound, Sage and Buck Bean (of each 2 handsful), Vipers just killed and cut into very small pieces, and Hog's Lard one pint. Let all these infuse in the mead four or five days (the bag of Æthrops being put to them) and drink half a pint, three or four times a day, or for common drink.[1]

And here may fittingly be cited another instance of the hold superstition took upon the peasantry. The Rev. Gilbert White, writing from Selborne to the Hon. Daines Barrington, under date of January 8, 1776, tells him that at the time of writing, there stood in

a farm-yard near the middle of the village a row of pollard ashes which by the seams and long cicatrices down their sides, manifestly showed that in former times they had been cleft asunder. These trees when young and flexible were severed and held open by wedges, while diseased children in a state of nudity were pushed by their parents through the apertures under the impression that they would be cured of their infirmities. As soon as the operation was over the tree in the suffering part was plastered with loam and carefully swathed up. If the parts coalesced and soldered together, as usually fell out where the feat was performed with any adroitness at all, the party was cured ; but where the cleft continued to gape, the operation it was supposed would prove ineffectual.

The same writer goes on to state that, at the south corner of the Plestor, or area near the church of Selborne, there had stood

a very grotesque old pollard ash, which for ages had been looked upon with no small veneration as a shrew ash—whose twigs or

[1] Rev. A. J. Wale, *My Grandfather's Pocket-Book*, p. 296.

branches when gently applied to the limbs of cattle will immediately relieve the pains which a beast suffers from the running of a shrew mouse over the part affected. A shrew ash was made thus :—Into the body of the tree a deep hole was bored with an auger, and a poor devoted shrew mouse was thrust in alive and plugged in, no doubt with several quaint incantations.

It is not too much to say that, during this period there was not a single city, town, village, or remote hamlet throughout the length and breadth of England in which belief in witches and their craft was not as deeply rooted as in the Middle Ages, doubtless resting its foundation on a mistaken interpretation of the Levitical condemnation, 'Thou shalt not suffer a witch to live.' There was still a disposition among the peasantry to impute certain calamities to the agency of witchcraft. If a death occurred suddenly in a household, if the cattle died of the murrain, if the dairymaid could not make the butter come, if the hens refused to lay, if there was a bad harvest, or a spell of tempestuous weather, if a river overflowed its banks, or a season of drought occurred, or a shock of earthquake was felt, the cry often was, 'Some witch has done this!' Suspicion would inevitably fall upon some wretched hag living in the neighbourhood, who had sold herself body and soul to the Enemy of mankind, had signed a contract with her own blood, and had been presented by him in due course with a 'familiar spirit' in the form of a black cat, or a toad, who rendered her assistance in her spells and machinations. Any poor harmless old crone who lived in loneliness and retirement at this time soon procured the unenviable distinction of being a witch, and when once that fact was proclaimed abroad, there were plenty of her neighbours ready to come forward and swear by all that was sacred that they had actually beheld her flying through the air at midnight, mounted on a broomstick, or taking her walks abroad in the shape of a cat, a raven, or a hare. Even a sinister and malicious look on the face of an old woman's cat was sometimes sufficient of itself to cause her mistress to be suspected of dealing with the Prince of Darkness.

The secret of this lay in the fact that for the first quarter of a century witchcraft was still numbered among capital crimes. It was not until 1736 that the odious penal enactment

of the British Solomon was erased from the statute book which
it had been so long allowed to disgrace, and consequently it is
not surprising that an ignorant and credulous peasantry should
have retained the time-honoured notions of the punishment
meet for witches, when as yet there had been no rejection
of them on the part of the highest legal authorities in the
kingdom.   There is much reason to believe that this hateful
superstition won the assent of many men of transcendent intellectual powers who flourished in England during the eighteenth
century.   Joseph Addison, for example, does not seem to have
been altogether able to divest his mind of the superstition; for,
says he, writing in No. 117 of the 'Spectator':—

> When I consider the question whether there are such persons
> in the world as those we call witches, my mind is divided between
> two opposite opinions ; or rather, to speak my thoughts freely, I
> believe in general that there is, and has been, such a thing as witch-
> craft, but at the same time can give no credit to any particular
> instance of it.

Dr. Johnson, too, when asked by the Laird of Auchinleck, during the course of a conversation which took place in
April 1772, as to what the term witches properly signified, made use of the following expression : 'Why, sir,
they properly mean those who make use of the aid of evil
spirits.'   To which Boswell answered, 'There is no doubt, sir,
a general report and belief of their having existed ; ' and was
met by the sage observing, 'You have not only the general
report and belief, but you have many solemn voluntary confes-
sions.'   So again, John Wesley, the greatest religious leader of
the eighteenth century, in his 'Journal,' one of the most remarkable embodiments of the solemn outpourings of the spirit
ever given to the world, recorded that with his latest breath he
would bear testimony against giving up to infidels one great
proof of the unseen world : that of witchcraft and apparitions
confirmed by the testimony of all ages.[1]   The legal mind is not
one where superstition might be supposed to lurk, yet Sir
William Blackstone, one of the acutest lawyers of his age, did
not hesitate to assert that, although witchcraft was excluded from

[1] *Journal,* v. 190.

the list of crimes, it was not to be construed into a denial of the possibility of such an offence.

The last judicial execution for witchcraft in England took place at Huntingdon on Saturday, July 17, 1716, when a certain Mrs. Mary Hicks, and her daughter Elizabeth, barely eleven years of age, were both hanged for having, on their confession, sold their souls to the devil, caused their neighbours to vomit pins, and having, by pulling off their stockings and making a lather of soap, raised a storm at sea by which a certain ship nearly foundered. Four years before, a woman named Jane Wenham, the witch of Walkerne, near Stevenage, was tried and convicted at Hertford for practising her craft, the prosecutors being the Worshipful Sir Henry Chauncy, knight, the erudite compiler of the 'Historical Antiquities of Herts,' and the spiritual overseer of the parish in which she resided ; but she escaped capital punishment. Two persons were hanged at Northampton on March 17, 1705, and five in the same place on July 22, 1712, for witchcraft.[1] The abolition of penal enactments against witchcraft did not eradicate the popular belief in it. It lingered on here and there in remote villages and half-civilised districts, as proved by the contemporaneous records of occasional victims in the various ordeals (species of Lynch law) commonly known as 'sinking or swimming,' 'ducking,' and 'weighing.'

. The Rev. Humphrey Michel, rector of Blaston and Horninghold, in the county of Leicester, narrates in his manuscript diary under date of June 11, 1709, the following circumstance :—

Being St. Barnabas Festival and Whitsun Eve, one Thomas Holmes of Horninghold, a labourer, was dowsed three times for a witch, and did not sink but swim, though his hands and feet were all tyed fast together, and all this was done in the Dungeon pit in Blaston, before 500 people (they say), and by commutation of punishment for stealing Mr. Atkins' malt. June 17 :—Being Whitsun Week, one Elizabeth Ridgway and Jane Barlow of Horninghold were both by consent dowsed for witches and did not sink but swim, though their hands and feet were tyed together, before some thousands of people, at the Dungeon pit in Blaston lordship.

---

[1] *Works of Dr. Samuel Parr*, ed. Johnstone, 1828, vol. iv, 181-2.

On August 15, 1709, the same divine records that

One Ffrances Sharp, the wife of Thomas Sharp, was buryed, and was in all probability bewitched to death by one Widow Ridgway ; for the other confessed that the said Ridgway appeared to her in very terrible shapes, and before she dyed she neither ate nor drank of eleven days, but said she could have done both very heartily, but that the little thing in her bosom told her she must do neither, and while the White Witch of Kibworth, one Clow, had ordered a charm to be sewed, and kept it about her bosom, she did eat and drink, but when she had scratted it away she never ate nor drank more.

Lastly, under date of October 2, 1709, he records that ' a wench of the widow Barlow, a supposed witch, went out of the church when I had named and read my text, Deut. chap. 18, where is the word witch.' These entries prove conclusively that the influence which belief in witchcraft exercised at this period extended to the clergy as much as it did to the laity.

According to the January number of the ' Gentleman's Magazine ' 1731, in the month of September 1730, the child of one Wheeler, resident at Frome in Somersetshire,

being seiz'd with strange fits, the mother was advised by a cunning man to hang a bottle of water mixed with some of the child's hair close chopped, over the fire, that the witch would thereupon come and break it. The account, which is taken from the ' Daily Journal,' does not mention the success, but a poor old woman in the neighbourhood was taken up, and the old trial by Water Ordeal revived. They dragged her, shivering with an ague, out of her house, set her astride on the pomel of a saddle and carried her about two miles to a mill pond, stript off her upper cloaths, tied her legs, and with a rope about her middle, threw her in, two hundred spectators huzzaing and abetting the riot. They affirm she swam like a cork, though forced several times under the water, and when almost spent, they poured in brandy to revive her, drew her to a stable, threw her on some litter in her wet cloaths, where in about an hour after she expired. The coroner upon his inquest could make no discovery of the ringleaders, although above forty persons assisted in the act, yet none of them could be persuaded to accuse his neighbour ; so that they were able to charge only three of them with manslaughter.

The impression conveyed to the reader by a perusal of these instructive notices will be that the rural districts were in miserable plight.

In 1735 a married woman upwards of sixty years of age,

who resided in the village of Oakley about three miles from Bedford, underwent the two ordinary popular modes of trying persons suspected of practising witchcraft. Having long lain under an imputation of witchcraft, the wretched woman at last, through anxiety not only for herself but her children to be cleared of it, consented to be ducked. The spot selected for her trial by the parish officers was by a mill on the banks of the Ouse. A concourse of people assembled, and on the woman presenting herself, she was tied up in a wet sheet. Her face was left uncovered, her feet and hands were tied together, and a rope was fastened round her body. As pins were supposed to prevent a witch from swimming, her person was searched for them. None being discovered, the woman was lifted up and thrown into the river, where the malignant vigilance of the bystanders was gratified in beholding that she floated, though her head was all the while under water. Seeing this the spectators instantly jumped to the conclusion that she was a witch, and a cry arose of ' A witch ! Drown her ! Hang her !' After remaining in the water for a few minutes, the woman was pulled out more dead than alive. As soon as she had recovered her breath, she was a second time placed in the river, and was again seen to float, which the ignorant multitude considered an infallible proof of her guilt. A little later she was hauled out of the water and laid down upon the grassy bank, speechless and in a dying condition. This, so far from exciting the pity or compassion of the bystanders, moved them one and all only to load her with abuse and reproach. Before long, however, she regained consciousness, but as her persecutors were far from satisfied, they proposed to try her by another experiment, that of weighing her against the big Bible of the parish church ; under the impression that, if really guilty, it would be impossible for her to outweigh it, as the Bible was undoubtedly the word of God, and consequently would prevail against the works of the devil. The question being carried, the wretched woman was weighed against the Bible of Oakley Church, which weighed about twelve pounds, with the result that she outweighed it. This convinced some of the spectators, and staggered others, but the parson of the parish went away firmly convinced that his unfortunate parishioner was a witch, and endeavoured to impress others with the same belief.[1] This shameful outrage, be it noted, was perpetrated in a village about fifty-three miles from the capital in 1735. Did then these spectacles, remnants or survivals of barbarous passions and of ignorant ages, cease after that date in England? Assuredly not entirely until the closing years of the eighteenth century. Some instances of these witch trials have been recorded, but we are tempted to reason from the known to the unknown, and to suppose that many took place which were never recorded. The subjoined curious entry is extracted from the parish register of Monk's Sleigh, a small parish in Norfolk :—'December 19, 1748.—Alice, the wife of Thomas Green, labourer, was swum, malicious and evil people having raised an ill-report of her for being a, witch.' The Oakley witch trial, already referred to, was paralleled by an occurrence which took place in April 1751 at Tring, in Hertford-shire. An innkeeper who resided in that village informed his neighbours that he had been bewitched by a man named Osborne and his wife, two harmless people, each upwards of seventy years of age. Not content with this, he caused it to be announced at several market towns in the vicinity that on a certain day they would both be tried by ducking. The day appointed came at last, and a vast concourse of people poured into Tring. The parish officers had prudently removed the old couple from the workhouse into the church. Baulked of their prey, the mob pro-ceeded to smash the workhouse windows, expended their fury upon the palings, demolished part of the house, and seizing the governor threatened to set fire to the town by igniting a quantity of straw, which they had brought with them, if he failed to comply with their demands. In these circumstances the frightened governor had no course open to him but to deliver up his charge. The church door was opened, the hapless couple were brought out, and given over to their persecutors, who after stripping them, and tying their thumbs to their toes, dragged them a distance of two miles and flung them into a muddy stream. After the crowd had ducked and ill-

[1] *London Magazine*, 1735.

used them, they dragged them out, and laid them on the bank, where the old woman soon afterwards expired. Even here the inhuman violence of the populace did not abate, for after having kicked and beaten the bodies with sticks, they heightened their barbarity by tying the wounded man to his dead wife, and putting them to bed, where the wretched victim soon breathed his last. A coroner's inquest was held not long afterwards, and a verdict of wilful murder was brought in against nine known men, and twenty others whose names could not be ascertained.[1]

An instance of the frivolous pretexts upon which women were sometimes charged as witches occurs in the Chronicle of the 'Annual Register' for 1759. There it is stated, that in February of that year, an elderly woman named Susanna Hannokes, resident at Wingrove, near Aylesbury, in Buckinghamshire, was accused by a neighbour of having bewitched her spinning wheel, so that she was unable to make it move round. Declaring that she would testify to the truth of what she asserted on oath before a magistrate, if necessary, the husband of Mrs. Hannokes, in order to justify her, insisted upon her being tried by means of the Church Bible, in the presence of her accuser. The accused was accordingly conducted to the door of the parish church, divested of her apparel, and weighed in the balance against the Bible, when to the no small mortification of her prosecutor, she was seen to outweigh it, and consequently was honourably acquitted of the charge. No more instructive commentary upon the credulity of the peasantry in the rural districts of England in the last century can be found than in the local records of this character.

The year 1760 witnessed another addition to the catalogue of those who perished from the detestable superstition.

They write from Glen in the county of Leicester (says the Chronicle of the 'Annual Register' under date of June 20, in that year), that on Wednesday sevennight last, a dispute arose between two old women of that town, one of whom called the other witch, and she affirming that she was no more a witch than herself, a challenge ensued, and they both agreed to be dipt by way of trial; they accordingly stript to their shifts, had their thumbs and great toes tied across, and with a cart rope about

---

[1] *Gent.'s Mag.* xxi. p. 186.

their middles, suffered themselves to be thrown into a pool of water ; one of them is said to have sank, whilst the other continued struggling upon the surface, which the mob called swimming, and deemed an infallible sign of her being a witch, insisting upon her impeaching her accomplices in the craft ; she accordingly told them that in the neighbouring village of Burton, there were several other old women as much witches as she was. These suspicions being confirmed by a student in astrology, who was referred to on account of a young woman said to be afflicted with an uncommon disorder, and pronounced to be bewitched, the mob, in consequence of this intelligence, next day repaired to Burton, and after a little consultation proceeded to the old woman's house on whom they had fixed the strongest suspicion ; the poor old creature on their approach locked the house door and went into a chamber, and from the window asked what they wanted ; they informed her that she was charged with being guilty of witchcraft, which they were come to try her for by ducking ; remonstrating at the same time upon the necessity there was of her giving proof whether she was a witch or no ; but upon her persisting in a positive refusal to come down, they broke open the house, went into the chamber, carried her downstairs, and by force took her to a deep gravel pit full of water, tied her thumbs and toes as above, then threw her in, where they kept her during pleasure. The same day the mob tried the experiment upon another poor old woman, and on Thursday a third underwent a like discipline. Several of the ringleaders in this, we hear, have been apprehended and carried before a justice ; two of which have been bound over to the sessions, and others ordered to pay small fines.

A correspondent writing from Wilton to the 'Public Advertiser' of Thursday, January 1, 1761, says :—

A few days ago one Sarah Jellicoat of this town escaped undergoing the whole discipline usually inflicted by the unmerciful and unthinking vulgar on witches, under pretence that she had bewitched a farmer's servant maid and a tallow chandler's soap which failed in the operation, only by the favourable interposition of some humane gentlemen and the vigilance of a discreet magistrate, who stopped the proceedings before the violence thereof had gone to a great pitch, by binding over the aggressors by recognisance to appear at the next assizes, there to justify if they can the parts they severally acted in the execution of their pretended witch law.

In the year 1762 six children, all of one family, died one after the other at a village called Wattisham near Needham Market in Suffolk, their feet mortifying and dropping off. It has since been demonstrated very clearly that their death may have been, and most probably was, caused by a too frequent use of deleterious food—the presence of ergot in their rye bread —yet in that village nothing would persuade the gossips that death had not resulted in consequence of the machinations of some neighbouring witch.[1]

On Sunday, December 28, 1762,

A number of people surrounded the house of John Pritchers, of West Langdon in Kent, and under a notion of her bewitching one Ladd, a boy about 13 years old, dragged out his wife by violence and compelled her to go to the said Ladd's father's house, about a mile from her own, where they forced her into the room where the boy was, scratched her arms and face in a most cruel manner, to draw blood as they said of the witch, and then threatened to swim her, but some people of condition interposing, the poor woman's life was happily preserved ; and the persons concerned in carrying on the imposture, particularly one Beard and Ladd's wife, being carried before a magistrate and compelled to make satisfaction to the unhappy injured woman, the mob dispersed, and the country that was everywhere in tumult is again quieted. The boy pretended to void needles and pins from his body, and his father and mother upheld the deceit, and collected large sums of money of those whose compassion was excited by so melancholy a situation.

In 1769 the compiler of the Historical Chronicle of the ' Gentleman's Magazine,' under date of Wednesday, August 23, records that 'a farmer at Grantchester in Cambridgeshire was bound over to the quarter sessions by the humanity of the Rev. Dr. Plumtree, for forcing a poor woman of Caldecot into the water to prove her a witch, and otherwise maltreating her.'

It was an article of the popular belief that a horse-shoe, an owl, or a hawk nailed on the door was a sure preservative against witchcraft and sorcery.

About the latter end of last month (says the August number of the ' Gentleman's Magazine' 1785), a poor woman of Mear's Ashby, in Northamptonshire, being suspected of witchcraft, voluntarily offered herself to trial. The vulgar notion is, that a witch if thrown into the water will swim ; but this poor woman being thrown into a pond, sunk instantly, and was with difficulty saved. On which the cry was, ' No witch ! No witch !' and the poor woman met with pity.

So late as 1795 a poor woman 'went through the usual sufferings ' in a pond close to the churchyard of Stanningfield

[1] *Royal Ag. Soc. Journal*, ii. 16.

near Bury St. Edmunds, in Suffolk. Her name was Greygoose, and her 'imps' were six in number.[1]

The belief in the existence of apparitions and haunted houses kept pace with the belief in witchcraft among all classes of the community. There was not a manor house but had a white lady or a headless gentleman who either paced up and down the leafy avenue before it at unseasonable hours of the night, or else terrified the domestics out of their lives by unexpectedly appearing in the corridors. The following story is transcribed from the parish register of Brisley Church, Norfolk :—

December 12, 1706.—I, Robert Withers, M.A., Vicar at Gately, do insert here a story which I had from undoubted hands, for I have all the moral certainty of the truth of it possible. Mr. Grove went to see Mr. Shaw on the 2nd of August last. As they sat talking in the evening, says Mr. Shaw, 'On the 21st of last month, as I was smoking my pipe and reading in my study between eleven and twelve at night, in comes Mr. Naylor (formerly Fellow of St. John's College, but had been dead full four years). When I saw him I was not much affrighted, and I asked him to sit down, which accordingly he did for about two hours, and we talked together. I asked him how it fared with him. He said "Very well." I asked are any of our old acquaintances with you ? " No," he said (at which I was much concerned) ; "but Mr. Orchard will be with me soon, and yourself not long after." As he was going away I asked if he would stay a little longer, but he refused. I asked him if he would call again. He said " No ; I have but three days' leave of absence and I have other business."' N.B.—Mr. Orchard died soon after, Mr. Shaw is now dead. He was formerly Fellow of St. John's College, an ingenious good man. I knew him there, but at his death he had a college living in Oxfordshire, and there he saw the apparition.

One morning early in the summer of 1745 (wrote the Rev. Percival Stockdale, Vicar of Lesbury and Longhoughton, Northumberland, in his Memoirs), while my mother and I were walking in the garden, my father called the servant to his bedside, for he had not yet risen. He desired her attentively to observe and remember what he was going to communicate to her. He had dreamed (he told her) in a very striking and impressive manner, that his long departed friend Mr. Townson (a clergyman of excellent parts and a fine scholar) came into his apartment and conversed with him. He assured him of the eternal felicity of the just, incommunicable to mortal ear, because inconceivable to mortal mind, which felicity he should enjoy for ever with his old friend, and on which he was to enter within seven years. My father likewise expressed his perfect certainty of his death at the time which was appointed for it in his dream. Accordingly he died on the seventh of April, 1755. The servant, as he had desired, did not communicate the dream to my mother and me till after the sorrowful event.[1]

Here is another remarkable ghost story of the times taken from the same source, 1783, in a memorandum found among the papers of the Rev. Edward Mores, rector of Leyton, Essex, who died in the year 1778 :—[2]

Mr. John Bonnell was a commoner of Queen's College (Oxford) ; he was remarkable in his person and his gait, and had a particular manner of holding up his gown behind, so that to anyone who had but once seen him he might be known by his back as easily as by his face. On Sunday, November 18, 1750, at noon, Mr. Ballard, who was then of Magd. Coll., and myself were talking together at Parker's door. I was then waiting for the sound of the trumpet, and suddenly Mr. Ballard cried out, ' Lad have mercy upon me, who is that coming out of your college ?' I looked, and saw, as I supposed, Mr. Bonnell, and replied, ' He is a gentleman of our house, and his name is Bonnell ; he comes from Stanton Harcourt.' ' My God !' said Mr. Ballard, ' I never saw such a face in all my life.' I answered slightly, ' His face is much the same as it always is ; I think it is a little more inflamed and swelled than it is some-times, perhaps he has buckled his band too tight ; but I should not have observed it if you had not spoken.' ' Well,' said Mr. Ballard again, ' I never shall forget him as long as I live,' and seemed to be much disconcerted and frightened. This figure I saw without any emotion or suspicion ; it came down the quadrangle, came out at the gate, and walked up the High Street ; we followed it with our eyes till it came to Cat Street, where it was lost. The trumpet then sounded, and Mr. Ballard and I parted, and I went into the hall and thought no more of Mr. Bonnell. In the evening the prayers of the chapel were desired for one who was in a very sick and dangerous condition. When I came out of the chapel, I in-quired of one of the scholars, James Harrison, in the hearing of several others who were standing before the kitchen fire, who it was that was prayed for ? and was answered ' Mr. Bonnell, sen.' ' Bonnell, sen ,' said I with astonishment, ' what's the matter with him ? He was very well to-day, for I saw him go out to dinner.' ' You are very much mistaken,' answered the scholar, ' for he has not been out of his bed for some days.' I then asserted more positively that I had seen him, and that a gentleman was with me who had seen him too. This came presently to the ears of Dr. Fothergill, who had been my tutor. After supper he took me aside and questioned me about it, and said he was very sorry I had

---

[1] *Memoirs*, i. 71-2.   [2] *Gent's Mag.*, ii. 848.

mentioned the matter so publicly, for Mr. B. was dangerously ill. I replied, I was very sorry too, but I had done it innocently ; and the next day Mr. B. died.

We shall now pass on to consider some of the notable impostors who visited the metropolis at different times during the eighteenth century, and at the head of the list must be placed the name of George Psalmanazar. This man, who gave himself out as a converted savage from the island of Formosa, is mentioned by Smollett in 'Humphry Clinker,' and several times by Boswell in his 'Life of Johnson.' His real name was never known ; but it is supposed that he was a Frenchman by birth. Having received instruction in the humanities at a Jesuit seminary in the South of France, Psalmanazar in preference to a settled profession chose the life of a vagabond. Experiencing great difficulty, however, in eking out a subsistence, he conceived the idea of shamming a Japanese convert, and as such entered the service of the Elector of Cologne, but the colonel of his corps soon saw fit to discharge him on account of his stature being below the standard. He next enlisted in a corps in Dutch pay at Cologne, and accompanied it to Sluys, where he attracted the notice of a Scotch brigadier named Lauder, and Innes the chaplain of his regiment, who endeavoured to convert him from the Paganism which he still counterfeited to Christianity, in order that he might make a merit of it to the then Bishop of London, Dr. Henry Compton. In a short time Psalmanazar expressed his assent to the Anglican formularies and was baptized by Innes, though not before that gentleman had artfully obtained proofs positive that he was an impostor. Innes, who was a very disreputable character, then wrote to Bishop Compton announcing his success, and received from him a letter inviting him and his convert to England. Psalmanazar, glad at any price to procure his discharge from the army, consented to accompany Innes, promising to maintain the imposture. The pair arrived in London in 1704, and quickly made themselves known to the diocesan, who, after introducing them in turn to all the great men in church and state with a generosity which did more credit to his heart than to his head, offered to send Psalmanazar to the University of Oxford. The bishop's gracious offer was accepted, but not before Innes had persuaded Psalmanazar, then scarcely twenty years old, to hatch up a 'History of Formosa,' for credit and profit.   In the space of two months this work, a tissue of lies from beginning to end, was written in Latin, translated by Innes, dedicated to Dr. Compton, and placed in the bookseller's hands.   Filled as it was with the wildest absurdities, it must have pleased the public immensely, for in 1705 the author was fain to relinquish his studies at Oxford in order to superintend the publication of a second edition in London.   Innes in the meantime having secured through the instrumentality of Bishop Compton the appointment of chaplain-general to the English forces in Portugal, left his dupe to his own devices.   The result was that Psalmanazar soon overreached himself.   In a long preface to the second edition of his 'Historical and Geographical Description of Formosa, an Island subject to the Emperor of Japan,' he stated that about a year previously he had had the honour of meeting Captain Halley (Savilian Professor of Mathematics in the University of Oxford) 'with some other gentlemen at a tavern ;' and that he had returned satisfactory answers to all their inquiries respecting the position of the sun at mid-day in Formosa, as well as of the duration of twilight.   When the attention of Captain Halley and these 'other gentlemen' (Drs. Mead and Woodward) was drawn to these assertions, they gave them the lie direct, and asserted that to their questions Psalmanazar had returned answers the exact reverse of satisfactory. Putting this and other things together, these scientists came to the conclusion that the Formosan convert was nothing short of a thoroughpaced impostor, an opinion which they were not slow in recording for the information of the public, and in inducing it to share with them.   Psalmanazar seeing the tide turn against him, had the good sense to abandon his dishonest courses and embrace honest ones, which he did by seeking employment as a hack writer for the booksellers.   Portions of the ' Universal History ' were written by him, as well as a history of printing.   It was while engaged in this capacity that he became acquainted with Johnson, who reverenced him for his piety.   Mrs. Piozzi says that Psalmanazar's 'pious and patient endurance of a tedious illness ending in an exemplary death (1763) confirmed the strong impression which his merit had made upon the mind of Dr. Johnson.'[1] A correspondent of the 'Gentleman's Magazine' for February 1763 describes him as 'a middle-sized, well-shaped man, of a fair complexion.' In the 'Memoirs of * * * *,' *i.e.* Psalmanazar, which were published in 1765 for the benefit of his executrix, an old woman whose residence he had shared ; he confesses that 'out of Europe he was not born nor educated, nor ever travelled,' and expresses deep contrition for 'the base and shameful imposture of passing upon the world for a native of Formosa and a convert to Christianity, and backing it with a fictitious account of that island, and of my own travels, conversion, &c., all or most of it hatched in my own brain without regard to truth or honesty.'

Toward the close of the year 1715 and the beginning of the year following the Wesley family, who then tenanted the vicarage at Epworth in the Isle of Axholme, Lincolnshire, were thrown into a state of great consternation by certain strange disturbances or spiritual manifestations, the facts of which were carefully investigated by Samuel Wesley and his brother Charles. In after years a narrative of them, based upon notes and memoranda made by various members of the family, was published by John Wesley in the pages of the 'Arminian Magazine.' Dr. Joseph Priestley, by whom the account was first made public, was of opinion that the disturbances were not of supernatural origin, but were attributable to the pranks either of the servants or of the neighbours. Although most of Wesley's biographers have referred these disturbances to supernatural agency, the rappings and noises were no doubt caused by one of the family (in all probability Hetty Wesley), whom Dr. Adam Clarke describes, in his 'Memoirs of the Wesley Family,' as 'gay and sprightly, full of mirth, good humour, and keen wit.' It is evident that the founder of Wesleyanism entertained no such suspicion. Southey, in his 'Life of Wesley,' asserts that 'many of the circumstances could not be explained by the supposition of imposture, neither by any legerdemain, nor by ventriloquism,

---

[1] *Croker's Boswell*, p. 602.

nor by any secret of acoustics,' and in answer to Dr. Priestley's demand as to what imaginable purpose could have been served by such a miracle, says that 'it was perhaps purpose enough if thereby one of those unhappy persons who, looking through the dim glass of infidelity see nothing beyond this life and the narrow sphere of mortal existence, could be led to admit that there are more things in heaven and earth than are dreamt of in their philosophy.'[1]

In the month of November 1726 another gross impostor started up at Godalming in Surrey, and speedily became the talk of the capital. Mary Tofts, the ignorant and credulous wife of Joshua Tofts, a journeyman clothier in humble circumstances who resided in that town, was persuaded by a friend that if she were to give out that she had given birth to a number of rabbits, it would have the effect of raising her from penury to affluence. Acting on this advice Mary Tofts did so, and completely deceived John Howard, a surgeon at Guildford, Molyneux, secretary to the Prince of Wales, and several local practitioners. Tidings of the great event reaching the ears of King George I. caused him to despatch Cyriacus Ahlers, surgeon to the household, to Godalming. So convinced was he of the truth of the woman's story, that he promised to secure a pension for her. Nathaniel St. André, chief surgeon and anatomist to the king, was then commanded to proceed to Guildford for the purpose of testing this extraordinary story, and he likewise returned to London fully impressed with the truth of it. The rabbits, which he had brought with him, were dissected in the presence of the king, and elaborate reports respecting them were drawn up by his express command, and subsequently published. London, as Pope said, was divided into factions over Mary Tofts. A fierce paper war ensued between those who credited and those who discredited the miracle so-called, and among those who took the woman's side was the eccentric William Whiston, who published a pamphlet in which he went so far as to declare that Mary Tofts was none other than the Woman of Babylon, with seven heads and ten horns, whose

[1] *Life of Wesley*, i. 27.

advent had been foretold in the prophecy of Esdras, which 'woman' Anglican divines had always held as emblematic of the Latin communion. In the ranks of those who refused to credit the imposture was Sir Richard Manningham, a physician of some eminence, and one of the Fellows of the Royal Society. He visited Guildford, and having examined Tofts, suggested her removal to London, where she would be out of the reach of accomplices. To the metropolis therefore she was conveyed. Manningham soon became so convinced that she was a rogue, that he threatened to punish her, and Sir Thomas Clarges, one of the king's justices of the peace, threatened her with imprisonment if she did not confess. These threats made a great impression upon Mary Tofts, so much so indeed, that on Wednesday December 7, 1726, in the presence of the Duke of Montagu, Lord Baltimore, Dr. Douglas, and Sir Richard Manningham, she made a full confession of her fraud. She was forced to hide her diminished head within the precincts of the Bridewell in Tothill Fields.[1] Pope and Pulteney wrote a joint ballad on the occasion of Mary Tofts's confession.

Nearly twenty-seven years after the collapse of the Godalming rabbit breeder, another case of imposture was brought prominently before the London public, well calculated to excite its curiosity and attention, more especially as it had enjoyed so long an interval of repose. The issue of the 'London Daily Advertiser' for January 31, 1753, contained a paragraph of which the following is a transcript :—

On Monday Night the young Woman who was advertised as left in Houndsditch on New Year's day last, about Nine in the Evening, came Home to her Mother, who lives in Aldermanbury Postern, and gave the following extraordinary Account of her being forced away and detained. She had been at Saltpetre Bank, near Rosemary Lane, to see her Uncle and Aunt, who came with her as far as Houndsditch in her Way Home, where she desired them to return. She went from thence into Moorfields by Bethlehem Wall, as the nighest Way Home ; there she was met and attacked by two Fellows, who pulled off her Hat and Gown, cut off her Apron, then gagged her, and threatened her, with bitter Imprecations if she cried

---

[1] John Howard, *The Wonder of Wonders*, 1726.

out, to cut her Throat. They forcibly carried her to Enfield, to a House kept by one Mother Wells, near the Wash, by the ten Mile Stone, which place they reached about Four o'clock in the Morning. The Fellows left her in that House, and she has not seen them since. The woman of the House, with her own Hands and with the horridest Execrations, forced her into a Room, where she was kept upon Bread and Water. She broke her Way through a Window and in a wretched Condition came Home. She left several unhappy young Women in the House, whose Misfortune she has providentially escaped.

The object of this outrage was a young domestic servant named Elizabeth Canning, and her tale of her sufferings (which was subsequently proved to be a web of falsehood from beginning to end) excited widespread sympathy, which culminated in the arrest of Mother Wells and a gipsy named Squires, and at their trial before Justice Henry Fielding (the novelist), Canning's evidence was corroborated by Virtue Hall, a servant in the employ of Canning. The jury found both guilty. Wells was ordered to be branded and to be imprisoned for six months. Squires was sentenced to death, and would have paid the penalty had not a respite been granted her on the interposition of Sir Crisp Gascoyne, lord mayor of London, to whom the verdict had failed to give satisfaction. The press poured pamphlet after pamphlet defending and opposing Canning, from Henry Fielding and Dr. Hill down to the hacks of Grub Street. All the ignorant prejudices of the multitude were now aroused. A subscription was opened at White's Chocolate House on her behalf. Charles Churchill, in his poem of 'The Ghost,' remarked that the case of Betty Canning had afforded the quidnuncs, 'with Gascoyne's help, a six months' feast.' Squires, having brought numerous witnesses to prove that at the time she was sworn to by Canning she was wandering in certain districts of the West of England, received through the instrumentality of Sir Crisp Gascoyne a free pardon. For this, the rabble, who for the most part espoused the cause of Canning, selected Sir Crisp as an object of their opprobrium. But the more Canning's evidence was investigated, the more extraordinary became the discrepancies in it, and this became so apparent that a warrant was issued for her apprehension on a charge of perjury. Her trial at the Old Bailey began on April 29, 1754, and resulted in her story being proved absolutely fictitious. On May 30, 1754, she received sentence of seven years' transportation. Three months later these shores knew her no more.[1]

There was a lull for about eight years after the discomfiture of Elizabeth Canning until the month of February 1762, when the absurd Cock Lane Ghost, so designated from the locality of the imposture, appeared, and engrossed the attention of the public for fully five years afterwards. The main facts are too well known to need any recapitulation, and may be read by the curious in a pamphlet entitled 'The Mystery Revealed,' pubblished anonymously in 1762, but in reality the production of the author of 'The Vicar of Wakefield.' Looking back from the vantage of an enlightened and scientific age, the only wonder is how such an impudent imposture could have been carried on so long without being detected, and it affords an indubitable evidence of the state of credulity and superstition in which even town society still lay hidebound. Cock Lane, near West Smithfield, was visited night after night by hundreds of every rank and station. People went out into the wilderness in expectation of seeing a prophet, and found but a reed shaken with the wind. For a time the ghost furnished an inexhaustible topic of conversation :—

> I could send you volumes on the ghost (wrote Walpole in a letter to George Montagu, dated Feb. 2, 1762), and I believe if I were to stay a little I might send its *life*, dedicated to my Lord Dartmouth, by the ordinary of Newgate, its two great patrons. A drunken parish clerk set it on foot out of revenge, the Methodists have adopted it, and the whole town of London thinks of nothing else. Elizabeth Canning and the Rabbit woman were modest impostors in comparison of this, which goes on without saving the least appearances. The Archbishop, who would not suffer the 'Minor' to be acted in ridicule of the Methodists, permits this farce to be played every night, and I shall not be surprised if they perform in the great hall at Lambeth. I went to hear it, for it

---

[1] *Gent.'s Mag.* 1753–4 ; *Genuine and Impartial Memoirs of Canning,* 1754 ; Lawrence's *Life of Fielding*; Stephen, *Hist. Crim. Law of England,* i. 423 ; Howell's *State Trials,* xix. 262–75 ; Caulfeild's *Remarkable Characters,* iii. 108–48.

is not an *apparition* but an *audition*. We set out from the Opera,
changed our clothes at Northumberland House, the Duke of York,
Lady Northumberland, Lady Mary Coke, Lord Hertford, and I,
all in one hackney coach, and drove to the spot. It rained in
torrents ; yet the lane was full of mob and the house full. We
could not get in. At last they discovered it was the Duke of York ;
and the company squeezed themselves into one another's pockets
to make room for us. The house, which is borrowed, and to which
the ghost has adjourned, is wretchedly small and miserable. When
we opened the chamber, in which were fifty people, with no light
but one tallow candle at the end, we tumbled over the bed of the
child to whom the ghost comes. At the top of the room are ropes
to dry clothes. I asked if we were to have rope-dancing between
the acts. We heard nothing. We staid till half an hour after one.
Provisions are sent in like forage, and all the taverns and alehouses
in the neighbourhood make fortunes.[1]

There is no necessity to tell again an oft-told story ; suffice
it to say that the promoters of this, one of the biggest impostures of modern times, got their deserts at the hands of the
law, although it would seem that the populace were not of
the same way of thinking. Ten years afterwards (in 1772)
what was supposed to be a ghost began to alarm the inhabitants of Stockwell, then a small village near London—the cause
of it being a servant girl named Robinson. The ghost began
its vagaries on Twelfth Day, and for a time bade fair, by the
excitement it aroused, to eclipse the fame of the Cock Lane
Ghost.[2]

In July 1776 the famous Italian impostor and pretender to
the science of alchemy, Giuseppe Balsamo, better known under
his assumed name of Count Alessandro di Medina Cagliostro,
thinking that he had shed the light of his countenance on
fashionable Parisian society quite long enough, determined to
visit this seagirt isle. Accompanied by his wife and secretary,
with three thousand pounds in specie, jewels, and money, the
count sailed for England, and on reaching London engaged
apartments in Whitcomb Street, near by Hedge Lane, Pall
Mall, for a laboratory, and began there as a professor of occult
sciences and judge of lucky numbers in lotteries. Three
swindling knaves, named respectively 'Lord and Lady Scott,'

[1] *Walpole's Letters*, ed. Cunningham, iii. 481-2.
[2] Hone's *Year Book*, p. 62.

(*alias* Fry,) and Vitellini, selected the count and his spouse as their victims. No sooner had they introduced themselves, than they began to trade on their ignorance of English language and law, and left them no peace until they had extracted from them nearly half their gains. They who had succeeded in victimising continental nations were now being victimised in turn. To crown all, Lady Scott, a female swindler whose real name was Fry, caused the poor count to be arrested for a fictitious debt of one hundred and ninety pounds, and subsequently on a charge of practising witchcraft. Of both these charges, however, Cagliostro was acquitted, only to be incarcerated in the King's Bench Prison at the instance of a surety named Badioli. After much difficulty he regained his freedom, and though repeatedly pressed by his friends to prosecute those who had perjured and swindled him, he declined to do so, and with but a remnant of the great possessions with which he had landed, set sail for France. On June 2, 1786, after the last . scene in what Carlyle calls ' the miserable pickle-herring tragedy of the Diamond Necklace ' had been enacted, Count Cagliostro, who had figured conspicuously in the trial, was commanded in the king's name to quit Paris within three days, and France within three weeks. Reaching Boulogne he again departed for these shores, and proceeding to London took a house in Sloane Street. By some means or other he secured the friendship of the fanatical Lord George Gordon, who soon warmly espoused his cause. Finding many other believers in him the count was induced to publish a memorial accusing the Marquis de Launay, Governor of the Bastile, of having embezzled his money and jewels. Matters were proceeding smoothly enough when he ventured to assert in one of his lectures that the denizens of Medina were accustomed to rid themselves of the ferocious wild animals with which the country was infested by fattening pigs with arsenic, and then driving them out into the woods and forests to be devoured. To these assertions, however, M. de Morande, the editor of a journal called the 'Courrier de l'Europe,' took great exception, and this so enraged the count that he sent a letter to the ' Public Advertiser,' September 5, 1786, inviting M. Morande to breakfast with him on November

9, 1786, at which the principal dish was to consist of a sucking-pig fattened after the manner in vogue at Medina.

The day after that of our breakfast (he wrote) one or more of four things will happen. Either both of us shall die, or we neither of us shall die, or you shall die and I survive, or I shall die and you survive. Of these four chances I give you three, and I bet you 5,000 guineas that on the day after our breakfast, you shall die and I be perfectly well. You must either accept the challenge or acknowledge that you are an ignorant fellow, and that you have foolishly ridiculed a thing which is totally out of your knowledge.

Replying to Cagliostro's communication in the columns of the same journal, M. de Morande not only declined to accept the count's challenge, but took the opportunity of branding him as ' the greatest impostor of this or any other age.' Such a correspondence, as might be expected, awoke the slumbering memories of several of the count's former enemies, who speedily renewed their old persecutions. Fearing a repetition of what they had experienced on their previous visit, the count and his wife resolved to depart, and so accordingly in May 1787 they shook the dust of English soil from off their feet and quitted the country never to return.[1] By the efforts of these impostors, and others like them, London society was drugged with a potion compared with which Eldonine was a salutary draught.

[1] *Vie de Joseph Balsamo*, 2nd ed. Paris, 1791, ci.-iii. ; *Mémoire Authentique pour servir à l'histoire de Cagliostro.*

CHAPTER IX.

CONCERNING QUACKS AND QUACKERY.

England overrun with quacks in the last century—The evil traced to its source—The methods which quack doctors employed—Specimens of quack advertising—Queen Anne and Sir William Read—Sir John Hill—Doctor Rock—Quack medicines—Dr. James's fever powder—The Bishop of Cloyne and the tar-water controversy—Female quacks—Mrs. Mapp, the Epsom bone-setter—Mrs. Joanna Stephens and senatorial stupidity—Foreign quacks—Dominicetti and his scented baths—The wonders of Herr Katterfelto—Itinerant empirics—Dr. Graham and his Temple of Health—His celestial bed—Animal magnetism—Dr. de Mainauduc and Philip Loutherbourg.

DISCOURSING upon ' the knowledge of ourselves' in the second book of his immortal treatise on the ' Advancement of Learning,' Lord Bacon makes an observation to the effect that ' the weakness of men is such as they will often prefer a montabank or a witch before a learned physician.' Had the great philosopher's words been written with direct reference to the men and women of Hanoverian England, instead of the English people of the wonder and miracle-loving age of Queen Elizabeth, they could hardly have been more appropriate. Our fellow-countrymen in the last century had, as we have seen in the foregoing chapter, barely succeeded in emancipating themselves from the shackles of mediæval superstition, and in the forcible language of the author of 'Past and Present,' were ' governed very infallibly by the " sham-hero " whose name is Quack, whose work and governance is Plausibility, and also is Falsity and Fatuity.' If, as is easily demonstrable, men of all classes and grades of intellect, men of great and distinguished talents, placed implicit credence in the existence of fairies and witches, in the potency of charms and spells, of talismans and divining rods, in the properties of the *elixir vitæ*, in the doctrine of the transmutation of metals, and if, moreover, the principles of chemical analysis had not yet been established, if the regular medical practitioners were but too often imperfectly acquainted with the very art they professed to exercise, can it be a matter for astonishment that when girded in on every side by quacks and quackery, they pinned their faith to the alleged life-giving properties of their nostrums also, grossly ignorant as they must have necessarily been both of the principles of therapeutic science and of pathological anatomy?

Throughout the eighteenth century, England was a by-word among the nations to denote the Elysian fields of professional charlatanry and empiricism. King Quack, surrounded by his votaries, sat enthroned in the capital, then as much as it is now the needy villain's home ; and those excellent people who are apt to stand aghast at the extraordinary amount of success which apparently attends the efforts of the numerous quacks of our own day, would doubtless have stood still more aghast could they have witnessed the facility with which innumerable ignorant and impudent charlatans, who with their remedies warranted of course to be of universal efficacy in the treatment of all the physical maladies that afflict humanity, succeeded in taking advantage of the credulity of the British public during the eighteenth century. How often it happened that a bricklayer who chanced to be the seventh son of his father, or a sharp-witted cobbler, picked up an antiquated collection of mediæval recipes, and conned it in the brief intervals of leisure which his craft afforded him ! Gathering from it that a dram of Venice soap given twice a day, either in pills or dissolved in some proper liquor, would effect the cure of cancer, or that the juice of the wild cucumber was efficacious in the treatment of dropsy, or that snails beaten together with bay salt and mallows, when laid to the feet of the patient, assuaged ague—straightway flung down the awl or the trowel, and established himself in a favourable locality as a vendor of

Infusions and lotions,
Decoctions, and gargles, and pills,
Electuaries, powders, and potions,
Spermaceti, salts, scammony, squills,

Horse aloes, burnt alum, and agaric,
Balms, benzoin, bloodstone, and dill,
  Castor, camphor, and acid tartaric,
With specifics for every ill.

If, possessed of more than average intelligence, he perceived that some mark of academical distinction was requisite to give him status in the eyes of the world, that mark was not difficult in those days to obtain. Armed with a diploma of this kind, and using all the arts and cunning of which he was master, he might hope to rise in time to the dignity of a court physician in that age of blind ignorance and superstition.

Professions, it has been truly said, contrive to preserve their chief characteristics in a remarkable degree. The English quack of the Georgian era is the English quack of the Victorian era, minus his gold-laced hat, his bag-wig, and his sumptuous attire. The methods employed by the quacks of those credulous times, therefore, will be found to vary but little, if indeed at all, from those which are employed by the most flourishing of their nineteenth-century successors, and it needs only to be said that they were those methods which Richard Brinsley Sheridan so happily described once for all in his amusing farce of 'The Critic'—the puff direct, the puff preliminary, the puff collateral, the puff collusive, and the puff oblique, or puff by implication ! Fully impressed with the truth of the old adage, ' out of sight, out of mind,' these rascally pretenders to the healing art systematically flooded the columns of the newspapers with puffs, bogus testimonials, and advertisements calling attention to their nostrums professing to cure every disease in the nosology, besides enlisting the services of the dregs of the population for the task of distributing their hand-bills in every important thoroughfare, the practices with which, in these days of patent medicines, even the most desultory of newspaper readers are much more familiar than they might wish to be, and which it may be safely asserted, then as now, were the only means by which one-half the quack medicines that were sold maintained an existence at all.

In the first edition of the ' Spectator ' several quack advertisements may be seen. Here is a transcript of one :—

An admirable confect, which effectually cures stuttering and stammering in children or grown persons though never so bad, causing them to speak distinct and free without any trouble or difficulty ; it remedies all manner of impediments of the speech or disorders of the voice of any kind, proceeding from what cause soever, rendering those persons capable of speaking easily and free and with a clear voice who before were not able to utter a sentence without hesitation. Its stupendous effects in so quickly and effectually curing stuttering and stammering and all disorders of the voice and difficulty in the delivery of the speech are really wonderful. Price 2s. 6d. per pot, with directions. Sold only at Mr. Osborn's toy shop, at the Rose and Crown, under St. Dunstan's Church, Fleet Street.

Here is an exact copy of another, taken from the pages of the same periodical :—

Loss of Memory or Forgetfulness certainly cured by a grateful electuary peculiarly adapted for that end. It strikes at the primary source which few apprehend of forgetfulness—makes the head clear and easy—the spirits free, active, and undisturbed—corroborates and revives all the noble faculties of the soul, such as thought, judgment, apprehensions, reason, and memory ; which last in particular it so strengthens as to render that faculty exceeding quick and good beyond imagination ; thereby enabling those whose memory was before almost totally lost to remember the minutest circumstances of their affairs, &c., to a wonder. Price 2s. 6d. a pot. Sold only at Mr. Payne's, at the Angel and Crown in St. Paul's Churchyard, with directions.

The extraordinary hold which these rogues had upon society did not escape the notice of the episcopal bench. Indeed, one of its number, Dr. Zachary Pearce, who occupied the see of Rochester, discussed quacks and their little ways in a pleasantly written paper which appeared in No. 572 of the 'Spectator' (July 6, 1714), in which he assigns one or two excellent reasons why they succeeded.

The desire of life (observes the prelate) is so natural and strong a passion, that I have long ceased to wonder at the great encouragement which the practice of medicine finds among us. Those who have little or no faith in the abilities of a quack will apply themselves to him, either because he is willing to sell health at a reasonable profit, or because the patient, like a drowning man, catches at every twig, and hopes for relief from the most ignorant, when the most able physicians give him none. Though impudence and many words are as necessary to these itinerary Galens as a laced hat to a merry-andrew, yet they would turn very little to the advantage of the owner

if there were not some inward disposition in the sick man to favour
the pretensions of the mountebank. Love of life in the one and
of money in the other creates a good correspondence between
them.

Some examples of the quack advertisements inserted in the
newspapers of this time have just been quoted. Here is
another specimen extracted from the issue of the 'Evening
Post' for August 6, 1717, the candour of which is quite re-
freshing :—

> This is to give notice, that Dr. Benjamin Thornhill, sworn servant
> to his Majesty King George, Seventh Son of the Seventh Son, who
> has kept a stage in the rounds of West Smithfield for several months
> past, will continue to be advised with every day in the week,
> from eight in the morning till eight at night, at his lodgings at
> the Swan Inn, West Smithfield, till Michaelmas, for the good of
> all people that lie languishing under distempers, he knowing
> that *Talenta in agro non est abscondita*—that a talent ought not
> to be hid in the earth. Therefore he exposes himself in public for
> the good of the poor. The many cures he has performed has given
> the world great satisfaction, having cured 1,500 people of the king's
> evil, and several hundreds that have been blind, lame, deaf, and
> diseased. God Almighty having been pleased to bestow upon him
> so great a talent, he thinks himself bound in duty to be helpful to all
> sorts of persons that are afflicted with any distemper. He will tell
> you in a minute what distemper you are troubled with and whether
> you are curable or not. If not curable he will not take anyone in hand
> if he might have five hundred pounds for a reward. N.B. The
> Doctor has an infallible cure for the gout, which in a few hours
> gives ease, and in a short time makes a perfect cure ; likewise a
> never-failing remedy for the colic.

The writer of this bold and impudent advertisement, who
was popularly known as the 'Stuttering Unborn Doctor,' enjoyed an extensive practice in Smithfield, and, if Steele is to be
credited, 'died worth five hundred pounds per annum, though
he was not born to a halfpenny.' Asked by a patient upon
one occasion to explain the extraordinary title with which he
had dubbed himself, the fellow stammered, 'Well, you s-s-s-see,
s-s-sir, I w-w-was not born a d-d-d-doctor, and s-s-so I am an
u-un-b-b-born d-d-doctor !' Logically conclusive, of course!
It was mainly, it may be supposed, with the view of counter-
acting the baneful influence exerted by such notorious cheats
as these that one of the craft caused the following paragraph to

be inserted in the 'Original Weekly Journal' of December 28, 1723 :—

An appeal to the judicious part of mankind (it runs), if it is not the grossest imposition imaginable to cram the public prints in so fulsome a manner with infallible specifics, Arcana's Italian boluses, and innumerable quack medicines put to sale at toy shops and other places, only to hide the shame and screen from the resentment of injured people the preparers. For your own sake apply [to a] man of ingenuity and probity, who appears to justify his [pretensions] by his success, one of which invites you to his house at [the Gold]en Heart and Square Lamp in Crane Court near Fetter [Lane.] Ask for the surgeon, who is to be advised with every morn[ing of] eleven o'clock, and from two till nine at night, in any dis[ease of the] neck.

Sometimes the quack's puff took the form indicated in the subjoined transcript :—

The following letter was some time since sent from a young Lady of Distinction to Legrange's Medicinal Warehouse in New Street, Covent Garden. 'Madam, a young Lady who had been given over with a violent cough and consumption, being cured by only taking two bottles of Boerhave's Pectoral Drops, sold by you, sends these Lines, and thanks you for being an instrument of her Recovery ; would be more particular but on Account of some Circumstances in regard to those who before attended, which beg you'll excuse ; I shall recommend to every Body I can. MIRANDA.'

Again, it would assume the fashion akin to that following, the original of which will be found in the 'Public Advertiser' of June 2, 1755 :—

Sir, although you may frequently have the satisfaction of hearing of the success of your Water, yet extraordinary cures can scarcely come under your Notice, and few of those such as you can lay before the Public ; rather from the mistaken Delicacy of some in refusing to publish them, or Obscurity of others that their Veracity would be suspected ; therefore I imagine that you will be pleased to hear that your Water has happily restored a child of mine from a complaint that was hurrying it to the grave. He was long indisposed, when your Water was recommended, as so remarkable in purging the Blood and restoring the Appetite, that there would be a strong probability of performing a cure, I gave it him, rather from Despair than Confident of Success. As it was as pleasant as Spring water he took it very regular, and he is now perfectly well. To see this in print may be of public utility and give a Pleasure to, Sir, your obedient humble servant, Nich. Farnborough, at the Plough in Leadenhall Street, May 20, 1755. The

above letter was sent to the Proprietor of the Old Iron Pear-Tree
Water, at the Green and Gold Lamp in Parliament Street, Westminster, where only the above water is to be had.

Another would-be benefactor of humanity informs the
editor of the ' Public Advertiser '

that the Public are now too knowing to be any longer imposed
by Quacks and Pretenders; and I who have been regularly educat
in Medicine, can venture to affirm that the surgeons of
nation at least equal any in Europe. The surprising ef
the bougie has very deservedly met with the highest a
and it is highly worthy the attention of the gentlemer
profession. Very great improvements have been made on
many unhappy persons in the most deplorable circumstan
many years have, when given over by others, been happily
from all their grievous complaints; and out of the great num
have recommended to the care of a surgeon of great merit an
perience, I can venture to affirm upon the word of an honest n
that no one has failed of a perfect cure; the truth of which w
easily appear to any persons afflicted by applying to Mr. Buck-
master, baker, opposite Surgeon's Theatre in the Old Bailey.[1]

By these pompous pretences, and indirect puffs, is it any
wonder that these irregular practitioners obtained that confidence to which neither success nor experience entitled them?

In the issue of the ' Grub Street Journal' for January 9,
1735, there is to be found a list, communicated by a correspondent signing himself ' Bavius,' professing to enumerate the most
notorious quacks which the century up to that date had produced, and which enables us, at this distance of time, to see
very plainly what manner of men they were. The list is not a
long one, but it contains the names of several quacks who had
paid the debt of nature before the close of the preceding century, so that those only who belong to the period we are considering will be here noticed. Foremost among these stands—
1. ' Sir William Read, Mountebank, Oculist, and Sworn Operator
for the Eyes,' of whom it is recorded that he ' could not read
one word, but was knighted and kept a chariot. He was a
tailor by trade.' For the greater part of her life Queen Anne
suffered from a weakness of the eyes, and when she failed to
derive benefit from the court physicians, never hesitated to call

---

[1] *Public Advertiser,* June 3, 1755.

in the aid of any empirical rascal whose name was submitted to her.   Read, an impudent quack who practised by the light of nature in the city of Oxford, was one of those who were thus honoured, and as the queen experienced, or rather imagined she had experienced, relief from his operations, she not only knighted him, but appointed him court oculist, an appointment which he enjoyed under her successor till his death, which occurred at Rochester on May 24, 1715.   In one of his advertisements which were inserted in the 'Tatler,' Read asserted that he had been established 'thirty-five years in the practice of couching cataracts, taking off all sorts of wens, curing wry necks, and hare lips, without blemish though never so deformed.'

2. 'Roger Grant, originally a tinker,' was another notorious quack, who posed first as a cobbler and then as a tinker. Disdaining pots and pans, Grant took a religious turn, and was led to seek a reputation as an Anabaptist preacher.   But the profession of physician of the soul did not agree with him long, and he turned quack physician of the body, or rather of the eyes.   He, like Sir William Read, had the good fortune to be summoned to the court, in order to prescribe for Queen Anne's eyesight, which caused a town wag to sing :—

> Her Majesty sure was in a surprise,
> Or else was very short-sighted,
> When a tinker was sworn to look after her eyes,
> And the mountebank Read was knighted !

3. 'Doctor Hancock, who recommended cold water and stewed prunes as a general panacea.   He was a shining light till he was put out by the writings of some men of superior sense.'   Dr. John Hancock was rector of St. Margaret's, Lothbury, and chaplain to the Duke of Bedford.   Impressed with the elder Pliny's account of the water cure to which the Roman citizens of his time commonly resorted, this divine sedulously inculcated its adoption by English people from the pulpit, and in 1723 he published a work dealing at great length with the same topic, entitled ' Febrifugium Magnum, or Common Water the Best Cure for Fevers,' which enjoyed considerable popularity.

4. 'Doctor Anodyne, the inventor of the necklaces which bear

his name to assist children in cutting their teeth.' 'After the wearing of them,' runs his advertisement, 'but one night children have immediately cut their teeth with safety, who but just before were on the brink of the grave with their teeth, fits, fevers, convulsions, &c., all proceeding from the teeth, and have almost miraculously recovered.' Five shillings and sixpence was the price of these remarkable necklaces, which their maker asserted were 'patronised by the king for the royal children,' which is extremely likely. Of this retailer of health, Bavius says : 'One year he informs us gratis, that all the woodcocks and cuckoos go annually to the moon. Another year he presents us (gratis also, good man !) with an almanack crammed with many valuable secrets, particularly one receipt to choke noxious vermin, and another to make sack whey.'

5. 'The worm doctor in Lawrence Pountney Lane.' John Moore was the name in which this quack rejoiced, and 'the worm-doctor' was the designation under which he was popularly known, on account of a certain worm-powder that he sold. Moore was apostrophised in one of the minor effusions of Pope, who bade him bear in mind that his 'art' was but 'vain,' and that worms would eventually destroy his own body.

> O learned friend of Abchurch Lane,　　　　*ı*
> Who sett'st our entrails free,
> Vain is thy art, thy powder vain,
> Since worms shall eat e'en thee.

The list of quack doctors which has been cited concludes with the name of Doctor Joshua Ward, described by Pope as one who 'tried on puppies and the poor his drop.' Ward, who combined the profession of Galen with that of a Thames Street drysalter, began life as a footman, and while serving in this capacity in Paris acquired, through the agency of some monks, a number of medicinal recipes, by means of which, on his return to his native country in 1733, he made divers extraordinary concoctions designated 'Friar's Balsams,' which enjoyed an extensive sale. It is recorded that on the recommendation of Lord Chief Justice Reynolds and General Churchill, he was commanded to attend George II. for the purpose of setting

his majesty's sprained thumb.[1]   Whether his nostrums proved
efficacious it is impossible to say, but certain it is that while
he was in attendance the king recovered, and soon afterwards
Doctor Ward was accorded the best thanks of the House of
Commons, and at his own request he was allowed the privilege
of driving his carriage through St. James's Park – an ægis
which effectually shielded him from the animadversions of the
College of Physicians.   Ward died in 1761.

Among other eminent pretenders in the Æsculapian line
was Dr. Richard Rock, whose personal appearance is described
by Goldsmith in one of his celebrated ' Chinese Letters.'

This great man (says he) is short of stature, is fat and waddles
as he walks.   He always wears a white three-tailed wig, nicely
combed and frizzled upon each cheek.   Sometimes he carries a
cane, but a hat never.   He is usually drawn at the top of his own
bills sitting in his arm-chair, holding a little bottle between his finger
and thumb, and surrounded with rotten teeth, nippers, pills,
packets, and gallipots.   No man can promise fairer or better than
he ; ' for,' as he observes, ' be your disorder never so far gone, be
under no uneasiness, make yourself quite easy, I can cure you.'

Equal to any of his brethren in impudence and unblushing
charlatanry was Doctor John Hill, whom Kit Smart once
addressed as

Pimp ! Poet ! Puffer ! 'Pothecary ! Player !

all of which vocations he assumed by turns, but found none more
agreeable or more lucrative than that of trading on the credulity
of his fellow-men.   Dr. Hill's great health-restoring specific was
an essence of dock, sage, valerian, and other herbs, which in consequence of persistent puffing was so extensively sold in London that he was enabled, by the profits of it, to clothe himself
in purple and fine linen, and to fare sumptuously every day,
much to the chagrin of his enemies, who shot their arrows of
wit and sarcasm at him right and left.   One of his assailants
addressed him thus :—

Thou essence of dock, valerian, and sage,
At once the disgrace and the pest of the age,
The worst that we wish thee for all of thy crimes,
Is to take thy own physic and read thy own rhymes.

---

[1] Smith's *Recollections*, p. 27.

A request which another capped by the following :—

> The wish must be in form reversed
> To suit the Doctor's crimes,
> For if he takes his physic first,
> He *ne'er* will read his rhymes.

While Garrick said of him :—

> For physic and farces his equal there scarce is,
> His farces are physic, and physic his farce is.

It may be worth while now to turn aside from the quack doctors of the age for a brief space, to notice some of the infallible antidotes which they so assiduously vended. To the ' Gentleman's Magazine' for August 1748 a correspondent signing himself Poplicola communicated what he called a ' Pharmacopeia Emperica, or methodical list of the Nostrums and their manufacturers then in vogue, and in which their professed objects, their inventors, patentees, and prices are all duly specified.' Anyone, after a careful study of this list (which extends to the number of two hundred and two, their vendors being about half the number) would be compelled to record his conclusion that it speaks volumes for the gullibility of the English nation in the reign of George II. The prices of these nostrums, when viewed in comparison with those of the quack medicines of the present day, must be pronounced exorbitant. The majority of them run as high as half a guinea per box ; a few run as low as five shillings and even less. Dr. Belloste's pills for rheumatism cost one guinea per box ; Mr. Parker's pills for the stone two and sixpence per pill. The most popular medicines appear to have been Daffy's Elixir ; Godfrey's Cordial (which so late as 1756 is named in the list of medicines which were employed by the nurses attached to the Foundling Hospital in quieting children); Scots pills, and Indian root, of which Lord Hervey appears to have thought very highly, and Dr. James's Antimonial Fever Powder, in which Horace Walpole and Hannah More were such firm believers.[1] Respecting the last named, it should be mentioned that Dr. James was a qualified practitioner, and it is to be regretted

---

[1] *Lord Gambier's Memorials,* i. 178.

that his name has always been associated with a nostrum. James was of the early friends of Samuel Johnson, and in 1743 he published a dictionary of medicine which he dedicated to Dr. Mead. Pressed by necessity in the early days of his career, Dr. James, by combining oxide of antimony and phosphate of lead, produced a powder which being vended by his agent Newbery at his establishment in St. Paul's Churchyard, proved very successful in allaying the progress of several maladies. It will be remembered that on the night of Friday, March 25, 1774, when his life was fast hastening to a close, Dr. William Hawes found Oliver Goldsmith

complaining of violent pain extending over all the fore-part of his breast, his tongue moist, his pulse at ninety, and his mind made up that he should be cured by James's fever powders. He had derived such benefit from this fashionable medicine in previous attacks that it seems to have left him with as obstinate a sense of its universal efficacy as Horace Walpole had, who swore he should take it if the house were on fire.[1]

Walpole, when commenting on Goldsmith's death, did not hesitate to express his conviction, that if he had continued using James's fever powders, his life would have been prolonged.

No remedy was more popular during the second half of the eighteenth century in England than tar-water. From 1734 to 1752, the see of Cloyne, a remote corner of Ireland, was occupied by Dr. George Berkeley, one of the greatest metaphysicians as well as one of the most amiable prelates of the times in which he lived. During a residence of seven years in Rhode Island, Berkeley, to whom Pope assigned 'every virtue under heaven,' had seen tar-water used by the natives medicinally, and happening to derive benefit from its use himself when suffering from an attack of colic, he was induced at a time when the small-pox was raging with great violence in his own diocese, to try the effects of it upon some of the afflicted peasantry. Encouraged by the success that he met with, Berkeley thought that its general adoption by the medical faculty would be productive of much good to the community

---

[1] Forster's *Life of Goldsmith*, iv. c. xxi.

at large, and accordingly, in the little leisure which the duties of his very extensive diocese allowed him, he devoted his energies to the composition of a work of a half-medical, half-metaphysical nature, which he entitled ' Siris, or a Chain of Philosophical Reflections,' eulogising its virtues. This work was published at London in April 1744, and the popularity which it attained was extraordinary. Several editions of it were called for, and it was translated into four continental languages. But great was the storm which, by the publication of ' Siris,' Berkeley drew down upon himself in England. Owing to his recommendation of tar-water as a catholicon, it gave rise to a fierce controversy, which, extending over several years, benefited the nostrum by procuring for it an enormous sale. The fashionable world of London went half crazy over tar-water.

It is impossible (wrote Duncombe, under date of June 1744, to his friend Dr. Thomas Herring, Archbishop of York) to write a letter now without tincturing the ink with tar-water. This is the common topic of discourse both among the rich and poor, high and low, and the Bishop of Cloyne has made it as fashionable as going to Vauxhall or Ranelagh. . . . However, the faculty in general, and the whole posse of apothecaries, are very angry both with the author and the book, which makes many people suspect it is a good thing.

The virtues of tar-water were further recommended by Bishop Berkeley in three letters written to his intimate friend and convert, Thomas Prior, the Irish patriot, between the years 1744, 1745, and 1746 ; in a letter to Dr. Hale in 1747, and in a work published the year before his death, ' Further Thoughts on Tar Water,' 1752. Several establishments, it is stated, were opened in London after the publication of 'Siris,' for the manufacture of tar-water in accordance with Berkeley's rules.[1]

Reverting once more to the quack doctors of the last century, it might be supposed, as nothing has yet been said to the contrary, that the field was one which was monopolised by the lords of creation. The very reverse. The ladies strove with them for the mastery, two in particular, Mrs. Sarah Mapp and Mrs. Joanna Stephens. In the first quarter of the last

---

[1] Berkeley's *Works*, ed. Fraser, ii. pp. 552–3 ; iii. pp. 461–507.

century the town of Epsom occupied a position analogous to that occupied by Brighton at the present time, in other words it was a watering-place so close to London that all its gay and fashionable company, with but very few exceptions, would often be found congregating there at one time.

A young woman at Epsom (says a paragraph in the August number of the 'London Magazine' 1736), who though not very regular, it is said, in her conduct, has wrought such cures that seem miraculous in the bone-setting way. The concourse of people on this occasion to Epsom is incredible, and 'tis reckoned she gets near 20 guineas a day, she executing what she does in a quick manner.

Who was this young woman? The daughter of a bone-setter named Wallin, of Hindon in Wiltshire. In consequence of some family disagreement she quitted the parental roof, and after wandering

up and down the country in a very miserable manner, calling herself 'Crazy Sally,' she took up her abode in Epsom, where by her eccentric behaviour and her remarkable successes in the art of bone-setting she achieved great notoriety, and thereby occasioned Epsom to become so great a resort that the town offered her 100 guineas to continue there a year.

So tempting an offer was readily accepted. The success with which her exertions had been attended was now increased in a tenfold degree. In an evil hour, 'Crazy Sally' *alias* Sarah Wallin, decided to wed, and on August 11, 1736, she was united to Hill Mapp, a footman in the employ of a Ludgate Hill mercer named Ibbetson. It would seem, however, that Mrs. Mapp's sojourn in the estate matrimonial was not only very brief but far from a pleasant one, judging from the following paragraph which appeared in the 'Grub Street Journal' for April 19, 1736 :—

We hear that the husband of Mrs. Mapp, the famous bone-setter at Epsom, ran away from her last week, taking with him upwards of a hundred guineas and such other portable things as lay next to his hand. Several letters from Epsom mention that the footman whom the fair bone-setter married the week before had taken a sudden journey from thence with what money his wife had earned, and that her concern was at first very great, but as soon as the surprise was over she grew gay, and seems to think the money well disposed of, as it was like to rid her of a husband.

Her husband's desertion did not interfere with her profession, as it is stated in the September number of the 'Gentleman's Magazine' that 'Mrs. Mapp, the famous bone-setter at Epsom, continues making extraordinary cures.   She has now set up an equipage, and this day (September 19) came to Kensington and waited on her Majesty.'   The Historical Chronicle of the same miscellany records under date of Saturday, October 16, that Mrs. Mapp, in company with Dr. Taylor the oculist, visited the playhouse in Lincoln's Inn Fields on the first night of the production of a comedy called 'The Husband's Relief ; with the Female Bone-Setter and Worm Doctor.'   The play drew a full house, and Mrs. Mapp had the satisfaction of hearing her skill eulogised in the epilogue, and in a song of which the two following verses may serve as a specimen :—

> You Surgeons of London who puzzle your Pates
> To ride in your Coaches and purchase Estates,
> Give over for shame, for your Pride has a fall,
> And ye Doctress of Epsom has outdone you all.
> Derry Down, &c.

> Dame Nature has given her a Doctor's Degree,
> She gets all ye Patients, and pockets the Fee ;
> So if you don't instantly prove her a Cheat,
> She'll loll in her Chariot whilst you walk ye Street.
> Derry Down, &c.

A figure of Mrs. Mapp was introduced by Hogarth into his print of the Undertaker's Arms, between those of Taylor and Ward, two famous quacks whose friendship she enjoyed. Between Epsom and the metropolis the doctress was accustomed to travel twice a week in a chariot drawn by four horses, and to exercise her skill upon London patients in the Grecian coffee-house, invariably placing the crutches they had used in her chariot, and carrying them back with her in order to be exhibited in attestation of her powers.   Mrs. Mapp, who in her short day must have realised large sums of money, died on December 10, 1737, at her lodgings near the Seven Dials, 'so poor that the parish were forced to bury her.'[1]

Contemporaneously with Mrs. Mapp, there flourished another female pretender to the amelioration of the miseries and

---

[1] *Gent.'s Mag.* Dec. 1737.

sufferings of her fellow-creatures, Mrs. Joanna Stephens, of the city of Westminster. This woman began her career by informing the public that she had discovered an infallible medicine for the cure of an ill, which she 'proposed to make publick' in consideration of 5,000*l.*, to be raised by voluntary subscription, and lodged with a banker named Drummond. The morbid inquisitiveness of the public being aroused, subscriptions began to pour in from lords spiritual, lords temporal, baronets, generals, and people of all classes and grades of intellect. One thousand three hundred and fifty-six pounds three shillings in this way was deposited in the hands of the banker. But this sum failed to afford satisfaction to Mrs. Stephens, who was resolute in her determination not to part with her precious secrets for less than she had fixed. Finding, however, that the public were tardy in subscribing, she induced some of her many influential friends to bring the matter under the notice of the legislature. What resulted? One of the most deplorable instances of legislative stupidity of which there is any record. It seems scarcely credible that in the twelfth year of the reign of George II. (1739) an Act of Parliament was passed 'for providing a reward to Joanna Stephens upon a proper discovery to be made by her for the use of the publick, of the medicines prepared by her for the cure of the stone.' Five thousand pounds were accordingly voted by the Treasury to Mrs. Stephens out of the supplies. And what does the reader suppose these medicines were? Three : a powder, a decoction, and pills. The powder was compounded of calcined eggshells and snails ; the decoction was made by boiling herbs and a ball (composed of soap, swine's cresse burnt to blackness, and honey) in water ; and the pills consisted of calcined snails, wild carrot seeds, burdock seeds, ashen keys, hips and haws, burnt to blackness and mixed with soap and honey.

The last quarter of the eighteenth century did not lag behind the preceding quarters so far as quacks and quackeries were concerned. Some of that intense interest which had been excited among the upper classes of continental society in mesmerism, electro-biology, and other pseudo-sciences and fooleries, spread to England. One of the earliest comers was Gustavus Katterfelto, whose memory was embalmed by Cowper in a line of his 'Task,' and who united in his person the functions of conjurer and empiric.

The following is a transcript of one of Katterfelto's advertisements inserted in the 'Morning Post' of July 31, 1782 :—

Wonders, wonders, wonders, and wonders ! are now to be seen at No. 22 Piccadilly, by Mr. Katterfelto's new improved and greatly admired solar microscope. Mr. Katterfelto has by a very long and laborious study, discovered at last such a variety of wonderful experiments in natural and experimental philosophy and mathematicks as will surprise all the world. Mr. Katterfelto will show the surprising insects on the hedge larger than ever, and those insects which caused the late influenza as large as a bird, and in a drop of water, the size of a pin-head, there will be seen above 50,000 insects. N.B. After his evening lecture he will discover all the various arts on dice, card, billiards, and E.O. tables. Admittance, front seats 3*s.*, second seats 2*s.*, and back seats 1*s.* only. Mr. Katterfelto likewise makes and sells Dr. Bato's medicines at 5*s.* a bottle.

' Every sensible person, wrote a fellow-countryman of him, 'considers Katterfelto as a puppy, an ignoramus, a braggadocio, and an impostor ; notwithstanding which he has a number of followers.' [1]

Dr. Bossy was another foreign quack who flourished in London during the closing years of last century. It is stated by Angelo, whose testimony is corroborated by that of Francis Place, who frequently saw him, that he was the last of the itinerant empirics who dispensed medicines and practised the healing art publicly and gratuitously. This he was well able to do by reason of the extensive private practice which he enjoyed in consequence of his reputation as a skilful operator. Accompanied by a livery servant, Dr. Bossy was accustomed to drive in a chariot every Thursday to Covent Garden, where, under the north-west colonnade, a covered platform was erected. On one side of this platform, which was hollow in front and was ascended by means of a broad ladder, stood a table with drawers, on which were placed the doctor's medicine chest and surgical apparatus. In the centre of the stage was placed an armchair in which the patient was seated. Before he com-

[1] Moritz's *Reise eines Deutschen*, 1782, p. 42.

menced his operations Bossy advanced, and having taken off his gold-laced cocked hat and bowed to the right and left, began addressing the populace which crowded before him.[1] The itinerant physician is rarely seen in the metropolis in these days ; the vendors of patent medicines having driven him completely out of the field. In the last century he carried on his operations without let or hindrance.

Through Moorfields (records Judge Curwen in his 'Journal' under date of June 22, 1781). Came across a mountebank or stage doctor, on an elevated scaffold covered with a ragged blanket, discoursing to the more dirty-faced ragged mob ; demonstrating, to their satisfaction no doubt, the superior excellence of his nostrums to those of the dispensary, and the more safe and secure state of patients under his management than hospitals and common receptacles of sick and wounded poor, whose lives, health, and ease, he said truly, were as dear to them as those of the best gentry or higher nobility in the land, and he further added, of as much use to the public.[2]

Whatever celebrity the three quacks who have been mentioned may have earned for themselves, faded away when the star of James Graham arose. He in the year 1780 settled in a house situated on the Royal Adelphi Terrace, looking on to the river midway between the Blackfriars and Westminster Bridges. The front of this house Graham caused to be ornamented with an enormous gilt sun, and in letters of gold to be inscribed on its portals the words *Templum Æsculapio Sacrum.* Every room in the house was furnished on a most lavish scale, and the walls were hung with mirrors in order that visitors might imagine themselves in some enchanted oriental palace. In this Temple of Health, as it was designated, the proprietor, who possessed great command of language, was accustomed to deliver lectures nightly on the application of magnetism and electricity to health, and to disclose 'the whole art of enjoying health and vigour of body and mind, and of preserving and exalting personal honour and loveliness ; or, in other words, of living with health, honour, and happiness in the world for at least a hundred years.' For admission to these lectures Graham charged two guineas, and the result was that his

---

[1] Angelo's *Reminiscences*, i. pp. 134, 135.
[2] *Journal*, p. 317.

establishment became the resort of crowds of fashionable, wealthy, and dissipated people, which increased when it was known that he had enlisted the services of a beautiful damsel to personate Hebe Vestina, the Goddess of Youth and Health, and to deliver a concluding discourse after he had brought his own lecture to a close.   It has been asserted that his fair colleague was Amy Lyons, or, as she preferred to style herself, Emma Hart, who subsequently became the spouse of Sir William Hamilton and the personal favourite of the hero of Trafalgar, but this is stoutly denied by Henry Angelo, the famous fencing-master, who appears to have seen her on several occasions.[1]   Graham hired two individuals of enormous stature, arrayed in gold-laced cocked hats and gorgeous liveries, and bearing long staves with ornamental silver heads, to parade the town and distribute his handbills from door to door.   Before he had been six months in London Graham found himself famous.   He was able to keep an equipage, to maintain a splendid retinue, and to accept invitations to the tables of many people of the highest rank.   His name was on everybody's lips, and among the distinguished people of the time whose curiosity prompted them to visit the Temple of Health was Horace Walpole, who in writing to the Countess of Ossory under date of August 23, 1780, stigmatised it as

the most impudent puppet show of imposition he ever saw, and the mountebank himself the dullest of his profession, except that he made the spectators pay a crown apiece.   We were eighteen (he continues).   A young officer of the Guards affected humour and tired me still more.   A woman, invisible, warbled to clarionets on the stairs.   The decorations are pretty and odd ; and the apothecary, who comes up a trapdoor for no purpose, since he might as well come upstairs, is a novelty.   The electrical experiments are nothing at all singular, and a poor air-pump that only bursts a bladder, pieces out the farce.   The doctor is like Jenkinson in person, and as flimsy a puppet.[2]

Brissot was another eminent visitor to Graham's temple.   He had met the quack, it seems, in the French capital, where he had attracted great attention.   Speaking of him in his 'Mémoires sur ses Contemporains,' Brissot says :—

[1] *Reminiscences*, i. 127.
[2] *Walpole's Letters*, ed. Cunningham, vii. 427; Reynolds's *Life and Times*, i. 153–5.

Graham avait une belle figure, une taille avantageuse, une contenance noble et majestueuse, des regards qui semblaient commander le respect, surtout lorsqu'il parlait; il développait ses opinions avec une pompe qui s'accordait assez bien avec l'idée qu'il voulait donner de son système. Tel était l'effet qu'il me semblait opérer sur nos Parisiennes ; un jour que je me promenais avec lui sur les boulevarts, tous les yeux étaient fixés sur lui. . . . Graham observait avec le scrupule le plus rigoureux l'abstinence de vin.[1]

Graham subsequently transferred his temple from Adelphi Terrace to Schomberg House in Pall Mall, where he continued his lectures. Finding, however, that they were not so well patronised, he lowered the charge for admission to them, first to one guinea, then to half a guinea, a third time to five shillings, and, as a last resource, 'for the benefit of all,' as he said, to half a crown. By degrees even this failed to draw visitors, and then he threw open the Temple of Health for the public inspection at a charge of one shilling per head. Subjoined is a transcript of one of the advertisements, or rather puffs, which Dr. Graham caused to be inserted about this time in the columns of the 'Morning Post':—

Temple of Health, Pall Mall, will be opened This and Every Evening This Week, as a Grand Elysian Promenade, which will now for the first time be conducted by Dr. Graham himself with that decency and decorum, with that ease and eloquence, with that peace and propriety, which he flatters himself will insure the satisfaction and happiness of the nobility and gentry of both sexes who honour him with their presence, and the approbation and protection of all upright and disinterested Magistrates.

N.B. The rooms will be superbly illuminated with Virgin Wax, Aromatic Odour, and Harmonious Sounds will be breathed forth from the Altar of the Great Electrical Temple ; and the Whole Electrical Apparatus, which is infinitely larger and more magnificent than any other that ever was erected in the World, will be displayed in all the celestial brilliancy of that universal, most resplendent and tremendous fire. The doors will be opened at eight o'clock, the Promenade will begin at nine, and Dr. Graham will withdraw from the rooms precisely at twelve. The admission (refreshments included) will be only Half a Crown.

For this week only, the magnificent Pile of musical Machinery, the Medico-electrical Apparatus, and the suite of brilliant apartments in the Temple of Health, will be all exhibited daily, from ten o'clock in the morning till four in the afternoon. Admittance only 1s.

---

[1] *Mémoires de Brissot*, ii. 233, 234.

Nothing, according to contemporaneous accounts, was more superb than the internal embellishment of the temple. Electric fire ascended in radiating streams. Crystal globes of radiant colours dazzled the eye in every corner. Rich vases, filled with the rarest perfumes, were to be found in every apartment. The great attraction of the Temple, however, was the Celestial Bed, the construction of which, according to Graham's account, cost him 60,000*l.*, a statement which must be received with considerable qualification. This bed, which was ornamented with hangings of splendid and costly workmanship, stood on glass legs, and to all married couples who reposed upon it the proprietor guaranteed an offspring of surpassing loveliness. For the enjoyment of this privilege the fee was 500*l.* a night, a sum which it is said was actually paid by several of the nobility. Graham also found people foolish enough to pay him a guinea for his treatise on health, and others still more foolish to pay him 1,000*l.* for regular supplies of bottles of the *Elixir of Life* which he professed to have discovered.[1] A sketch of his establishment at this time is afforded us in the journal of Samuel Curwen, who gives the following particulars of his visit to it under date of February 19, 1783 :—

Evening at Dr. Graham's lecture on health in his Temple of Health, in Pall Mall, near St. James's. The first room entered was properly a vestibule, from whence, through folding doors, one passes into the apartment holding the electric bed, about seven feet square, raised three feet from the floor ; over the frame at the head are fixed two balls gilded of four inches diameter and one inch apart, to receive the electric spark from the machine above, continued down in a glass tube through the floor. Passing this you enter the room of Apollo, through a narrow entry, having on each hand two or three niches containing statues, gilded, about half the natural size. The first object that meets the eye is the temple of Apollo, being a round cupola, five feet in diameter, supported by six fluted pillars of the Corinthian order, and eight feet high, in imitation of Scagliola ; in the centre stands a tripodal frame with concave sides on which rests in each angle a lion *couchant*, supporting a long frame for the branch of six or eight lamps, adorned (or rather over-charged) with crystals, whose tremulous action, by the company's walking, adds great brilliancy to the appearance, the walls all around having many branches with three candles each, besides two

[1] Angelo's *Reminiscences*, i. 128 ; Archenholz's *Picture of England*, p. 103 ; also Captain Grose's curious medley, *A Guide to Health*, pp. 24 8.

more large central branches, suspended by gilt chains from the ceiling. The decorations in the frippery kind are in great profusion in this as well as in the other room, consisting of glass in various forms and sizes, inlaid, and hanging ; many gilt statues of Apollo, Venus, Hercules, Æsculapius, etc., besides a few pictures. The master discovered a ready elocution, a great medical knowledge, and appeared well qualified to support the character he assumes.[1]

The year 1783 witnessed Dr. Graham's departure from his Temple of Health in Pall Mall, which was soon numbered among the things that had been. The world next heard of him as delivering lectures in which he recommended earth-bathing, not only by precept, but also by practice. For one hour daily, the public were admitted, on payment of 1*s.*, to a room in Panton Street, Haymarket ; there to behold him and the Goddess of Health immersed in the warm earth to their chins, their heads being full dressed and powdered in accordance with the ridiculous fashion of the day.

I was present at one of his evening lectures upon the benefits arising from earth-bathing as he called it (says Henry Angelo, in his amusing ' Reminiscences,'), and in addition to a crowded audience of men, many ladies were there. In the centre of the room was a pile of earth, in the middle of which was a pit, where a stool was placed ; we waited some time, when much impatience was manifested, and after repeated calls ' Doctor, doctor ! ' he actually made his appearance. After making his bow he seated himself on the stool, when two men with shovels began to place the mould in the cavity. . . . The earth being up to the chin . . . he began his lecture, expatiating on the excellent qualities of the earth-bath, how invigorating, etc. Whether it was that the men felt they had had quite enough of his imposing information, which lasted above an hour, either the hearers got tired, or some wags wished to make themselves merry at the Doctor's expense, and there was a cry of ' Doctor, a song, a song ! ' The Doctor nodded assent, and after a few preparatory hems, he sang, or rather repeated,

> Ye fair married dames, who so often deplore,
> That a lover once lost is a lover no more :

Mrs. Abingdon's song in ' The Way to Keep Him.'

---

[1] *Journal*, ed. 1842, p. 369 ; see also a curious account of the Temple of Health in Archenholz's *Picture of England*, pp. 102-108 ; likewise vol. i. of Kay's *Edinburgh Portraits*, where there is a print representing Dr. Graham in the act of delivering a lecture to the sons of pleasure.

The doctor was a tall, handsome man, about forty, his manner pleasing, and much information was derived from his lectures in this way.[1]

There is no sunshine without its shadow. In 1783 the Goddess of Health fell sick and died, in consequence, the wags of the day declared, of her having contracted a chill from the damp sheets of the celestial bed. The vast sums of money which he had expended on the internal adornments of his temple, which involved him in heavy difficulties, coupled with unguarded expressions respecting the Anglican clergy which raised him many enemies, who denounced him as a thorough impostor, led to Dr. Graham's withdrawal from the garish lights of London to the provinces in March 1784. After visiting the chief country towns he proceeded to Scotland, where the reception he met with among people of education and distinction was extraordinary. Judging from some of the numerous tracts which he published about this time, it would seem as if he had become a convert to the mystical doctrines enunciated by Emmanuel Swedenborg and his disciples. It is at least clear, that when he crossed the Border he put away his quack practices for a season, seeing that Sir James Mackintosh states in his ' Memoirs ' that in the winter of 1784–5 Graham was one of his fellow-students at the University of Edinburgh.[2] Ten years later, in June 1794, he paid the debt of nature at Edinburgh, and was buried in the Grey Friars' Cemetery in that city by the generosity of a Genevese gentleman, who, in recognition of the pleasure he had derived from a perusal of one of his pamphlets, had allowed him an annuity of 50*l.*

After Graham had retired from publicity, the field of quackery in England was occupied chiefly by Dr. de Mainauduc, Mr. and Mrs. Loutherbourg, and Mr. Benjamin Douglas Perkins.

Dr. de Mainauduc first introduced himself to the English public in 1785, in the city of Bristol, by lecturing upon the

---

[1] *Reminiscences*, ii. 60–2.

[2] Mackintosh's *Memoirs*, i. 28. A number of Graham's brochures are preserved among the valuable collection of the King's Pamphlets in the British Museum.

wonderful curative properties latent in animal magnetism, and upon the principles of Friedrich Antoine Mesmer, the famous Viennese quack, one of whose pupils he avowed himself to have been. Dr. George Winter, in his 'History of Animal Magnetism,' asserts that 'Dr. de Mainauduc's subjects numbered 127, among whom there were one duke, one duchess, one marchioness, two countesses, one earl, one baron, three baronesses, one bishop, five right honourable gentlemen and ladies, two baronets, seven members of parliament, one clergyman, two physicians, seven surgeons, besides ninety-two ladies and gentlemen of respectability.' It was not long before Dr. de Mainauduc found his way to the metropolis, where his lectures continued to be crowned with complete success :—

> Lady Palmerston, Mrs. Crewe, Mrs. Sheridan, and Miss Crewe (wrote Sir Gilbert Elliot to his spouse from Park Street under date of July 4, 1786) have been twice at Mainauduc's. They were all infidels the first day except Mrs. Crewe, who seemed staggered a little by the number and variety of the people she saw affected by the *crisis*. The next time Mrs. Sheridan and Miss Crewe were both magnetised, and both had what is called a crisis—that is, they both fell into a sort of trance, or waking sleep, in which they could hear what passed, but had no power of speaking or moving, and they describe it as very like the effects of laudanum.

Four days later, Sir Gilbert wrote as follows :—

> All the fine people have been magnetised, and are learning to magnetise others. The Prince of Wales had a crisis—that is to say, became sick and faint. The Duchess of Devonshire had one ; Lady Talbot, as she was coming out of her crisis, was asked whether she wanted anything ; and she, not being quite come to herself, and not sensible of where, or in what company she was, spoke plain English. This, however, is Hugh's story, and something short of gospel. I went yesterday (17th) to Mainauduc's, but saw nothing even to entertain me. It seemed the grossest dupery imaginable, but there were several people one knows among the dupes.[1]

When Dr. de Mainauduc perceived that the public had been sufficiently mesmerised, he published a proposal for the establishment of a Hygeian Society, and met with such encouragement that Hannah More, writing to Horace Walpole in reference to what she called his 'demoniacal mummeries,'

---

[1] *Letters of Sir G. Elliot*, ed. Countess of Minto, i. 111-3.

under date of September 1788, said that he was likely to realise the sum of one hundred thousand pounds by them, as Mesmer had succeeded in doing at Paris. There is no proof, however, that De Mainauduc effected his purpose.

It should be mentioned that about three years before De Mainauduc made his first appearance in London, the last of the pretenders to the Spagiric art, or science of alchemy, as it is more generally termed, proclaimed himself. This was a man named James Price, who announced to the public that he had gained possession of a tincture whereby metals weighing between thirty and sixty times its own weight could be changed into gold. But the London public just then could attend to no one else but Dr. Graham, and consequently Price's appeal to its favour failed to secure any attention.

Among the residents at Hammersmith in the year 1789 was Philip James de Loutherbourg, a native of Alsace, a landscape painter, and superintendent of the stage scenery at Drury Lane Theatre under Garrick. This man and his wife professed that they had received direct from on high the power of healing all human maladies by means of sympathy. As they charged no fee, they found many people, especially among the poor, to believe in them, and their residence was perpetually crowded with the diseased of every rank and degree. Admission was obtained only by tickets, which it will scarcely be believed sold at prices ranging from one guinea to three. One of Loutherbourg's enthusiastic devotees, a woman named Pratt, who compiled a list of all those who had been cured, or who fancied they had been cured, by the imposition of his hands, states that 'report' said that as many as three thousand people at a time had waited outside his doors on healing days, which it is quite possible may have been the case. Accumulated proofs are brought forward by Pratt to demonstrate the reality of Loutherbourg's cures, but it is sufficient to cite the case of Mrs. Hook, of the Stable Yard, St. James's, whose two deaf and dumb daughters, she gravely assures her readers, waited on Mrs. Loutherbourg, who 'looked upon them with an eye of benignity and healed them.' A prophet is not without honour save in his own country ; consequently the reader will not be surprised to learn that, after having suffered 'all the malignity that man could suffer, joined to ungrateful behaviour and tumult,' curses instead of thanks from their patients, for example, Philip Loutherbourg and his wife wisely relinquished the practice of sympathetic healing, which had reflected more credit upon their hearts than upon their heads, and retired into private life. The outbreak of the French Revolution, combined with the movements of Napoleon Bonaparte, drove animal magnetism out of the minds of Englishmen until 1798, when it was revived for a short time, but without any marked success, by an American Quaker, named Benjamin Douglas Perkins.

Carlyle has said that the reign of superstition ended with the French Revolution. Doubtless when the revolutionary wave came rolling in, bearing high on its crest triumphant democracy, chanting her wild song, 'Liberty, Equality, and Fraternity,' when each cherished institution began to be rudely challenged, when the streets of Paris were running with the blood of the inhabitants, and when the citizens whom Gibbon characterised as 'the savages of Gaul' were worshipping the Goddess of Reason, quacks and quackery found no abiding-place in the sprightly capital, and vanished like as the mist before the rising sun. But in England, although the vibration that was shaking all the thrones in Europe was severely felt, quackery contrived to lift up its head and to reach a point that may be called monstrous. The gullibility of the people did not expire with the eighteenth century, and in the very last year of its course an observant German traveller felt justified in informing his countrymen in the pages of a short record of his sojourn on British soil, that the country was disgraced by the presence of impostors and ignorant quacks 'beyond any other in the whole world.'[1] Doubtless, in those days, mankind found that the pleasure of being cheated was as great as that of cheating.

[1] P. A. Nemnich, *Beschreibung einer in Sommer* 1799 *nach und durch England geschehenen Reise*, p. 473.

CHAPTER X.

WARS AND RUMOURS OF WARS.

Pugnacity of the English nation in the last century—Victories by land and sea—Rumours of invasion—Ludicrous invasion panics—The unsatisfactory state of the navy—Naval mutinies—Impressment and its abuses Privateers and privateering—Condition of the army—Its defects and severity of discipline—The slave-trade and its abominations—Testimony of various writers to its inhumanity—Prevalence of smuggling—' Kentish Knockers'—Connivance at ' free-trading.'

At a time like the present, a time characterised, comparatively speaking, by peace and tranquillity both at home and abroad, no conception, or at best a very imperfect one, can be formed of the combative spirit which our forefathers displayed in the last century. Never were they so truly in their element as when, figuratively or actually, they were imbruing their hands or their swords in the blood of their enemies ; never were they so unfeignedly delighted as when 'the latest advices' from distant lands communicated to them the welcome intelligence of England's ' brilliant victories' and 'glorious actions' by land or sea. The nation needed sorely to be taught that the peacemakers blessed are. Patriotism and martial zeal burnt so deeply and so strongly among men that what was at one time a nation of shopkeepers became at another a nation of volunteers, and every other profession save that of arms was neglected. The ploughman left his team to be drilled, the tailor flung aside his goose in order to become used to war's alarms, and the tradesman quitted his establishment for the purpose of attending parade. The pruning hook became a sword, and the plough-share was metamorphosed into a spear. The prospect of a war sent a thrill of pleasurable excitement through the community.

It literally made men's blood boil. Peace with them meant dulness and monotony. War signified activity and progress. A large proportion of the yearly taxation was spent in unwise and needless wars, the consequence being that from the dawn to the close of the eighteenth century our forces were almost incessantly engaged in either military or naval warfare with those of nations far distant from our shores. Momentous events and brilliant episodes crowd upon the mind as it recalls the martial annals of England under the House of Guelph.

On the accession of Queen Anne in 1702 hostilities commenced against France, and everywhere our banners, to borrow the language of Gray, were 'fanned by conquests' crimson wing.' In 1703 the English army under the command of the Earl of Marlborough attempted to wrest the whole of the Spanish dominions from Philip, in favour of the Archduke Charles of Austria. In 1704 Marlborough and Prince Eugene of Savoy defeated the French and Bavarians at the village of Blenheim in Bavaria. In the same year Admiral Rooke effected the capture of Gibraltar. The following year, the city of Barcelona was taken by the Earl of Peterborough. In 1706 Marlborough defeated Villeroi at Ramillies in Belgium, Marshal Vendôme at Oudenarde on the Scheldt in 1708, and Villars at Malplaquet in Flanders a year afterwards. Peace was concluded at Utrecht in 1713. Five years later the Quadruple Alliance was formed against Spain. Admiral Byng defeated the Spaniards off Cape Passaro in Sicily on August 11. Throughout the eighteenth century there was a constant feeling of national pride and national prejudice against France. It was this soreness, combined with an undercurrent of royal and courtly inclination, that forced Sir Robert Walpole in 1739 into a war with Spain, one of the greatest blots in the chronicles of the realm. In 1743 King George II. defeated the French and Bavarians at Dettingen on the Main, in Bavaria, memorable as the last battle in which an English monarch personally engaged. In 1756 the Seven Years War began. The English at one time appeared to be destined to go as far as the arm of conquest could reach, or the waters of the ocean extend. The faculty of appropriating to themselves vast spaces of earth, and of establishing supremacy over men of every tongue and nation was extraordinary. As the dominant passion of the French was military glory, so the dominant passion of the English was the acquisition of empire. In 1757 Robert Clive recaptured Calcutta, and defeated the Surajah Dowlah on June 23 of that year, at the battle of Plassey in Bengal, a victory which not only avenged the foul crimes of the Black Hole, but laid the foundations of the British Empire in Hindostan, and enabled the influence of Europe to tell for the first time since the days of Alexander on the nations of the East. In 1759 Canada was wrested from the French, and about the same time an English fleet took possession of the Island of Guadaloupe. George III. had scarcely ascended the throne than the maritime power of France was almost annihilated by British seamen. Admiral Hawke gained a complete victory over the French navy in Quiberon Bay, while Sir Eyre Coote struck a fatal blow to French power in India by the capture of Pondicherry near Madras. In 1762 war was declared against Spain, and was attended with victory. Simultaneously there were British conquests in America and the East Indies, and these proved so disastrous that peace was sued for in 1763 by both France and Spain. In 1765 the British government rashly projected a scheme for the taxation of the American colonies, in order that a revenue might be raised from them. Three acts were accordingly passed ; the first prohibiting the contraband trade in which the British and Spanish colonists extensively engaged, the second imposed upon them the payment of certain duties in cash, and the third was the Stamp Act. All these three were productive of the greatest indignation beyond the Atlantic, and the vigorous opposition to them eventually drew the British nation into the disastrous American war, which began in 1775 and continued with varying success until 1782, resulting in the complete severance of the ties which had hitherto bound the colonies to the mother-country, and plunging it into debt to an unprecedented extent. From 1790 to 1792 war was waged fiercely in the peninsula of Hindostan. Towards the close of that year France proclaimed war against England and Holland, and the tranquillity which it had for some time enjoyed was again ruffled. This led to the capture of Toulon by Lord Hood in 1794. Nor was Britain less successful in other quarters of the globe. To the West Indies an expedition was despatched in 1794, commanded by Sir Charles Grey and Sir John Jervis. The result was the capture of several of the islands. During the course of the same year the French evacuated Corsica, which thereby was placed under British sovereignty, and on June 1 the French fleet was severely repulsed off Brest by Lord Howe. The year following, the French fleet was attacked by Lord Bridport, near Port l'Orient, and lost three ships. Soon afterwards two sail of the line belonging to a fleet which had set out from Toulon, bent upon the capture of Corsica, fell a prey to Vice-admiral Hotham in the Mediterranean, off the coast of Genoa. February 14, 1797, witnessed a great naval triumph by Sir John Jervis in the utter defeat of the Spanish fleet, bent upon the invasion of England, off Cape St. Vincent. Similar triumphs were in store for British naval forces in 1797. Sir John Jervis, then newly created Earl St. Vincent, blockaded Cadiz, while Admiral Duncan routed a Dutch squadron near Camperdown. A year later, England was thrown into a state of apprehension and alarm by the movements of Napoleon Bonaparte, who was bent upon the seizure and colonisation of Egypt with a view to opening up a path to India. A fleet was however despatched from England to Egypt under command of Admiral Nelson, who destroyed his fleet in Aboukir Bay. In 1799, the war in the Carnatic, which had been continued by Tippoo Saib, king of Mysore in Southern India, since 1783, terminated by the death of that monarch in the capture of Seringapatam.

Throughout the eighteenth century, the narrow bounds of latitude and longitude which Nature had marked out for Great Britain furnished our forefathers with the gravest apprehensions as to its immunity from the attacks of neighbouring powers, more especially France and Spain. Several attempts at an invasion of England were made at different times during the eighteenth century, but none were successful. In 1715 the Chevalier St. George, direct heir to the throne of the Stuarts, who was called the Pretender, attempted to invade England. But the insurgents were defeated. Twenty-five years later, Charles, called the Young Pretender, grandson of James II., arriving in Scotland, gained a victory over the loyalists at Prestonpans, and afterwards entering England, reduced Carlisle, established his quarters at Manchester, and penetrated as far as Derby, whence he was forced to beat a retreat. In the early part of 1756 the country became alarmed at the report which was circulated that the French were making preparations for a more formidable invasion than any with which the kingdom had been threatened for many generations. In 1759 there was another similar rumour. In 1779, 1782, and 1783, the same report was put into circulation, but nothing resulted. In 1796 the French Directory, receiving an invitation from a number of malcontents in Ireland, despatched seventeen vessels, carrying an army of eighteen thousand men, under command of General Hoche, for the purpose of invading that country. The expedition made its appearance in Bantry Bay on the west coast of Ireland, but it effected practically nothing. In the same year the Directory, having organised a force of some twelve hundred and fifty felons and galley slaves, arrayed in black regimentals and dignified with the title of *La Légion Noire*, despatched them under the command of Colonel Tate to the shores of England. Proceeding up the Bristol Channel, they anchored at Ilfracombe on February 22, and after scuttling some merchant ships, steered their course in the direction of Pembrokeshire, where, anchoring in Fishguard Bay, they succeeded in effecting a landing and in pillaging the cottages of the inhabitants. In the end the would-be invaders were forced to give themselves up to Lord Cawdor as prisoners of war. In 1798 rebellion broke out in Ireland. The ever-watchful eye of General Napoleon Bonaparte detected in this a favourable opportunity for striking a deadly blow at his invincible enemy, by following the train of Julius Cæsar, in the invasion of Britain. When it became known that a vast armament was at Boulogne, the enormity of the danger was recognized. To conclude a lasting peace with so inveterate a foe was seen to be hopeless. Every seaman in the island was armed. The suspense was terrible: but the destination of the army proved to be not England but Egypt, and soon all alarm died away.

That there was some ground for England's apprehensions will be readily apparent, and that as soon as reports arrived men should have hastened to defend their hearths, their homes, and their household gods, determined that, come what might, their country should never lie at the proud feet of a conqueror, was but natural. Several ludicrous stories are on record of the impetuosity manifested by people in expectation of invasion. Thus, at Deal, in the eventful winter of 1744, when folk lived in daily, or rather nightly, anticipation of a French invasion, when the regular soldiers in the kingdom were few in number and scarcely any of them in the country, the inhabitants were rudely awakened in the dead of one November night by a man galloping furiously through the town, yelling out, 'I am John Redman of Walmer, come to tell you that six hundred Frenchmen are landed at the Castle.' John Redman's repute among the townsfolk of Deal was great, and this alarming intelligence he communicated was by them implicitly believed. Consternation became general. The inhabitants turned out in a body, and John Redman was examined by the mayor. He persisted in his story, and others who had come from the same place amply confirmed it. The drums now beat hastily to arms ; the church bells rang out the alarm ; the townsmen took with all expedition to their arms ; the women screamed and the children squalled. After a while some persons were sent out, in accordance with the practice of the best generals, for intelligence, while the rest awaited their return. Morning dawned at length, and the scouts returned with joyful exultation, safe and sound. They had found that John Redman was merely the echo of an old woman's exclamation at the pranks of two idle drunken young men, who had got into Walmer Castle, and were amusing themselves by uttering discordant noises. Will it be credited that Walmer Castle was then—a time of danger be it noted—defended by two women ; that there was no gunner, and that the porter was a pilot who was then in the capital?[1]

[1] Pennington's *Memoirs of Mrs. Carter*, i. 108-111.

Another ridiculous invasion panic occurred in January 1756. It was in that month that the marriage of the Hon. John Spencer with Miss Poyntz was celebrated, and the bride and bridegroom saw fit to come to town from Althorp in Northamptonshire in three coaches drawn by six horses, and accompanied by horsemen to the number of two hundred. The consternation that the progress of this splendid equipage created, as it proceeded through the sleepy country villages, was immense. Some of the people shut themselves up in their cottages, while others assumed a warlike attitude, and emerged brandishing pitchforks, spits, and spades, and vociferously informing their weak-kneed brethren that 'the invasion was come,' firmly impressed with the idea that the Pretender and the King of France had both at last carried into effect their long-standing threats of landing on British soil. The country folk breathed freely only when the formidable cavalcade had rolled by without firing their cottages and slaying them wholesale.[1]

The state of the British navy when the eighteenth century dawned was bad, and bad it remained till the age closed. Yet, notwithstanding, some of the greatest and most distinguished characters in naval annals were reared in its midst. Lords Howe, Hawke, St. Vincent, and Nelson are some of the names which occur to the mind when it reflects upon the British admirals of the eighteenth century. These won renown at a time when, to use the words of Sir John Barrow, 'there was very little system observed in the navy and very little science.' What the abominations of the dockyards, and naval abuses in general, were like at that time, few or none have now any conception.

It was in the early part of June 1749 that Lord Sandwich, who had recently taken his seat at the Board of Admiralty, set out on a visitation of all the dockyards and other naval establishments, which until then had been entirely neglected. Sir John Barrow, in his 'Life of Lord Anson,' says that there is nothing on record to show that they had ever been visited officially by any preceding Board of Admiralty, or even by the

[1] *Autob. and Corr. of Mrs. Delany,* ed. Lady Llanover, iii. 401, 402.

Commissioners of the Navy, under whose control they were more immediately placed.[1] Gross negligence, irregularities, waste, and embezzlement were so palpable that the visitors ordered notices to be set up in various parts of all the yards, offering encouragement and protection to such as should discover any misdemeanors committed either by the officers or workmen, or any other abuse whatever.[2] It was nothing uncommon for borough-mongers to buy ships, and to hire them out as transports to the government, which required their votes, at vast profit to themselves. The number of brave fellows whose lives were sacrificed in order that these harpies might be fattened, who is he that can tell? The secret rests where ' the fiery fight is heard no more, and where the storm has ceased to blow.' Greater abuses prevailed during the second half of the eighteenth century. 'You had your hand in the bag, sir, why did you not help yourself?' was the reply which a purser, who had been a commissary, received from a corrupt minister of the Crown in 1783, in response to the plea of poverty.[3] The numerous departments of the naval service were Augean stables of corruption. 'It was a common expression with the receiving clerks in the dockyards,' says Captain Edward Brenton in his entertaining ' Life of Lord St. Vincent,' 'to say that they had not been "hampered," as a reason for refusing to receive inferior articles into store, when supplied by the contractors.'[4] The term 'hampered' signified in plain English the giving of a bribe in the shape of a hamper of wine or some other expensive present, as the price of a certificate setting forth that the articles supplied had been found suitable for his Majesty's service, when they were really more fit to be flung upon the dunghill. Careful observers did not fail to note, during the progress of the American War, that the English gunpowder was invariably inferior to that in use among the colonists, and that British shot never failed to fall short, while that which they did use usually went over the heads of the enemy. The clothing with which seamen were supplied was of the quality

[1] C. v.   [2] *Ibid.* p. 216.
[3] Capt. Brenton, *Life and Corr. of Earl St. Vincent*, ii. 154.
[4] *Ibid.* p. 158.

commonly denominated 'slop clothing,' and even that was sold to them at shamefully exorbitant prices. In the dockyards the peculation that went on almost exceeds belief. The copper bolts by which vessels were secured were, in nine cases out of every ten, copper only at the ends, all the best of the metal having been purloined and wood substituted in its place. Dr. Patrick Colquhoun, in preparing a report on the state of the English police, published in 1796, asserted, to the best of his belief and knowledge, that the Government was then being systematically plundered from the dockyards alone at the rate of one million sterling per annum, and when this statement appeared in print its author was roundly accused of the grossest exaggeration. Captain Brenton, however, saw good reason for believing, from the results of personal observation and close investigation, that Colquhoun's estimate, so far from being an exaggerated one, fell far short of the true mark.[1]

Culpably negligent as the Government was in permitting abuses and evils to increase and multiply, it is not surprising that mutinies became of constant occurrence. Mutiny was a most inadvisable and unlawful policy to pursue, and it was one obviously attended with the greatest dangers, yet seamen at this time had absolutely no other means in their power by which they could hope to call the attention of the naval authorities to the grievous wrongs under which they suffered. In January 1758 seventy of the crew of the ship ' Namur,' then lying in Portsmouth harbour, exasperated by the vile provisions with which they were supplied, left the vessel, forced their way into the dock, and thence set out for London, in order to lay their grievances before the Lords of the Admiralty. Arriving in the capital, fifteen of them attempted to obtain an audience, but this was denied them, and orders were issued for them to be put into irons and carried back to Portsmouth, in order to be tried by a court-martial for mutiny.[2] Greater wisdom would the Admiralty have displayed, if it had instituted proceedings against the provision contractor. In December 1794, a letter signed 'A Delegate' was ad-

[1] *Life of Earl St. Vincent,* ii. 139.
[2] *Ann. Reg.* 1758, p. 78.

dressed to Lord Bridport, then second in command of the 'Culloden' (Lord Howe being absent), from the crew, numbering seventy-four, who were all in a state of mutiny arising from their apprehensions of the vessel not being seaworthy in consequence of her having been aground. Two of the ringleaders were acquitted, five were executed, and three received a pardon. In the month of September in the year following there were disturbances on board the 'Cæsar.' In April 1797 there was a mutiny at Spithead. There the causes which had induced the sailors to break out into revolt were not wholly unjustifiable. First, they submitted that their pay was still fixed at the same rate at which it had been fixed in the second half of the preceding century, notwithstanding the notorious fact that the prices of commodities had risen thirty per cent. since that time ; next, that their provisions were not only insufficient, but unfit for consumption, a state of affairs directly traceable to the rapacity and downright dishonesty of the pursers ; thirdly, that while the Chelsea pensions had been raised to thirteen pounds, the Greenwich pensions still remained at little more than half that sum ; fourthly, they demanded that when wounded in defence of their country's flag, they should continue to receive their pay until they were sufficiently restored to health and had received their discharge ; lastly, they entreated some relaxation of the hard-and-fast regulations respecting going ashore when in port. The Board of Admiralty, displaying more sense than some of their predecessors had done, acceded to most of these demands.

In connection with the navy, a few words may be said upon the subject of impressment. In legal theory none but seamen could be impressed, but in actual practice the gang exercised no such discrimination. All fish came to net. The working classes, in particular, who were accounted of no value at all, but rather as excrescences of the soil, were taken by the press-gangs whenever they were required, not only without the least ceremony, but almost invariably without complaint on the part of any except the sufferers themselves. Few sympathised with the victims of this unjust tyranny, because scarcely any one then regarded that treatment as an outrage. Yet the upper grades of society did not always escape. It will be remembered that Lord Fellamar, in Fielding's novel of 'Tom Jones,' is represented as engaging a pressgang at the instigation of Lady Bellaston for the purpose of impressing that edifying young hero, an artifice in which he is foiled only by force of circumstances. At times almost every merchant's ship was boarded by a pressgang on its return into port, and every able-bodied man among the crew immediately pressed into his Majesty's service. The most distressing scenes were sometimes witnessed by the inhabitants of seaport towns, in consequence of the harsh and cruel proceedings which were justified and sanctioned under the Recruiting Act. Wives, mothers, children, and lovers, waiting in the harbours to meet gallant tars, were rudely snatched from their very embrace, perhaps after long years of absence from one another, and transported to the tender-ship without being permitted to exchange one parting word. Had even the most ordinary attention been paid by those whose duty it was to pay it, to the comfort and the welfare of sailors, impressment would have had no justification whatever. But all this was quite contrary to the spirit and aim of the Admiralty in the eighteenth century. Regulations for the comfort and welfare of any except themselves they studiously neglected to devise ; the very words 'comfort and welfare' themselves were unknown in their vocabulary. Every human being possessed of the commonest sense, who directed his thoughts towards entering the navy, knew perfectly well that on board ship he would be submitted to a discipline compared with which the yoke of an Asiatic despot was a light one ; that he would be subjected to innumerable privations and petty vexations of a character which could not be realised except by actual experience ; and that in the end it was a hundred chances to one if he ever received for his services that which was his lawful due. Some of his pay he might receive, but the rest would be certain to be sent on a journey to Jupiter. The full knowledge of all this was not likely to fire many with a desire to taste the sweets of life on the high seas, and the consequence was that few or none entered the service of their own accord. The honour of England's flag

upon the seas must be maintained at all costs ; this was the
justification of pressgangs, and such little paragraphs as the
following, transcribed from contemporary records, will convey
an idea of the extent to which they carried on their operations :
'Saturday, Feb. 2, 1754, Gosport Impress Warrants being issued
out, the Press was very brisk at Cowes and in the harbour, and
a great many useful hands were picked up.' [1]   The 22nd of June,
1758, 'was the hottest press for seamen on the Thames that has
ever been known since the war began, no regard being had to
protections and upwards of 800 swept away.   The crew of the
"Prince of Wales," a letter of marque ship, stood to arms and
saved themselves by their resolution.' [2] Again, 'The Press began
on the river for sailors, when five hundred men were carry'd off.'
In another place : 'His Majesty's yachts are cruising in the
Channel to pick out all able-bodied seamen out of the homeward bound vessels.' 'Last night there was a very hot press
on the river, no less than forty pressgangs being out, who
picked up above one thousand hands and even took the mates
of ships.' Again : 'An embargo was laid on all the shipping in
the ports of England and Ireland, and the hottest press began
for seamen that ever was known, all protections being disre-
garded and the hands pressed from the merchantmen to the
very mate and master.   At the same time an order was sent to
the justices of the respective counties to take up all able-bodied
vagrant poor, and to send such of them as refused to serve in
the army on board the tenders.   Orders were likewise sent to
Scotland to lay an embargo on all the shipping there.' Written
in pencil by Benjamin Franklin on the margin of Judge Forster's
report, containing his argument in vindication of the impressment of seamen, was this trite observation :—

When the personal service of every man is called for, then the
burden is equal.   Not so when the service of part is called for and
others excused.   If the alphabet should say, Let us all fight for the
defence of the whole, that is equal, and may therefore be just. But
if they should say, Let A, B, C, and D go and fight for us while we
stay at home and sleep in whole skins, that is not equal, and cannot
therefore be just. [3]

[1] *Gent.'s Mag.* Feb. 1754, p. 92.
[2] *Ann. Reg.* 1758, p. 99 ; see also Palmer's *Yarmouth*, i. 294-5 ; and
Hutchinson's *Diary and Letters*, ii. 113 and 264
[3] Franklin's *Works*, i. 332.

This odious system was one of those which did not escape the keen observation of Voltaire when he was sojourning in England. In one of those clever letters of his upon our manners and institutions the philosopher of Ferney observes :—

Un jour, en me promenant sur la Tamise, l'un de mes rameurs, voyant que j'étais français, se mit à m'exalter d'un air fier la liberté de son pays, et me dit, jurant Dieu, qu'il aimait mieux être batelier sur la Tamise qu'archevêque en France. Le lendemain je vis mon homme dans une prison auprès de laquelle je passais ; il avait les fers aux pieds et tendait la main aux passants à travers la grille. Je lui demandai s'il faisait toujours aussi peu de cas d'un archevêque en France. Il me reconnut. ' Ah, Monsieur, l'abominable gouvernement que celui-ci! On m'a élevé par force pour aller servir sur un vaisseau du Roi en Norvège. On m'arrache ma femme et mes enfans, et on me jette dans une prison, les fers aux pieds, jusqu'au jour de l'embarquement, de peur que je ne m'enfui.' Le malheur de cette homme et une injustice si criante me touchèrent sensiblement. Un Français qui était avec moi m'avoua qu'il sentait une joie maligne de voir que les anglais, qui nous reprochent si hautement notre servitude, étaient esclaves aussi bien que nous.

Nearly one hundred of the seamen who had been impressed on Thursday, May 8, 1755, rose and got ashore at the chalk-pits down the river. In the ' Public Advertiser ' for January 27, 1755, it is stated that

on Thursday night the press for seamen was very low below Bridge, and on Friday there was a very warm press for landmen to man the guardships. His Majesty's yachts are cruising in the Channel to pick out able-bodied seamen out of the homeward bound vessels.

An extract from a letter dated Bristol, April 10, 1755, printed in the ' Public Advertiser,' says :—

The press for Seamen to serve on board his Majesty's fleet has continued here near six weeks with the greatest assiduity, in which time a great number of hands have been impressed and many entered, which has so effectually cleared our keys of sailors that the captains of merchantmen etc. have been obliged to advertise for hands to convey their ships to their respective ports.

The ' London Packet ' for November 8, 1770, records :—
' Yesterday a man stood in the pillory in Catherine Street in the Strand for keeping a disorderly house in the same street A pressgang attended, and picked up several useful men.' One

of the cleverest of James Gilray's numerous caricatures was that which he called the 'Liberty of the Subject,' published in October 1779, and which depicted a villainous-looking press-gang hauling off to the tender ship a poor miserable tailor, whom his wife is endeavouring to rescue by seizing the unkempt locks of the foremost of the band. Now and then the pressgangs rendered some service to the protection of life and property, as the following paragraphs transcribed from the 'Public Advertiser' for September 21, 1782, plainly demonstrate :—

On Friday night a pressgang having received intelligence of a house near Poplar where the thieves skulk till the evening, when they commence their depredations, went very unexpectedly and surrounded the house, from which they took 17 and carried them away to the tender at the Tower.

Monday, April 4, 1790.—The kingdom was unexpectedly alarmed by all the seamen, unemployed persons, etc. in the outports being impressed, or otherwise obliged to enter on board the king's ships. Tuesday, 5.—This night a very hot press also took place on the River Thames.

It must not be supposed that the action of pressgangs never brooked opposition. Desperate struggles took place in the streets and houses, not only in London, but in provincial towns and villages, between the pressgangs and those whom they selected as their victims. In 1755 a gang broke into the cottage of a man named Sparrow, situated near the town of Calne in Wiltshire. He was discovered in bed, whereupon they bade him rise and go with them, which he consented to do on condition that they refrained from binding him. As soon as he was up, however, one of the gang attempted to bind him, whereupon Sparrow produced a knife and stabbed him to the heart with it. At Hull some time later, three hundred pressed men, confined beneath the hatches in a tender ship during a spell of sultry weather, broke on a sudden into open revolt, fought their way on deck, killed the captain, pitched one of the lieutenants overboard into the Humber, slashed the cheeks of another, overpowered the guard, and effected their escape. By far the greater number of these had accepted the alternative which had been offered them by the judge who presided over the assizes at Pontefract, in place of taking their trial. A similar story is recorded in the 'Annual Register' for 1759. In May of that year thirty impressed men on board a tender at Sunderland forcibly made their escape. The leader having been hoisted on deck by his companions, wrested the halbert from the sentinel on duty, and defended himself with one hand while with the other he lowered a ladder into the hold for the use of his comrades, who soon clambered up and overpowered the crew. On one occasion a pressgang, while giving chase to a sailor who had almost succeeded in eluding them on Tower Hill, despatched a bull-dog in pursuit, and the animal, tearing after him, caught hold of one of his calves and bit it completely off. At another time the victim of a pressgang offered his persecutors the sum of forty guineas for his release, which offer being refused, he deliberately cut off the forefinger of his left hand, but was impressed notwithstanding. Very often when the advent of a gang was expected in a certain neighbourhood the signal of its approach was given by a shrill blast on a cowhorn, on hearing which every man took, of course, to his heels. Sometimes the proceedings of a pressgang were enlivened by a touch of humour. One day two vigilant catchpoles dogged the footsteps of a naval captain (who had neglected to discharge his debts with that promptitude which his creditors thought essential) along Ratcliffe Highway. Seizing a favourable opportunity one of them tapped him on the shoulder. Scarcely had he done so than a pressgang trooped out of a court hard by and marched the pair off to a tender-ship.

This week (runs a paragraph for January 23, 1761) there has been a smart impress on the River Thames and all parts adjacent thereunto, and a great number of seamen and other persons fit to serve his Majesty have been ferreted from their lurking holes, and sent on board the men-of-war that are ready for war.

An extract from a letter dated Bristol, June 3, printed in the issue of the ' Daily Advertiser' for June 6, 1778, sets forth that

on Friday last there was a very warm Press in this City for seamen, and the vessels in the road were all stripped of their hands. The pressgang attempting to board an outward-bound vessel in King Road were fired upon by the crew, when one man was killed on the spot and another wounded, and the boat beat off; but the tender immediately weighed anchor, and came alongside of the vessel, boarded her, and took every one of the hands.

Professor Pryme of Cambridge stated late in life that he well recollected as a child being an eye-witness at Hull in 1797 of a very determined and, as it proved, effectual resistance which was offered to a pressgang by the mercantile crew of the 'Blenheim,' a Greenland whaling-ship, upon its arrival in that port.

That fishery (said he) required a number of hands on each ship; the sailors, armed with their harpoons, knives, and lances, resisted the attempt of the pressgang to board them, and one of the latter was so severely wounded that he died shortly afterwards. The master of the 'Blenheim' was tried for murder at the next assizes, but was acquitted on the proof that his sailors had confined him (probably no unwilling prisoner) to his cabin during the conflict.[1]

Throughout the eighteenth century the pressgang was in full force as a Government institution, and by its instrumentality the ranks of the navy were mainly recruited. Advocates of this system were wont to urge in justification of it, that it was one of the obvious necessities of the age. There is a probability it may have been so, but it should not be forgotten that the conditions of the naval service at this time were such as to compel all but those of the very lowest stamp to avoid it. No better commentary on the dreadful state of it can be found than Smollett's 'Roderick Random,' and no higher testimony can be borne to the veracity of the clever novelist than that of the great Admiral Earl St. Vincent, who told Captain Pelham Brenton, his sympathetic biographer, that the scenes which he beheld with his own eyes when he entered the navy fully bore out the correctness of Smollett's descriptions. It is evident from the word-portraits of naval captains and lieutenants which are preserved for all time in the novels of Smollett, that they were either scandalously incompetent or else brutal and tyrannical to the last degree, and when this is considered, it is not surprising that a seafaring life became an object of dread and detestation. Whosoever had not the golden key had small hopes of even entry into the navy, much less promotion while there. The naval officials were corrupt

---

[1] *Autobiographic Recollections*, p. 27. It is a curious and interesting fact that there was living at Wavertree, near Liverpool, in 1872, a man named John Taylor, then in his ninety-ninth year, who in 1796 had been pressed at Yarmouth and sent on H.M.S. *Bellerophon*, then lying in the Roads.

and abominable to the very core. If there were exceptions, they were like those of men born either blind or lame. When one day in 1741 Roderick Random (or to speak more correctly, George Tobias Smollett, since 'Roderick Random' partakes largely of an autobiographical character) and his companions delivered their letters of qualification for the appointment of surgeon's mate at the Navy Office before one o'clock, the secretary opened and read them. Roderick confesses that he was mightily pleased to find himself fully qualified for the post of second mate of a third-rate vessel. After he and his companions had left the presence of this august official, they conferred together on their expectations ; and then it was that Random understood that each of them had been recommended to one or other of the commissioners, and that both of them had been promised the first vacancy that should fall, but that none of them relied on that interest without a present to the secretary, 'with whom some of the commissioners went snacks.' The others had taken the precaution to provide a small purse, and Roderick was asked what he proposed to give—'a vexatious question to me,' he observes, 'who far from being in a capacity to gratify a ravenous secretary, had not wherewithal to purchase a dinner.'[1]

Smollett sailed in the capacity of surgeon's mate on board of a ship of the line to South America in 1741, and in discharge of the same office accompanied the expedition to Carthagena. Something of the loathsome scenes and sights that met his gaze on the voyage out, he causes Roderick Random to relate in the following passage :—

When I followed him (*i.e.* the surgeon) with the medicines into the sick berth or hospital, I was much less surprised that people should die on board than that any sick person should recover. Here I saw about fifty miserable distempered wretches suspended in rows, so huddled one upon another, that not more than fourteen inches space was allotted for each with his bed and bedding, and destitute of every convenience necessary for persons in that helpless condition.[2]

Two years before the accession of George III. one who was not a novelist, but a sober essayist, could say that

[1] C. xviii.   [2] C. xxv.

he had known a thousand men confined together in a guardship, of whom several hundred possessed neither a bed nor so much as a change of linen ; and that he had seen many of them brought into the hospital wearing the same clothes and shirts they were wearing when pressed several months previously.

To such a system as this the appointment of the naval commanders was due. So doughty a sea-commander as Captain Oakum, for example (under whose command Roderick Random sailed from St. Helen's ' on the ever-memorable expedition of Carthagena '), who on the morning after the ship had quitted the port, when he had perused the sick list handed to him according to custom by the first mate, cried with a stern countenance, ' Blood and oons ! sixty-one sick people on board of my ship ! Harkee ! you sir, I'll have no sick in my ship, by God.'[1] To such a system as this his successor, Captain Whiffle, owed his appointment. That remarkable character, we read, when he entered into command of the ship on her homeward voyage, sought the sweets of repose on a couch with a wrapper of fine chintz about his body and a muslin cap with lace about his head. The air which he displayed, we are further told, was a languishing one, and his head was ' supported by his *valet-de-chambre*, who from time to time applied a smelling-bottle to his nose.'[2]

The practice of privateering, in other words the practice of commissioning vessels and authorising their crews to rob the merchant ships of other nations on the high seas, was widely prevalent during the century. During the time of the American and French War, several hundred Gallican prisoners were brought into Liverpool by privateers. Dr. Benjamin Franklin, who stigmatised the practice as ' the universal bent of the English nation,' records that during the American War no less than seven hundred such were commissioned and fitted out by merchants for the purpose of plundering other merchants who had never done them any harm whatever.[3] The newspapers of that time teem with announcements having reference to privateers. In an extract of a letter from Penryn inserted in the ' Morning Chronicle ' for November 4, 1779, it is stated that

---

[1] *Roderick Random*, c. xxvii.   [2] c. xxxiv. and xxxv.
[3] Dr. Franklin's *Works*, ed. Sparks, Boston, 1836, ii. 483-6.

Last Friday morning the ' Revenge' privateer, belonging to this place, fell in with a French privateer on our coast, when a smart and bloody engagement ensued, which lasted three glasses ; but at length a nine-pound ball from the ' Revenge ' entered the French privateer close to the surface of the water, and she immediately filled and sank in ten minutes, and all the crew were drowned. The ' Revenge's ' people gave them three cheers as they went down. Several men were wounded on board the ' Revenge,' but none killed : her rigging was much shattered.

From the outbreak of the war with France in July 1778 to the month of May in the year following, the Liverpool privateers alone took prizes to the value of 1,025,600*l.* On October 3, 1779, the ' Amazon' of Liverpool and the ' Ranger ' of Bristol succeeded in capturing off the Azores a ship of 800 tons proceeding homewards from Manila. She was deeply laden with gold, silver, silk, coffee, china, cochineal, and indigo ; and also carried great private adventures which were not registered. The value of the whole was supposed to exceed 300,000*l.* Nearly about the same time the ' Shark ' of London and the ' Sprightly' of Guernsey effected the capture of a ship returning from the South Seas, containing among other valuable treasures three chests of doubloons, forty-seven chests of silver, two hundred thousand dollars, one chest of white silver, two hundred and seventy marks, nine small chests of gold, four hundred tons of cocoa, fifteen bales of fur, and one hundred and fifty tons of bar copper. Not unfrequently the crews of English privateers changed their characters, and became in effect pirates, attacking, as such, English ships. Thus the ' Annual Register ' records under date of March 23, 1759, that

the society of merchants and insurers of ships having received information that divers neutral ships have been plundered of their cargoes by pretended English privateers, have renewed their reward of one hundred pounds for detecting and convicting all such pirates, over and above the reward offered by the Lords of the Admiralty.

There is a similar record in the Historical Chronicle of the ' Gentleman's Magazine,' under date of April 3, 1759 :—

Two gentlemen, passengers from Holland, landed at Margate. They affirm they were in the evening boarded in sight of the North Foreland by an English privateer cutter, whose crew in disguise confined the captain and the crew of their vessel in the cabin, and then plundered it of goods to the value of 2,000*l.*, demanded the captain's money and took what the passengers had.

In the month of August in the preceding year the Lords of the Admiralty received intelligence that a Dutch vessel having on board the baggage and domestics of the Marquis de Pigna-telli, ambassador from the Court of Spain to the King of Denmark, was boarded no fewer than three successive times by the crews of three different English privateers, who after forcing the hatches and rummaging the hold, burst open and rifled the trunks of the ambassador, insulted, stripped, and cruelly bruised his servants, and crowned all by carrying off his effects, together with letters of credit and a bill of exchange.[1]

'The Public Advertiser' for January 14, 1761, records that

information having been sent to Capt. Harden of the 'Hornet' priva-teer belonging to Dover, that two large ships bound from Marseilles to Havre, laden with sundry sorts of merchandise to a considerable amount, were drove by contrary winds off Dungeness, he met with the crew of the privateer and seized them, and they are gone to ride quarantine. The information coming from very good hands of their cargoes being French property, there is great reason to believe they will be condemned. The crews of the French privateers (says another paragraph in the same journal) taken by our ships, are found to consist nearly in a proportion of two-thirds foreigners, especially Spaniards and Portuguese, who allured by the prospect of gain and uncommon success, the enemy have had flock to France in shoals.

Michael Kelly, manager of the King's Theatre in the Hay-market, in speaking of a voyage that he took when a youth, from Dublin to Naples in May 1779, while the American War was raging, on board a Swedish merchantman sailing under a neutral flag, says :—

In the Bay of Biscay we were hailed by an American privateer. Our captain lay to, while a set of the greatest raga-muffins my eyes ever beheld boarded us. They swore the vessel was under false colours, and proceeded to overhaul the captain's papers and seize everything they could lay their hands on. . . . The captain finding that our vessel was really a neutral left us. The next day we were boarded and examined by an English sloop of war.[2]

---

[1] *Gent.'s Mag.* 1758, p. 391.

[2] *Reminiscences*, p. 23 ; see also Beatson's *Naval and Military Memoirs*, iii. 65, 228, 231 ; *Malmesbury Corr.* i. 49 ; and *Diary and Letters of Thomas Hutchinson*, ii. 263.

The character, circumstances, and conditions of army service, from the colonel to the recruit, under the House of Brunswick were of a piece throughout—that is to say, they were all thoroughly bad. In the army at that time the ruling principles were the systems of purchase and the sale of commissions. The days of competitive examination and professional qualification were not dreamt of in the philosophy of the legislative assembly, and the only wonder is, with the army in such a state of deterioration, how the eighteenth century came to be what it incontestably is—one of the most brilliant periods in the military annals of the country. Some years ago a distinguished statesman, since passed from among us, described the military and naval services as 'a gigantic system of out-door relief for members of the aristocracy.' As applied to the services in the eighteenth century these words would have been equally appropriate. Army commissions were utilised by statesmen with the most barefaced audacity for the gratification of political designs, and even for the provision of their nephews and nieces. Sir Robert Walpole, after straining every effort to shunt William Pitt, one of his most uncompromising opponents, resorted to the expedient of depriving him of the cornetcy of horse to which he had been gazetted. From one year's end to another soldiers were condemned to keep in the ranks without the smallest prospect of promotion unless they chose to pay for it, or to secure influential interest on their behalf. It was commonly said in those times that the worse man was the better soldier, as it was believed that a certain amount of recklessness was requisite in order to give a man the courage to risk his life. The consequence was that young men who had lost both their characters and their situations, men who in the rural districts were poachers, who in the towns were thieves, were regarded as the lawful prey of the recruiting sergeants. By lies they lured them, by liquor they tempted them, and when they were dead drunk they forced a shilling into their fists. Stern repression followed, and oftentimes the poor dupes had to be imprisoned and flogged in order that they might realise that they were no longer their own masters. To expect promotion without interest was considered about as reasonable as to command a mountain to be removed and cast into the sea. Smollett emphasises this in his novel 'The Expedition of Humphry Clinker.' While staying at an inn in Durham Mr. Matthew Bramble and company make the acquaintance of Lieutenant Lismahago, a tall meagre figure answering with his horse the description given by Cervantes of Don Quixote mounted on Rozinante :—

We were immediately interested in behalf of this veteran (says Melford, writing to Sir Watkin Phillips), but our pity was warmed with indignation when we learned that in the course of two sanguinary wars he had been wounded, maimed, mutilated, taken, and enslaved, without ever having attained a higher rank than that of a lieutenant. My uncle's eyes gleamed, and his nether lip quivered, while he exclaimed, 'I vow to God, sir, your case is a reproach to the service. The injustice you have met with is so flagrant.' 'I must crave your pardon, sir,' cried the other, interrupting him ; 'I complain of no injustice. I purchased an ensigncy thirty years ago, and in the course of service rose to be a lieutenant according to my seniority.' 'But in such a length of time,' resumed the Squire, 'you must have seen a great many young officers put over your head.' 'Nevertheless,' said he, 'I have no cause to murmur ; they bought their preferment with their money. I had no money to carry to market ; that was my misfortune, but nobody was to blame.' 'What ! no friend to advance a sum of money ?' said Mr. Bramble. 'Perhaps I might have borrowed money for the purchase of a company,' answered the other, 'but that loan I must have refunded, and I did not chuse to incumber myself with a debt of a thousand pounds, to be paid from an income of ten shillings a day.'

Collins relates that in 1756 William Wentworth of Henbury, Dorsetshire, 'had a cornet's commission in a regiment of dragoons when he was but two years old.' As to the other abuses which had crept into the regular army by this time, they were simply scandalous. The worst of them are enumerated in one of the papers which Sir Walter Scott contributed to the pages of the 'Edinburgh Weekly Journal' :—

No science was required on the part of a candidate for a commission in the army, no term of service as a cadet, no previous experience whatever, the promotion went on equally unimpeded ; the boy let loose from school last week might in the course of a month be a field officer if his friends were disposed to be liberal of money and influence. Others there were against whom there could be no complaint for want of length of service, although it might be difficult to see how their experience was improved by it. It was no uncommon thing for a commission to be obtained for a child in the cradle, and when he came from college the fortunate youth was at least lieutenant of some standing by dint of fair promotion. To sum up this catalogue of abuses, *commissions* were in some instances bestowed upon *young ladies*, when pensions could not be had.

Sir Walter concludes by saying that he had himself known one fair dame who drew the pay of a captain in the dragoons, and who, as he says, 'was probably not much less fit for the service than some who at that period actually did duty.'[1]

It may be well believed that in those times many incorrigible blackguards drifted into the army and disgraced it by their presence, requiring the administration of a stern discipline before their evil tendencies could be repressed, much less eradicated, yet the severity of discipline which characterised the army until late in the eighteenth century was barbarous. Thus a paragraph in the issue of the 'Times' for January 7, 1797, states that

On Thursday a private who had been found guilty of deserting from the West London Regiment of Militia after having received the bounty, and entering into his Majesty's corps of Marines, and also for embezzling a sum of money with which he was entrusted to pay his sick comrades, was sentenced to receive *three hundred lashes* as his punishment. The sentence was inflicted in a field in front of White Conduit House, where the culprit was placed on a wooden frame, with his hands made fast to the post. When he had received 100 lashes, the officers ordered him to be taken into the house for his wounds to be dressed.

The mass of human misery created by the abominations of the African Slave Trade now blotted the escutcheon of England. For the ports of Bristol, Liverpool, and Lancaster, it constituted one of the branches of commerce, and large numbers of seamen were engaged in it. Thomas Clarkson, to whom the priority of originating the great design of the abolition of slavery belongs, confesses in his 'History' that when pursuing his inquiries into its nature, on whatever branch of the system he turned his eyes, he found it equally barbarous. While he saw that numbers of vessels were engaged in it, and hundreds of persons were concerned in it, comparatively few supported its abolition.

[1] Ed. *Weekly Journ.* Jan. 10, 1827, quoted by Lady Llanover, i 47.

The seamen who were enticed into the traffic were of two classes. The first consisted of those who were ignorant of its real nature, and to whom false representations of advantage accruing from it were made ; and the second class consisted of seamen who by means of a regular system connived at by captains and mates, had been purposely brought by their land-lords into distress, from which extrication was possible only by engaging in so hateful an employment.' [1]

We, the British Senate (wrote Walpole to Sir Horace Mann from Strawberry Hill, on Feb. 25, 1750), that temple of liberty and bulwark of Protestant Christianity, have this fortnight been pondering methods to make more effectual that horrid traffic of selling negroes. It has appeared to us that six and forty thousand of these wretches are sold every year to our plantations alone ! It chills one's blood. I would not have to say that I voted in it for the continent of America. [2]

In a tract upon this subject written by an English merchant in 1745, the writer contended that the African slave trade is ' the great pillar and support of the British plantation trade in North America.' He was of opinion that,

were it possible for white men to answer the end of negroes, our colonies would interfere with the manufacture of these kingdoms ; in such case we might have just reason to dread the prosperity of our colonies, but while we can abundantly supply them with negroes, we need be under no such apprehension.

The following description of a slave ship is transcribed from the ' Annual Register ' for 1762 :—

On Friday, the men slaves being very sullen and unruly, having had no sustenance of any kind for forty-eight hours except a dram, we put one half of the strongest of them in irons. On Saturday and Sunday all hands, night and day, could scarce keep the ship clear, and were constantly under arms. On Monday morning many of the slaves had got out of irons, and were attempting to break up the gratings ; and the seamen not daring to go down the hold to clear our pumps, we were obliged, for the preservation of our own lives, to kill fifty of the ringleaders and stoutest of them. It is impossible to describe the misery the poor slaves underwent, having had no fresh water for five days. Their dismal cries and shrieks, and most frightful looks, added a great deal to our mis-

---

[1] Clarkson's *Hist. of the Abolition of Slave Trade*, i. 294.
[2] Walpole's *Letters*, ed. Cunningham, ii. 197.

fortunes ; four of them were found dead, and one drowned herself in the hold.[1]

It was computed that on an average each slave-trading transport lost on the voyage out about ten per cent. of the human cargo with which it started, and that this was caused either by sickness, starvation, brutal usage, or deliberate murder. As these were days distinguished for dignified episcopal sloth, it is a pleasure to record that there was one member of the right reverend bench who had the courage of his opinions. In a very excellent discourse delivered on February 21, 1766, by William Warburton, the learned Bishop of Gloucester, on behalf of the Society for the Propagation of the Gospel in Foreign Parts, there occurs this striking passage : —

> In excuse of the violation of all things civil and sacred, it hath been pretended that, though indeed these miserable outcasts of the race of Adam be torn from their homes and native wilds by force and fraud, yet this violation of the rights of humanity improves their condition and renders them less unhappy. But who are you who pretend to judge of another man's happiness ?—that state which each man under the instinctive guidance of his Creator forms for himself, and not one man for another. To know what constitutes mine or your happiness is the sole prerogative of Him who made us, and cast our minds into different moulds. Did these unhappy slaves ever complain to you of their unhappiness amid their native woods and deserts ? or rather, let me ask, did they ever cease complaining of their condition under you, their lordly masters ?—where they see, indeed, the accommodations of civil life, but, the more to embitter their miseries, see them all pass by to others, unbenefited by them. Be so gracious then, ye petty tyrants over human freedom, to let your slaves judge for themselves what it is which makes their own happiness, and see whether they do not rather place it in their return to their own country than in the contemplation of your grandeur, of which their distresses make so large a part.[2]

Very often it happened that West India planters brought with them, during their flying visits to this country, slaves— ' black boys '—to England, and the kind treatment with which they noticed English servants were treated often caused them to abscond, more especially when they became cognisant of an opinion firmly held in many quarters, that all baptized

---

[1] *Ann. Reg.* 1762, p. 118 ; see also Gardiner's *Reminiscences*, iii. 67.
[2] *Warburton's Sermons*, vol. iii. 82-4.

persons became free. Consequently, when they absconded they generally prevailed upon some pious divine to baptize them, and some kind-hearted citizen to act as sponsor. Planters and merchants found to their dismay that their slaves ran away so often that in 1729 they applied to both the Attorney-General and the Solicitor-General of that day (York and Talbot), in order to solicit their opinion upon the baptism of slaves. This opinion they were not slow in giving, to the effect that no slave coming into the British Isles from the West Indies became free, and that baptism had no power whatever to absolve them from their condition. The planters lost no time in giving publicity to an opinion so favourable to themselves, and publishing advertisements proclaiming rewards for the apprehension of all runaway slaves. Nor was that all. People in no wise concerned with them commenced trading in slaves by making agreements with the captains of ships bound for the West Indies to carry them at a stipulated price.[1] Clarkson, in his ' History of the Slave Trade,' instances three cases of this. One dark night in 1770 a certain Robert Stapylton of Chelsea, in conjunction with two watchmen named respectively John Malony and Edward Armstrong, seized the person of Thomas Lewis, an African slave, whom they dragged to a boat lying in the Thames, where, having gagged him and bound him with a cord, they rowed him down the river to a ship, and placed him on board to be sold in Jamaica as a slave. This seizure occurred near the garden attached to a house in the occupation of the mother of Sir Joseph Banks. The shouts of the victim caused the servants to run to his assistance, but the boat was out of sight before they arrived. Mrs. Banks soon communicated this occurrence to the celebrated Granville Sharp, and expressed her readiness to defray any of the expenses that might be incurred in bringing the delinquents to justice. Sharp, whose indignation burnt against injustice and wrong, lost no time in procuring a *habeas corpus*, and by means of it he secured Lewis at Gravesend just as the vessel was on the eve of sailing. Stapylton was tried for his action, but the jury came to the conclusion that the plaintiff was not the property of the defendant.[2]

[1] Clarkson's *Hist. of Slave Trade*, i. 66.   [2] *Ibid.* i. 73-4.

One or two significant facts relative to the deep atrocity of this subject occur in the ' Memoirs' of Gilbert Wakefield.   He states that since the conclusion of the American War it had come out in evidence on a trial in Westminster Hall, that a ship freighted with negroes was reduced to great scarcity of water, and that the captain caused the handcuffed blacks to be brought one by one out of their dungeon on to the deck, and pitched overboard to the number of one hundred and thirty.[1]   Beilby Porteus, Bishop of London, alluding to this same fact in a sermon preached in February 1783, fixed the number at one hundred and forty.   Wakefield also relates, that once while sojourning at Buxton he heard a Liverpool captain informing the company in which he happened to be that a female slave during her voyage fretted herself to a very great degree over an infant child which she had brought with her.   'Apprehensive for her health, I snatched the child,' said this monster, glorying in his unparalleled brutality, ' I snatched the child from her arms, knocked its head against the side of the ship, and threw it into the sea.'[2]

Out of the eight hundred and fourteen thousand slaves, which it appears were conveyed from the coast of Africa to the West Indies in the thirteen years 1783-1795, no fewer than four hundred and seventeen thousand were conveyed in the vessels belonging to Liverpool merchants.[3]   During the first quarter of the year which preceded the outbreak of the Revolutionary War there were a hundred and thirty-six ships of Liverpool engaged in the African slave trade, and according to Baines, the historian of Liverpool, the tonnage on them constituted about a twelfth part of that which entered the port.

Against this monster iniquity, which fairly outstripped all abhorrence and baffled all exaggeration, which converted one corner of the earth into the nearest possible resemblance to the infernal regions, which reversed every law of Christianity, and openly defied the divine vengeance—with zeal, with patience,

[1] *Memoirs*, i. 194.
[2] *Ibid.* p. 195; see also Roberts's *Memoirs of H. More*, i. 25, and Lord Gambier's *Memorials*, i. 178.
[3] Baines, *Hist. Liv.* p. 719; see also Bandinel's *History of Slave Trade*.

and courage did William Wilberforce, the member for Yorkshire, occupy night and day in a ceaseless crusade in the House of Commons and out of it, for many a long year from 1787 onwards; labouring in spite of calumny, in spite of delays the most disheartening and in the teeth of difficulties the most formidable, calling public attention to the cruel wrongs that were being inflicted upon the negroes throughout the British dominions. Unfortunately, in that age, public attention was anything but the forerunner of public action. The eighteenth century passed away without witnessing any amelioration of their lot, and the sceptre was destined to pass from the House of Hanover before Wilberforce was permitted to see the desire of his eyes.

It was the common practice for the London agents of the East India Company, without one jot or tittle of a legal right empowering them to do so, to organise bands composed of the lees and feculence of society (denominated 'crimps' or 'kidnappers'), to entrap lusty youths in the metropolis and to cause them to be detained in establishments scattered here and there in the capital, rented for the purpose, until they could be sold into the hands of Bengal ship captains, who employed them in the service of the Company, in Hindustan. Other kidnapping establishments existed for the detention of youths and men until they could be sold to Pennsylvanian and North American planters, unless ransomed in the meantime by their friends if apprised as to where they were located. An instance of an attempt at kidnapping is recorded in the 'Annual Register' under date of February 24, 1760 :—

An apothecary in Devonshire Street, near Queen's Square, was one night last month attacked by two ruffians in Red Lion Street, who, presenting firearms and menacing him with death if he cried out or resisted, carried him to Black Mary's Hole [a lonely spot situated, as near as can now be ascertained, where the present Somers Town lies], when, by the light of a lantern, perceiving that he was not the intended person, they left him there without robbing him. This mysterious transaction has not yet been cleared up, though they are suspected to be the same fellows who lately sent threatening letters to Mr. Nelson, an apothecary in Holborn, and another tradesman.

One of the crimps met with a young fellow and told him he would treat him with a pot of beer if he would only say he was

just enlisted to serve in the East India Company. The man refused; on which the man pulled a paper out of his pocket, and
said he had a warrant against him for stealing a silver tankard, a
trick to get the young man into a lock-up house; a trick generally
used to get young men into lock-up houses, where they are confined in such a manner as to make it impossible they should acquaint
their friends with their situation.[1]

In 1768 the master of a lock-up house in Chancery Lane
was tried before Lord Chief Justice Mansfield, on an indictment for a conspiracy with a Middlesex magistrate, to inveigle,
kidnap, and carry several persons out of the kingdom. It
appeared that great cruelties had been perpetrated on a man
who had been unjustly confined in this hole, by beating him
with the thick end of a horsewhip, &c., and carrying him away
under a strong guard in the dead of the night on board a ship
lying off Gravesend. He was found guilty on the clearest
evidence.[2] 'The scandalous method,' said Lord Clive, 'by
which the Company raise their militia should be abolished.
There is but one season of the year when they can raise them
at all, and then they are shut up in lock houses.'[3] It seems
strange that such practices should have been permitted to
flourish on until the closing decades of the century, and yet
there is evidence to prove that they were. An instance of a
determined attempt at this kind of thing is recorded in the
issue of the 'British Gazette' for August 4, 1782, the paragraph running to this effect:—

Wednesday evening one of the most horrid scenes was discovered near Leicester Fields that ever disgraced any civilised
country. A young lad was perceived running from thence towards
the Haymarket, and two or three fellows crying after him, 'Stop
thief!' Some of the passengers no sooner stopped him as such
than he told them he was no thief, but had been kidnapped by his
pursuers, who had chained him in a cellar with about nine more in
order to be shipped off for India, and that he had made his escape
so far by mere desperation, swearing he would run the first through
with a penknife he held open in his hand. The youth was instantly liberated, and the whole fury of the populace fell on his
kidnapping pursuers, one of whom was heartily ducked in the
mews pond. All the remaining youths were taken from the place
of confinement by the intervention of the populace. These robbers
of human flesh, it seems, not only intoxicate country lads till they

---

[1] *Ann. Reg.* 1767, p. 83.   [2] *Ibid.*, 1768, p. 123.
[3] Speech in 1769. Cavendish, *Debates*, i. 262.

can confine them, but have been known to stop people in the streets and carry them to their horrid dens, under the various pretences of their being deserters, pickpockets, etc. They likewise attend register offices, and hire youths there for servants, whom they immediately confine, and sell them either to the military or to the India kidnapping contractors. The master of this infamous house behaved in a most insolent manner before Justice Hyde, and was committed to the watch-house black hole till this day at eleven o'clock, when he is to be re-examined.

This state of affairs was bad enough in all conscience, but it is paralleled by a similar occurrence recorded in the issue of the 'Craftsman' for January 7, 1788 :—

Saturday evening about nine o'clock, a most uncommon scene presented itself near Charing Cross, viz., a young man about eighteen, with a hot poker in his hand, running full speed, and two crimps pursuing him, crying out 'Murder!' and 'Stop thief!' It seems the lad being obstreperous had been put to bed about eight o'clock for security, but that after forcing open the chamber door, he rushed into the tap-room, and seizing the poker that was then in the fire, defended himself against upwards of a dozen crimps and others, some of whom were much bruised. The lad was stopped in St. Martin's Lane, but soon rescued by the populace, who, it seems, had been in a similar situation with the young lad but a short time ago. The former had been met with coming out of a register office, and trepanned under the pretence of carrying a letter to the house where he had been detained.

That a vast amount of smuggling, or free-trading as it was euphemistically termed, went on during the eighteenth century needs hardly to be mentioned. As the century increased in years, so the smugglers increased in number, defying the fiscal laws, and cheating the king's customs on a gigantic scale. People of mark, ladies as well as gentlemen, smuggled prodigiously without scruple costly articles of foreign manufacture, and when they were unable to do so themselves aided and abetted others in doing it for them. The Selwyn Correspondence affords much evidence of this. The Earl of March, writing to George Selwyn under date of Tuesday, July 19, 1763, says : 'All my stockings have been *seized by not being taken out of the paper and rolled up, which would have made them pass for old stockings.*'[1] Gilly Williams, writing to George Selwyn from Brighthelmstone on August 25, 1784, observes :—

[1] Jesse's *Selwyn*, i. 257.

The pattern of velvet you sent me is so pretty that it has made me alter my intentions, and *determines me to risk the vigilance of the custom house officers, but the master of the packet here tells me he can do it with much more ease and security*, therefore I wish you would order the suit of clothes immediately, and send them well-packed directed to Captain Killick, to be left with Mr. Ballard at Dieppe.

The owners of small ships succeeded in driving a very profitable business in facilitating the conveyance to their clients of high degree of large quantities of smuggled goods from France and Germany. The Hon. Henry St. John, writing to George Selwyn from his residence in Sackville Street, Piccadilly, under date of January 11, 1765, says :—

If you are not already loaded with commissions, which I am sensible are not in general very agreeable, I own I should be exceedingly glad if you would order for me one dozen pair of silk stockings ; eight pair of them to be of the finest white silk that can possibly be made, and four pair of a lightish grey ; the feet to be exceedingly long and the legs to be of the same size as your own. *There is no difficulty in passing them*, if washed and marked, but I will not give you that trouble also, but will endeavour to find some opportunity of getting them safe here.[1]

Other passages in the Selwyn Correspondence show conclusively how widely prevalent among the upper classes of English society in the last century was the practice of smuggling finery. 'It is feared old Gunning will die,' says one correspondent, 'and defeat all the smuggled finery of the earl and countess for the ensuing day.' 'Pray do not leave the shoes behind you,' writes another. 'Unpack the box and let John put them in his pocket ; if he bribes the custom house officers I will reimburse him.' Ladies of title chiefly smuggled, or employed their friends to smuggle for them, French and Flemish lace. In 1767 a custom house officer seized Flanders lace to the value of four hundred pounds which had been carefully concealed in the hollow of the buoy of a vessel. The revenue officers became very vigilant ; perpetually placed guard ; but still the fair smugglers came off victorious. Huge quantities of lace shirts and ruffles would be thrust into coffins and conveyed

---

[1] Jesse's *Selwyn*, i. 348 ; see also Smith's *Life and Times of Nollekens*, i. 17.

across as dead bodies from Calais to Dover, the High Sheriff of Westminster running in this manner six thousand pounds worth of French lace in the coffin of Dr. Francis Atterbury, the exiled Bishop of Rochester, who died in Paris in 1731.

If the fine ladies and gentlemen saw nothing very venial in smuggling, the lower orders saw even less. The population of entire villages was supported by this occupation.. Common smugglers were of two classes, between whom it might be said there was a great gulf fixed—sailors who were intimately acquainted with the coasts, and 'long-shore men,' bold, venturesome spirits, whose business it was to 'run' the tubs or bales from the coasts, and by this means to send them up the country. Every sea-coast town or village, especially in the western and south-western counties of England, by reason of their proximity to France, had some 'free traders,' as they were called among the inhabitants, whose operations were generally connived at by the neighbouring gentry and clergy. The skill, ingenuity, and caution which they displayed in running their goods ashore, and the expedition with which they were wont to hurry them inland to places of security were worthy of a better cause. Emboldened by impunity the smugglers resorted to the practice of turning the many unfrequented holes. and corners of London into depôts of safety for the concealment of contraband goods, even carting them, if report holds true, into the hallowed precincts of the Fleet Prison itself. Desperate struggles between whole bands of smugglers and troops of soldiers occasionally took place in the streets of the metropolis in the closing years of the eighteenth century. A paragraph in the issue of the ' Public Advertiser ' for October 29, 1774, states that

on Wednesday morning early, three custom house officers stopped a postchaise and four on the Deptford road, in which were Indian goods to the amount of some hundred pounds which they seized. It is said they were designed for a capital smuggler at the west end of the town, and that the officers got the information by making one of his servants drunk.

Again, in a paragraph in the ' British Chronicle ' for May 1 to 4, 1778, it is stated that three officers of the excise having received intelligence that a gang would pass over Blackfriars Bridge into Surrey on Monday morning, between the hours of twelve and two, applied for the assistance of the military in order to make a seizure of the goods; they were accordingly attended by a sergeant and twenty-two horse grenadiers, who secured the gate, while the remainder concealed themselves on the London side of the bridge to cut off their retreat. Soon after two the smugglers came upon the bridge to the number of two-and-thirty, but found themselves stopped by the gate being secured, and at the other end the grenadiers were drawn up in a line, with their firelocks and bayonets fixed. The smugglers, however, formed in two lines, placing their loaded horses in the rear, and rushing upon the soldiers' bayonets, broke through and got clear off, except one man, who was stopped and his goods seized. One of the smugglers' horses dropped down dead in the Old Bailey, being pierced in several places with the bayonets. Many of the others were wounded, and one of the men had his leg cut in three places. The grenadiers were ordered to fire, but expecting no resistance, their pieces were not loaded. Several of them were hurt by being thrown down and trampled upon by the horses. The value of the goods was supposed to be about 1,000*l.*

Travellers accounted it nothing uncommon until long after this date to meet gangs of forty or fifty 'Kentish Knockers,' as they were called, on the Dover and Brighton roads, well mounted on strong, lusty horses, drawing waggons containing ankers of brandy and Hollands, proceeding up to the metropolis, fully prepared to cross Westminster Bridge in defiance of the custom house officers. Dwellers in isolated parts of the southern counties near the high roads would be frequently roused from sleep at night by weird sounds much resembling those which the ignorant and superstitious peasantry of the Black Forest are wont to declare herald the approach of the spectre huntsman, the tramp of horses, the hum of voices, and the jingling of little bells, which proved on investigation to be a number of heavy laden smugglers proceeding to London with contraband goods. The New Forest and the Hampshire and Dorsetshire coasts were the happy hunting grounds of these desperadoes, who with their confederates were far too impregnable for the ordinary custom house officials, who even when they brought extra pressure to bear upon them, generally got the worst of the encounter. They who were acquainted with the character of the smugglers generally did their best to evade coming into hostile contact with them, and the consequence was that their operations were more often connived at than disturbed.[1]

The 'Public Advertiser' for January 27, 1761, sets forth :—

Liverpool, January 23.—On Friday last a sloop laden with one ton of tea and six casks of brandy from the Isle of Man, belonging to one Macguire, was seized by the officers of his Majesty's revenue in the river.   The smugglers perceiving the boatmen coming towards the sloop, made their escape on shore, and it is said that the officers' shares will amount to 30*l*. each at least.

In the issue of the 'Daily Advertiser' for June 8, 1778, there is printed an extract of a letter from Blandford, written seven days previously, which runs to the following effect :—

A few days ago James Vinen, supervisor, William Ellis, Philip Jenkins, and six other excise officers, having information of 32 cwt. and a quarter of tea and twelve casks of brandy, being concealed in a poor shepherd's house, situate in a wood at Woodcot, ten miles from this place, seized the same, having brought it three or four miles, were beset by twenty-five smugglers armed and disguised, who presented pistols, fired upon them, and recovered half the goods ; the remainder was brought safe to the supervisor's house. In the evening about 100 of these ruffians surrounded the town, part of whom paraded the streets with loaded blunderbusses and suffering none to pass or repass, while the other part surrounded Mr. Vinen's house, demolished the windows, broke in, and presenting a pistol to his wife's breast, threatened immediate death if the goods were not instantly discovered, which she was of necessity obliged to comply with ; after having distributed part of the goods among the populace, they mounted their horses and rode off in triumph.

An extract from a letter dated Newport, Isle of Wight, October 27, 1779, in the 'Morning Post,' states

that on Monday last as Mr. Stephen Phillips, officer of excise, was returning from John Bowerman's, Esq., of Brook, where he had been on a visit, he unfortunately (on Apes Down near this place) fell in with a large gang of smugglers and requested some of them to strike their goods, which they all refused, swearing if he attempted to obstruct them they would murder him ; Mr. Phillips still persisting he would have some of the goods, one of them with a drawn cutlass struck at him, and in endeavouring to repeat his blow Mr. Phillips having a pistol, shot him, which so irritated the rest, that they immediately surrounded him, and cut and beat him in so inhuman a manner that it is impossible he can survive.

[1] See Roberts's *Social Hist. of Southern Counties*, pp. 370–5 ; and *Diary and Letters* of Thomas Hutchinson, ii. 53.

The 'London Chronicle' for December 29, 1782, records that a letter from Chichester

brings advice that a large smuggling vessel, in attempting to run ashore to land some goods near the above city, got on a sandbank, where she stuck fast ; and before the tide rose to get her off, two revenue cutters came up, on which the smugglers got on shore, made off, and left their vessel to the custom house officers, who took possession of her ; and the next tide she was got off, and they sailed with her for Portsmouth ; she was deep loaded with divers sorts of 'smuggled goods.'

As the east coast of England at that time was, by reason of its proximity to Holland, most favourably situated for the transport of contraband merchandise, it is not surprising to find it recorded in the columns of the same journal that a considerable seizure of tea, cambric, and other smuggled goods had been made only the week before by a party of dragoons near Long Melford in Suffolk, after a desperate scuffle with upwards of twenty armed smugglers, of whom several were wounded.[1] In January 1782 a smuggling vessel landed her cargo within three miles of the village of Shoreham in Sussex ; when the crew had finished despatching the forbidden merchandise to places of security in carts and on horses, they proceeded to two farmhouses in the neighbourhood, plundered them of the cash and articles of value in the possession of their owners, and captured twenty fat sheep, which they carried to a vessel bound for the French coast. The authority for this account adds that the farmers were not much pitied, as they had not long before been very assiduous in assisting smugglers to run their goods into the kingdom. So late as 1790 the 'Public Advertiser' informs its readers that in December of that year 'Messrs. Raglers and Whitcomb, riding officers, seized from a gang of smugglers on the sea-beach near Selsea Island, eighty casks of brandy, rum, and geneva, and lodged the same in his Majesty's custom house at Chichester.' Formidable as was the amount of smuggling that went on, there is reason to think that the evil may be traced distinctly to the action of some of the statesmen to whose

---

[1] Further evidence of the smuggling that went on along the seaboard of the Eastern Counties may be found on consulting Palmer's *Perlustration of Yarmouth*, ii. 267.

charge the national interests were for the time being entrusted. The imposition of high and extravagant duties, in itself a principle as wholly and completely opposed to justice as it was contrary to all sound principles of legislation, was the primary means of rendering the smuggler a sort of popular hero, whom his neighbours, so far from viewing as a criminal, came to regard in the light of a benefactor who supplied them with some of the necessaries and all the luxuries of life at the lowest possible rates. Up to 1784 the duty upon tea, to mention one article, had been raised by successive additions to 119 per cent., and in consequence, it was estimated that on an average the revenue was defrauded to the extent of over 100,000*l.* sterling per annum.

END OF THE FIRST VOLUME.

PRINTED BY
SPOTTISWOODE AND CO., NEW-STREET SQUARE
LONDON.

www.ingramcontent.com/pod-product-compliance
Lightning Source LLC
Chambersburg PA
CBHW030912270326
41929CB00008B/662